MAKING
THE
FASCIST STATE

Fortune, being a woman, is always a lover of young men, for they are less cautious, more violent, and with more audacity command her.

(Machiavelli: *The Prince*. Ch. xxv.)

MAKING THE
FASCIST STATE

BY

HERBERT W. SCHNEIDER

NEW YORK
OXFORD UNIVERSITY PRESS
LONDON   TORONTO   MELBOURNE   BOMBAY
MCMXXVIII

FOREWORD

THIS book is the result of studies carried on in Italy during 1926–7 when I was a Fellow of the National Social Science Research Council. The generosity of this Council and the kindly interest of its President, Professor Charles E. Merriam, have made this work possible.

My guiding aim in this study was to investigate the construction of fascist theories in terms of the varying practical situations into which the movement was forced by dint of circumstances. The fascist mind and imagination hold the foreground of this picture, while enough of the political history and economic problems of the movement is brought into the background to make clear how the *fascisti* intended their ideas to be applied. The interaction between fact and philosophic fiction, between practical exigencies and social theories, between mind and body, forms the dominant theme of the following interpretation of fascism. To the practical politicians both within and without the movement the greater part of this ideology is mere froth. But to the student of the workings of the human mind such froth is not negligible. Philosophies may not reveal the ultimate and universal nature of things, nor are they prime movers; but they are significant symptoms of social pathology and entertaining forms of human energy. I make this explicit statement here of my method, to save the reader the trouble of discovering for himself that this book is intended as both more and less than a history of fascism; it is a laboratory study of the mind and imagination at work.

I have been helped more than I can well express by distinguished Italians, by ex-ministers, senators and many others actively engaged in politics, whom I should like to name here, were it prudent under the present political circumstances to do so. But in order not to repay their kindness by causing them embarrassment, I content myself with acknowledging my indebtedness to them collectively. I wish to express my appreciation to various fascist officials, to librarians, to university administrators, and to Italians generally, for their courteous and hospitable treatment of an inquisitive stranger.

To my colleagues, Professors John Dewey, John J. Coss and Dino Bigongiari, I am indebted for their encouragement, advice and criticism. To Carol Smith Schneider, who has written and rewritten all of this many times, and who has seen the manuscript through its many stages and vicissitudes, the reader owes more than he realizes, and I more than I can say.

H. W. S.

COLUMBIA UNIVERSITY
MAY 1928.

TABLE OF CONTENTS

* Figures in parentheses represent page folios in the text.

CHAPTER V

FASCIST CULTURE 215

APPENDIX

SELECTIONS FROM FASCIST LITERATURE AND DOCUMENTS OF FASCIST HISTORY

PART I

PART II

PART III

PART IV

PART V

CHAPTER I

WAR AND EMPIRE

I. *Interventionism*

DEPRETIS used to say, "When I see a foreign policy cloud arising on the European horizon, I open my umbrella and wait until it passes." This might well be taken as the motto of Italian foreign policy between Cavour and Crispi. If Gladstone thought it reasonable to adopt a "little England" policy, it would seem almost axiomatic that the new-born Italian state must adopt a policy of "little Italy." Cavour, who had played the diplomatic game to the limit, had found it exceedingly difficult and treacherous, and his ultimate success might well be attributed to his good fortune rather than to his power. The New Italy seemed to be launched into a sea of enemies. Austria was of course an enemy, but so also was France, which has frustrated the early hopes of Italian unity and had kept a garrison in Civitavecchia from 1850 to 1870. The pioneer Italian socialist, Pisacane, who was at the same time a soldier of the *Risorgimento*, had taught the doctrine that Italy must face not only her open enemy, Austria, but also France, and in a measure England, "who deserve our contempt as well as our hatred since they are our enemies only in secret." [1] Certainly after 1870 and during the rule of Bismarck the European waters looked less favorable than ever for any ambitious Italian statesman who might venture to fish in them.

Depretis took this for granted; Crispi learned it by bitter experience. For Crispi, who might be called an Italian Disraeli and whom the *fascisti* now regard as their direct predecessor, was the first statesman of the New Italy to conceive his country as a world power. Hitherto Italian nationalists had dreamed of no higher bliss than seeing Italy a national state, that is, seeing all of *Italia irredenta* united to the Italian state. And this was no mean ambition, for *Italia irredenta* was a large territory. But Crispi, probably more from despair for irredentism than from faith in a new imperialism, decided that Italy's expansion must take other forms. Following up the success of his internal anti-

[1] Quoted in Michels: *Soczialismus und Faszismus*. Vol. II, pp. 30–31.

clerical policy, and floating on the wave of anti-French sentiment, he spread the doctrine that France and not Austria was Italy's greater enemy, that Italy's manifest destiny lay not so much in the Adriatic as in the Mediterranean, and that instead of a policy of political expansion to the territories on the northeast, Italy must undertake an economic expansion to the southeast of the Mediterranean; Italy must become an economic imperial power before it could be a unified national state. In pursuance of this policy he put a damper on irredentism; then he approached Bismarck, who sent him to Vienna to make peace there, after which the Triple Alliance was concluded. German capital began to pour into Italy and the combination of German capital and Italian labor gave industry and commerce a fresh impulse and a prosperity which paved the way for "economic expansion." The actual industrial development of Italy was, of course, accomplished by financiers and industrialists, both German and Italian, more than by politicians; and it was from these economic leaders that the slogan of Italy's "sacred egoism" and the economic interpretation of Italy's policy first came — a doctrine which later became the gospel of Italian politicians.

Bitter regrets now began to be heard that Depretis had failed to take Tunis when he might have had it easily. Now that this was impossible, France having taken advantage of Italy's renunciation, Italy should seize Tripoli immediately before it was too late. Crispi therefore set out in 1882 to gain Tripoli, but instead of adopting the fairly easy route from Egypt into Tripoli, which would have been possible had he co-operated with England, he undertook a more ambitious plan of starting at the Red Sea, going around Egypt and thence into Tripoli, thus laying the foundations of a vast colonial territory from Arabia to Tunis. Assab was besieged in 1882, Massaua in 1885 and the expedition dragged on until the disaster at Adua in 1896, which led immediately to Crispi's fall and to the abandonment of his whole foreign policy. Italy was also forced to sign a humiliating treaty with respect to Tunis, the result of which was to prevent the Italian majority in Tunis from building adequate Italian schools and to subject them to the French language and culture, as well as to French economic domination. Then came England's growing opposition to Germany and finally the Triple Entente. This upset Italy's position completely, and she was forced to follow the confused policy of "alliance with the central powers and friendship with the others."

Such a policy was but a symptom of the fundamental dilemma which Italy's ambitions were compelled to face; a nationalistic expansion of its boundaries meant conflict with Austria, an imperialistic expansion in the Mediterranean meant conflict with France and England. One or the other of these ambitions would have to be sacrificed, but Italy would renounce neither and hence she could do nothing but fall back on Depretis' umbrella.

It was Germany and Austria who finally helped her out of the dilemma, for by their new Balkan and Eastern policy and by their friendship with Turkey, they made themselves more serious obstacles to Italy's ambitions in the eastern Mediterranean than were France and England. The latter powers immediately took advantage of the changed conditions and cultivated Italy's " friendship " by patching up their differences. As early as 1903 Austria began to protest against this growing friendship, and in the following years Italy's adherence to the Triple Alliance became more and more formal and perfunctory, until the Lybian War of 1911 made it perfectly clear that the dilemma was broken and that both in its nationalistic and in its imperialistic aims Italy's chief enemy was Austria.

Along with this clarification of foreign policy the Lybian War brought with it, as perhaps its chief result for the Italian people, a renewed confidence in Italy's power and independence. For the mere fact that Italy had been able to fight its own war for its own ends, instead of being forced beggarly to pick its way through the intricacies of the policies and alliances of other states, impressed the Italians as the first real evidence of their national liberty and as the beginning of their career as a world power.

The elder statesmen, to be sure, were still conscious of Italy's weakness. Giolitti had prepared the diplomatic ground with extraordinary caution, and had undertaken the war not so much because he was enthusiastic about it as because he needed it to strengthen his internal political position. He and his colleagues evidently sighed with relief when it was all happily over.

But this older generation, with its nineteenth century background of discouraging experience, was now confronted by a younger generation, the New Italy, as it styled itself, full of confidence, exuberant and bursting with national pride and patriotic sentiment. The Lybian War of 1911 was to some extent a result of the rise of this generation, but to a much greater extent was its cause. Nationalistic doctrine had been developing of course ever since Mazzini, but in 1910 the Nationalistic Association was formed by a small group of intellectuals and their young disciples, and after 1911 their movement grew enormously. Enrico Corradini's newspaper, the *Idea Nazionale* (now combined with the *Tribuna*), became a popular and powerful organ of public opinion for the younger generation. In 1913 the Nationalist Association was transformed into a political party, which at its first elections sent six deputies to Parliament. This comparatively meager strength of the Nationalist Party is, however, no adequate measure of the growth of national sentiment in the country. For in all the parties, notably among the Syndicalists and Republicans, the military spirit carried large groups away with it. Even the Socialists, by their very benevolent neutrality, had lent passive but none the less impressive support to the war. Certainly among the younger generation in the non-socialist parties the Tripoli War fanned nationalism into a flame. Heretofore there had been little organized propaganda either for or against nationalism, but now it became a vital political issue.

The more significant forms of nationalism, however, went beyond party politics and became a cultural heritage of the new generation. The already influential society, *Dante Alighieri,* doubled its membership between 1905 and 1914, and became the chief organ of irredentism and an almost official guardian for all Italians living beyond the confines of Italy. Soon another irredentist society, the *Pro Trento e Trieste,* was founded to carry on the propaganda for northern *Italia irredenta.* The geographer Ettore Tolomei developed the theory of the *italianità* of the south Tyrol, and other Italian scientists came to his support with the discovery of Italy's " natural " frontiers, which, it happened, were considerably beyond the language boundaries. These conceptions soon became the common property not merely of the intellectuals, but, by means of school texts, maps, and travelling guides, of the Italian public at large.

A whole philosophy of nationalism was also developed at this time, which, though it then represented little more than the journalism and propaganda of leaders like Corradini, has since then been taken over bodily by the *fascisti,* and recognized as a serious and integral part of their political theory. The general ideas which underlay the nationalism of practically all European states in the nineteenth century need not be rehearsed here. The outlines of the Italian nationalists' theory were taken over bodily from Maurras and the *Action Française,* and thus indirectly from De Maistre and De Bonald; but there are certain special characteristics of the Italian version which are fundamental to an understanding of fascism.

First and foremost is the theory of the disparity between national potentialities and the pre-war government of Italy. At its beginnings the nationalist party was in a sense revolutionary, in that it was frankly opposed to the existing parliamentary regime. According to it the national characteristics of the Italian people, not of its government, are as a matter of fact those of a rejuvenated rising people. The population is growing by a vigorous birth-rate, spreading with enormous rapidity over ever new areas, penetrating into the German regions in the north, and into France on the west, dotting practically the whole Mediterranean coast with Italian cities, colonies or settlements, and emigrating to the Americas by the million. This process is called by the nationalists "the imperialism of the poor." In practically all parts of the world, by the productive labor of this growing people new areas are being opened up, railroads built, deserts irrigated, coal and iron mined. The Mediterranean basin especially is being developed by Italians. Nor has this creative energy of Italians today merely an economic form. Wherever they go they feel themselves part of the Italian people, representatives of its traditions and culture, members of a single nation. This sentiment of unity, this unwillingness to be individually independent, this consciousness of the higher value and ultimate indivisibility of the national whole, is, they say, a common fact. But of this fact the pre-war Italian state and its government took no notice; instead it represented just the opposite. It was old and weak, subservient to other states, and incapable of expansion. Internally it was divided into rival classes and parties, and externally it failed to unite politically the masses of Italians who had been forced beyond its narrow confines. Based on individual rights and independence, it claimed to be but the servant of its individual citizens, not the organic embodiment of a national unity. In this situation the state had to give way. No political government can resist the primary social forces by which national life is ruled. The governing class, which was but a vestige of an antiquated past and no longer really ruled, had to give place to a fresh *classe dirigente*, who share the new expansive energies of the people and who can bring the Italian state into harmony with Italian national life.

Above all, the nationalists have taught the primary duty of disciplining the nation for the struggle with other nations. Foreign policy must have the first place, and it must be frankly imperialistic and expansive as is the Italian nation. Italy must be taught to expect international competition in normal times and war in times of crisis. In order to make the devotion of the people to the people spontaneous and whole-hearted, the cult of the nation must become a veritable religion, a myth, in the Sorellian sense. "Nothing for the individual, all for Italy" must be the motto.

In practice, of course, the nationalists were not, as their theory pretended, the embodiment of the nation. As Corradini put it, they were representative of the nation only in the sense that they represented the true interests of the nation! They were little more than a handful of young intellectuals, students and journalists, whose patriotic pride and youthful enthusiasm were usually exploited by the calculating agents of financial and industrial interests. Their own recognition of their kinship to the Liberal (*i.e.*, the conservative) party testifies to this, as does also their career after the World War. Nevertheless they themselves were conservatives neither in theory nor in spirit. They were fighters who had transferred their pugnacity from the class-struggle, with which most Italians of the last generation or two had been preoccupied, to the struggle between nations. War appeared to them a more hopeful means of saving the Italian proletariat than the class-struggle by which the socialists were keeping the country in internal turmoil and perpetual poverty.

It was with this temper and under the stimulation of these ideas that the younger generation of Italian politicians faced the World War. Many had already been converted by the Tripoli War in 1911. But not all were converted so easily. For example, among those socialists who refused to be side-tracked from the class struggle by a merely imperialistic war, was a young journalist named Benito Mussolini. He was at the time editing " The Class Struggle " at Forli in Romagna. When the Tripoli War broke out, he successfully organized a general strike of protest against the war, for which he spent several months in jail. In defending his anti-war speech before the court he said:

" Between us Socialists and the Nationalists, there is this difference of view: they want a vast Italy, what I want is an Italy well cultivated, rich and free. I would rather be a citizen of Denmark than a subject of the Chinese Emperor. I took my stand then on love of country. I may have been a little incoherent in my remarks, for I have been accused of having shown a weakness for nationalism. If I had wished to take a strictly internationalist and revolutionary line I should, in reflecting on the Lybian Expedition, have rejoiced after the fashion of the Christian over the decadance of the Roman Empire: ' What matters it to me that the Empire is falling into ruins, as upon these ruins will rise the Cross of Christ? ' I should have gone on to say: ' And if official Italy is going to embark upon a venture which will cost her blood and treasure she will be the less able to offer resistance to the dissemination of our ideas and to the blows dealt her by the revolution.' But, because I am an Italian and love the land in which I was born and whose language I speak, therefore in my capacity as a good Italian citizen I expressed, on the basis of economic and geographical facts, my opinion that this enterprise was calculated to injure gravely the interests of the nation, with which are bound up indissolubly the interests of the proletariat. I have written and said what I have written and said because the Italy I want to see, the Italy I would love, is one which would strive to fulfil the duty which now at last is recognized: the

duty of freeing her children from economic and moral impoverishment.
. . . I say to you, Gentlemen of the Tribunal, that if you acquit me
you will do me a kindness, because you will restore me to my work and
to society. But if you condemn me you will do me an honor because
you find yourselves in the presence not of a malefactor, but of an asserter
of ideas, of an agitator for conscience' sake, of a soldier of a creed which
calls for your respect in that it bears within itself the visions of the
future and the great strength of the truth." [2]

However, such irreconcilable hostility on the part of revolutionary socialists was characteristic of only a small minority; the reformist socialist majority half-heartedly supported the government during
the war.

The case of Mussolini is nevertheless typical in one sense, for though
he was still opposed to imperialism, he had for some years espoused
nationalism. Though a nationalist, he was not an "Africanist," as the
imperialists were contemptuously called. Before he came to Forli
he had been active in Italian propaganda in the Trentino and had
even been associated with Cesare Battisti in the editorship of an irredentist journal in that region. Hence, when war broke out between
Austria and Serbia in July 1914, his attitude was quite different from
what it had been toward the war of 1911. As editor of the radical
socialist paper, the *Avanti*, and one of the spokesmen of the party,
he immediately denounced the Triple Alliance and came out for
"absolute neutrality." This stand pleased everyone, the nationalists because they saw it as a blow to Austria, the orthodox socialists
because they interpreted it as an instance of proletarian hostility
to war.

Meanwhile among the non-socialist parties interventionism was growing rapidly. In Florence, Genoa, and other northern centers of patriotic sentiment, influential groups were openly in favor of war.
Among these the writers represented by the *Voce* of Florence were
important. They were a group of young intellectual adventurers,
Prezzolini, Papini, etc., "militant idealists" eager for almost anything
new, and fired by the idealistic philosophy of Gentile as well as by a
sincere and spontaneous patriotism. [3]

[2] Quoted from Margherita G. Sarfatti: *Benito Mussolini*, pp. 174–5.
[3] A typical idealistic war argument may be found in the *Voce* of April 28, 1914,
where Prezzolini, on the occasion of Wilson's war on Mexico in the interests of
international peace, wrote an article on "World Coöperation" in which he developed the thesis that internationalism is possible only by means of war. The article
closes as follows: "One is always right in opposing this or that war in its particular
forms with such and such results. To justify war, one must rise to the consideration
of war as a form of the world's activity."

Numerous groups (*fasci*) of interventionists began to form all over the country. Within a few months a Garibaldi Brigade had volunteered for the Argonne front, including Corridoni and a number of his patriotic syndicalist followers.

A more boisterous form of interventionism came from the futurists. In September 1914 Marinetti and several others were arrested for burning Austrian flags in the *piazza* at Milan and for pro-war demonstrations during the battle of the Marne. No sooner out of jail than Marinetti continued preaching war as " the world's only hygiene." He addressed a crowd of students as follows: "We . . . futurists have always considered war as the only inspiration of art, the only moral purifier, the only leaven for the human mass. Only war can rejuvenate, accelerate, stimulate human intelligence, give relief and airing to the nerves, free us from our daily burdens, give a thousand flavors to life and a little genius to imbeciles. War is the only measure of altitude for the new aeroplane life which we are preparing. War, intensified futurism, will never kill war, as the *passé*-ists hope, but will kill *passé*-ism. War is the culminating and perfect synthesis of progress (aggressive velocity plus violent simplification of efforts towards well-being). War is a lightning stroke of courage, energy and intelligence falling on everyone. A compulsory school of ambition and heroism; fulness of life and complete freedom in surrender to one's country.

" For a poor and prolific nation war is a business proposition; to purchase the needed land by the over-supply of blood. . . . The war will exhaust all the Country's enemies; diplomats, professors, philosophers, archeologists, critics, cultural obsessions, greek, latin, history, senility, museums, libraries, tourist industry. The war will develop gymnastics, sport, schools of practical agriculture, commerce and industry. The war will rejuvenate Italy, will enrich it with men of action, will force it to live no longer on its past, its ruins, and its gentle climate but on its own national forces." [4]

Such interventionism, however, did not represent large groups. The attitude of the socialist masses was much more important, and much more uncertain. The government at the time could not venture a war without socialist support, and hence Mussolini's stand was awaited eagerly and was critical if not nationally decisive. Up until the middle of September he seemed to cling to his absolute neutrality formula, but even before then his casual remarks expressed his sympathy for the Entente and by the middle of October he had definitely slid into the interventionist camp. His conversion came out only indirectly at first.

---

[4] Marinetti: *Futurismo e fascismo*, pp. 96–7. Also compare the war chart inserted between these pages. See also Appendix No. 3.

It began by putting his neutrality into the form of a demand for an official outspoken denunciation of the Triple Alliance on the part of the Government. Then, being an ardent admirer of the violent French socialist, Blanqui, he defended "Blanquism" against the German Marx. He transformed the attacks made by Turati and Treves against the German military machine into ringing denunciations of the "Teutonic order." Several of his personal friends had become interventionists, notably Corridoni, and to these Mussolini had expressed his personal judgment in favor of war with Austria. Soon the pacifism in his public writing became more and more dubious.

During October, in his paper, *Avanti*, he engaged in polemics with the *Giornale d'Italia* and the *Resto del Carlino* (liberal papers), which made his position still more equivocal. Prezzolini commented on them as follows: "I believe Mussolini is sincere but his position is not clear and there is a conflict in him between his own determined and superior nature and his socialistic attachments, his sacrifice to his party. Nevertheless the polemic has been useful in that it has forced Mussolini to confess his sympathy for a war against Austria and has freed the government from any fear of the attitude of the Socialist Party in case of action." [5]

Mussolini was immediately called before the Grand Council of the Party at Bologna to give an account of himself, and after an editorial in the *Avanti* against the pacifistic *pecore belanti*, he was asked to resign from the paper. The Milan section of the Party met to recommend his expulsion from the Party and gave him an opportunity to defend himself. He accepted the challenge. In the face of the whistling and hissing which greeted him, he pounded on the table, swore a round provincial oath and shaking his forefinger at his accusers said: "You hate me because you still love me. . . . You are going to strike at me tonight with ostracism and with banishment from the public squares and streets of Italy. Very well; I solemnly wager that I shall continue to speak, and that in a few years the masses of Italy will follow and applaud me, when you will no longer speak nor have a following." [6] And at his formal expulsion from the Party, November 25, 1914, he said: "I tell you from this moment on I shall have no remorse nor pity for those who in this tragic hour do not speak out their minds for fear of hisses and cat-calls. I shall have no remorse nor pity for such vile wretches. And you will see me once more at your side. Do not believe that the bourgeoisie is enthusiastic about our interventionism. It is grumbling, accusing us of rashness and evidently fears that the

[5] *La Voce*, October 13, 1914.
[6] Domenico Russo: *Mussolini et le Fascisme*, p. 60.

proletariat once armed with the bayonet will be able to use it for its own ends. Do not imagine that by tearing up my membership card in the Socialist Party you can forbid my socialist faith or prevent me from continuing to work for the cause of socialism and of the revolution." [7]

For Mussolini the issue was an intimately personal one; it was a conflict between his temperament and his philosophy. It was physically impossible for a man who had been picking fights for years, and who was habitually devoted to continuous conflict, to preach neutrality when at last a real fight actually presented itself. For months he had supported Battisti at Trent in a journalistic attack on Austria. How could he now be passive while Battisti was on the way to martyrdom? As the above quoted passage shows, he could not honestly conceal his desire to be in the fray, and he naturally concluded that other socialists were pacifists insincerely or out of fear. In fact his momentary " neutrality " meant to him personally rather an energetic opposition to the government in case it should join Germany and Austria. He was an Italian fighter by nature and a socialist by circumstance. For in time of peace socialism offered the only opportunity to wage war. Of course, he was a fighter politically and intellectually, not physically. (He seems to have had little physical courage or military enthusiasm,[8] and had left Italy apparently to avoid military service.) As early as 1912 Sorel is supposed to have said of him: " Our Mussolini is no ordinary socialist. You may expect to see him some day saluting the Italian flag, sword in hand at the head of some Holy Brigade. He is an Italian of the fifteenth century, a *condottiero*." [9]

It was therefore merely a matter of time until he should find the proper ideas to justify his temperamental preferences.

In *Il Popolo d'Italia*, his newspaper, which appeared three weeks after his expulsion, there was ample opportunity to expound and develop a pro-war philosophy. Mussolini's ideas were not notable for inner unity, which fact in itself would indicate that they were trumped up *ex post facto*. Nevertheless it was during these months of reconstruction of his philosophy on the basis of his own personal experience that he formulated those ideas which later came to be characteristic of fascism. The new journal was headed " *Il Popolo d'Italia*, a Socialist Daily." In the upper left-hand corner was a quotation from Blanqui: " He who has steel, has bread," and in the right-hand corner, from Napoleon: " The revolution is an idea that has found bayonets." Mus-

[7] Benito Mussolini: *Discorsi*. First edition, p. 17.

[8] Cf. Angelica Balabanoff in *La France de Nice et du Sud-Est*, February 25, 1927, p. 6.

[9] Cipriano Giachetti: *Fascismo Liberatore*, p. 87.

solini's first editorial was headed " Audacity " [10] and it closed with this appeal: " To you, youths of Italy, youths from offices and classrooms, young in years and young in spirit, you who belong to the generation to whom fate has allotted the making of history, it is to you that I direct my cry of greeting, in the assurance that among your ranks it will find a loud echo and abundant sympathy. The cry is a word which I would never have uttered in normal times but which today I raise loud and clear, without dissimulation, with a sure faith — a fearful and fascinating word — War! "

Among the prominent contributors to the early numbers appear Alceste De Ambris, Di Staso, Agostino Lanzillo, Longobardi, Giovanni Papini, Giuseppe Prezzolini, Sergio Panunzio, Arturo Rossato and Salvemini. These authors directed their fire against various anti-interventionists, for various motives and from various points of view, but Mussolini tried to unify them all into a joint attack on a single external enemy, Austria, and on a triple internal one, *viz.*, " the bourgeoisie, the priests, and the socialist party." Especially the pacifistic " priests and politicians," " the eunuchs of the spirit," were assailed. It was suggested that the bourgeoisie should pay for the war by heavy inheritance taxes. Papini called the " Germans of the *Banca Commerciale* " the " real bosses of Italy " against whom the revolution must be directed primarily. The same writer then sailed into the Pope's powerless peace encyclical, abusing priests in general and urging the King to do something practical for the war. By several writers, including Mussolini, the King was threatened: " Either the risk of war or the risk of the crown! " Prezzolini blamed Giolitti and the parliamentary bureaucracy for its disgraceful dallying and dilatory tactics. In short, by one author or another every conceivable kind of appeal was made to push Italy into the war.

The arguments which were emphasized by Mussolini personally were:

(1) Italy will sooner or later be forced into the war anyway, it is therefore both more honorable and more profitable for Italy to *will* the war, to enter it freely, immediately and for her own interests. No further motive or cause is necessary.

(2) Salandra's policy of " sacred egoism," of bargaining with both sides to see who would promise Italy the most for her neutrality, is both disgraceful and useless. Italy must fight, must make sacrifices, if she expects to gain anything by the war. Italy will be isolated and despised after the war if she stands aloof now.

(3) All the other national proletariats are fighting, hence the princi-

[10] See Appendix No. 1.

ple of proletarian solidarity demands that the Italian proletariat should do likewise. Moreover "war and socialism are incompatible only when taken in the universal meanings of the terms, but every age and every people has its wars. Life is relative; the absolute does not exist save as a cold and barren abstraction. He who cares too much for his own skin will not go to fight in the trenches, but neither will you find him on that day of battling in the streets. . . . We must act, do something, fight and if needs be die. Neutrals have never dominated events; they have always submitted to them. It is *blood* that gives motion to the clanging wheels of history." [11]

(4) For Italy the war must be a revolutionary war. The people must arm itself and overthrow first foreign oppression and then its internal autocratic masters. "For us socialists the aims of the war are higher and more far-reaching: the war to weaken Austria and to humiliate Germany, the war which is to free Italy from servitude to the Triple Alliance, must necessarily create an atmosphere more propitious to the realization of the demands of the working class." [12] "Today it is war, tomorrow it will be the revolution." [13]

(5) Italy must fight a *national* war as a necessary preliminary to an international order, "for there will never be an international order until the people have reached their national boundaries." [14]

Such ideas were evidently those of a socialist, intended to convert fellow socialists. But the group which now gathered around Mussolini did not come from the rank and file of the Party, for to the socialist politicians and their followers Mussolini was anathema. They branded him as sold to the bourgeoisie. The fact that he was practically penniless when he left the *Avanti* coupled with the appearance after only a few weeks of his own full-sized daily paper, contributed to by a number of very competent writers, gave a certain plausibility to this charge in its most literal meaning, and led to a bitter polemic. As a result *Il Popolo d'Italia* assumed a violent anti-socialist-party character right at the start and it became practically impossible for Mussolini to make his paper merely a "parallel" to the *Avanti*, as had been his original intention.[15] Although the paper carried the "Socialist Daily" caption until 1919, and although Mussolini continued to call himself a socialist, he was soon aware that he could hope for no following among bona fide socialists, and he began to look about for support wherever he could

[11] Speech at Parma, December 13, 1914. First edition of *Discorsi*, pp. 30–31.
[12] Mussolini in *Popolo d'Italia*, December 27, 1914.
[13] Mussolini in *Popolo d'Italia*, January 24, 1915. Also in *Diuturna*, p. 15.
[14] Mussolini speech at Parma, December 13, 1914. First edition of *Discorsi*, p. 28.
[15] v. T. Nanni: *Bolscevismo e Fascismo*, pp. 189–203.

find it. On March 30, 1915, at Milan, he and his followers even went so far as to hold a joint interventionist convention with the Republicans, the arch-enemies of socialism in Romagna. In general it became difficult for him to insist on the distinction between socialists and the socialist party and on January 8, 1915, on the occasion of the funeral for Bruno Garibaldi, who had been killed in action, he cried: " Your day has passed, O socialists of Italy; when our dead live, some of our living must die."

Mussolini's supporters were therefore a mixed lot from the start, neither bourgeois nor proletarian. Many of them were, like himself, young men who were misfits in any of the old parties. They were mostly " white collar " men, young men from offices and universities who felt an inner urge, left-wing nationalists, futurists, individualistic idealists, militant labor leaders too " subversive " for the socialist party, etc. In some regions (for example Tuscany) they were mostly ardent patriots of the Garibaldi type. In others (as in Romagna) they were violent anarchists. In still others they were student groups. On the whole they were restless spirits, radicals and revolutionists, who were disgusted with the neutralist attitude both of official socialism and of the bourgeois parties, and who out of temperament as well as policy were anxious to join the other nations in war. Augusto Turati, now Secretary General of the Fascist Party, in a letter to a friend written at the front in 1916, characterized them well when he wrote: " I will not hide from you that I love war: we grew up with an unsatisfied longing for greatness, a longing nourished by medieval duels, by Garibaldine achievement or rather by the revolutionary exploits of Garibaldi, by plumes and songs, and we found ourselves keeping accounts and scribbling for ten-cent magazines. We were malcontents then and shall be after the war; for the present I am at my post. I assure you modern war is not merry; nevertheless I like it." [16]

Naturally enough these young men, eager for Italian participation in the war, organized quite spontaneously and regardless of party into little bands (*fasci*) of patriots. Within the patriotic parties, of course, this was natural and to be taken for granted. The groups of whom we are now speaking constituted merely the left wing of the interventionist movement. The Milan *fascio,* of which Mussolini was the leader, was only one of a number of similar but largely independent *fasci* scattered throughout Italy. *Il Popolo d'Italia* naturally became the chief organ of publicity for such groups and it, even more than Mussolini personally, helped to give a semblance of form and unity.

[16] Augusto Turati: *Ragioni Ideali di Vita Fascista,* pp. 154–5.

On January 24, 1915, they held their first general convention at Milan. The list of speakers was: G. Vidali, M. Bianchi, T. Masotti, B. Mussolini, F. Corridoni, M. Gibelli, O. Olivetti, Alceste De Ambris, A. Bottai, D. Papa, Madame Sorgue. They agreed to give their various groups a national organization and to call them " *Fasci d'Azione rivoluzionaria,*" bands for revolutionary action. The word " *fascio* " was, of course, not their invention, being a common word, nor did they mean to give it any new or profound connotation. In the nineties there had been " revolutionary *fasci* " among the socialists of Sicily, a movement led by the deputy, Giuseppe De Felice Giuffrida, and since then the word had retained a certain vogue among revolutionists. Moreover it was politically a neutral term and this had its advantages for a movement that expressly sought to be non-political.

Mussolini's speech [17] outlining what he thought ought to be Italy's war aims and foreign policy is highly interesting, not so much because it was important at the time, as in view of what happened after the war. He admitted that the *fasci* could not threaten a revolution since they lacked the necessary power, but he claimed that the *fasci* could contribute toward creating a public opinion for the war so strong that if the government should refuse to make war, a revolution would result. He discussed the simplest way of bringing about a *casus belli,* and then outlined Italy's objectives in going to war. He explicitly denounced an irredentist war — such a war could be left to the Republicans and Nationalists. All he wanted was a war to unify the Italian nation. He argued for the " Napoleonic boundary " of Bolzano and Trieste not only on the ground that it marked the northern limit of the bi-lingual zone but also because it was strategically easily defensible. For the non-Italian population of Trieste he pleaded the widest possible national liberty. The problem of Fiume and Dalmatia he thought wise to postpone altogether for later diplomatic agreements. A few days after this speech, in the *Popolo d'Italia,* Prezzolini argued on economic grounds for annexing Fiume as well as Trieste; to which Mussolini replied that he had no " prejudices," but that if Fiume is to be annexed it should be done for better reasons than economic.

By his general pragmatic flexibility, by his policy of not having " prejudices," and by thus keeping constantly a middle ground, he succeeded in gaining a personal leadership over the *fasci* and in organizing them into concerted action. By the end of February 1915 there were already 105 *fasci* with 9,000 members. Street demonstrations were the ordinary activity of these " revolutionary " bands, though occasionally acts of intimidation and violence were resorted to against the neutralist

[17] Published in *Discorsi,* first edition.

leaders. On April 12, at Rome, Mussolini, Marinetti, Settimelli and several others were arrested for interventionist demonstrations. After the declaration of war, in May, Mussolini devoted his paper and what little influence he had to subordinating all issues to those of a military victory. In the fall of 1915 he was drafted and served as corporal until the spring of 1917 when he was wounded by the explosion of a trench mortar. On being dismissed after recovery he returned to his paper. He was an unsparing critic of the politicians who both before and after the great defeat at Caporetto failed to support the military chiefs. And he was among the first of the journalists to herald the final failure of the Austrian offensive and their consequent retreat as "the victory of Vittorio Veneto," the achievement of the Italian army and the decisive battle of the war, by which Italy could claim really to have won the war.

II. Down with Parliament

The course of the war added at least two major themes to fascist ideology. One was the emphasis on military discipline as opposed to a parliamentary government and democratic liberty, the other was imperialism. Even before the declaration of war, the interventionists became impatient with the parliamentary tactics of delay and debate. On the eve of Italy's entrance into the war Mussolini wrote an exasperated editorial in the *Popolo* entitled "Down with Parliament," in which he said: "These deputies who should be at the head of the nation to give it strength and courage, instead of to depress and degrade it as they are doing — these deputies should be brought before a war tribunal. Discipline must begin at the top if it is to be respected lower down. As for me, I am ever more firmly convinced that for the welfare of Italy a dozen or so of deputies should be shot in the back, shot I say, and at least a couple of ex-ministers should be sent to jail. Not only this, but I believe with an ever profounder conviction that the Italian parliament is the noxious boil which poisons the blood of the nation. It should be extirpated." [18]

During the war he became even more disgusted, if possible, and extended his condemnation to democratic institutions and ideas in general. Especially after his own return from the front, it appeared ridiculous to him that the whole nation should not be mobilized for war, disciplined by a military hierarchy and willing to sacrifice its normal extravagances. Luxury, frivolity, leisure, liberty, everything that did not contribute to the "moral discipline of the nation" ought to be abandoned without question. The whole nation must be militarized and

[18] *Diuturna*, pp. 49–50.

must " assume the aspect of an arsenal." [19]　From this point of view, which appeared to him obviously justified after the defeat of Caporetto and during the tense winter of 1917–18, the checks which parliament imposed on military authority, and the lengthy debates about civil liberties, free speech, rights of labor and similar problems, together with the whole traditional business of party bargaining for cabinet portfolios, impressed him as little short of treason.　On February 24, 1918, he finally let loose as follows: " In May 1915 we committed a grave error for which we have since atoned bitterly.　We who willed the war, we should have seized the power. . . .　They spoke of ' political liberty!' Ah, liberty to betray, to assassinate our country, to make more blood flow. . . .　This political liberty is paradoxical.　It is criminal to think of drafting, clothing, arming and sending off to be killed one group of men, of denying these every liberty of word or protest, punishing terribly any soldier who perpetrates the least act or word contrary to the established order, and at the same time, behind their backs, in secret convention, among groups of drunken brutish men and in the sacristies to permit the deliberation of deeds and the uttering of phrases which would kill the war. . . .　The poor soldier in the trenches asks himself: Why should I suffer and die, while at Rome they are still debating whether or not to make war?　When at Rome those who should be directing the affairs of Italy are still in doubt whether it is right or wrong to wage war!　Gentlemen, I call this a deplorable and criminal crowd of academics.　And now, even after Caporetto, even after the defeat, this crowd of irresponsibles is still permitted to obstruct the war." [20]　" We young men made a mistake at that time, a mistake for which we have paid dearly; we put thus our flaming youth into the hands of the most ruinous old age.　When I say ' old,' I do not mean in point of time.　I think some people are born old.　I speak of those aged persons, who are antiquated and outworn, who are but incumbrances. They have not understood, they have not realized a single fundamental fact of the war.　It is the people . . . who have grasped the meaning of this war, and two other classes of persons too — the poets and the industrialists. . . .　To these two classes should be added also the journalists, who are sufficiently poetical not to be industrialists and sufficiently industrial not to be poets." [21]

[19] v. *Disciplina di Guerra*, November 9, 1917.　In *Diuturna*, pp. 147–150.
[20] *Discorsi*, first edition, pp. 33–39 *passim*.
[21] *Discorsi*, first edition, p. 46.

III. Imperial Rome

This picture of a nation morally unified and disciplined for combat, an idea which was natural enough in the face of military defeat, was revived by the *fascisti* after the war and under circumstances which we shall describe later. For the present we must return to a second concept which was developed during the war — imperialism. As we have already noted, Mussolini was violently opposed to the imperialism of the Tripoli War and was at least very indifferent to the imperialistic aims of the nationalists at the outset of the World War. But as the war went on, he and his revolutionary *fasci* were gradually by almost imperceptible stages converted to an imperialism of the most extreme type.

One of Mussolini's first expressions in this direction is to be found in an editorial of August 16, 1915, which he wrote on the occasion of Greece's maneuvers for entering the war on the side of the Allies. He frankly opposed Greece's bid and recommended that in order to humiliate her and her pan-hellenism, the penalty of neutrality be inflicted on her. The world can be saved without Greece, he said, and moreover Greece would not be essential to the " new Balkan constellation." Greece should be considered a " moral " enemy of Italy. The article closes as follows: " Italy can not and must not remain aloof from the eastern Mediterranean which is destined to be our field of expansion tomorrow." [22]

The ensuing hardships and struggles of the war, which proved to be greater than had been anticipated, naturally encouraged the idea that after the victory Italy would be entitled to all she might want. Certainly the interventionists, Mussolini among them, would have been the last to suggest limits to Italy's ambitions. When the Austrian offensive finally broke in June 1918 and the Italians were able to pursue their enemy across the Piave, and when " peace-talk " began immediately afterwards, patriotic Italians were quick to sense their glory. Mussolini consciously cultivated a feeling of national pride, and expounded what has been called " the heroic lie that saved Italy," [23] namely, that the Italians had won a positive strategic victory at Vittorio Veneto and that this victory had really won the war for the Allies. Nothing, therefore, could be too good for heroic Italy! In this spirit of pride over the victory and in the confidence that Italy had attained her objectives, the peace conference was awaited.

Then there came unexpectedly, out of a clear blue, the great disillusionment, or as the nationalists called it, " the great humiliation of

[22] *Diuturna*, p. 66.   [23] v. *Banchelli* in Appendix No. 13.

Versailles." Italian achievements were discounted, Italian imperialism was denounced, culminating in Wilson's obstinate opposition to the secret treaties and in the diplomatic embarrassment of the Italian delegates.

Mussolini did not hesitate to come to Italy's defense. This thing they call imperialism, he said, is nothing unusual or new, nothing to be alarmed at. It is but the natural need of expansion which all healthy individuals or nations feel. " Imperialism is the eternal and immutable law of life. At bottom it is but the need, desire and will for expansion which every individual and every live and virile people have inside them. . . . President Wilson, in a sense, as is not difficult to demonstrate, is the greatest and most fortunate of all the imperialists." [24] France and England, he emphasized, were busily cementing their new imperial holdings, and it was only poor Italy who was being cheated out of her rights by the diplomatic hypocrisy of her plutocratic neighbors and by the renunciations of her decrepit statesmen.

The internal aspects of the situation, however, soon overshadowed the defeats at Versailles. One after another the old statesmen began to talk as though the war had proved to be a delusion for Italy. And, what was more, the masses began to feel the delusion. A depreciating currency, enormous debts, general unemployment (especially for the thousands of demobilized veterans), rising prices — rapidly created an economic situation which smacked of anything but of a glorious victory. The ensuing strikes merely aggravated the evils. The theory that Italy had been deluded therefore found congenial soil.

It spread all the more easily because it was embedded in a tradition much older than the war, that is, in the economic interpretation of history. Marxian sociologists had found it easy enough to explain Italy's economic poverty and political weakness by her lack of natural resources, which lack was also claimed to have produced inevitably a lack of capacity in the Italian people. Italians were said to be the poor products of a poor soil. The elaboration of this theory had been a favorite theme of Italian scientists for decades, and taking their clue from the would-be " pure " scientists, socialistic propagandists found it useful to their purposes to harp on the theme still more. If Italy was doomed to poverty and disgrace under the present economic order, good Italians could easily be converted into earnest socialists. Southern writers then began to use the theory against the politics of the industrial north. Giustino Fortunato was especially influential in popularizing " the problem of the south," and in his hands the theory took a definitely anti-nationalistic turn. It was pointed out that the political

[24] *Diuturna*, p. 228. v. Appendix No. 4.

union of Italy was not an unmixed blessing; that the north would always be retarded in its economic development by a naturally poorer south, and that the south in turn was handicapped in its agricultural development by the politics and tariffs imposed upon it by the more powerful north. Shortly before the war these ideas were made more popular than ever by the brilliant writings of a young democratic leader, Francesco Saverio Nitti.[25] In his hands they ceased to be ideas of revolt and took on a cynical and pessimistic flavor.[26] Italy's poverty and subserviency were taken as more or less ultimate decrees of fate to be faced without wincing and accepted grimly. Hence whatever misfortunes befell Italy were all grist for Nitti's mill. Even during the war and with greater assurance during the peace negotiations and the economic disasters after the war, these pessimists simply said: " I told you so! What else can you expect? We are now bound by iron necessity and must make the best of it." The more Italy went on the rocks, the more they proclaimed their insight into Italian politics and their claim to "leadership." The "humiliation of Versailles" and the economic crisis were therefore heralded as the natural consequences of the war, which any scientifically minded man might have foreseen, and the responsibility for which was to be placed on the shoulders of those young irresponsibles who had so gaily "willed" the war.

Mussolini was quick to sense this danger for the ex-interventionists and tried to place his opponents, not himself, on the defensive. He began his attack during the darkest days of the war, following the defeat of Caporetto, when the pessimists merely smiled a bitter smile, not daring at the time to come out with their thoughts. Mussolini guessed them and attacked them at once: " The factor ' man ' is the fundamental one and all the mechanical means of the world are insufficient to give victory if the soldier's spirit is found wanting and *vice versa*. . . . Destiny is in us, for what is called destiny is but the confession of our imperfect knowledge of the causes which govern the turns of human fortune. The cause of the defeat is in us. . . . The forces of recovery are in us. . . . There exists an external mechanical fatality in things, but there exists also a human will, which does not whine under the blows that seem unforeseen, but dominates them and gathers experience from them. The ' fatality,' if one may call it so, of Caporetto has been dominated by our will for victory." [27] In June when victory seemed to support his argument, he continued as follows: " If October 24 was, as it actually was, a moral defeat, then today is our great moral victory.

[25] See for example his *Nord e Sud*.
[26] v. Gentile: *Che cosa è il fascismo*, pp. 245 ff. Also Appendix No. 29.
[27] *Diuturna*, pp. 163, 175–6.

Very well then, without taking on the airs of chauvinism, which is out of the question, we may be allowed to show our pride at being Italians, the intimate joy of belonging to this people, capable of finding itself again, of beginning anew, of remaking itself, while other peoples, cast into the depths, no longer find the energy for regaining their feet and going ahead." [28]

For a while Mussolini took the defensive with this idea. He defended the war, claimed that its major objectives had been attained,[29] urged the ratification of the Treaty of Rapallo and even publicly opposed d'Annunzio's obstructionism. But when he saw the drift of events, the growing discontent with the terms of Versailles, the success of d'Annunzio's defiance, and the exasperation of the people over economic conditions, he shifted his tactics and took the offensive. He admitted that the " war had been won and the peace lost," and that Italy had a perfect right to be disillusioned. But whose fault was it? Not the natural poverty nor the moral inferiority of the Italian people was to blame; not her readiness to fight the war and to make enormous sacrifices; but rather that handful of pessimistic, timid, degenerate old " statesmen " who threw away what Italy had dearly won. Nitti especially was seized upon as the personification of " defeatism " and cynicism and the hatred and abuse which were vented on him far exceeded anything he might have deserved personally. He and his materialistic *disprezzo* of the Italian people were made the scapegoats of the terrible aftermath of the war.

And ever since, the idea of the supremacy of moral over material forces has been a favorite theme with the *fascisti*. Especially in 1919, when Nitti seemed triumphant, it was revived louder than ever, as one of the cornerstones of the fascist faith. But it was now enlarged to include not only Italy's capacity to win the war, but Italy's capacity to found a new empire, to revive the glories and primacy of ancient Rome.

At this point the tradition of philosophic idealism in Italy came to the fascists' support. During the nineteenth century, while pessimistic materialism and positivism were developing in the north, from the south there came a vigorous strain of patriotic idealism, led by the most distinguished of Italian philosophers. It is customary in Italy to begin this tradition with Giam Battista Vico, who has been erected into the father of Italian philosophy and science, as Descartes has been for the French. He laid the foundations for the attack on the French rationalists, an attack intended in part as a defense of the Catholic tradition which always has been supreme in the south of Italy, and in part as an attempt at the " new science " which attempted to give an Italian basis

[28] *Diuturna*, p. 193.   [29] v. *Diuturna*, pp. 251 ff.

for the science of international relations. This double interest again found a champion in Vincenzo Cuoco, an Italian Edmund Burke, who, disillusioned by the failure of the Neapolitan Revolution of 1799, denounced the pretensions of the French Enlightenment and reasserted the necessity of cultivating tradition, especially, of course, Catholic Italian tradition.

In the nineteenth century, parallel with the revival of Italy's national political ambitions, Italianism in philosophy was cultivated by a whole line of famous scholars and men of letters, on the literary and political side by Alfieri, Mancini, Foscolo, Botta, Leopardi, Carducci and Mazzini; on the side of historical and philosophical interpretations, by Rosmini, Gioberti, Spaventa, and Croce.

The classic expression of the patriotism embedded in Italian philosophic idealism is to be found in Gioberti's " *Del Primato Morale e Civile degli Italiani* " (On the Moral and Civil Primacy of the Italians). In opposition to the French and the German schools of philosophy which were then dominant in Italy, he developed a Catholic idealism. The starting point of his philosophy is neither reason nor sense but *creation*, as a primary, simple datum. God or Universal Being creates particular existences, and all things participate in the divine process in so far as they are creative. " The protological formula: ' Being creates existences,' when applied to human society in general becomes: religion creates morality and human civilization, . . . from which most general truth we are led to this practical conclusion: the Catholic religion has created the morality and civilization of Italy. Christianity created all the European nations; but especially Italy, for it elected her as its firstborn, and established its throne in her and in her attained the height of its splendor. Hence sprang our own precocious civilization, for we were already cultured and de-paganized when the rest of Europe was still dormant and toiling in barbarism. Providence chose the Italian land for this high destiny, nourishing a spark of truth in it *ab antico* and molding there a race wonderfully adapted in genius and intelligence for subjecting the whole world in Christian obedience. . . . Italy is the priestly nation among the great body of redeemed peoples; Christianity's head, as other peoples should be its arms, as they actually were in the long war waged by civilization against the sword of the Saracens. Nor did the inhabitants of this peninsula give to other peoples merely divine gifts, but also every other civil and human good; and all the great intellects of Europe, who enhanced in any measure the glory of their countries, lit their lamps at the living flame of Italian genius." [30]

" France and the whole of Europe proportionally are heading towards

[30] Gioberti: *Del Buono.* 1843.

barbarism and are nearly at the doors of a second Middle Age. . . . To repair these none too remote perils, European civilization must be reestablished a second time, by recalling it to its Christian and Catholic origins and extinguishing the heterodoxy which for two centuries reigns in all its parts. . . . When a civilization is to be rebuilt a moral center of action must be established where the source of motion may reside and whence movement may be spread to all its parts as from the center to the circumference. History teaches us that every civilization has its special seat in one country or city as its base, which becomes morally the capital of the civilized world. . . . The center of ideal civilization should be there where the knowledge of its principles is maintained whole and intact. . . . The knowledge of the principles can only be found in the revealed word. . . . The revealed word being inseparable from the ecclesiastical word, the Catholic Church is the only guardian of the ideal principles. . . . Therefore the center of the civilizing process is there where the center of Catholicism is. . . . Now since Italy is the center of the latter it follows that Italy is the true head of civilization and Rome is the ideal metropolis of the world. . . . Rome morally speaking is not only the eternal city but the innate city, that is, born with the first of men. . . . For the civil and cosmopolitan primacy of Italy the mere safeguarding of principle does not suffice; in addition their unfolding must take place in the double form of science and action, of ideas and facts. . . . Italians, therefore, have the special duty of cultivating encyclopedic knowledge and art in all their achievements in order to enable them to exercise in practice the primacy which they potentially possess and can rightfully claim." [31]

This thesis was expanded into the two large volumes of the *Primato*, in which Gioberti outdoes the Hegelian philosophy of history and which he hoped would initiate the spiritual and political *risorgimento* of Italy. Though his own "realistic" scheme of union failed, the general success of the *risorgimento* assured a prominent place to the theme of the *Primato*. The variations which it received were too numerous to describe here. I select one only, and that from the writings of Bertrando Spaventa, by whom it was given a Hegelian flavor.

"Italian philosophy is everywhere and in itself the whole of philosophy. It is not a particular movement of thought, but, I would almost say, thought itself in its fulness, the totality of all its movements. I am not speaking of ancient Italy; its philosophy belongs to that of Greece. I speak of modern Italy, of that Italy which must be, as a true phrase puts it, the Italy of the Italians. This universality in which all opposites meet, this harmonious unity in which all aspects of European

[31] Gioberti: *Sul Progresso.* Ch. III.

genius are united is precisely our national genius. It recalls the universal character of ancient Rome, without however its abstract form. This forceful, variegated and complicated nature requires a long and difficult undertaking to complete itself. It must struggle not only with other people but with itself. To really be, it must overcome itself. Hence it is not without reason that Italy has been the last to be seated at the table of the nations and that Italy must still struggle for mastery over itself." [32]

By Benedetto Croce this idea was further developed, as a contribution to the history of philosophy. The philosophy of Gioberti had been obviously part of his political propaganda; the researches of Croce were more disinterested. Having learned from Spaventa and from Hegel directly that the history of ideas has itself an ideal structure, he began to investigate the history of Italian philosophy from this point of view. He soon succeeded in giving a new form to the history of European thought, which not only revealed a distinctive and continuous Italian tradition, but also made this tradition an indispensable element for the interpretation of the evolution of philosophy in general. In short, it was discovered that almost unconsciously Italy had been developing its " idea " and that this idea was an indispensable unit in the dialectic of history.

Croce, as we have said, had no political axe to grind in all this, but his slightly younger colleague, Giovanni Gentile, made a political gospel out of it, which though it received a vague formulation even before the rise of fascism needed only the stimulus of the fascist revolution to put it on its feet. Gentile's version is evidently reminiscent of Gioberti. According to him and his fascist disciples there are two Italies: the classic and the living, the accomplishments of the past and the deeds of today, Italy as it can be seen in its monuments and Italy as it can be felt in the process of creating itself. The *risorgimento* itself, which marks the beginning of Italy's rebirth, had become little more than a literary tradition until fascism brought it back to life. For the *risorgimento*, so the fascist historians say, was infected a bit by the poison of the French Revolution. The *carbonari* spread the French doctrines of federalism and constitutionalism and democracy, but these ideas were gradually supplanted by the strictly Italian ones — those of the nation, liberty from foreign oppression and the necessity of sacrifice and ideal devotion. The pioneers of the *risorgimento* revived Dante's idea of the nation, Machiavelli's idea of the need of unity and Vico's spiritual conception of Italian social life; and these ideas were synthesized by Mazzini and Gioberti, who mark the intellectual culmination of

[32] Quoted in *Gerarchia*, November 1926, p. 739.

the *risorgimento*. But the new Italian state turned its back on this Italian intellectual orientation of the *risorgimento* and tried to live on the imported principles of the French Revolution. It fumbled along for decades in this way, until finally fascism rescued it, denounced the democratic French ideology, reinstated Mazzini and Gioberti, and followed the pure Italian tradition built up by Dante, Machiavelli and Vico. Hence fascism, though a revolution, is really to be regarded as the completion of the work of the *risorgimento*. The new Italy could not rise on the basis of French abstractions, but had to be nourished from the living streams of its own national experience. With fascism the new Italy passed from abstract conception into practical reality. And with it, Italian idealism too passed from speculative formulation into concrete actuality, from idea into act.[33] The emphasis on Italian tradition therefore represents an attack on so-called abstract and speculative German idealism. Croce himself is criticized by the younger disciples as having yielded too much to the methods and concepts of Hegel. True idealism, they say, is based not on German concepts but on Italian action. In short the traditionalism of the Italian idealists from Cuoco down is really an empiricism, an upholding of their own experience in the face of foreign dialectical systems.

Italy's participation in the war and her subsequent policy of expansion, when set against this philosophic background, no longer appear as a " sacred egoism " in pursuit of material aggrandizement, but as the very essence of idealism, a demonstration that God, the immanent spirit, had moved from Germany and is now manifesting himself in Italy, his new abode in the creative process of history.

Thus Italian idealism came to conclusions which were most congenial to the ideas of Mussolini and his associates, though the background and philosophic orientation were quite different.

But the first group to give imperialism a fresh impetus after the war was neither Mussolini and his associates, nor the idealists; it was the nationalists. They were the first to suspect the trend of events at Versailles, and were also the most indignant at it. They " saw through " the war at once, realized that Italy had been deluded and prepared for the greater fight to come. In December 1918 the veteran Nationalists, Francesco Coppola and Alfredo Rocco, founded their review, *Politica*. It opened with a ringing " manifesto," which gave the signal for national revolt. It pointed out the great gulf between the ideology of the

---

[33] On this subject in addition to the writings of Gentile (see Appendix No. 29), see Valentino Piccoli in *Critica Fascista*, January 1, 1927, pp. 6–7; Agostino Savelli: *Risorgimento e Fascismo* in *Il Giornale di Politica e di Letteratura*, January 1927, pp. 3–17.

war and the real motives and issues of the war. The war for democracy, individualism, peace, self-determination and internationalism was really a struggle for existence of peoples and empires, a war for world dominion. This "corruption of ideology" was traced back to the French Revolution and it was pointed out that, from the first, democratic philosophy was more or less of a blind to the real facts. In France it concealed a rising commercial bourgeoisie; in England a conservative industrial class and in America an "instinctive spiritual imperialism." The deceit was kept up during the war partly out of habit, partly because statesmen thought it would be easier to win the support of the masses by appealing to them in terms of these sacred principles and rights than in terms of national self-interest, duty and sacrifice. Now the Italian nationalists proposed to tear down the blind and face the facts. In place of the ideology of the French Revolution they suggested the philosophy of Rome, both of the Roman Empire and the Roman Church. They suggested that the struggle between nations is so intense that internal class struggle must cease. The state must be made strong (in the Machiavellian, not in the "materialistic German, sense") and it must frankly cease to be merely national and become imperial. The manifesto culminates as follows: "Everything calls Italy to the resumption of her imperial mission: the tradition of Rome, of Venice and of Genoa; the political genius of the race, which has always made it a master in the art of governing peoples; her geographical position, which links her by land to continental Europe and at the same time bids her dominate the whole Mediterranean basin, where today the heart of three continents beats.

"Here lies the duty and the mission of Italy, for, as history teaches, whenever life returns to this peninsular land of destiny, welding it into an ethnic and political unity, into a strong and organized power, the iron necessity of things has driven it beyond its boundaries towards that sea of three continents which washes its shores and for which it has a natural and historic vocation superior to every force and to every opposing will." [34]

Politica immediately became the most important spokesman of nationalist doctrine and of an aggressive foreign policy. And what is more, many of its contributors were idealists (Gentile contributed to the first number) and fascists, so that it early became the intellectual center of the movement which was destined soon to unite these various groups.

The fascist propagandists now carried the notion of the New Italy to its extremest forms. Italy, they said, was about to take up again the

[34] *Politica*, December 1918, pp. 1–17.

great thread of the Roman Empire. Italy is by its very nature and by long tradition imperial, expansive, dominating, pioneering. But this empire need not take the traditional military form, it would take the form of peaceful growth, economic conquest and above all an imposing merchant marine. Mussolini, for example, wrote: " We wish to convince Italians that beside the vile, putrid and pestiferous Italy of the politicians, who are jousting in the House of Parliament — really but filthy parasites on the better blood of the nation — there is another Italy: one which causes foreigners to sit up and take notice, the Italy which is working, preparing itself, striving to live and to conquer, the Italy of tomorrow, which will populate the sky with swift aeroplanes and the sea with powerful ships, which will no longer have its generations of small employees and scribblers of useless paper, but generations of sailors, who will carry the tri-color of Italy over all the oceans and all the shores of the world." [35] " The Mediterranean is destined to return to us. Rome is destined to become once more the city which directs the civilization of the whole of Western Europe. Let us raise the banner of the Empire, of our Imperialism, not to be confused with the Prussian and English types. Let us pass on to the new and rising generation this flame of our passion to make Italy one of the nations without which it is impossible to conceive the future history of humanity." [36]

Imperialism now became rampant. The adoption of the black uniforms and rituals of the Fiume *Arditi* and the Romanism of the d'Annunzian faction gave the empire visible symbols. The March on Rome naturally fanned the flame still more. On January 12, 1924, the editors of the newspaper *l'Impero*, with the coöperation of Corradini, erected a tablet in the Chigi Palace to the memory of Crispi, " the last hero of the *risorgimento* and the first of Italy's greatness." Mussolini's personal bearing and public utterances have become increasingly imperial; and his followers far surpass him in their wild exaggerations and bold metaphors. Italy has regained, they say, not merely her dignity but her moral primacy. The talk of Caesar and Napoleon is a commonplace. Italy is now more than a nation, it is an Empire.

This passage from nationalism to imperialism is supposed to mean much more than the mere resumption of " Africanism " and more too than the *Mare Nostrum* policy. It means a revolution in the moral structure and aims of the Italian people. " A nation is based on an immanent idea and value; an empire on a transcendent value. A nation is, at bottom, economic (hedonistic); an empire is ethical. . . . A

[35] *Diuturna*, p. 264.
[36] From his Trieste Speech, February 6, 1921. First edition of *Discorsi*, pp. 155–170; see Appendix No. 4.

nation serves its citizens, but subjects serve an empire. A nation is a practical concern; an empire is a duty; the former may be a conviction, the latter is an inspiration. . . . The traditional nature of our people is abandoning the old conception of the nation . . . and inclining towards that of empire. Just as our Church is in essence imperial. The problem of the modern world is in fact no longer a dialectic of nations but of empires that supersede nations. There is the industrial and colonial empire of the British, and now also the money and banking empire of the Americans; and Germany got in the way of both. . . . These empires are the dominant forces of our time and the undoubted products of the liberal and rationalist type of mind; but they are destined to an ephemeral career, for they lack the two essential elements of every imperial organization, inspiration and strength. And to avoid their fate they are trying to retrace their steps and bind themselves together in the democratic compromise of the League of Nations. . . . It is high time that the chirping of these egoistic, prattling and villainous nations and scoundrel-nations disgust and irritate all of us. We do not want Italy to be like that." [37]

IV. Fascist Foreign Policy

The concrete working out of this imperial program proved somewhat tortuous. Foreign policy has been Mussolini's prime personal interest, and until the Matteotti crisis in 1924, almost his exclusive concern. Mussolini seemed to have the idea that after the March on Rome the internal situation would take care of itself, and that the "internal and financial consolidation of the country" opened the doors for an aggressive foreign policy. But this statement had to be repeated year after year, as internal problems kept looming up, until the Matteotti murder and the "economic battle" forced Mussolini to take a more realistic view of Italy's condition and to temper his ambitions to his actual resources.

The Italian Parliament never did know what was going on in the realm of foreign affairs and during the fascist regime, with the abolition of the superfluous Parliamentary Committee for Foreign Policy, the ministry has had a perfectly free hand. Furthermore now that the government controls the press, it can exercise an almost absolute sway over so-called public opinion and can give the appearance of "moral and intellectual solidarity of the Italian nation" in its relations with other nations, and in its interpretation of "incidents."

[37] Pellizzi: *Fascismo Aristocrazià*, p. 164–5, 173–4.

The only idea which has remained constant and basic is distrust of the League of Nations, and of internationalism in general and reliance on specific economic agreements with as many countries as might be useful to Italy's commercial expansion. *" Niente per niente "* was Mussolini's laconic formula. He put his faith in bargaining for specific objectives rather than in legislating for the universe.

Fascist contempt for the League of Nations is perfectly frank. It is true that immediately after the war, when Italy still felt its victory and imagined that along with France and England it too had finally " arrived," Wilsonian internationalism was given a hearty welcome. Mussolini himself on October 20, 1918, as a delegate for the wounded veterans at a League of Nations meeting in Milan, had made an ardent plea for the League.[38] He claimed that a crisis in history had been reached and that justice could at last rule the nations. He pointed out that Italy was really the home of internationalism, witness Cattaneo and Mazzini! However, he dwelt at length on the initial difficulties, of which he seemed very conscious. Again during the next spring, when resentment over the war was already becoming alarming, Mussolini defended the democratic ideas of Wilson and the outcome of the war. At the founding of the *fasci di combattimento* in Milan, March 23, 1919, Mussolini said: " The war has achieved positive results, for in none of the victorious nations is there a triumph of reaction. In all of them there is a progress toward the broadest political and economic democracy. . . . The war, in spite of certain details which may be offensive for the more or less intelligent, has given us all that we asked." [39]   But he continued more guardedly as follows: " The Congress of the twenty-third of March declares itself opposed to the imperialism of other peoples at the expense of Italy, and to any Italian imperialism at the expense of other peoples, and accepts the supreme postulate of the League of Nations, which presupposed the integration of each of the nations, an integration which in the case of Italy should be realized on the Alps and on the Adriatic with the vindication and annexation of Fiume and Dalmatia. . . . Imperialism is based on the vital forces of every people that naturally tends to expand economically and spiritually. What distinguishes the various imperialisms are the means used. Now the means which we can and shall choose will never be the means of barbarous penetration such as those adopted by the Germans. And we claim: let all be idealists or none, one's own interest must be looked after. We do not understand why idealism should be preached by those nations that are in favorable positions

[38] v. First Edition *Discorsi*, pp. 147–153.
[39] v. First edition *Discorsi*, p. 63.

to those that are suffering, for that is too easy. We want our place in the world because we have a right to it.

"We reaffirm . . . the federal postulate of the League of Nations. It is also ours in its general aim, but let there be no misunderstanding; if the League of Nations is to be a solemn conclave on the part of the rich nations against the proletarian nations for the purpose of fixing and making permanent the conditions of equilibrium which actually obtain in the world at present, let us look it square in the face. I understand perfectly that the nations that have already arrived are able to establish such insurance premiums for their wealth and present position of domination. But this is not idealism, it is profiteering and self-interest."

Less than a year later, in his Trieste speech outlining fascist foreign policy, he said flatly: "Fascism does not believe in the vitality nor in the principles which inspire the so-called League of Nations." [40] And he went on to maintain that Italy must gradually free herself from the "Holy Alliance of the plutocratic western nations" and conduct an independent foreign policy of eastward expansion. Later he became still more outspoken and said frankly that the only reason Italy did not withdraw from the "Anglo-French duet at Geneva" was because it would do no good and would merely remove Italy's only chance to offer a bit of resistance to their domination. [41]

The talk of disarmament, of international peace and coöperation is generally regarded as the sheerest hypocrisy. The discussion of the so-called "protocol" at the League of Nations was characterized by Mussolini as "lyric, with a tendency toward mysticism." [42] Other fascist writers are inclined to be more violent in their language. The "Christian internationalism of the Presbyterian Wilson" and the "Jewish internationalism" of the bolshevists were alike regarded as ideological nonsense, each invented to serve as a screen for the growing imperial powers respectively of Wall Street and of Moscow.

Resentment toward the allies far outweighs hatred toward Austria and Germany. [43] The entrance of Germany into the League has mollified Italy's attitude somewhat, since it makes the League Council amenable to a continuation of the Locarno diplomacy. But in the meantime foreign policy has gone so far in Italy without the League

[40] v. Appendix Nos. 4, 5, 6.

[41] *La Nuova Politica*, II, pp. 102–4.

[42] *La Nuova Politica*, III, p. 505.

[43] In this connection see Count Antonio Cippico: *Italy the Central Problem of the Mediterranean*; esp. pp. xi, 44–47, 64–65, 71–72.

that there is little danger of a revival of internationalist sentiment or League diplomacy, and Spain's withdrawal is held up as the beginning of the end.

Nor is fascism in the least interested in cutting down Italy's army or navy. Though the regular army has been reduced, the militia more than compensates for the reduction both in point of men and of money, and though it may be expensive it at least gives an honorable occupation to many who would otherwise be unemployed.

An increased maritime power is one of the major objectives of the regime. First of all a great merchant marine is aimed at, but naturally as a consequence the navy must be big enough to dominate the Mediterranean. Mussolini's "lecture" at the University of Perugia, October 5, 1926, on the sea power of ancient Rome, was no mere academic foible. In the spring of 1927 Mussolini frankly declined Coolidge's invitation to another naval conference on the ground that Italy could not further weaken its naval power in the face of its Mediterranean neighbors, who were not signatories of the Washington agreements. It does not follow from such a policy that Italy is consciously preparing for war. On the contrary the *fascisti* are convinced that in the present conflict of national interests, a nation that disarms merely invites war upon itself.

It is impossible to go into the detailed course of fascist foreign policy but we might point out the chief general changes of front which have taken place in response to changing conditions.

At first, and up until the disillusionment, the general picture of Italy's rôle in the world was, as Mussolini put it, to take part in the struggle of East against West, of England, France and Italy against Germany, Russia and the East in general. At that time the imagination of Italian politicians was still dominated on the one hand by the fear of Austria and Germany and on the other by the expectation that Italy's policy of eastward expansion would find its chief foe in Russia. A minor but closer enemy would be Greece. Mussolini was prepared to patch up a temporary peace with Jugoslavia and to free his hands for spreading Italian influence in the direction of Montenegro, Albania, the Greek Islands, and thence up into the Black Sea. The economic alliance between Germany and Russia seemed to confirm this policy. Hence immediately after the March on Rome Mussolini's own *Popolo d'Italia* suggested to him the advisability of inflicting further guarantees on Austria and of erecting a neutral East Alpine Confederation under Italian protection between Austria and Germany.

To the surprise of all, Mussolini promptly and officially repudiated the idea. He also put a stop to the irredentist propaganda against Switzer-

land for the annexation of Italian Switzerland.[44] At the same time he
urged an economic treaty with Germany. For in the meantime he had
conceived quite another policy — a policy of resentment against the
Allies, and first of all against the " Anglo-Saxon world." Italy's debts
to England and to the United States, the depreciation of Italian currency on the English market, capped by the immigration exclusion act
of the United States, produced a spirit of bitterness, or rather of covetous
contempt, for the English-speaking world.[45] Italy must learn to stand
alone, to shake off its subserviency to the " plutocratic western nations,"
whom Italian labor has enriched and Italian victory defended, but who
now turn and trample on their poorer and weaker ally. The resentment against the United States gradually was transformed into a frank
admiration of its " economic imperialism " and a pious awe of its all-
engrossing financial power.[46]

For practical purposes the Entente had been destroyed and Italian
foreign policy now took a definitely anti-British form. The revived
" Mediterranean for the Mediterraneans " formula was directed first
of all against England. A month before the March on Rome Mussolini
wrote in the *Popolo d'Italia:* " We must be prepared for the possibility
of putting an anti-British policy into practical operation. It is not in
Italy's interest to contribute to the maintenance of British imperialism;
rather it is in her interest to help in its destruction. The doctrine of
the rise and fall of empires now became a current theme of speculation.
The stars of Russia and of Italy were rising. The sun had just set on
the dreams of a Teutonic Empire. Would the British be the next to
collapse? Each difficulty which England had to face was heralded as
the beginning of the end. The coal strike, especially, caused Mussolini
and his disciples to " stand in awe " as they watched the unrolling of
the " historic fate " which presides over the fortunes of empires and
decrees that " one people shall rise and another decline "!

Some fascist writers wanted to encourage the British possessions in
the Mediterranean (especially Malta) to revolt.[47] Turkey was to be
befriended in its struggle both against Greece and against England.
Economic agreements were to be made with Russia not only to offset
the agreements being made between England and Russia, but also to

[44] On the Swiss dispute see *Popolo d'Italia*, May 9 and 22, 1924; Gerarchia III,
p. 683 ff; Mussolini: *La Nuova Politica*, III, p. 444.

[45] This theme was revived after the Thoiry agreements. See for example Coppola in *Politica*, August 1926. v. Appendix No. 9.

[46] v. Quotations from Soffici, Carli, etc.; in Appendix Nos. 7, 8, 10, 11.
Also Mussolini's report as Minister of Foreign Affairs, June 1928.

[47] v. Gorgolini, *Il Fascismo nella vita italiana*, p. 169 ff.

get coal and other raw materials through Mediterranean channels, instead of from Great Britain. In a series of editorials published immediately after the treaty of Rapallo and during the Fiume excitement Mussolini pleaded with the nationalists to let the Dalmatian issue rest for the present and to turn to the wider issues of imperial expansion. Let another generation finish the conquest of Dalmatia, he said. We have done our bit in this direction and can do no more under the present international line-up. Our expansion must take new and bolder forms. " I am more of an imperialist than you," he told them. He pointed out the possibilities of trade with Russia, of coal and other resources which could be brought to Italy from the Black Sea basin on more favorable terms than the northern powers could grant. This policy would give Italy an immediate opportunity to build up a great merchant marine in the Mediterranean. " I wish to demonstrate," he wrote, " that by an eastward policy Italy may attain her emancipation from the plutocracy of the west and may turn toward the vastest and most promising possibilities of economic and spiritual expansion. . . . To free itself from the yoke of occidental plutocracy, Italy has no other row to hoe but the one already indicated for it by the dominant power." [48]

This high-sounding doctrine continued to be preached until about the time of the Corfu affair, in September 1923, but for various reasons it was becoming increasingly difficult to maintain. Mussolini had made little diplomatic headway against England, and after the Corfu affair he practically gave up trying. Instead he cultivated England's coöperation, or perhaps more accurately, he accommodated himself to England's foreign policy; for the English seem to have taken the initiative. In May 1923 the British royal couple visited Rome. In September came the Corfu "blunder." Next spring the royal visit was returned by the Italian king and queen. Things now began to go more smoothly and the urge to the east took on a practical form with the definite annexation of the Dodecanese Islands and Rhodes, the pacification of Tripoli, the acquisition of Jubaland from England, the partition of Abyssinia, and the treaty with Yemen. Quite recently it has even been suggested that Palestine would make an ideal mandate for Italy, both because of the historic connections between Rome and Jerusalem and because Italy is least troubled by the Semitic problem.

Meanwhile England had shifted Italy's attentions from Greece to Turkey, and had used the Italian threat against Turkey in order to acquire Mosul for itself. England practically put a stop to Italy's attempts at extensive commercial agreements with Russia and convinced Italy that Russia had better be an enemy. To compensate, however,

[48] *Diuturna*, p. 269.

England supported Italy's Balkan policy, undermining the French hegemony.

Against this France naturally protested, as well as against the English-Italian agreements about Abyssinia and Arabia, in which France was not consulted. Italy replied that France had excluded her from the Tangiers Conference, and that the Thoiry agreement with Germany had undermined both the Entente and Locarno and had forced each nation to look after its own interests.

In the negotiations with Germany over reparations Italy initially sided with France against England and Mussolini sent Italian engineers into the Ruhr. But when the occupation of the Ruhr proved to be a military expedition of the French rather than a joint commission of engineers as Mussolini had been led to believe, he withdrew, and from then on England and Italy were usually allied against France in the negotiations. Meanwhile the nationalists on whom Mussolini became increasingly dependent insisted on keeping alive the Dalmatia issue, thus offending Jugoslavia and indirectly France.

All things now pointed to France rather than to England as the chief enemy of Italy's Mediterranean policy. France is a very popular enemy in Italy anyway. The French interference in the politics of the *risorgimento* is not forgotten. The " problem " of Savoy and Nice is hinted at every now and then and occasionally articles about the " Italian island of Corsica " appear. Crispi was revived with great ceremony and proclaimed a predecessor of fascism. Extraordinary solicitation began to be felt for the fate of the Italians in Tunis. Spain was encouraged to resist France in Tangiers and finally the Spanish-Italian alliance made it evident to all that France was aimed at. Count Sforza had already been forced to resign as ambassador to France because he refused to take part in an anti-French diplomacy. Most serious of all were the incidents centering about the anti-fascist *émigrés* in France and the attempts on Mussolini's life, all of which were capitalized to the utmost by the Italian press to stir up bad feeling against France. The newspaper, *Impero,* went so far as to suggest an immediate alliance with Germany and the government itself became unusually friendly toward Germany. Nevertheless Italian anti-French policy probably aims less at war than at forcing France by diplomatic maneuvers to make colonial concessions in Africa or Syria.

The Thoiry conference in the summer of 1926 between French and German industrialists created a sensation, for it was a severe blow to Italy's attempt at isolating France. It was the occasion of a strengthening of the Anglo-Italian friendship and was followed by a much advertised and very cordial meeting between Chamberlain and Mussolini. "Locarno is threatened!" was the cry; England and Italy must take steps immediately to safeguard their future. There was evident joy in the Italian press when the Thoiry policy met obstacles and the pessimism of Italy over a French-German *rapprochement* proved to be unfounded.

Turkey joined hands with Russia. Then came Italy's recognition of Albanian independence and its declaration to uphold the existing pro-Italian regime. Whereupon Jugoslavia immediately turned to Russia. Italy, having already made a very friendly commercial treaty with Roumania in the summer of 1926, took occasion during the Anglo-Russian dispute over China to recognize formally the annexation of Bessarabia. This recognition had been agreed on at the time the treaty was negotiated but Italy was at the time still unwilling to offend Russia by its publication. Coming when it did the offense was peculiarly timely, especially for England. Economic treaties were negotiated with Austria, Czecho-Slovakia, Bulgaria and Hungary with an unusual display of friendship. In May 1927 Mussolini revived the Brenner Pass issue and pretended to see in Germany's " steel helmet parade " and in Austria's moves for union, an imminent danger. Again in February 1928, the problem of the harsh treatment of the German minorities in the Upper Adige flared up, but as quickly subsided. All this was evidently done for effect and served to draw attention from the Jugoslavian frontier, where the real trouble is expected. Overtures to Greece were apparently without success. The government of Pangalos had sought Italy's aid against Turkey and in general had been very friendly toward Italy. But his fall from power upset the cordial relations and the present Greek government is allying itself with Jugoslavia.

In March 1927 Italy's whole policy was put to a concrete test by the war-scare between Jugoslavia and Italy over Albanian intrigues. Italy discovered, much to her satisfaction, that Jugoslavia was fairly well isolated except for her French support. A similar test case came the following winter when Italy was caught sending arms to Hungary. The incident revealed the fact that Italy had considerably weakened the Little Entente, that Roumania was in an embarrassing position, but on the whole still under French control, and that the League of Nations found it difficult to take decisive steps in such cases. The signing of the Franco-Jugoslavia Treaty was the signal for a general anti-French outburst in the Italian press, an outburst so violent that England as well as France took steps toward a reconciliation. The arrival at Rome of the new French Ambassador in January 1928 was heralded in the

English and French presses as a sign of *rapprochement;* but in Italy, the event merely served to raise hopes that France would make concessions. Accordingly Tunis, Syria, Corsica and other territories were mentioned as compensation for French interference in Jugoslavia. If only England could be detached from France, or France from Jugoslavia! Otherwise diplomatic lines and policy are now taking fairly definite form. England and Italy versus Russia, Jugoslavia, Greece and Turkey — this much seems clear. The position of Hungary, Bulgaria and Poland is practically certain. Roumania, France and Germany are still the big puzzles of Italian diplomacy.

It would be ridiculous, of course, at present to regard this as a military line-up of alliances ready for war, at least as long as England and France are on good terms. It is little more than the picture of international relations which dominates the popular imagination of the *fascisti* and which to a certain extent controls their foreign policy. The economic situation is as yet favorable. But obviously war is expected before long. Mussolini in his speech of May 26, 1927, said: "We must be ready at a given moment to mobilize five million men and be able to arm them; we must strengthen our navy and also our aviation, in which I believe more and more, and which must be so numerous and so powerful that the roar of its motors can drown out every other noise on the peninsula and the surface of its wings hide the sun from our land. Then tomorrow, when, between 1935 and 1940, we shall be at a point which I would call crucial for European history, we shall be able to make our voice heard and to see our rights finally recognized." In his report as Minister of Foreign Affairs, June 1928, Mussolini referred to this statement of a year previously and softened it a little by explaining that the "crucial point" did not necessarily mean war.

Meanwhile the government sticks to its formula of "peaceful economic expansion" in all countries, and seems to be well aware that a war, even a small one, at this time would be disastrous. On the other hand the rank and file of the fascist party are more than ready for war, preferably with France or Jugoslavia, and will be greatly disappointed if they fail to get one soon. The press is inflammatory, to say the least, and the militia is eager to display its valor. The ex-squadrists and so-called intransigent fascists want war, almost cry for it.[49] The rebirth of the military spirit is welcomed almost universally and is acclaimed by the *fascisti* as one of their most basic virtues. The general opinion, as I have heard it from many representative fascists, is that Italy must either fight or explode. "We are forty millions," said Mus-

[49] v. Carli, Appendix No. 12.

solini, " squeezed into our narrow but adorable peninsula, with its too many mountains and its soil which cannot nourish so many. There are around Italy countries that have a population smaller than ours and a territory double the size of ours. Hence it is obvious that the problem of Italian expansion in the world is a problem of life and death for the Italian race. I say expansion: expansion in every sense: moral, political, economic, demographical." [50] In spite of this apparently explicit and official declaration of conquest, the context of these words as well as the activities of the government indicate that the immediate emphasis falls on the " economic battle," especially in the matter of emigration and colonial policy.

Colonial development of course plays a large rôle in the fascist imperial politics. It is the chief concern of Federzoni, Minister of Colonies, and in general of the nationalist wing of the Party. Mussolini's voyage to Tripoli in 1926 and the Tripoli Exposition of 1927 have attracted unusual interest to this colony. It is being developed rapidly. The colonial treaties with Great Britain and the Arab States are also indicative of a renewed and aggressive " Africanism." Nevertheless Italy cannot hope to find room in its own colonies in the near future for its whole surplus population. " Tripoli," said a young fascist to me, " will take at least twenty years to develop, and we need immediate relief. We need land like Asia Minor which can give us two crops a year now; or like Tunis which has already been opened up." Italy has repeatedly demanded a colonial mandate from her former allies, preferably Syria, and makes no secret of her desire for part of the Turkish coast. But such aspirations seem hopeless unless war is resorted to.[51]

Barring this, expansion by emigration must still be the dominant concern of Italian foreign policy. It is a more serious problem than ever now that the doors are being closed and the consequent number of pent-in emigrants, calculated on the normal flow, is mounting into the millions. The country is physically forced to expand, they say. Emigration is to be encouraged systematically, but (and this is the fascist emphasis) the emigrants are to be protected, organized, linked to the mother country by cultural and economic ties, so that they form an integral part of the Italian nation. " And this is but our right," say Rossoni, who was himself an emigrant, " for others have always come into Italy to oppress and rob us, whereas we, when we leave Italy, have

[50] Mussolini: *La Nuova Politica*, I, p. 101.

[51] See in this connection Robert Michels: *Sozialismus und Faszismus*, II, pp. 5? 139; Roberto Cantalupo: *Politica e agricultura nel Nord Africa*, in *Gerarchia*, Ju 1926, pp. 418–429; and Federzoni: *Venti mesi di azione coloniale*.

always gone with our art, our labor, our blood, with the red shirts of Garibaldi to fight for the liberty of other peoples." [52]

Such a policy is aimed primarily at France, for in Tunis and southern France, where Italian immigration has noticeably increased since the war, the problem of de-nationalization has been most acute. France is being reproached continually for trying to rebuild its dwindling population and repopulate its abandoned farms by importing Italians, who are practically forced to become naturalized and soon become almost indistinguishable from the native French. Italy has been more than glad to encourage this emigration, and has submitted per force to the French policy. But now the fascist formula is: we are willing to give you our labor, but you must not take our men. "Our Latin brothers know very well that we willingly give them (for it is also in our own interest) the sweat of the Italian brow to make fruitful the French lands abandoned by them in their selfishness; but they must remember that souls can not be sold nor is blood given for merely material compensation." [53]

But it is evident to Italians and no doubt to their government that such a policy if rigorously insisted upon is bound to bring them into conflict with their neighbors and ultimately into war. Such a prospect, however, is faced not merely with confidence and courage but with positive exhilaration in the overflowing energies of the race, for it is but another tribute to its Imperial destiny.

Apart from the theory that the Roman Empire never had a fall but merely a temporary relapse and that fascism is now reinstating the ancient and natural primacy of Roman civilization, little has been done as yet in developing a theory to sanction the practical aspirations of the new Italy. Being realistically minded, the *fascisti* are contented to accept their political exigencies with a minimum of intellectual fancywork. Nevertheless even among these realists the question of right is raised from time to time, and an answer is being sought to the rather academic demand: What *right* has Italy to expand? The older theory, suggested by the nationalists before the Tripoli War and later developed by the patriotic syndicalists, that Italy as a whole is a proletarian nation and must wage a class struggle with its wealthy neighbors, might be regarded as a sufficient answer, so long as socialist theory was generally accepted, but now that the theory of the class struggle has been discarded some new ideology must be found.

I might give an example, which though trifling in itself is symptomatic

[52] Rossoni: *Idee della ricostruzione*, p. 62.

[53] Antonio Toniolo: In *Vita Nova*, September 1926, p. 28. On Tunis see also Michels: *Sozialismus und Faszismus*, II, pp. 130–133; Cippico: Italy, pp. 58–62; and F. N. Massuero: *Ombre e luci di due continenti*. Milan, Alpes, 1926.

of the intellectual situation. In November 1926 the *Critica Fascista*, which is solicitous for the " cultural " enhancement of fascism, printed an article (incidentally by a French author) outlining very frankly the way in which Italy had been cheated out of colonial expansion since the war by her allies and concluding that either France and England in a fit of unheard-of generosity would give Italy and Germany a few colonies, or else there would " inevitably be war at a day less distant than might be supposed." The editors in a note agree in general with these conclusions but take the author to task for his " historical materialism, now *passé* " and say: " We too think that (unless there is a radical revision of mandates) no one can prevent the inevitable. But do not forget that if this should be the result of an excessive pressure on the economic factors necessary to the life of a great nation in its development, it would be reinforced by those *moral* elements from which all wars and all victories spring, and which no one likes to admit, perhaps in order to avoid blushing." [54]

This points to the need of an unblushing fascist morality in international relations, which, though in harmony with material facts, raises these to a higher, spiritual level, and transforms economic exigencies into moral rights and duties. The beginnings of such a doctrine in a more or less systematic form may be found in Luigi Valli's *Il diritto dei popoli alla terra* (Milan, Alpes, 1926). Here the theory is developed that the need of land has always been one of the most fundamental factors in governing the actual relations between nations, that in the face of it all the traditional principles of Grotius, Rousseau or Wilson have crumbled, that its power might as well be frankly recognized and that in place of the ever-violated immutable rights of the past, the absolute right of peoples to land must be recognized. Such a principle, though absolute, is not abstract, for it cannot be applied once and for all, but implies continuous readjustment in view of the continually changing " dynamic demographic " facts. It centers upon the living nations in their fluctuating needs and capacities, not upon their historical claims or " legitimate " boundaries.

It also offers a substitute for the ancient claim to *imperium*, now anachronistic, but nevertheless implied in the modern concepts of imperialism, expansion, etc. The traditional language of imperialism is a poor instrument for regulating modern demographic relationships, and merely serves to arouse the passions. Moral indignation against imperialism or moral elation over expansion leave the actual moral problems untouched. The same thing applies to our moral judgments on war and

[54] Philippe de Zara: *Il nuovo aspetto della politica coloniale italiana*, in *Critica Fascista*, November 1, 1926, p. 402.

peace in general. What is needed, therefore, are moral categories that enable us to make distinctions between particular imperialisms and between particular wars, and that hence yield judgments on particular issues.

The right of peoples to land is analogous and supplementary to the idea of the right of capital to markets. The latter notion will seem plausible to other nations, and for the same reason the former appears axiomatic to Italy.

Facing these facts frankly, the author concludes, Italy must face war, especially now that growing immigration barriers are transforming the emigration problem into a political and military problem. The limited opportunities for emigration, for internal economic development and even for the practice of the immoral neo-Malthusian art are but palliatives and hopelessly inadequate to cope with the enormous "demographic" energy which at present characterizes the Italian people. There can be no peace for a people which irrepressibly overflows its narrow confines.

Perhaps a word might be added at this point on the subject of the birth rate and birth control, not because it is a serious problem from an Italian point of view, but because foreigners continually hold it up to Italy as a panacea. As for deliberately diminishing the birth rate, quite apart from its immorality according to Catholic standards, such a policy would be politically ridiculous, a confession of national shame or at least of racial weariness. "Apart from the fact that the Italians are proud of their highly civilized humanity," writes a representative fascist, "I know of no people, even decadent or barbarous, which would willingly accommodate itself to accepting the teachings of these apostles of infanticide." [55]

There is some concern that the Italian birth rate may follow the example of the French and that Italy may become in the near future "physically decadent." The pretended growth of celibacy and the recent tax on celibates aroused a little discussion on this subject; but in general the Italian people were quick to realize that the tax was a financial, not a eugenic measure. Mussolini, on the other hand, in his big speech before Parliament, May 26, 1927, attempted to arouse a general concern on the subject of population and birth rate. After giving some of the vital statistics showing a falling off in the birth rate in some of the industrial regions, he said: "Some unintelligent persons may say: there are already too many of us. Intelligent persons reply: there are too few of us. . . . Let us speak plainly. What are 40 million Italians to 90 million Germans and 200 million Slavs? Turn west-

[55] Cippico: *Italy*, p. 42.

ward: What are 40 million Italians to 40 million French plus their 90 million colonial inhabitants, or to 46 million English plus the 450 millions in their colonies? Gentlemen, if Italy wants to count for something, it must appear on the threshold of the second half of the century with a population of not less than 60 million inhabitants. . . . If we fall off, Gentlemen, we can not make an empire, we shall become a colony." Accordingly Mussolini recommended in addition to the bachelor's tax a possible tax on childless marriages and above all an effort to re-ruralize Italy. For the high birth rates and the vigorous race are products of the soil! In commenting on this part of the speech, the newspaper *l'Impero*, in its characteristic manner, outdid Mussolini, saying: " Not to have children, when it is not a misfortune, should be considered as the most serious and shameful of crimes. And it is not enough to stop after the first or second. Every couple should leave behind it its own equivalent plus *x*, that is at least three or four children."

It is therefore obvious that far from considering relief by birth control, the Italians are anxious to become still more numerous. Italy's high birth rate and its consequent abundance of labor power is regarded as the most vital, precious and " creative " of its " natural resources." Italy is, as it always has been, heroic. It is prepared to suffer, to fight, to make whatever sacrifices may be necessary in order to make room for itself, but it can not surrender nor consciously curb its natural growth. Or, if some day it should, it will be because the young Italy of fascism will have passed and the inevitable doom which overtakes each empire in turn will put a political end to a nation already morally dead.

Exuberant confidence in Italy's future and youthful enthusiasm for conflict are certainly the most obvious traits of the fascist mind and imagination. And they represent a remarkable achievement. It should naturally have been the interventionists, the war party, on whom the blame for the disasters following the war should have been heaped and it was they who should have gone under in the wave of disillusion. Instead they were able not only to throw off the responsibility for the disasters, but to renew the war in imagination. In 1920 a disgusted and wretched Italy never wanted to hear of war again. Today a " new " Italy believes confidently that the real war has but begun and is arming itself morally and economically for the greater struggle of the morrow. " I regard Italy as in a permanent state of war," said Mussolini, " and the war bread which we have revived is our daily reminder and symbol." Thus war weariness within a very few years was turned into a military morale in anticipation of future war and national struggle. " The enemy " is as conspicuous in Italy as ever, for the economic burden of the people has not been lightened; but it is no longer an internal enemy, an Italian bourgeoisie to be fought by strikes and riots; it is an external "plutocracy" which the whole nation must face unitedly and with the weapons of "production." Hence the greater the economic pressure, the greater the patriotism! Here lies the stronghold of the fascist philosophy.

But it must be remembered that it is of the fascist imagination that we are speaking, not of the fascist government. In practice, of course, the government must be much less boisterous, more circumspect than it is on paper. Fascist philosophy, or any other philosophy for that matter, should be interpreted psycho-analytically not literally. The press, the parades and the other symptoms of *giovinezza* are themselves "equivalents for war," in William James' phrase, whether they are "moral" or not. The military spirit so recently reawakened in Italy is looked upon as a symptom of national recovery rather than as a source for future trouble. Hence there is no attempt to curb it. But instead the government has attempted to turn it into economic channels. The emphasis on "the battle of the *lira*," the "economic battle," the "battle of grain," etc., is more than a metaphor. It is a recognition by the government of the necessity of bending all of the country's energies to economic "conquests," and of giving a productive form to the nation's militant enthusiasm. The continued menacing of France and Jugoslavia in particular and of the plutocratic nations in general, which the government encourages in the press and on the platform, is probably intended partly as a safety valve, partly as a threat to force concessions, and is not to be taken literally as an open challenge to war. How long and how far the government can safely play with this fire of the imagination remains to be seen. The gospel of discipline, which is still being preached daily and primarily for the benefit of the militant *fasci* themselves, may find itself powerless in a crisis, and the diplomacy of the government may kindle a conflagration which it can not control. Fascism overthrew one government and it may overthrow another. On the other hand, it is by no means impossible that the present diplomacy may lead to fortunate alliances and successful wars and that Rome in a not distant future may once more feel the actual burden of an empire which it now enjoys in imagination.

CHAPTER II

REVOLUTIONS

I. Squadrism

LONG after the war was over there were still battles in Italy between interventionists and neutralists. Not only were the same men involved in these conflicts before and after the war, but the issues apparently remained unchanged. ✓Fascism has rightly been called a post-war interventionism.✓

But originally, strictly speaking, there were many fascisms, each springing spontaneously from local causes and each local situation having its own peculiarities. The earliest symptoms of the movement were agrarian and arose out of the unique economic and political situation of the lower valley of the Po. This valley is the most fertile and wealthy agricultural district of Italy, but it was made so by the concerted efforts of generations of men and by the investment of huge capital, both by individuals and by the state. Therefore agriculture in this region has assumed an almost purely industrial form; great financial interests control vast areas and these are worked to a large extent by day laborers (*braccianti*) whose lot is little different from that of industrial workers. The recent development of the sugar-beet and similar agricultural industries has but accentuated this economic characteristic of the region. Naturally this was fertile ground for socialism. And so it happened that while Italy was fighting the war, the local administration of most of Romagna and Emilia was in the hands of socialists. Bologna, for example, had a socialist government steadily from 1914 to 1920. Nor was this local socialism of the bourgeois type that characterized Italian and parliamentary socialism. Especially during the war, when labor was comparatively scarce and conditions in general were favorable, the labor bosses, indirectly through the municipal administrations and directly through the Chambers of Labor and the so-called "Red Leagues," were able to establish an absolute dictatorship. They parcelled out laborers as they pleased, forcing landowners to pay their wages whether they needed them or not. They controlled the selling and renting of land. They frequently dictated the crops to be raised and of course they determined labor conditions. Any laborer who tried to remain independent of the leagues, or any farmer who hired non-union labor, was boycotted (that is, he and his family could buy nothing of any sort anywhere, frequently not even medical service, or burial). Tenant farmers were subjected to all sorts of restrictions and inconveniences to force them into becoming laborers on the wage basis. Production was cut down to the point where it yielded the maximum return per labor hour, and frequently whole crops were allowed to rot on account of strikes or boycotts. In the cities similar conditions prevailed, though the dictatorship could not be carried to such lengths.

After the war the situation became rapidly worse. It became practically impossible to find work for all the returned soldiers, even by imposing them forcibly on "employers." With inflation and rising prices there was a continual demand for increases in wages, and the masses stood by the leagues to the limit, believing them to be their only refuge against starvation. "Either Red or Starve" was their argument. When the economic situation became unbearable, the labor leaders fanned the flame of revolt to white heat and their tactics became more violent. The revolution was preached as the only hope of salvation, and with the growing chaos it was generally believed to be imminent. "The worse, the better" was the general cry. Several times during the period between August 1919 and December 1920, a date was set for the grand event, which when the time came proved to be more a riot than a revolution. All seemed to expect that the universal despair would create a revolution by spontaneous combustion. Meanwhile they vented their wrath on two chief enemies, patriots and non-union men.

As wages kept soaring, the temptation to hire non-union labor increased, and as unemployment increased, the opportunities for getting non-union labor increased also. Of the incidents which now occurred no adequate account can be given here. One typical case must suffice. On a Sunday in the summer of 1919 a group of independent threshers set up their machine in the square of the little town of Medicina. Anticipating trouble they had gone to the league headquarters several times previously and had been assured that they would not be molested. Next morning shortly after they had begun work, they were attacked by a band of peasants led by the brother of the head of the league. Shots were fired from behind walls. The foreman of the threshers was killed, his body riddled with bullets, his purse stolen, and his wife dragged to the scene and threatened with similar treatment. Most of the other threshers were wounded. At Bazzano, Molinella and other towns similar incidents took place. Though the violence was worst around Modena, Ferrara and Bologna, it was bad throughout Romagna, Emilia and Tuscany and in the big agricultural establishments in the southern province of Puglia. In the circumstances landholders, tenants and independent laborers naturally looked about for defense.

For such conditions the socialist masses naturally blamed the war. Even during the war the local socialist administrations had opposed national policy to an extent which probably no other government would have tolerated. The war was openly condemned. Russian bolshevists were entertained like heroes, immediate peace was urged, and in general municipalities constituted an " anti-state within the state." After the war the veterans were publicly abused and insulted, often even beaten up or stabbed, the red flag was commonly displayed in place of the national tri-color and all men in uniform, police as well as soldiers, were regarded as assassins hired by the bourgeoisie. Not infrequently from the windows and doorways of their houses women would throw bottles, pans, dishwater, anything at soldiers as they passed by in the streets. Trolley cars had a habit of refusing to go when a man in uniform got on. Monuments to fallen soldiers were destroyed and even military funeral processions were occasionally attacked. Memorial celebrations were particularly offensive. As for the ambitious patriotism of d'Annunzio and the nationalists, it was regarded as worse than criminal.

The first sign of resistance to this " bolshevism " came during the war. After the defeat of Caporetto, when " defeatism " was spreading rapidly among the masses, a parliamentary *fascio di resistenza* was formed, being a group of deputies from several parties, organized for national defense. Patriotic clubs then sprang up in great number. In Bologna, for example, the nationalists organized the *Pro Patria* and in 1918 the more democratic parties, headed by the republicans, organized a rival *fascio democratico di resistenza*. Then came the *arditi*, armed squads of young nationalists and combatants, who after the war continued their military organization and were ready for any kind of patriotic service. It was the *arditi* who first wore the black shirts and carried the black banner, and who furnished d'Annunzio with his volunteers for Fiume. A little later the nationalist leader, Paolucci, organized the *Sempre Pronti*, or *camicie azzure*, militiamen of the Nationalist Party, who wore blue shirt uniforms, and who regard themselves as among the pioneers and the aristocrats of the whole movement. The liberals organized squads of " grey shirts." The Association of Veterans was naturally a powerful influence, though on the whole the combatants were more interested in getting jobs for each other and in caring for their crippled than in patriotic demonstrations. They had more a business than a sentimental interest in fascism. It was their younger brothers in the universities and offices who made most of the noise. Strongly attracted by the shirts, the banners, the parades and other rites and ceremonies, and filled with the patriotic idealism inspired by the war, they organized in large numbers and were the first to " descend into the *piazza*," as the technical phrase goes, singing patriotic hymns, flying the national colors and carrying guns and clubs.

These blacks and blues were met by the " red guards " and later by the *arditi del popolo*, who resorted to the same tactics, sang the *bandiera rossa* song, flew the red flag, shouted for Russia and the Revolution, and occasionally threw bombs for it. The *piazza* became a battle ground. The general discontent found expression in organized combat, for the masses now had a visible object of attack and an organized enemy, on whom to vent their wrath. The parades and demonstrations usually ended up in general beatings, clubs being used freely and occasional shots being fired. On the whole, however, it must be said that these " bloody battles " and "massacres " of which the current literature is full, really turn out on close examination to be nine tenths noise.

In the cities, besides the " parade fights " of which we have spoken, and the reprisals and feuds which grew out of them, violence most frequently was caused by strikes. These increased rapidly both in number and violence. During the metal industry strikes in Turin, for example, a student, Sonnino, and a jailor, Scimola, were condemned by a communist " military tribunal " for opposing the strikers. The workers wanted them thrown into the furnaces, but these had gone out on account of the strike, so they were shot instead.

On both sides fighting was indulged in much more freely than mere utilitarian motives would have called for. Both sides deliberately outraged each other's sentiments. The *fascisti* made it a practice to display fanatic patriotism, apparently for no other reason than to anger the communists; and the latter, in turn, fanatically persecuted soldiers and patriots to the ultimate undoing of their economic tactics. The political leaders on both sides were unable to stop the conflagration at the time when they realized that it no longer served any practical purpose. The worst violence came *after* the worst communism, when both sides were in a rage of fear and anger. They were literally *arditi*. They killed their enemies and suffered " martyrdom " with true religious fervor. Though the crisis no doubt was in its causes and origins economic, the struggle soon assumed a character which no economic interpretation could possibly explain.

Economic motives were more obvious, however, in the bloody and businesslike punitive expeditions into the countrysides. These were raids, mostly at night, by automobile loads of armed men coming out from the cities into the villages where the reds were intrenched, where they had used violence against some landlord or free laborers, or in general where the reds had particularly strong "nests." In such raids there was always a generous amount of shooting on both sides, frequently bombs were thrown, houses burnt, especially labor headquarters, resulting usually in the loss of several lives and the terrorization of a whole countryside. These expeditions were not infrequently financed by rich agrarians, who used them to defend their own interests, but their members who actually did the fighting were on the whole fairly disinterested, bonafide ex-combatants or would-be combatants, who participated either out of patriotic motives or for the sheer excitement of the thing.

Squadrism was common in all the "red provinces," Venetia, Romagna, Emilia, Lombardy, Piedmont, Tuscany, Umbria, the Marches and Puglia. In these provinces violence was practically unrestrained on both sides, for the police were controlled by rival groups of politicians and were helpless to intervene. When the reds made a raid, the local authorities kept the police at home and when the *fascisti* made a raid the national government ordered the police to maintain a benevolent neutrality. But even when the police did intervene, they often merely added to the violence, for they were seldom strong enough or energetic enough to dominate the situation. *Fascisti* were arrested and jailed by the dozen, but as soon as they were freed they resumed their activities. Nitti, who headed the government up to September 1920, adopted a *laissez faire* attitude both out of principle and policy; then Giolitti, after the local power of the revolutionists had been checked, tried to reassert government authority, but in practice this meant that the police merely supported the *fascisti*.

The central fact of the whole movement was that the government, either purposely or through weakness, had adopted a policy of *laissez faire* in the face of the economic disturbances and that as they became increasingly violent the government could not intervene in any clear and consistent manner. In other words, the government practically abdicated, and let private individuals take the initiative in solving the problem. Naturally army officers, police officers, and in general young men with a military training were the first to take a hand, *fascisti* as well as others, and the government morally supported whichever side seemed to serve its interests in particular cases. This is the basis for the *fascisti*'s contention that they did not destroy public order nor overthrow the state, but that the state itself resigned its functions, — its executive and police functions in 1919-20 and its legislative functions in 1922.

II. Local Color

These were the general causes and characteristics of squadrism, but the movement had significantly diverse forms in different regions of the country. In Romagna, for instance, especially in the smaller centers like Mussolini's home town, Forli, political life even before the war centered on the struggle between republicans and socialists, who were respectively the bourgeois and the proletarian revolutionists. Consequently after the war, when socialism became violent, it was but natural that the republicans should give battle. In these regions, as elsewhere too for that matter, especially in Tuscany and the Abruzzi, we find many republican *fascisti*, and some of the early *fasci* were explicitly republican organizations. This accounts in part for the fact that Mussolini seemed to take for granted that when he began fighting socialists he would have to turn republican.

In Bologna the nationalists maintained their preponderance and gave the movement a definitely reactionary character. They were shocked at the war conduct of the socialists and tried to combat the local indifference or even hostility to the aggressive foreign policy, to which the nationalists were primarily devoted. They felt more than justified in trying to overthrow what they regarded as a treasonable " anti-state " within the state. But there were local issues as well. In Bologna, Reggio-Emilia and neighboring cities the socialist coöperatives had established practical monopolies in the business of the cities, which threatened to ruin private enterprises and which were almost as oppressive as the labor leagues were in agriculture. Fascism's strength therefore lay in the lower middle classes, merchants, whose economic position was exceedingly precarious and whose sentiments were outraged, intellectuals, students and small shopkeepers, but it received both moral and financial support from the big commercial and agrarian corporations, whose private interests dominated the economic life of the whole region and who were most seriously menaced by the peasants' revolt. The struggle in Bologna came to a dramatic culmination on November 21, 1920. In the local elections of October the socialists had won by a narrow margin. Whereupon certain nationalist and veterans' organs announced that they would not permit the new administration to function. The *fascisti* had threatened trouble if the red flag instead of the tri-color were displayed from the balcony of the city hall, but they were promised by the authorities that the tri-color would be displayed as legally prescribed. Nevertheless the *fascisti* posted threatening signs on the day before the opening of the New Municipal Council, and advised women and children to stay away from the *piazza.* The socialists, badly scared, came armed with pistols and hand grenades. Both sides staged demonstrations in the *piazza,* and both tri-color and red flags were to be seen on the balcony. A few shots were fired and, fearing an attack, some socialists threw grenades from the balcony into the crowd. In the Council Chamber the majority members at once inferred that an attack had begun and shouted at the minority, holding them responsible for a plot. At the same time four or five men, no one knows just who, started firing point blank at the five minority members. The ex-combatant, Giulio Giordani, was killed and two others wounded. The news of the event caused consternation all over Italy. Giordani immediately became a martyr and fascism for the first time moved into the foreground of the national stage. In Bologna the *fascisti* soon took reprisals, burned the Labor Hall, beat up some of the maximalist leaders and put an end to the socialist regime.

At Ferrara and Parma events took a somewhat different turn. Here the movement was dominated by the middle class of the rural population, the tenants and small independent farmers, whose interests were contrary to the politics both of the labor leaders and of the big landed aristocracy. Under the leadership of the squadrists in the cities they organized patriotic syndicates which, together with the usual squadrist violence, compelled the labor leagues on the one hand to recognize their independence and their tenant contracts, and on the other forced many of the big landowners to break up their holdings into small farms. In this way the labor dictatorship passed from the red leagues to the patriotic peasant syndicates. Ferrara is held up, especially by syndicalists, as the outstanding proof that fascism is not merely a bourgeois reaction, nor a defense of private interests, but that it fought its own labor fights on occasion, developed its own labor movement, and when necessary conducted its own strikes. The spirit and aims of these syndicalistic *fasci* may be gathered from the following excerpt from a speech by Mussolini at Ferrara:

" . . . We *fascisti* have a great affection for the workers, for the laboring class. But our love, being pure, is strictly disinterested and steadfast. We love not by the burning of grains of incense, not by creating new idols and new majesties; we love by speaking plain truth always and everywhere. The more this truth may be unwelcome the more necessary it is to speak it openly. Very well then, if this is our love for the affairs of labor, we *fascisti,* calumniated until yesterday, slandered until yesterday, have decided to continue the war in order to obtain the right of free circulation in Italy. We *fascisti* are the first not to yield to a base sort of demagogy, but to maintain that the rights of the laboring class of the nation are sacred and that the rights of those who cultivate the soil are all the more sacred. And in this connection I am glad to applaud heartily the *fascisti* of Ferrara who by deeds and not by the foolish prattle of politicians have begun that agrarian revolution which gradually, without epileptic fits, ought to give the peasants the definite possession of the soil. I give my hearty encouragement to the *fascisti* of Ferrara to continue in this direction and to place themselves in the vanguard of the agrarian fascist movement of the whole of Italy. How can they say that we are sold out to the bourgeoisie, to capitalism, and to the government? Our adversaries now no longer dare maintain this accusation; it is too ribald and ridiculous."

At Cremona a type of local control was established very early, which since then has come to be called "*ras*-ism" ("*ras*" = an Ethiopian chieftain). Roberto Farinacci, a railroad worker and socialist politician under Bissolati, and a telegraph operator during the war, succeeded after the war in becoming a prominent labor leader, establishing himself as absolute dictator, *ras*, or boss of Cremona and its environment. The "red leagues" of the communists had been early supplanted by the "white leagues" of the Popular Party, organized by the Catholic deputy Miglioli. These enjoyed much the same monopoly here that the reds still enjoyed lower down the valley, and by their oppressive tactics made themselves just as obnoxious. The socialists under Bissolati and the anti-clericals in general combined against them, and out of this combination grew the *fasci* when the fight became violent. This circumstance made Cremona fascism retain certain proletarian and socialist aspects without being "bolshevist" or unpatriotic. Farinacci and his squads completely destroyed the power of the white leagues, and by an intelligent use of his own resources he soon made himself a very popular dictator, enjoying the unquestioning loyalty of the majority and the well-grounded fear of the remainder. He took orders from no one and served no one's private interests slavishly. Later on, for example, when a fascist minister tried to turn over the railroads of Farinacci's province to a private concern, he opposed it and had the contract rescinded. Farinacci attained an immense prestige nationally as well as locally and was rivalled in the popular imagination only by Mussolini. He is usually held up as the leader and model of the squadrist and "intransigent" type of fascist. His brand of fascism has its own peculiar characteristics. It is not so anti-socialist as the nationalist wing and certainly less of a middle class affair. Then too it is, or was, violently anti-clerical and positivistic and affiliated with the Masonic Order. Of his activities as National Secretary of the Fascist Party, we shall speak later.

In Venetia, and especially in the newly "redeemed" territories, fascism had a very special function. In Trieste early in 1919, on the initiative of Captain Francesco Giunta of Florence and Professor Ruggero Conforto, a *fascio* was founded to combat the Slav minorities who were beginning to organize. Almost immediately on its foundation it attacked the *Sedi Riunite*, a Slav headquarters, and the *Balkan*, the headquarters of the Slav communists. And ever after, Trieste remained one of the centers of violence. For similar functions a *fascio* was founded at Bolzano. The German majority in that region was vigorously combated. On April 24, 1921, a German parade was broken up by *fascisti* and in October 1922 a thoroughgoing attack was launched on the city administration without any government interference. The German mayor was forced to resign, the best schoolhouse in town turned over to Italians, German signs pulled down, and German law and language forbidden wherever possible and in general a violent effort was made at Italianization.

In Florence (and Pisa) fascism was predominantly "cultural" and found its strength in literary and university circles. It grew out of the activities of those futurists, idealists, anti-Teutonic intellectuals, etc., groups who had been leaders among the interventionists. But beside this "high-brow" group, and occasionally in opposition to it, grew up a squadrist group of ex-soldiers, who made Florence one of the worst centers of violence. Here again the immediate cause of the violence was agrarian. A general revolt broke out among Tuscan peasants against a growing tenant system (*métayage*), which was threatening a general revival of feudal tenure and big estates, to the undoing of the socialist labor organizations.

Early in 1919 a Florentine lawyer named Terzaghi and a number of veterans, among them Amerigo Dumini and Umberto Banchelli, formed the Alliance for Civic Defense. In a very short time this group collected about a million *lire* from the frightened bourgeoisie. Part of the money was used to fight the revolting peasants and intimidate the city communists, but most of it went no one knows where. In the fall the leaders of the Civic Alliance transformed it into a political body and set up candidates for the elections. The squadrists became disgusted with such tactics and split off.

A famous incident of Florentine fascism was the "martyrdom" of Giovanni Berta. His father owned a large factory and the workers had gone on strike. Unable to get all their demands, though some concessions were made, some workers, men and women, one morning waylaid their employer's eighteen-year-old son on the iron bridge, as he was on his way to the factory. They beat him up and threw him overboard. He tried to save himself by clinging to the bridge and yelling "Mamma," whereupon they cut off his hands and he dropped into the river. The father then closed up the factory and retired from business, and several hundred workers were out of employment.

For a brief period the *fascio* tried to deal with the economic problem of the city. A detachment of squadrists under Banchelli was ordered to see that prices came down. They gave the merchants a few days within which to lower prices. After the time was up, beatings began. Recalcitrant shopkeepers were first beaten and then brought to " trial." After repeated offense, their shops were padlocked and a sign hung up " Closed for continued robbery." Next these squadrists planted the " tri-color among the vegetables " in the market and tried to control the prices asked by the peasant vendors. But the political *fascisti* of the town soon put an end to all this for, as Banchelli says, ' they were caught between the duty of being the friend of the people and the pitiful tears of the merchants, business men and industrialists from whom they had received money." In other ways too the *fascio* tried to gain the favor of the working classes, but all attempts failed, because of the too conspicuous sons of rich merchants and landed proprietors, who had joined.

The leader of the fighters and perhaps the most notorious of all fascist squadrists was Amerigo Dumini. He and his squads not only " filled Florence with the smell of powder," but also went on numerous punitive expeditions to most of the neighboring villages, and then all over Tuscany, Umbria, as far north as Sarzana (above Pisa) and as far south as Perugia. The Sarzana debacle in July 1921 proved the culmination of the activities of this group of squadrists. A large band made a night march on that town with the purpose of freeing some of their prisoners and in general of subduing the peasants in the neighborhood. Hardly past the railroad station they were met by the police, who fired on them, causing a few casualties and sending the rest pell-mell over the countryside, where many of them fell into the hands of ambushed peasants. Reprisals for this defeat were taken a few nights later at the neighboring village of Roccastrada.[1]

[1] An entertaining account of this expedition, as well as of the history of the Florentine *fascio* from a squadrist's point of view, is to be found in Umberto Banchelli: *Le Memorie di un fascista 1919–1922*, selections of which are given in Appendix No. 13. Bianchelli was expelled from the fascist party for conduct unbecoming a fascist, and was recently involved in a petty straw hat business

The case of Siena is worth mentioning chiefly because here the municipal administration had been wrested from the socialists, but the countryside and the deputies to Parliament were still red. Otherwise the conflicts were much like those of Bolzano and Florence. Ex-soldiers and ex-republicans took a prominent part in the early exploits. The "*Casa del popolo*," socialist headquarters, was one of the first things to be destroyed. Then came frequent expeditions breaking up peasant strikes, defending peasants who harvested against orders from headquarters, avenging the "martyrs," etc.[2]

In Umbria, with Perugia as its center, we find another variation of the same theme. In this province of small farms there had been very little extreme labor organization except around Terni, where the big hydro-electric plant was a labor center. Politics had always been in the hands of the middle class liberal party. During the war, however, a number of war industries arose in Perugia, and these closed down suddenly at the same time that thousands of soldiers were returning home, and at the time of the general economic depression following the war. As a result the election in the fall of 1919 suddenly put not only Perugia but over fifty other Umbrian towns in the hands of the maximalists. The middle classes were paralyzed. In this situation a young liberal, a biologist just returned from Red Cross service, Alfredo Misuri, attempted to rally whatever forces he could to "save the country." Before the elections he tried to organize an anti-bolshevist committee, but he failed completely. After the elections all middle class political action seemed futile. Consequently he and his friends organized a *Unione Sindacale del Lavoro*, " dedicated to the representation of specific economic interests (categories) in place of that of classes, keeping in view exclusively their economic and social functions; and dedicated to the union of such forces into a *fascio* with the aim of promoting a more rapid and peaceful social evolution by means of the creation of a potent weapon of defense for the rights of the various categories."[3] Camouflaged in this way as a labor organization for strictly non-political purposes, this *fascio* of " all the good citizens " made some headway. I quote from Misuri's own account of what followed: " The syndica

---

swindle in South America (for which he is now, I think, in jail). Dumini, after having served his brief sentence for the Matteotti murder, was finally sentenced to five years imprisonment for an " offense against the President of the Council. He is said to have remarked, "If they give me five years, they ought to give the President of the Council twenty."

[2] An account of these activities can be found in Giorgio A. Chiurco: *Fascismo Senese*, Siena 1923.

[3] Appendix No. 1 in Misuri: *Rivolta Morale*.

organization of the middle classes was as slow and difficult as ever; an organization of the lower classes was not even thinkable, given the infatuated hostility which dominated all of them. We kept on agitating, nevertheless, getting a little inspiration for our ideas from the fascist movement already begun at Milan and adapting it to local circumstances, but not being able to realize it in Umbria, both because the political temperament of certain members did not permit it, and because the local situation was not yet ripe for it. While we were making these first efforts, it should be said for the sake of the truth, there was not even a trace visible of the then shining lights of official fascism, and this lasted for over a year longer.

" . . . Thus we came to the administrative elections of 1920, which we confronted by uniting into a bloc, the *Unione Sindacale del Lavoro,* the veterans, the liberals and the economic associations. I succeeded in being elected at the head of the minority list, falling only 56 votes behind the socialist mayor and obtaining a majority in the city itself. . . .

" We all felt that a political program was necessary to make our activities more effective. . . . Accordingly I constructed a political program to which most of the groups allied during the municipal campaign adhered, and we called it *Democrazia Sociale.* . . . But this new political body, for several reasons, failed to meet with the success it deserved. Events were moving on. . . . Among us too in the industrial establishments the 'red guards' were being formed; the atmosphere became electrified when the news came to us from the northern provinces of the first deeds of the *fascisti* and *arditi* at Milan, then of the massacre at the City Hall of Bologna, and still later of the battle of San Frediano at Florence. Then the period of genuine conspiracy began in earnest. Subscription lists for the *Popolo d'Italia* were drawn up; the first group of volunteers began to circulate to get members for a *fascio di combattimento.* For now political formulas and campaigns no longer sufficed; it was necessary to identify ourselves with the movement which was coming to the rescue of the nation. In January 1921 Captain Zamboni of the *fascio* of Florence came to Perugia, and a score or two of us founded the Perugian *fascio di combattimento.* The day following the foundation of the *fascio* there came a collision between several young fascist students and the red guard. A student named Sanvico was seriously wounded. The tension grew continually until March 1921, when one evening one of our meetings was broken up by the report of firearms in the street. The socialist-communists had put an end to the life of a student named Romeo. We rushed into the streets with revolvers in hand and began an irresistible action which lasted for five days in Perugia, with the help of the Florentine squad, and which spread in a few weeks' time over the whole region. Soon the red flags began to disappear from public buildings and, with the violence which was absolutely indispensable, liberty for all was established." [4]

In the south, except for the province of Puglia which we have already mentioned, fascism was practically unknown before the March on Rome. Political life and labor organization are both very backward in these parts, and since neither nationalism nor anti-nationalism has made much headway, naturally neither has fascism. The south was dominated by the Catholic Popular Party immediately upon its formation in 1919, and labor began to be organized into "white syndicates." After the March on Rome these organizations were gradually transferred by means of political pressure to the fascist syndicates. What conflict there was in the south was an extension of the conflict which arose in certain northern sections, where the white syndicates were fought by the *fascisti,* and in general was the result of the attempts of the Masonic forces to utilize the *fascisti* in promoting anti-clericalism. The most serious fights in the south, however, were between nationalists and fascists. Many young men of the middle classes, on returning from the war, had organized nationalist *fasci,* which were usually of the most reactionary temper and served the interests of the big landholders. Later, when the *fascisti* came in and tried to organize similar *fasci,* personal rivalries ensued and the *fascisti* made the reactionary character of the nationalists a pretext for appealing to the masses in their attempt to dislodge them. These fights, however, were not widespread nor of long duration and in the south as well as the north nationalism and fascism have fused.

Into minor local differences of fascism we can not enter here. In some cases fascism was supported by the Catholics (for example, by Count Grosoli); in others it was under Masonic and anti-clerical influence (as for example, in Rome where General Capello, member of the Council of the Grand Orient, and now sentenced for complicity in an attempt on Mussolini's life, reviewed the first fascist parade, himself in fascist uniform). Some *fascisti* were violently anti-d'Annunzio, and others just as violently pro-d'Annunzio. Fascism, as Zibordi said, "took on local color" almost immediately and has only recently achieved a fair degree of national homogeneity.

III. Milan Facism

After these scattered examples of fascist origins and motives we must now turn back to headquarters, that is, to Milan, and follow the movements of this particular *fascio* in more detail. For though fascism did

[4] Misuri: *Rivolta Morale,* pp. 18–22 *passim.*

not originate in Milan nor spring from the brain of one man, the Milan *fascio* headed by Mussolini undoubtedly first gave the movements a formal organization and a national scope.

In Milan, Turin and Florence, the intellectuals and students played an exceptionally prominent part. Middle class youths had left their studies or professional practices and gone to war. More than the laborers, they felt on returning from the front a claim for recognition and honor to say nothing of employment. Most of them were officers in the army and expected to be leaders in civil life. Instead, they found it difficult to make up their losses, to pass their examinations, to find employment, and to enter into normal social relations. Within a short time the inflation had reduced their economic status below that of the laborers. Then came insult on injury. Instead of being treated as heroes they were persecuted as traitors. Consequently they were among the first to welcome the *fasci*, not only as an employment but as an opportunity to defend their personal honor. In the *fasci* of the above-named cities these students, journalists, lawyers and intellectuals were prominent, if not predominant.

A number of such radicals had already organized under the banner of futurism. Even before the end of the war, Marinetti, Settimelli and Carli had founded a paper in Rome, *Roma Futurista*. Mario Carli at Rome and Captain Vecchi at Milan succeeded in organizing the *arditi* into a national association and affiliating this with the futurist movement. *Roma Futurista* was to be the official organ of the *arditi*, but shortly afterward Vecchi founded *L'Ardito* at Milan, which practically made the *arditi* independent of the futurist organizations, though in their personnel there was considerable overlapping. To give themselves a political organization, the futurists in 1918 formed several *fasci politici futuristi*, which were to be the basis of a Futurist Party. These were especially strong at Rome, Florence and Milan. By February 1919 there were about twenty such *fasci*.

In the first number of *Roma Futurista* Settimelli wrote: "Futurism, which until now has carried on primarily an artistic program, proposes to carry on a unified political activity in order to coöperate in solving the urgent national problems. . . . The prejudice for pedantic and quietistic seriousness imposed on old Italy by soft-headed professors, by anti-Italian priests and by Giolitti's grafters tried to discredit the geniality of our daring youths and innovators.

"But the *true* Italy can not and will not remain, not even in part, in their incapable hands. The war has revealed the *true* Italian forces. They are young, violent, anti-traditional and ultra-Italian forces."

This is a comparatively mild and restrained statement of futurist politics. On the whole this group was so violent, so revolutionary, so ridiculously enraged against everything that has a past, that it was taken even less seriously in politics than in art. It attracted attention, however, because it was so ridiculous and served as good advertising and campaign material. In fact many of the early fascist propagandists and organizers were futurists; among them, in addition to those already mentioned, Castelli, Freddi, Fabbri, Bolzon, Bottai. (The two last named are now in the government.)

The forty-five men whom Mussolini called together at Milan on March 23, 1919, and who constituted themselves the first *fascio di combattimento*, were a very mixed lot. Many, but by no means all of them, were war veterans. A number of them were active *arditi* (*e.g.,* Vecchi), there were a few Republicans, a few syndicalists and agitators (like Michele Bianchi), an army general, and a generous representation of futurists. F. T. Marinetti, the national leader of the futurists, was there and *fasci futuristi* of various cities had sent representatives, among them Piero Bolzon, Enrico Rocca, and Mario Carli. In general this *fascio* represented much the same lot who had formed the *fasci d'azione rivoluzionaria* in 1915, and its chief aim now was to defend the war against the rising tide of "neutralists," against the "penitent Magdalenes," as Mussolini called them. One of the distinguishing characteristics of the Milan *fascio* was that it wanted to be revolutionary, proletarian, a band of fighters for a new Italy, not merely defenders of the existing social order and vested interests in the face of bolshevism. The "*combattimento*" was not meant against the threatened revolution but against the neutralism of the regime as well as of the communists. The motto was: "Fight for the revolutionary fruits of a revolutionary war." The *fascio* was formed at the time when the Italian socialists voted to join the Russian Third International, and the prime fear of the fascists was not economic bolshevism, but Russian, international anti-war bolshevism.

Here it must be recalled that Mussolini had entered the war as a revolutionary socialist, and had suggested, though vaguely, that after the war, as a result of it, the proletariat would be able to carry out its longed-for revolution. He had still not quite forgotten this idea and though he had been cured of his romantic revolutionism, he said, by the lesson of the Russian revolution, and though he now saw that a genuine revolution can be achieved only by "gaining mastery over long-standing and complicated economic forces," [5] he still clung to his 1917 formula of "giving a social content to the war." "The war must

[5] *Popolo d'Italia*, February 27, 1919. In *Diuturna*, p. 245.

lead to the material and moral elevation of the masses, to a profound renewal of our national life." [6] Now that the "material elevation of the masses" was far from visible, he harped on the "moral elevation" and to the hosts of the "deluded proletariat" and to the "penitent Magdalenes" he sang this heroic strain:

"From the point of view of social and economic renovation, the war has satisfied the most ardent hopes and the most far-reaching aspirations. The war has not driven the masses back into the pre-historic darkness of their life before the war, but has called them with a loud voice to reassert themselves. It has broken their chains. It has given them an extraordinary vindication. A war of masses ended with the triumph of the masses. Numbers exalt the numbers who aspire to rule human society. The paradise dreamed of by the Bellamys of socialism and relegated by them to the year 2000 has now been anticipated by a century. . . . What matters the immensity of the sacrifice in view of the wonderful possibilities of the immediate future? The centuries of celestial happiness which open up make us forget the four years of hell. The official socialists who foolishly opposed the war must exalt it lyrically today. . . . Their Ideal is within reach. I repeat: the Ideal. Penitent Magdalenes of all sorts and descriptions, do not stop at those details which may offend your taste and your affections. Look at the grand total. This is not the time for repentance. I venture to say it is the time for continuing in the sin, to say nothing of not renouncing it." [7]

This rhapsody was obviously too ironic to be convincing and Mussolini himself no doubt had misgivings. The idylls of "*primavera umana*" which he set up after the victory, seemed strangely out of place, and it evidently took effort to sing them. He soon changed the tune a little as follows:

"We interventionists are the only ones in Italy who have a right to talk about revolutions. . . . We need not await the revolution, as does the crowd of Party members; nor does the word frighten us, as it does those timid mediocre persons whose brains stopped working in 1914. We have already fought the revolution. In May 1915.

"The *fasci di combattimento* are revolutionary, for we take our departure from that May which was essentially and divinely revolutionary, in so far as it destroyed a shameful situation in our internal politics and decided the outcome of the World War. That was the first episode of the Revolution. It was the beginning. The Revolution continued under the name of war for forty months. It is not yet over. It may

[6] *Popolo d'Italia*, March 1919.
[7] *Popolo d'Italia*, March 5, 1919. In *Diuturna*, pp. 247–252.

or may not take a dramatic, sensational course. It may proceed on a faster tempo. But it is continuing. . . . As to the means? We have no formal principles (*prejudiciali*). We accept whatever means may become necessary, the legal and the so-called illegal. A period is opening in history which might be defined as that of mass politics or of democratic hypertrophy. We can not run counter to this movement. We must head it toward political democracy and economic democracy. The former can lead the masses back to the state and the latter can conciliate capital and labor on the basis of their common ground, namely, maximum production. From all this travail will rise new values and new hierarchies." [8] " Formal principles are iron and tin fetters. We have neither republican nor monarchist principles, neither catholic nor anti-catholic, socialist nor anti-socialist. We are problemists, realists, realizers." [9]

Nevertheless, when the time came, Mussolini saw fit to draw up a program or platform for the *fascio,* not a set of binding principles, he explained, but a program for immediate action. It was accepted by the *fascio,* published in the *Popolo d'Italia,* and may be summarized as follows:

1. Annexation of Fiume and the whole of Dalmatia.
2. Universal suffrage for men and women.
3. *Scrutin de liste* and proportional representation.
4. *Political elections as soon as demobilization is completed.*
5. Eligible age for deputies to be reduced from 31 to 25 years.
6. Deputies to be elected at the next elections to form a National Assembly.
7. The National Assembly to sit for three years.
8. The National Assembly to determine immediately a new form of government.
9. The Senate to be abolished.
10. Economic councils with legislative powers to be elected by professional groups.
11. Establishment of eight-hour day by law.
12. Management of industries by those workers' organizations which prove themselves capable of it, particularly the railroads by the railroad workers.
13. The formation of a national militia.
14. The nationalization of munitions plants.
15. A heavy capital levy.

[8] *Popolo d'Italia,* March 18, 1919.   [9] *Giornale d'Italia,* March 19, 1919.

16. Confiscation of certain church properties and abolition of certain clerical privileges.

17. A heavy inheritance tax.

18. The seizure of 85 per cent of the war profits and revision of military contracts.

That same evening at the celebration in the *piazza*, which has been called the Constituent Assembly of Fascism, the general formula was announced, " coöperation in production; class struggle in distribution," and three fundamental " declarations " of policy were read and approved:

(1) Recognition and honor to the veterans of the War and to the fallen heroes.

(2) Acceptance of the League of Nations, opposition to all imperialisms; annexation of Fiume and Dalmatia.

(3) Sabotage of all neutralist candidates in the elections.

Mussolini's general scheme at that time seems to have been the institution of a sort of Producers' Republic with a constitution modelled on the new German one. The syndicalist elements in it, the scheme for national economic councils, were suggested to him partly by Kurt Eisner's German plan which Mussolini quoted word for word, partly by the fact that the patriotic *Unione Italiana del Lavoro* was holding its national congress at the time and Mussolini hoped to establish an alliance with it.

His chief reliance, however, in the realization of such a program, was on the returned soldiers, the " proletariat of the trenches," who immediately after demobilization would rally to a program which was both patriotic and revolutionary. He changed the heading on the *Popolo d'Italia* from " A Socialist Daily " to " A daily for fighters and producers." In his speech at the first gathering in the *piazza* he expressed himself as follows: " We must go out to meet the labor which is returning from the trenches; for it would be disgraceful and bolshevik to deny recognition to those who fought the war. We must accept the principles of the laboring classes. We are placing ourselves on the ground of national syndicalism and contrary to the interference of the state when the latter seeks to kill the process of wealth production. I have the impression that the actual regime in Italy is opening the way for its successor. During the war, we all felt the incapacity of those who were governing us and we know that we won only by virtue of the Italian people, not by any intelligence or capacity on the part of the administration. Given the chance for a new regime, we must not be faint-hearted. Therefore we are constituting the *fasci*, bodies capable of creative action and capable of going out into the squares and crying: It is we who have the right to succeed this government, for it was we who pushed the country into the war and led it to victory. . . . From the next elections will come a national assembly which must determine the form of government of the Italian state. It will ask: Republic or Monarchy? and we, who have always had republican leanings, will then come forward and say: Republic."

On July 22, 1919, Mussolini made a campaign speech [10] which clearly revealed his preoccupation with the fall elections. He outlined a detailed program constructed of planks in the platforms of the parties of the left, especially the Republican, which he expected would be " a common denominator for the U. S. M., the *fasci di combattimento*, the Veterans' Association, the *arditi*, the Union of Demobilized Soldiers, the Association of Volunteers, the Garibaldist Association, the *Circolo Corridoni*, etc." He suggested:

1. Oppose the Socialist Party.

2. Stop striking and produce.

3. Financial provisions: (a) A loan of a million dollars, and (b) concessions in Asia Minor; both of these he expected Secretary Lansing to get for Italy in opposition to Clemenceau.

4. Only Fiume and the Dalmatian cities are possible annexations for the present and " Secretary Lansing promises substitutes in the Mediterranean for our sacrifices in Dalmatia."

5. Oppose a general strike under any conditions.

6. " Constructive " measures, it matters little whether they be called revolution or reaction. " My compass is: I favor whatever furthers the greatness of the Italian people."

7. No alliance with the Socialist Party. " I deny the utility and the opportunity of any sort of collaboration with that party."

8. Revise the Versailles Treaty, but oppose the projected general strike of protest against the treaty.

9. Syndical organization:

    (a) Absolute independence of all parties or sects.

    (b) Federalism and autonomy.

    (c) Reduction to a minimum of salaried officials.

    (d) Referendum on all issues.

10. " The electoral reform will be passed, with *scrutin de liste* and proportional representation. This will obviously determine some great coalitions. One, a socialist-Leninist; another, a clerico-popular; and a

10 v. *Discorsi*, first edition, pp. 69–80.

third, *ours*, which might be called The Alliance of the Component of Forces . . . a republican alliance or a concentration of the interventionist groups of the left." On October ninth he made another campaign speech which was strongly republican.[11]

The list of candidates set up at Milan for the election included Mussolini, Marinetti (futurist), Podrecca (leading anti-clerical), Toscanini (the distinguished and popular musician), Bolzon (futurist), Macchi (an aviator and a futurist), several republicans and several syndicalists. During the campaign Mussolini, Marinetti, Vecchi, Bolzon and fifteen *arditi* were locked up for twenty-one days for leading armed bands against state authorities. Carli, to escape arrest, fled to Fiume and joined the *arditi* under d'Annunzio.

These candidates and their program were ill-fated in practically all respects. They received but little support even among *fascisti*, and the events of the next few months made their program hopelessly obsolete. Its enthusiasm for democracy, which came largely from Versailles and the Wilsonian war propaganda, was soon buried under the revelation of what was actually going on at the Peace Conference. It was useless to talk of Dalmatia when the annexation even of Fiume seemed doubtful. The "proletariat of the trenches" joined the "red guards" in much greater numbers than they joined the *fasci*. The *Unione Italiana del Lavoro*, to which Mussolini had made overtures, failed to get a foothold. The masses flocked into the folds of the Socialist and Popular Party organizations. It soon began to look as though the revolution, far from being led by Mussolini, would take place in spite of him. The elections, which were to produce a grand coalition, gave Mussolini and Marinetti but a few thousand votes, scarcely worth counting, and the triumphant "reds" and "whites" were content to scoff at the "political corpses" of the *fascisti*.

For a while Mussolini thought he saw a ray of hope coming from an unexpected angle. In May 1919 the laborers in the metal works of Franchi-Gregorini at Dalmine near Bergamo felt the need of an increase in wages, as did everyone at the time. They feared to strike, for strikes, though expedient as political protests, were practically useless as means of getting higher wages, especially at that time of depression when surplus labor was plentiful and employers were already resorting to lockouts to get rid of labor. Influenced in part by the growing menace of lockouts and in part by the movement for workers' factory control, which was at the time being urged among labor circles in the northern industrial centers, these laborers hit upon the scheme

[11] v. *Discorsi*, first edition, pp. 81–88. Cited in part by Mussolini in *Diuturna*, p. 336–7.

of remaining in the factory night and day. Instead of stopping work, they "camped" on the job, refused to leave, and ran the factory with or against orders. To make their action still more irreproachable they hoisted the national tri-color over the factory. The "occupation" was successful and the employers yielded in a few days. This appealed to Mussolini immensely and he gladly accepted the invitation to address the "factory occupiers." He praised their "productive strike," gave them his hearty support and claimed that they had shown the people how to free itself from the political game and had opened up the horizon for the future.

The idea took hold rapidly and one factory after another was occupied, culminating in September 1920 in the occupation of practically all the metal works around Turin and Milan and of hundreds of others in all parts of Italy. Mussolini continued to support the workers. But when the red flag came to be hoisted more frequently than the tri-color, when the workers organized themselves into military "red guards," and when they threatened to put an end to private ownership altogether, Mussolini was placed in a predicament. He favored the attack on the industrialists, but he had a horror of a red revolution. It all seemed to turn on the color of the flag hoisted. By September 1920 it was clear that the movement had become the very essence of "bolshevism," and the terror-stricken industrialists and middle classes did not hesitate to declare war on it. Outside Milan the *fasci* themselves were openly fighting it. Mussolini weakened gradually, fearing first that the workers would not prove competent to carry on production, then asserting that the movement was being led by subversive labor leaders against the interests of the Italian nation. He finally tried to inject the nationalistic and patriotic issue into what he had maintained was a purely economic experiment. On the whole, however, he gave it his moral support until the end, ridiculing the idea that it was bolshevism, and asserting that there was absolutely no relation between such experiments in workers' democracy and the bolshevik tyranny in Russia. In fact, during this crisis, Mussolini and the *Popolo d'Italia* were really preoccupied with the Fiume excitement. In part, at least, his tactics seem to have been to try to divert attention from the internal and economic problems to that glorious revindication of national honor and prestige which the Fiume expedition signified to his mind. And he inclined strongly towards the contention of the nationalists, that all internal questions should be subordinated to a foreign policy and "the superior interests of the nation as a whole."

Meanwhile the problem was being solved by others, or rather it solved itself. The workers carried on as long as they could with the funds and raw materials available, but found out that the banks would neither give them credit nor turn over the factory funds to them. They faced the same problem when they came to buy new materials. In short, they very soon absolutely stopped and after using up what was on hand they had to come to terms with their employers. In the meantime the Giolitti government had intervened and finally succeeded in inducing the employers to accept a compromise whereby the factories were returned to their owners, factory committees with limited powers were established, and wages raised. Had not the government intervened, and had not the great majority of the workers voted for the compromise, industrial labor organization would probably have been crushed completely. For the industrialists would certainly have done what some of them did do a year later, when the elections were favorable. The Fiat Company, for example, forced each employee to sign a statement saying that he did not and would not belong to any labor union whatsoever. As it was, the government kept out long enough to let the workers feel their failure, but not long enough to let the employers dictate. The net result was that the revolution was broken, and the Giolitti government came out of the fray with a feather in its cap. Mussolini himself could do little else than support the government's action, throwing in a little scolding, as was his custom, for all three parties, — the employers for their initial stubbornness, the workers for their dangerous approach to bolshevism, and the government for its lack of promptness and decision.

The failure of the factory occupations really determined the fate of the revolution. Certainly fascism played no critical part in it one way or the other. The bulk of the squadrist-communist violence came after this event, and had an agrarian and not an industrial setting. Nevertheless the factory occupation had an important bearing on the subsequent development of fascism. For though it settled the practical issue quite independently of fascism, and marked the turning of the tide against maximalism even among the socialists, it did not calm the mental and emotional state of either side. Both sides now resorted increasingly to violence; the socialists, because, defeated in economic strategy, they had no other recourse; the employers, because they were terror-stricken and feared " a return of the beast." From now on the *fasci* had little trouble in collecting all the funds they needed.

IV. War on Bolshevism

Thus Mussolini's political and economic program of 1919 fizzled out miserably, but fascist squadrism was becoming increasingly active and important. The Milan squad itself, a few weeks after its formation, went into action. On the occasion of a general strike, which had been declared because the government had prohibited a celebration in honor of Lenin, the *fascisti* on April 15, 1919, broke up a parade of 10,000 of the strikers. And in the afternoon, a number of them joined the *arditi* under Vecchi and destroyed the offices and printing plant of the *Avanti*, not without bloodshed. This action was like a signal for similar enterprises all over the country. Strikes were broken up, parades were turned into street battles, labor offices were sacked and burned, guns, clubs and castor oil were used freely. We have already given some account at the beginning of this chapter of the nature of the ensuing violence. A mere list of " battles " as they were announced in the press may give the reader some idea of their extent.

1920, Sept. 12 — Conflicts in Turin, Como, Valdarno.

            23 — *Fascisti* destroy the Labor Hall of Pola.

            25 — End of factory occupation.

    Oct. 11 — Sonzini " assassinated " by communist jury.

            14 — Bloody incidents at Milan, Trieste, Brescia, Bologna. At Trieste the *fascisti* destroy the offices of the paper, *Lavoratore*.

            29 — Strike at Florence and conflicts between *fascisti* and socialists.

    Nov. 4 — Bloody conflicts at Verona, Bologna, Ancona, and Reggio Calabria between socialists and fascists. Bolshevik deputy, Scarabello, killed by a bomb he was carrying in a satchel.

            7 — Bloody conflicts at Florence.

            21 — Massacre at Bologna and murder of Giordani.

    Dec. 18 — Bloody riots of war cripples against Chamber of Deputies. Two deputies beaten at Bologna. Socialist riots in Chamber of Deputies.

            20 — Bloody attack of socialists on *fascisti* at Ferrara.

            26 — State of siege in Trieste, when masses of *fascisti* are arrested.

1921, Jan. 1 — Bloody conflicts between *fascisti* and socialists at Correggio.

            3 — Bloody conflicts between *fascisti* and socialists at Fusignano.

            9 — Bloody conflicts between *fascisti* and socialists at Bologna.

            19 — Bloody conflicts between *fascisti* and socialists at Castellamare di Stabia.

22 — Socialist aggression against *fascisti* at Modena.

24 — Ditto. In reprisal *fascisti* burn Labor Halls at Modena and Bologna.

25 — Socialist aggression against *fascisti* at Cecina.

26 — Fascist reprisal; burn office of socialist press.

30 — Bloody conflict between socialists and *fascisti* at Vittoria in Sicily.

Feb. 8 — Bloody riots at Trieste. Office of *Lavoratore* again attacked.

16 — Conflicts between socialists and *fascisti* around Cremona, Modena, Polesina, Puglia and elsewhere. General strike at Livorno.

20 — Conflicts between socialists and *fascisti* at Bra, Milan, Ferrara, Verona, Taranto, Bari.

24 — General strike at Bari. Bloody conflicts at Minervino.

26 — Conflicts between *fascisti* and socialists at Torre Annunziata and Rodigno.

27 — Conflicts between *fascisti* and socialists at Florence, Spezia and Cerignola.

1921, Mar. 1 — Barricades and bitter conflicts at Florence. Bolshevists trap *fascisti* in ambush at Canfanaro (Istria). Labor Hall of Trieste burned by *fascisti* and shipyards of San Marco by communists.

2 — Violent fights around Florence. Sailors and police massacred in ambush at Empoli.

4 — Disorders and conflicts throughout Tuscany.

6 — Bloody attack by communists on a parade at Casale.

13 — Fresh cruel encounters between *fascisti* and socialists.

22 — Conflicts in Puglia and Varesino.

23 — Terrible anarchist aggression at Diana Theatre, Milan.

24 — Communist aggressions on railroads and at Genoa. Conflicts in Tuscany and Puglia. Cruel deeds of communists in mines of Castelnuovo dei Sabbioni.

28 — Labor Hall of Foligno burned by *fascisti*. Bloody conflicts at Alessandria and in the Valley of Aosta.

Apr. 6 — Fiat works close down. Labor Hall of Padua burned.

8 — Bloody riots in Venetia. Labor Hall of Reggio Emilia burned. Mines of Albona are held by workers, captured by troops.

10 — Conflicts in Arezzo, Ferrara, Puglia and Sicily.

13–14 — Bloody fights at Livorno.

    17 — Bloody communist attack on *fascisti* at Foiano (Chiana). Fascist reprisal by burning Labor Hall of Voltri. Conflicts at Vaiano, Piano, Bozzano, Arezzo, etc.

And so it continues month after month until well into the summer of 1921, only to be resumed again though less intensively the following October. And this leaves out of account the series of fights for Fiume, which fall in the same period and aggravated the excitement and confusion.

It was not easy for Mussolini to adjust himself to this drift of events, for it demanded a radical reconstruction of the fascism of 1919 as he had first outlined it. It was he himself who had insisted on the word *combattimento,* but he had conceived it more in a political sense, not this literal and brutal fighting. At first he seems to have taken his political debacle more or less cynically. He began to seek comfort and salvation for his own individual soul in his former " absurd but always comforting religion of anarchy." [12] He joined in the general chorus, not only of " Down with the government! " but also of " Down with the state in general! " He talked much of the eternal wolf in human nature, of the joy which human beings find in fighting each other in the name of humanity, fraternity, and internationalism, [13] and that " strife is the origin of all things." [14] An editorial in the *Popolo d'Italia,* July 15, 1920, entitled *Amarissimo,* probably describes the general state of his mind. But he soon reconciled himself to the new situation. In February he still dropped occasional remarks about heavy inheritance taxes, war profits taxes, confiscation of big estates and similar ideas reminiscent of the original program. But by the time of the second National Congress in May, there was little mention of this sort of thing, and the program of the 1920 Congress was short and simple, consisting of three main planks, but really only one idea:

1. The defense of the war.
2. Revindication of the victory.
3. Opposition to the " theoretical and practical degeneration of politicians' socialism."

About all that was left of the radical program of the previous year was a general " expression of disgust for those men and those organizations of the political bourgeoisie who are demonstrating their in-

[12] v. *Diuturna,* pp. 284–5.

[13] v. *Diuturna,* pp. 280–1. Also Appendix No. 5.

[14] v. Trieste Speech, Appendix No. 6.

capacity to face the problems of both internal and foreign policy, who obstruct all far-reaching reforms and oppose any willing recognition of the rights of the people, merely accepting the concessions and renunciations which parliamentary calculations suggest to them." The Congress went on record as being opposed to a party organization, since fascism could not be forced into fixed programs, and it declared itself "free from any prejudices against existing institutions" (*i.e.*, the monarchy).

At this Marinetti and some of the futurists bolted. Already at the congress of Florence in October 1919, Marinetti had become a bit suspicious of his fascist allies. He approved their revised program in general, but he noticed "several serious omissions." Nothing was said about the church; he recommended that Italy be "de-vaticanized" and the Pope expelled. The program called for Senate reform; he recommended Senate abolition, and in its place a "stimulatorium (*eccitatorio*) of competent young men under thirty." The program called for school reform; he recommended "schools of physical courage and patriotism to replace the now prehistoric and antediluvian courses in Greek and Latin." Finally he resented the fact that no provisions had been made for the "proletariat of genius" and genuine "brain work." He wanted "free expositions of creative genius" in all cities. Consequently when the next congress abandoned both the anti-clerical and the anti-monarchist planks, he severed his connection with the *fasci*.

By September 5, at the fascist congress of Cremona, when no one could discover a generally acceptable program, Mussolini said frankly, "The *fascisti* are the gypsies of Italian politics; not being tied down to any fixed principles, they proceed unceasingly toward one goal, the future well-being of the Italian people." In his famous Trieste speech of September 20, he emphasized this still more. "We have no fixed principles (*prejudiziali*), and we have none because we are no church; we are a movement. We are not a party, we are an athletic body of free men." Then he went on to set up the two great pillars of fascism, as he called them. The one was precisely this quality of flexibility, the willingness to change with the times, the aversion to all panaceas and absolutes, a quality which Mussolini called "pragmatism and anti-demagogism." The other was fascism's revived consciousness of the ancient glories of Italy, of the Roman Empire, of the Renaissance, of the *risorgimento*, and the continuation of this tradition by intervention in the World War, by the heroism of d'Annunzio's legions and by the fascist struggle for a new imperial Rome, which would mark the culmination of Italy's traditional glory and leadership among the nations. All this led up to the battle cry: "We are ready to kill and be killed!"[15]

Though these sentiments were very congenial to the temper of squadrism and served to arouse the fighting spirit on both sides, they were inspired in Mussolini's own case more by the problem of Fiume and by foreign policy in general, than by the internal situation. For, as we have noted, throughout this period he seemed more enthusiastic about the revival of militant patriotism and the campaign of the nationalists against both the allies and the "renunciatory" Italian government, than he was about the so-called civil war. In fact, he persisted in trying to view the latter as merely corollary to the former, minimizing the economic basis of the strife and exaggerating the patriotic issues.

Many of the squadrists too, being *arditi*, were very much excited about Fiume, not a few of them joining the expedition. When, on Christmas Day 1920, the government ordered troops against d'Annunzio, these *fascisti* wanted to revolt immediately and overthrow the government. But Mussolini and the Milan group were content with words, merely heaping invectives on Giolitti. For they were not professed nationalists and though they were ardent for Fiume, they thought d'Annunzio had gone to useless extremes. For political reasons as well, these would-be radicals and republicans could not support d'Annunzio too slavishly. As a result there were serious splits in many of the *fasci*. For example, in the Florence *fascio,* which was then headed by Umberto Pasella, the republican Mussolini politician, most of the squadrists under Dumini, and the intellectual nationalists under the leadership of Professor Agnoletti, withdrew and formed the *Fascio Gabriele d'Annunzio.* But after this affair was settled such breaches were soon healed, not, however, without causing a notable growth in nationalist sentiment throughout the fascist movement.

V. The Fascist Party

Mussolini and his associates were by no means content to have fascism assume merely this squadrist character. For though it was admirably adapted to the needs of the moment, it could not be permanen and when the struggle was over it would degenerate into a sort o "Roman letter fraternity" or into one more patriotic social club o the Garibaldist type. He wanted fascism to be a permanent politica force, and to this he bent his efforts from the start. He had never bee a squadrist himself and had never conceived of fascism in militar terms. By 1921 he privately confessed he was tired of all the "Duce

[15] cf. *Popolo d'Italia*, October 17, 1920.

talk and the military spirit and wished he could settle down to being a civil leader of a civil movement.[16]

The trend of events had obviously spelled failure for his original political program, but it had not interrupted the work of political organization which he and his immediate associates had been carrying on assiduously, and which enabled fascism to enjoy continuity in action, however much its programs might change. Fascism, being multiple in its origins and aims, could not be expected to start out with a consistent and permanent program. That it achieved unity at all and a national organization is largely due to the persistent efforts of Mussolini to get and keep control of it.

Immediately after the first formal session of March 23, 1919, a hierarchy of officials was established; a secretary general, assistant secretary general, and provincial secretaries. Then a number of missionaries, or " confidential agents " (fiduciari) as they were called, were sent out into those provinces where fascism was just beginning and where such new units could be brought under the Milan control. Prominent among these early organizers were Umberto Pasella, Luigi Freddi, Alessandro Melchiorri, and Francesco Giunta. In Emilia and Romagna such agents were at home, so to speak, for the local organizers of these provinces coöperated continually with the Milan group and were represented at its meetings. But in Tuscany, Umbria, and regions south, these men were outsiders, sent to impose themselves on the local organizations. They were literally Mussolini's " trusties," mostly men of mediocre ability, whom Mussolini could control and who represented his point of view. Most of them were ex-labor organizers or some other kind of " subversive " politician. It is, of course, difficult to generalize in this matter, but on the whole it is safe to say that they worked in two chief directions:

(1) They gave what local organizations they found or created a political form and incorporated them in the general scheme. Where local leaders were too prominent and too insistent on autonomy, they tried to wrest control from them and focus all eyes on Mussolini. They naturally collected subscriptions for the Popolo d'Italia, the " official paper."

(2) They tried to win the lower classes.

As we have already pointed out the Milan group were more " proletarian " than others, certainly more so than the Tuscan and southern fasci. Occasionally it happened that Mussolini would declare a benevolent neutrality during squadrist raids, in order to discourage the impression that he was sold to the bourgeoisie. Mussolini's

[16] cf. Misuri: Rivolta Morale, p. 197.

agents, wherever they went, set to work to organize syndicates, to appeal to the masses, to gather together whatever malcontents and revolutionary spirits they could, and especially to welcome as many socialists and communists as could be converted. Naturally neither the means used for conversion nor the converts were always of the highest quality.

Politicians are politicians the world over, and the details of this story must be left to the reader's imagination. I mention a few samples and pass on. Umberto Pasella was made Secretary General and set out to organize Tuscany. He came to Florence, but found the squadrists and local politicians both hostile to his interference. Mussolini then worked directly through the local politicians. For a while an ex-captain Zamboni kept politicians and squadrists reconciled. But when the split came at the time of the Fiume crisis, Mussolini seized the opportunity to send his man Dino Perrone, the Provincial Secretary, who enjoyed rural support, to restore harmony and whip the Florentine *fascio* into line. Then followed incessant friction between local politicians like Agnoletti and Pirelli, and the official secretaries. Meanwhile Pasella had established a struggling syndical organization, but it made little headway because of the rich men's sons and middle class domination in the *fascio*. When the party was being organized in 1921, Cesare Rossi, the Assistant Secretary General and one of Mussolini's right-hand men (the other being Bianchi), took occasion to oust Pasella, because of a more or less personal dispute which Pasella had got into at Florence. Whereupon Pasella continued to lead a rival, autonomous *fascio* until 1922 when he was re-admitted.

The story of Perugia is somewhat similar. Misuri, of whose middle-class *Unione Sindacale* we have an account above, secured the services of one Guido Pighetti, a professional syndicalist organizer, and while Misuri, Bastianini, Ucelli and the old squadrists were out on their punitive expeditions, which they conducted with exceptional vigor and violence, Pighetti was busy collecting syndicate members. In August 1920 he succeeded in having himself appointed *fiduciario* by Rossi, the Milan Secretary, in order to organize an official *fascio di combattimento*. After its formation in January 1921, Misuri continued to direct the fighting and enjoyed the support of the nationalists and liberals. Pighetti, being a Mason, got the support of the Masonic organization and of the democrats with whom the Masons work. Then he raked in what labor elements he could by hook or crook and with these forces attacked Misuri. The Masons and democrats now used Pighetti to the limit to get control of the Perugian *fascio*, while Misuri rallied the conservative forces to his support. Pighetti finally won out in the local elections, but during the campaign Misuri had made remarks reflecting both on Pighetti's syndicalist tactics and on his private character. A duel was the inevitable consequence. Pighetti was wounded. Mussolini now sent an investigating committee, but before their report, which was favorable to Misuri, had come out, Misuri had launched his attack on the Milan clique in general and as a result was expelled from the Party.

These are but a few incidents in a vast network of political maneuvering and organization. Mussolini now became eloquent on the subjects of discipline and hierarchy, a gospel preached for the Italian nation, but intended immediately for the all too independent *fasci*. But of this more later.

Mussolini's political tactics and ambitions were suddenly given a new turn by Giolitti's decision in April 1921 to dissolve Parliament and call for new elections, in the hope that he might get a more tractable Chamber. He asked the *fascisti* and nationalists to coöperate with the other middle class groups in forming a " constitutional bloc " to offer a united front to the menacing Socialist and Popular Parties. Remembering their experience in 1919, the *fascisti* and nationalists were glad to accept the proposal and now made common cause, supporting each other's candidates. The result was that the Catholic south, where the Popular Party had almost undisputed sway, held its own, but in the north the constitutional bloc was able to rob the socialists of about twenty seats. Thirty-five *fascisti* found themselves in the Chamber of Deputies, together with ten nationalists and a still smaller group of national liberals. Except for a popular young professor of economics at Vincenza, Alberto De Stefani, whom his students had elected, all of the *fascisti* owed part of their support to the nationalist vote. Nevertheless they came out of the elections the strongest single group of a very weak nationalist bloc. The gains were too small to do Giolitti much good. Among the *fascisti* elected were Mussolini (deputy from Milan and Bologna), Farinacci (from Cremona), Paolucci and Gay (nationalistic fascists), Bottai (a republican), Acerbo (from the Abruzzi), Coda (violently monarchist), Misuri (from Perugia) and others representing in general a group of popular local leaders, a large proportion coming from Tuscany and the central provinces, where the bloc had been most successful.

This brought the Mussolini group of fascist politicians face to face with two serious problems: their relation to the other parliamentary groups and their relation to the fascist deputies. It seemed, off-hand, as though the Milan clique would have to play a minor rôle in both cases. But they played the game hard.

Immediately after the election Mussolini announced to Giolitti that he could not count on his support, that liberalism was a dead cause, that Giolitti would not have enough support from the masses anyway, and that he, Mussolini, felt no obligation to keep alive an artificial bloc. So much for the liberals.

Next, Cesare Rossi, the leader of the Milan clique, whispered to Mussolini that now would be a good time to announce " the republican tendency of fascism." This he did in a widely advertised newspaper article, and he emphasized it by absenting himself and his fascist co-deputies from the sitting at which the King read his address. This had the desired effect on the nationalists. They, being ardent monarchists, were duly scandalized, and the distinction between nationalists and fascists, which had practically disappeared during the electoral campaign, was vigorously reasserted. The bloc was broken up right at the start, and Mussolini felt free to step out as " the leader of the new Right." He and his comrades made themselves conspicuous by sitting on the extreme right, which position, as Mussolini put it, " was physically favorable for *combattimento*." He now made light of the democrats, liberals, and other middle-class groups, the groups from which most of the cabinet members and ex-cabinet members came, told them that the " liberal-democratic " state was doomed and that " the world is turning to the Right." The main lines of the program of this fascist right wing, as he outlined them in his address in the Chamber on July 21, were a strong foreign policy and an individualistic, *laissez faire* economic policy, coupled with a reassertion of the authority and integrity of the state in those matters which fall in its proper sphere.

At the same time he was building up this new Right, he was making peace with the socialists. Though he met with determined resistance both at the hands of the socialists and of his own followers, he was finally able to get a " Pact of Pacification " signed on August 3rd. Meanwhile, July 23, he had expounded to the Chamber of Deputies at some length his ideas about Church and State, which turned out to be surprisingly similar to those of the Popular Party. Then he suggested that the nation needed a government of coalition of the " three parties that really represented the masses," the Socialist, Popular and Fascist Parties. This proposal was quite ludicrous at the time, but a year later (that is, only a few months before the March on Rome), when the King consulted Filippo Turati, the reformist socialist leader, about the possibilities of his heading a cabinet, Mussolini immediately took the occasion to revive this idea. He wrote in the *Popolo d'Italia*, July 30, 1922, as follows: [17]

[17] In *Diuturna*, pp. 449–452.

"There is much talk these days of coalitions. In this matter I should like to say what may seem a paradox. I think that sooner or later, we are headed for a grand coalition between the three effective forces in the life of the country. There is no use talking of the democratic-liberals and of the social-democrats, who are *inside* but not *within* the country; but of socialism, which has already by the vote of the Confederation of Labor in regard to public services, shown its capacity to govern; of the Popular Party, a real and powerful force based on the force of Catholicism, and a third force, which gathers together the best energies of the country, *viz.* fascism. It will be this coalition which will have the merit of leading Italy toward her higher destinies."

How much of all this Mussolini really took seriously is difficult to say. It is true that it represents a final emergence of his early "prejudices" and aims. He may still have a suppressed desire to see himself at the head of Italian socialism, in revenge for his expulsion from the Party and in refutation of the charge which he will probably carry to his grave, that he betrayed the cause of socialism and of the masses to the enemy. No human mind can be absolutely relative, and it is but natural that even a Mussolini should feel occasional regrets for the causes he had left behind him. Certainly a man who aspired to be the leader of revolutionary masses may be excused a bit of rationalization when he finds himself at the head of a handful of extreme-right deputies.

The matter was more than personal bias, however. It was Milan politics, for these tactics had not been without effect within the fascist ranks. When the republican trend was announced, a number of the fascist deputies were no less upset than were the nationalists, for the republican urge among fascists had never been felt keenly outside Milan. The great majority of fascists were fairly indifferent on the subject. But many others had very decided prejudices in favor of the monarchy and regarded attacks on the King as treasonable. Several of the parliamentary group, as the deputies came to be called, openly told Mussolini that they would have none of his republican trend, and of the social-democrats, who are *inside* but not *within* the country, Misuri, for example, attended the royal session in defiance of Mussolini. At the first meeting of the parliamentary group at Milan the divergence was very evident and lines were clearly drawn between the Mussolini crowd and the independent deputies. Remarks were made about the crooked game of the Milan clique, and in return Mussolini said that the newcomers to fascism must not expect to have the broad outlook and familiarity with its traditions which characterized the founders. In short the deputies were told that fascism was not to be bossed from the benches of Parliament, and in return the deputies said they were not tied to a party and had a right to use their own judgment in their political conduct.

The opposition within the ranks to the republican trend was evidently much stronger than the Milan group had anticipated. Only a few days after the announcement had been made, and as soon as it had worked its desired effects, Mussolini beat a hasty retreat, explaining that fascism had no tendencies whatsoever, that it was neither monarchist nor republican, that the monarchy in fact had much for which to thank the *fascisti* and that the movement would continue to be without political prejudices, adopting always whatever policies might make for the moral elevation, etc.

Hardly was this excitement over, when a still worse internal crisis arose out of Mussolini's pact of pacification with the socialists. He had become worried over the continued fighting, and had noticed that the unnecessary and bloody fights of Sarzana, Roccastrada, Treviso, Terni, and Perugia had alienated the affections of a large part of the favorably inclined public. For by now public sentiment, even socialist sentiment, had abandoned the communists to such an extent that the danger of revolution seemed definitely removed. Since the *fascisti* enjoyed the support of public opinion, of press, and of government, they had nothing to fear, and further violence appeared to be sheer blood-thirstiness and brutal persecution of a vanquished enemy. For these reasons, Mussolini willingly accepted the suggestion of d'Annunzio and also of the government that a fascist-socialist truce was necessary. He explained to his squadrists that the need for fighting had passed, that fascism must now turn to its constructive tasks, and that "just as the nation welcomed us when our movement meant the breaking up of a tyranny, so the nation would repudiate us if our movement should assume the form of a new tyranny." [18]

The truce found practically no support outside Milan. The majority of fighting fascists favored war to the finish with socialism. They were somewhat annoyed by the Socialist Congress of Livorno in January 1921, which by a large majority repudiated communism and forced the maximalists out of the party. But they interpreted this as a sign of disintegration, the beginning of the end of socialism. A little more hammering and the fascist victory would be complete. Hence it appeared ridiculous to them that fascism "should ally itself with a corpse." [19] The communists at least were respected for their willingness to fight for their cause (only "they didn't know how to

18 *Popolo d'Italia*, July 27, 1921. In *Diuturna*, p. 344.
19 cf. Soffici: *Battaglie fra due vittorie*.

fight "), but for that bourgeois, reformist, politicians' socialism they had the same disgust which the pre-war Mussolini had. They regarded it as part of that sluggish, lifeless mass of political matter from which fascism was trying to free the Italian people. The *Partito Ufficiale Socialista* was nicknamed the *pus*. In short the theory was that fascism was fighting the communists because they were unpatriotic and the socialists because they were putrid. It was useless for Mussolini to argue, in rather tortuous fashion, that the pact merely signified a " return to fascism's original principles," [20] or to appeal to the national interests and the constructive problems awaiting fascism. The *fascisti*, especially the squadrists, saw no occasion for peace yet, and in fact obstructed the negotiations by new fights. The provincial meetings in Emilia, Romagna and Tuscany, lead on by Farinacci, officially rejected the pact. Thereupon Rossi, who apparently had inspired the pact and who had written a scathing article against continued fascist violence, resigned his office on the Directorate immediately. Mussolini was obliged to do likewise. He accompanied his resignation with the words: " During these last weeks I have made it clearly understood that I would feel unable to guide an undisciplined and chaotic movement any longer. . . . I willed and firmly willed a treaty of peace; however, hundreds of *fasci* did not want to hear of it and said so explicitly. It is not I who leave; it is the others who force me to go, for their vote strikes at me particularly and disqualifies me."

A few days later a meeting was held *at Milan,* the resignation was refused and the pact of pacification accepted. Nothing more was said about the matter, however occasional fights took place as before. In November at Rome where the *fascisti* held their annual national congress, a protest strike of tramway and transportation workers was declared. The *fascisti* tried to break it and violence was resorted to on both sides. This furnished Mussolini with a convenient occasion and adequate pretext for officially declaring the truce broken and the pact null and void.

Another and more fundamental issue was decided at Rome. The internal chaos in the fascist ranks and the parliamentary situation had led Mussolini and his group to demand a definite party organization for fascism. All the summer, the *Popolo d'Italia* had spread propaganda for the party, and before the congress met Mussolini announced that the party was a foregone conclusion. Nevertheless there was vigorous opposition and, as Mussolini later remarked, the Rome congress of November 1921 marked one of the most serious crises in the history of fascism. The chief issue centered on the nature of the party: was it

[20] v. *Popolo d'Italia,* August 3, 1921. In *Diuturna,* p. 348.

to be an ordinary political party, controlled by an official bureaucracy or not? Fundamentally it was a struggle between the Milan hierarchy and those forces that were making for loose local organization. Three main views were represented. Mussolini and Massimo Rocca defended the "New Right" conception of fascism. According to them there was need of a well organized parliamentary party of the right wing to counterbalance the Socialist and Popular Parties. Fascism was to continue the work of Cavour. It would accept the Treaty of Rapallo and carry on an imperialistic foreign policy, and counteract democratic and socialistic tendencies at home. They warned against revolutionary tactics in the current economic crisis, and against economic paternalism. They favored the organization of national economic councils of experts, but otherwise recommended an individualistic economic policy. Mussolini in particular emphasized that both the parasitic capitalists and the class-conscious workers must be subjected to the higher interests of the nation. Fascism must take a constructive, political form now that the violent and revolutionary phase was passed. He spoke as one with authority. He outlined his own political views and seemed to expect them to be accepted by all *fascisti* as a matter of party discipline.

A second point of view was defended by Dino Grandi, formerly a d'Annunzian nationalist. He was not radically opposed to any party organization whatsoever, but to a party which was merely political. He reminded Mussolini of the generally accepted principle that fascism was not a party but a movement. Furthermore, he insisted, it was a revolutionary movement, a movement of *combattimento*, fundamentally "romantic" like that of the traditional Left of Mazzini and Garibaldi. He urged d'Annunzian tactics, opposed the Treaty of Rappallo, opposed the pact with the socialists, and looked forward to a new kind of democracy, not parliamentarian but genuinely popular and syndicalistic. He summed up his program in the following formula: fascism should be a synthesis of the idealistic forces of *modernism, syndicalism,* and *nationalism,* which were generated even before the war, but which needed the war to liberate them from the reigning "materialistic" forces of *clericalism, liberalism,* and *socialism.* Fascism must be inspired, he insisted, by the nationalist philosophy of the state as a positive, organic, "spiritual" whole, in opposition to the negative individualistic philosophy of the state typified by the liberalism of Cavour. He preferred to see the fascist deputies seated, not on the right, but as a "mountain of the center."

A third view came from Pietro Marsich, of Venice, and was in general that of the national-liberals. It was closer to Grandi's than to Mussolini's, being opposed to a mere party and favoring syndical organization, but it reflected a conservative bias, an individualistic economics and in general a less romantic fighting spirit than Grandi's. Marsich was by far the most sober-minded, reasoned and critical of all the orators, but he was less interested in a practical plan for the moment, than in building up a comprehensive theory for the fascist state.

Behind these three views there lurked the deep-seated regional differences in the structure and aims of fascism, to say nothing of the conflicts between rival groups of politicians. After the speeches were over, a commission was appointed to draft a program synthesizing all three points of view and the congress closed with a general reconciliation and apparent agreement. The chief result was an overwhelming majority for the *Partito Nazionale Fascista*. While many of the squadrist fascists were preoccupied in the *piazza* and on the streets, fighting the strike, the new secretariat of the party, selected by a very small group and consisting entirely of Mussolini men, was formally installed in the auditorium of the *Augusteo*. It turned out afterwards that the synthetic harmony in which the convention closed was not so conspicuous in practice. Grandi was supplanted in the party hierarchy by Baroncini and Balbo, and as for Marsich, he disappeared from the arena altogether. The program appeared several weeks later, and was Mussolinian in its main lines, though it was so bedecked with nationalistic verbiage and platitudes that it could mean all things to all men. In defending it Mussolini fell back on the ever convenient gospel of relativism.[21] The program, he said, was perfectly fascist, for it was a program of action not of theoretical exposition, of general aims for the nation, not of the specific means which must always be left to the dictates of time and circumstance. "Fascism," he said, "is not a museum of dogmas and principles." This is but a symptom of the fundamental predicament in which Mussolini was placed, a predicament from which fascism in general has not yet freed itself. As a member of the Milan group, Mussolini's sympathies were decidedly to the Left; as a member of Parliament he had to play the game of the nationalist Right. Later Misuri summed up the situation succinctly: "The tendency toward the left, encouraged by the complicated and obscure activities of the most irresponsible and degenerate left-wing elements, was merely an opportunistic and demagogic show. In reality, fascism tends neither to the right nor to the left. The party has pretended to go to the left; the government has pretended to go to the right; but in fact both go zig-zag according to the dictates of the moment."[22] Such "gypsy politics" did not worry Mussolini, who was proud of

[21] v. *Popolo d'Italia*, November 22, 1921. In *Diuturna*, p. 374.
[22] Misuri: *Rivolta Morale*, p. 48.

being a relativist and a man of action; but it made it difficult for him to express his ideas.

Without implicating the program in any way, Mussolini dropped some casual remarks in an editorial, which throw some light on the direction his own thoughts were taking:

" It can not be maintained that we are headed for a period of greater liberty, of greater democracy with its various suffrage schemes. It is possible that the next decades will witness the inglorious end of all the so-called conquests of democracy. From government by many or by all, the extreme ideal of democracy, men will probably turn to government by a few or by one only. In economics the experiment of government by many or all has already failed; in Russia they are returning to dictators in the factories. Politics must inevitably follow economics. I do not see clearly how universal suffrage and its proportionalistic amendments will turn out. Before long it will be an old game. Men will, perhaps, long for a dictator." [23]

Whether he was already playing seriously with the idea of dictator, whether he was waiting for a preponderance of his party in Parliament, whether he felt it his duty to maintain a non-party, anti-parliamentary attitude, or whether he was merely disgusted with the talk of party bargainings in the Chamber of Deputies, the fact is that after the foundation of the party he took little active part in Parliament, and devoted himself to an intensive study of foreign relations, to strengthening his grip on the party machine, and to disciplining the militia.

In fact the forming of the militia was but the military aspect of the forming of the party. Both events signified the *inquadramento* of the fascist forces into an ordered hierarchy. And on the whole, the more ordered it was, the more orderly it became.

It was at this time that fascism acquired most of its rites and ritual. Not only the uniforms of the *arditi* were adopted but also their songs, symbols and organization. The Latinism and Romanism of d'Annunzio already suggested in Mussolini's Trieste speech became a dominant characteristic. April 21, the legendary date of the founding of Rome, was made a fascist holiday, on which day in place of the usual undisciplined crowds or of the old-fashioned parades and religious processions, the *fascisti* proposed to revive the severe " Roman march." The Roman salute, the lictor's rods and *fascia*, the cry of *eia-eia-a-la-là*, were adopted and popularized, and proved especially attractive to large bodies of students and to the middle-class youth in general, who joined in large numbers. The squads were also given a Roman military organization: they were formed into maniples, centuries, cohorts, and

[23] *Popolo d'Italia*, November 22, 1921. In *Diuturna*, p. 374.

legions. Mussolini became " Chief Honorary Corporal " of the legions. The whole organization was dignified with the term Militia, and was declared to be from then on devoted exclusively to the national service. Shortly before the March on Rome, De Vecchi, Fiume legionary and the real founder of the militia, drew up an " ethical decalogue " for " fascist soldiers " in which the duties and qualifications of a militiaman are laid down.

The chief activity now remaining for the militia was the comparatively peaceful one of strike-breaking. Strikes had decreased notably by 1922, especially in the rural regions, where the squadrists had done their work most thoroughly. The strike figures for 1920 were: in industry 1,267,935, in agriculture 1,045,732; in 1921 they fell to 644,564 in industry, and only 79,298 in agriculture.[24] The country had been saved from bolshevism! Nevertheless there were still serious disorders, especially railroad strikes. This invasion of bolshevism into the public services incurred the special wrath of *fascisti* and nationalists, not merely because it was a public nuisance, but because it undermined the moral conception of the state.

On the whole, however, in the summer of 1922 business was running low for the squadrists, and the *fasci* were filling up rapidly with college boys and other lads who enjoyed the marches, uniforms, salutes, and yells. The movement was becoming increasingly ceremonial. It was also becoming increasingly a politicians' game. The " constructive tasks " of which Mussolini spoke were too intangible and the " higher duties " too prosaic to interest *fascisti di combattimento*. Defections in the ranks spread. Something had to be done; work had to be found for idle arms.

VI. The Fascist Revolution

Fortunately work was at hand. Parliament was deadlocked. The elections on which Giolitti had relied to free him from socialist pressure had merely postponed the evil day a little. The situation was very complicated, but the root of the trouble was this. Thanks to proportional representation which had been introduced for the purpose in 1920, the middle-class groups had saved themselves from a complete rout and held about one half the Chamber, but the dominant parties were the socialists of the north and the popularists of the south. Because of this regional separation, as well as for other reasons, socialists and popularists were very jealous of each other. The middle-class government could not carry on without support from one or the other of them and tried to weaken these two opposition parties by playing them

[24] Bonomi: *From Socialism to Fascism*, p. 83.

off against each other. The socialists in their turn, being the largest
single group, wanted to head the ministry and have the lion's share of
the government. The Popular Party, holding the balance between right
and left, thought it ought to be at the head, a position which the centrist
parties of several other nations were enjoying at the time. The middle-
class groups would not listen to a socialist prime minister, whereupon
the socialists would not listen to any other. Endless party squabbling
ensued. Cabinet after cabinet failed to break the deadlock. Finally it
looked as though the King, having exhausted all possible middle-class
candidates, would be forced to call a socialist prime minister, and there
was some hope that Mussolini might be willing to join such a ministry.
But he insisted that he would welcome socialists and popularists in a
ministry headed by him, but would not enter a ministry headed by another. Meanwhile the press and public opinion was becoming daily more
exasperated, until by fall Parliament hardly had a single friend in the
country. The members themselves were disgusted with each other
and the King was weary of selecting impossible prime ministers. The
nationalists, anti-parliament by principle, now fused with the *fascisti*,
and together they launched an open attack not merely on the current
tactics of the parties, but on the whole parliamentary state as such.

The so-called *coup d'état* was by no means as sudden nor as violent
as is commonly believed. Certainly it was not made in secret. During
the spring and summer Mussolini had written extensively on the subject
of the fascist versus the liberal state.[25] On September 20, the anniversary of the capture of Rome in 1870, Mussolini announced at Udine
that the *fascisti* were ready to rule Italy, he spoke of the "fascist revolution," he raised the cry "On to Rome!" He also definitely made his
peace with the monarchy and said the change of political regime could
be brought about without disturbing the House of Savoy. The only
trouble with the present King being that he was not monarchic enough.
A number of speeches followed in rapid succession, each explaining
more definitely than the preceding how fascism hoped to establish the
fascist state. Immediately after the *fascisti* had overthrown the German
administration of Bolzano and had met no resistance from the national
government, Mussolini presented a series of demands to the Chamber,
declaring that they were the only possible remedy for the deadlock. If
they were not accepted he threatened force. The demands were, in
Mussolini's words, "the dissolving of the Chamber, electoral reform
and elections within a short time. We demanded that the state abandon
its grotesque neutrality between the forces of the nation and those of

[25] v. For example, *Popolo d'Italia*, April 30, 1922. In *Diuturna*, p. 423. *Gerarchia*. I: 6, pp. 295 ff.

the anti-nation. We demanded strenuous financial measures, we demanded reconsideration of the evacuation of the Dalmatian zone, and we demanded five portfolios besides the Commission of Aviation. We demanded, to be precise, the Ministry of the Exterior, of War, of the Navy, of Labor and of Public Works. . . . And included in this legal solution was the provision that my own direct participation in the government be excluded." [26] The parliamentary leaders naturally merely smiled at these demands and suggested that the *fascisti* might have a minister without portfolio or some "under-ministers." For in Parliament no one took fascism seriously. Politicians had listened to the bumptious fascist talk and gestures for several years, and seeing but the handful of deputies which resulted from it all, they were more amused than frightened by it, treated it condescendingly and never thought of taking it literally. In a sense this was true of the country at large, for though the movement was much more popular outside than inside Parliament, and though it was regarded as the symbol of the new spirit of Italy, it was not thought of as a major *political* force. But Mussolini did not share these views and insisted that "fascism would not enter the government by the service entrance." Consequently the events which now followed came as a surprise, though they had been heralded from the housetops for months previously.

During October the *fascisti,* who were already complete masters in most of the important cities of northern Italy, took possession of the prefectures and police headquarters of the others and spread their control to the southern centers. The railroads and telegraph offices, which had been defended by *fascisti* in recent strikes, were now "guarded" by them. On October 24th a national congress was called at Naples — at Naples, of course, in order to impress the comparatively indifferent south and to make the movement appear genuinely national in scope. The Revolution was discussed openly and Mussolini announced that if a legal solution were not found immediately a march on Rome would be necessary.

Facta, a very pleasant and peaceful old man, was officially the head of the government, but he was really powerless since he could not command a majority in the Chamber and had even less authority outside Parliament. He therefore let matters drift. The ministry resigned. Immediately after the Naples Convention, the *fascisti* hosts assembled at Civitavecchia, a little north of Rome. They were mobilized under military formation and military law by the dictatorial authority of a "secret quadrumvirate," Michele Bianchi, General De Bono, Captain DeVecchi, and Lieutenant Italo Balbo. Mussolini went

[26] From the Naples speech, October 24, 1922.

to Milan to await events. The march was ordered and on October 28th the legions of black shirts with a sprinkling of blue shirts, about 50,000 strong, began piling into Rome. The proclamation of the quadrumvirate stated that the march was not made against the army, nor the police, nor the King, nor against the " productive bourgeoisie," nor against the " masses that work in fields and offices," but only against " a political class of weaklings and defectives who for four years had not been able to give the nation a government." There was no fighting and no opposition. The troops assembled more peacefully than they had a year ago in the same place, when they had been met by a strike. Facta hastily declared a state of siege, but recalled the order almost immediately when the King refused to sign it. Rumor has it that the King was inclined to sign it but was dissuaded by the Duke of Aosta, on the ground that the army would not fight. Everything now waited for the King's action, since only the King could act under the circumstances. On the afternoon of the 28th, Salandra asked Mussolini if he would accept a cabinet post under him, which was of course refused. On the 29th Mussolini was called to the telephone and asked by the King to form a ministry. He took the next train to Rome, announcing as he left Milan, " Tomorrow Italy will have not a ministry but a government." He stopped at Civitavecchia and Santa Marinella, where the great bulk of the fascist forces (about 150,000) were still mobilized. By the evening of October 30th, the new ministry was formed and Mussolini ordered his Chief of Staff, much to the latter's amazement, to get the 50,000 *fascisti* out of Rome within twenty-four hours. The Revolution was over.

It is a metaphysical question whether the revolution was violent or not, or for that matter, whether or not there was a revolution at all. Some say the event was little more than a parade to celebrate a cabinet crisis, others regard it as comparable to the French Revolution. From the point of view of the careers of the *fascisti*, there can be no doubt of its significance. In a very few years they had risen from obscure journalists, labor agitators, soldiers, students, political and social nobodies, to the heads of the Italian state. They saw themselves transformed overnight, as it were, from boys to statesmen. They naturally imagined that all Italy had undergone a similar transformation, and in this they were not altogether mistaken. Whether they were the cause of it or not they certainly became the symbol and focus of as dramatic and radical a change in political sentiment and national feeling as has ever been witnessed. In 1919 the *fascisti* received about four thousand votes in 1924 about four million. Though these votes give an exaggerated impression of the extent of the revolution, they may be taken as a rough index of the shift of public opinion. It was a revolution in opinion rather than in practice. But among the *fascisti* whom it affected in practice, it created a ferment of emotion and ideation much more revolutionary than the event itself, and the picture which lives in the fascist mind has already assumed such heroic and mythological proportions as to bear little likeness to the reality which generated it. This living myth is perhaps more significant and will certainly be more enduring than the modest tangible achievements which it celebrates.

The idea that Italy has periodic rejuvenations is of course not new. Renaissance and *risorgimento* are unusually familiar themes in Italian tradition. Even before the war there was a general feeling that Italy was getting stale and needed a new start. The Tripoli War rejuvenated a few exceptionally sensitive romantics. When the World War came, the interventionists immediately were convinced that surely *this* war would start the re-birth. But no; after the war, pessimism and world-weariness ruled stronger than ever. This was attributed to the old age of the democratic, liberalistic order. It was represented as living on the husks handed down by several generations. Decadent in tastes, weak in politics, entangled in institutions which had long ago outlived their usefulness, and clinging to faiths long dead. Then to see groups of young men quite spontaneously rise up out of the very depths of this despair and carry the whole nation to a fresh confidence in its abilities and to new hopes for its future — *this* was the deed which several generations had longed to do but could not.

Believing this as they do, the *fascisti* have no patience with those who label them as reactionaries. Mussolini, when he was asked whether his government would go right or left, said he was not interested in "historic terminologies." In terms of traditional class theory, fascism may no doubt be called a lower-middle-class reaction. But "lower middle class" is obviously no adequate description of the leaders of the New Italy. Financially the *fascisti* may be neither poor nor rich, but intellectually and morally, they claim to be the cream of the nation. The fascist revolution is said to be a "reaction of idealists" in the interests of "a solid nation, impartiality, justice, spiritual, intellectual and moral light." [27] Though no one takes this literally, it is certainly true that the old categories can not be transplanted bodily into the revolutionary regime. Of its economic characteristics we shall speak in a later chapter, but morally and politically, fascism certainly represents something fresh, rather than something reactionary. The theory is that the *risorgimento* of the nineteenth century was successful in making the new Italy, but it failed to make the new Italians. In 1870

[27] Gorgolini: *Fascismo nella vita italiana*, p. 76.

Massimo d'Azeglio made his famous remark: "Italy is made, now we must make Italians." The *risorgimento* has now been completed, the new Italians have appeared on the scene and proved their worth.

There are, of course, more sophisticated versions of the philosophy of the revolution. Suckert, for example, makes fun of the idea that the old politicians, as d'Azeglio claimed, could "make Italians." The "real" Italians had never got into the politics of the old state, and these bourgeois politicians regarded them as *Italia barbara*. Now these "barbarians," the genuine old Italians, have asserted themselves, both against the old Italian state and against the whole so-called civilized world.[28] This is not reaction; it is counter-reformation. Massimo Rocca too sees in the fascist revolution a rescue of "Catholic" civilization, that is, of religion, idealism, the state and a productive economic order, from the "negative" tendencies (nihilism, scepticism, bolshevism, materialism, intellectualism, etc.) which had been piling up their evil fruits for several generations, and which reached their most violent forms in the Italian aftermath of the war.[29]

Corradini, the veteran nationalist, regards the revolution as the inevitable consequence of the war. The victory had made a new Italian nation, but the state tried to manage with the anachronistic residue of pre-war institutions, until fascism, itself a war product, burst the old fetters and established a state worthy of the new Italy.

Another and a very popular version is that just as the French Revolution marked the beginnings of the liberation of the middle classes, so the fascist revolution, the revolution, not of a class, but of the Italian people (*popolo d'Italia*), marks the beginning of the liberation of peoples the world over. There are innumerable other variations on the theme, but the central idea is always that of Italy's renovation, rejuvenation, *risorgimento*. Italy has been saved by her youth.

"Whose was the battle?" Mussolini cries.

"Ours," is the reply.

"Whose is the glory?"

"Ours!"

"Whose is Italy?"

"Ours!"

[28] v. Curzio Suckert: *Italia Barbara*. Also Appendix No. 30.
[29] v. Massimo Rocca: *Idee sul Fascismo*, pp. 318 ff.

CHAPTER III

THE FASCIST STATE

I. *Mussolini and His Parliament*

The fact was the revolution had barely begun. It will be remembered that Mussolini's "peaceful" demands on Parliament had included five fascist portfolios in the cabinet. Now that the government had refused these demands and fascism had used force and gained a complete victory, most fascists naturally expected a fascist government. Imagine their dismay next morning when they saw the following cabinet announced.

Minister of Foreign Affairs — Mussolini.

Minister of the Interior — Mussolini, with Michele Bianchi as his Under-secretary.

Minister of War — General Diaz.

Minister of Navy — Admiral Thaon de Revel.

Minister of National Economy — Teofilo Rossi, an industrialist of the Liberal Party retained from the Facta Cabinet.

Minister of Finance — Alberto De Stefani, fascist, but politically belonging to the Democratic group.

Minister of Public Works — Carnazza, Social-democrat.

Minister of Public Instruction — Giovanni Gentile, Liberal.

Minister of Labor — Cavazzoni, Popular Party.

Minister of Agriculture — de Capitani, Liberal.

Ministry of the Treasury — Tangorra, Liberal.

Ministry of Justice — Orviglio, fascist.

Minister of Liberated Territories — Giurati, fascist.

Minister of Colonies — Federzoni, Nationalist.

Postmaster General — Colonna di Cesaro, Liberal.

Only three regular *fascisti* besides Mussolini! In the assignment of under-secretaries the *fascisti* fared a little better: fifteen *Fascisti*, six Popular Party, three Liberals, three Nationals, three Democrats.

Of the effect of this announcement on the fascist ranks we shall speak later. Its effect on Parliament, with which we are now concerned, was very soothing. It was evidently to be a government of coalition; a

" national coalition " from which only the socialists had been excluded. It was, after all, not so much a revolution against Parliament and the " liberal state " as against socialism. It was Mussolini's revenge on the Socialist Party (and he told them so to their faces [1]) for having refused his offer of coalition in the summer.

After the initial excitement had died down a bit, on November 16, Mussolini presented himself and his government to Parliament.[2] Toward the Senate, the respectable resting place of the most respectable old men of the old Italy, he behaved with great deference; he apologized for the rudeness of his accession to power, promised to lead a strictly legal life thereafter, and proposed to conduct a policy of peace abroad and of as much liberty as possible at home.

His attitude toward the Chamber of Deputies was a marked contrast. He told them that he was " performing an act of formal deference," for which he " asked no special recognition." He continued: " To the melancholy zealots of superconstitutionalism I leave the task of making their more or less pitiful lamentations on recent events. I maintain that revolution has its rights. . . . With 300,000 youths fully armed, fully determined and almost mystically ready to act on any command of mine, I could have . . . made of this sordid, grey Assembly Hall a bivouac of squads; I could have kicked out Parliament and constructed a government exclusively of *fascisti.*. I could have, — but I did not want to, at least not for the present." Then, after outlining his program, he asked for unlimited powers for one year in order to make the necessary economies in the government. He promised to give complete account of his use of these powers to the Chamber, but he added that the " Chamber must be aware of the fact that it is subject to being dissolved within two days or two years." " You must either accept national sentiment or vanish." He closed his speech with the words: " Gentlemen, do not throw any more vain prattle at the nation. Fifty-two members scheduled to speak on my remarks are too many. Rather let us get to work with clean hearts and alert minds to bring prosperity and greatness to our country. And God help me to bring this my arduous task to a victorious end."

Many of the Honorable Gentlemen were shocked at being thus scolded in public by a youngster. Turati, the socialist leader, said he " preferred an outright dictatorship to the ghost of a parliament Mussolini is trying to set up." Others took it good-naturedly. Giolitti, when he was asked to come to the rescue of the Chamber's dignity, is said to have replied

---

[1] v. Speech in the Chamber, November 17, 1922.

[2] See Appendix No. 16.

simply that he thought the Chamber deserved the scolding. The Senate merely smiled at the "lower" house. In the press, and by the country in general the speech was not only approved but hailed with great enthusiasm. Thus isolated, the Chamber had but one choice. After 48 of the 52 speakers had made their comments, it passed by 306 to 116 votes a fascist resolution calling not exactly for a vote of confidence, for that would have implied resignation in case of an adverse vote, but for "confidence in the destinies of the nation and acceptance of the program of the government." That evening the demand for special powers was passed by a vote of 215 to 80. The opposition came almost exclusively from the socialists and communists. The constitution had been saved and Parliament had meekly accepted "the national sentiment," rather than "vanish."

It is impossible, however, to ascribe this vote and similar ones that followed merely to physical force and intimidation, nor even to the lack of public favor which Parliament enjoyed at the time. It was due in no small measure to the hypnotizing effect of Mussolini's person, his bearing, his speech, his career. The very novelty of it all was refreshing; and no doubt many were curious to see what he could do if he were given the chance. Certainly Mussolini achieved an immediate personal victory over Parliament, which he did not entirely lose even during the dark days of 1924. He "inspired confidence" and no one seemed to take his threats of violence seriously.

The collaboration which Mussolini magnanimously offered proved a bed of thorns. Senator Albertini had explicitly demanded that the coalition be bona fide and not merely a blind for imposing fascism on other parties. Mussolini's reply was somewhat equivocal, for though he was anxious to avoid parliamentary hostility, he was forced by his fascist followers to preach the completeness of the fascist victory and the initiation of the fascist state.

His chief worry was the attitude of the Popular Party, on which he was absolutely dependent for his parliamentary majority. Mussolini's theatrical and unheard-of appeal for divine aid in his speech before the Chamber had been for the particular benefit of the Catholic center. Don Sturzo, the leader of the popularists, realizing his strategic power, began almost immediately making demands. He complained of the meagre representation granted to his party in the Mussolini government. He protested against the fascist disrespect for liberty and democracy and its boastful imperialism. But above all he complained of the continued aggression by *fascisti* against his own organizations. For while Mussolini was officially collaborating, both his party politicians and his syndicates were busy locally wresting control of the south from the Popular Party organizations. Relations became increasingly strained.

In April 1923, at Turin, the Popular Party held its annual convention. Opposition to the *fascisti* ran high and it was with difficulty that Don Sturzo was able to prevent an open secession. The convention finally drew up its conditions for a continuation of the collaboration, emphasizing the maintenance of its independence as a party, the protection of individual liberty and the defense of religion and the Church against any and all attempts to corrupt it " in the name of a pantheistic state and a deified nation." Mussolini did not wait for an open break. One of the two popularist members of his Cabinet conveniently died and the other was asked to resign immediately after the convention.

Mussolini's parliamentary position now became increasingly precarious; and he saw that he could not carry on much longer. Consequently he revived the demand for electoral reform and new elections. A Reform Commission was appointed, headed by Giolitti, and composed of members of various parties; but the most active member was the fascist deputy, Acerbo, who was entrusted with drafting the bill. The purpose of the reform was frankly stated to be to put an end to bloc government, to give one party a clear majority and thus to avoid the danger of deadlocks and squabbles which had haunted the pre-fascist government and now loomed up again. The coalition system was declared to be not merely a practical nuisance but also a theoretical anachronism. In his election speech, for example, Mussolini said, " No more relations with the other parties. All parties must end, must fall. I want to see a panorama of ruins about me — the ruins of the other political forces — so that fascism may stand alone, gigantic and dominant." [3]

The bill provided that whichever party should get the plurality of votes in the nation as a whole, should be given two thirds of all the seats. In each electoral district, accordingly, two thirds of the seats automatically would go to this party, regardless of the local vote, and the other third would be distributed among the other parties according to their local strength. With this daring proposal Mussolini now faced Parliament. It received general support on the right and violent opposition on the left. The popularists were in a predicament; it was practically up to them to decide the issue. They charged that it violated the constitution, a charge which was evaded by the countercharge of the *fascisti* that if it were defeated another and a more violent revolution would become necessary, which would certainly destroy the constitution. The popularists knew that the electoral reform would reduce their power,

[3] v. *Gerarchia*, November 1926, p. 681.

but on the other hand, a revolution would not only put an end to their power absolutely, but they would be the greatest sufferers from the violence. In the midst of the conflict, Don Sturzo suddenly and mysteriously resigned, called off by the Vatican, presumably through fascist pressure. The discouraged popularists now made the best of a bad situation. Some of them thought they might have a chance at the elections, since they were then the strongest single group in Parliament. They offered an amendment to the effect that the leading party must poll at least forty per cent of the total vote in order to be assigned the two-thirds majority. This the *fascisti* accepted in principle but they modified the figures from forty per cent to twenty-five. The first vote on the general scheme, really the deciding vote was: 235 for, 139 against, 79 not voting. Those not voting were the popularists. The outright opposition was largely socialist. It was a narrow escape. Shortly before the final vote Mussolini himself took part in the debate. He wasted but few words on the popularists, condemning their equivocal position and challenging them to come out openly either for or against. Most of his speech was detailed answer to the socialist opposition. The final vote on July 21st was 223 for, and 123 against. It was fascism's decisive victory. The old Parliament had voted its own end; the new one would be made to order.

Counting on the traditional divisions among the right wing parties, the socialists and popularists seem to have nourished some hope that they might yet retrieve their misfortunes by the elections. But Mussolini took no chances. He laid the ground very carefully. Four or five men selected all the fascist candidates. They were selected from the various right wing parties as well as from the *fascisti* ranks, to form a "national list." The list was constructed with special care in the south, where southern candidates were set up and where the "national" list successfully camouflaged fascism. In localities where a heavy fascist plurality was expected, "minority fascist" lists were set up in addition, in order to capitalize their local strength to the utmost. Parliament was officially dissolved in January, though on account of growing opposition Mussolini had already closed the Chamber in December, and elections were not held until April. The fascist militia was mobilized on election day and naturally acted more according to local needs than according to Mussolini's orders to enforce an honest election. In many places the opposition parties were prevented from doing any public campaigning and were not even allowed to set up candidates for local offices. In short, the *fascisti* took abundant precautions, and made it their aim to get a clear fifty per cent of all votes cast. The result, however, came as a surprise even to them. The candidates of the

" national list " received two thirds of the total vote. The rough figures are:

Fascisti or National list (including minority fascist lists)	4,800,000
Socialists (of all parties)	over 1,000,000
Popularists	650,000
Opposition liberals, etc.	600,000

The popularist and socialist vote was probably cut down unduly by the fact that because of the novel ballots, over 1,000,000 votes were declared invalid, most of which no doubt came from the illiterate masses. But even allowing abundantly for error, corruption and intimidation, the *fascisti*, that is, the " national coalition," could certainly claim far over their necessary 25 per cent and probably a substantial majority, and were hence entitled to regard the election as a " plebescite of the nation " and themselves as " the people's choice."

Even before the election Mussolini had been asked what he would do with his parliament when he got it. Would he make its subserviency a pretext for practically discarding it altogether? Was this merely an indirect way of realizing his anti-parliamentarianism? To this he had replied in his one big campaign speech: " I'll tell you what I propose to do with it: to make Parliament function so that it will function. Gentlemen, you must not take my anti-parliamentary utterances too literally. My personal antipathies and sympathies are well known, but I do not base my politics on them. When I spoke of ' paper games ' and said that the ' legions are worth more than assemblies,' I merely did it to put the brakes on electoral impatience a little. . . . And what will we do when we have Parliament functioning regularly? We shall make our reforms more perfect." [4] In other word's, Mussolini's idea was that this purified Parliament would take up the reforms drafted by the government and give them a technical criticism and detailed examination before they became laws. He expected Parliament to be a body of political experts dispassionately weighing the merits of the details of the reforms proposed by the ministry.

He was therefore rudely shocked when the minorities in the new Chamber, immediately after its opening in May, began to protest the elections, charge illegal procedures and violence, criticise the fascist government in general and expound the programs of their respective parties — all in the good old-fashioned manner. The socialists, Amendola and Matteotti, were particularly irritating. The fascist deputies naturally replied in kind and the atmosphere became heated at once.

[4] Mussolini: *La Nuova Politica*, III, p. 33.

On June 7 Mussolini appeared before the Chamber, visibly peeved. He said he would point out to them the only possible basis for proceeding peacefully. He patiently went over the old ground for the benefit of each party in turn. Then finally he broke out: "I propose to make Parliament function. This need not surprise you. Fascism has always been electionistic, too much so; and now it would be ridiculous if being electionists, we would not accept the consequences of this our electionism, that is, parliament and legislative action. I have already told you that there would be no more decree-laws. What is needed now is to discuss the budgets, to accustom people to interpret figures; this is what constitutes genuine supervision. The government will present projects of laws to the Chamber, which will discuss them, amend them, approve them. That is how I understand the legislative function of the parliament of the future. . . .

Now let us put the problem in concrete terms: what are you thinking of doing? How do you expect to get on (I am not speaking of the communists for they are not in question) — how do you expect to get on with these rigid platforms of yours that hold you tight? By an attempt at insurrection? But that is certainly unthinkable, you don't think of that for a moment, it does not even pass through the cells of the antechambers of your brains; for you know that in twenty-four hours, or in twenty-four minutes, all would be over. . . . You certainly ought to undertake a little self-examination and ask yourselves: 'What is going to become of us?' For it is impossible to be forever absent, to be always on the outside; something either good or ill must be done or said; in your own interest you must carry on either a positive or a negative collaboration, for on that day on which you remain absent, indifferent, like Stilites on your columns waiting for a miracle, you will be condemned to a perpetual exile from history." [5]

Mussolini had the illusion that this speech had brought Parliament to its senses, that it showed signs of being willing to get down to work and that the reply of Matteotti would be conciliating. But within a week all his pious hopes were blasted forever by the murder of Matteotti.

The horror and indignation over the murder were soon buried under the general wave of disgust which followed on the revelations of the activities of the Fascist Party. The more of his close friends Mussolini sacrificed the greater grew the disgust. The socialists suddenly acquired an unheard-of repulsion and a moral indignation against violence. Nothing would satisfy the opposition now; the regime was condemned. It was demanded that Mussolini resign, that the militia be

[5] Mussolini: *La Nuova Politica*, III, p. 159.

abolished and that new elections on the basis of proportional representation be held immediately.

The revolt spread with alarming rapidity. What Mussolini feared most of all was defection on the part of the nationalists. To save himself, he quickly reconstructed his cabinet; put Federzoni, a nationalist, in as Minister of the Interior, Rocco, a nationalist, as Minister of Justice, and even inserted several nationalist leaders into the Grand Council of the Party itself. He took occasion for a general house cleaning in the government, and appeared before Parliament with a cabinet that was at least clean and fresh. He promised a thorough reorganization of the Party and an immediate suppression of violence. But on the other hand, he refused point-blank to resign his office, to touch the militia, or to call new elections. He pleaded most fervently a return to legality, but he had no intention of reviving the parliamentary coalition " normalcy " which the opposition wanted.

Hereupon most of the opposition absented itself from the Chamber, actually adopting the policy which Mussolini but a few days previously had characterized as preposterous. A hall was hired on the Aventine Hill, where headquarters were established and where the campaign of words and ink against fascism was continued.

Mussolini was seriously embarrassed by this move. Unwilling to face the empty seats in the House of Parliament, he assembled his faithful rump of about 350 deputies in the nearby Palazzo Venezia and explained the situation to them as follows:

" As for dissolving the Chamber, I ask you who are deputies and who feel yourselves regularly elected by the Italian people, I ask you if you intend to withdraw, to renounce your delegated office, to hand in your resignations to the nation, I would almost say to your own consciences. It goes without saying that this is no time in which to speak of elections and that it is an idea as grotesque as it is catastrophic to want to plunge the masses of the nation, who need quiet, calm and work, back into an electoral battle, which, given the present situation, would be of very uncertain issue. Therefore, to all the demands of the opposition, whether they are formulated by the party organizations in the country, or whether they come tomorrow from the parliamentary representatives of these parties, I believe the government and the majority can only reply with a firm unconditional solemn NO." . . . "The exodus, the secession of the opposition is a fact. Is this secession temporary? Is it permanent? That is the whole point and the whole delicacy of the situation. If the secession is temporary, the situation may clear up. If, on the other hand, the secession should be permanent, then the problem is put in new and relatively more serious terms. The problem which we must then face is whether or not Parliament can function with the majority deprived of the presence of the minority. This much is certain, that the majority must not pay the penalty for the minority. If tomorrow some minority group or other should withdraw from the Aventine, would that fact suffice to reëstablish the functioning of the Chamber? . . . If the opposition should take account of their responsibility and should return to the Chamber and give us their work of criticism, of surveillance and of opposition, even though it be rancorous, sectarian and prejudiced, we must endure, tolerate and at times even encourage it, since opposition which brings to light certain facts and conditions can be of the greatest usefulness; if this should happen, then we could say that the crisis was overcome." [6]

By July 22, Mussolini's attitude towards the Aventine Secession had changed somewhat. He addressed the faithful gathered again in the Palazzo Venezia, as follows: " The more the opposition swells the more it reveals its dropsy and impotence, and the nausea at the prolonged promiscuity becomes more acute. That the pile of the opposition appears huge, there is no doubt. There are in Italy at least ten anti-fascist parties and six or seven anti-fascist sects or groups. Let us line them up in single file. Some one may perhaps be growing proud of finding himself in so numerous a company — anarchists, communists, maximalists, unitary socialists, republicans, popularists, social-democrats, constitutional democrats, Peasant Party, the Sardinian and Lucan Party of action. We pass by the various local spiritual unions in the south; then the groups of Free Italy, For Country and Liberty, The Liberal Revolution, to say nothing of all the dissident more-or-less *fascisti*. To all these parties and groups we must add the hosts of Freemasonry, which have officially declared war on the fascist regime. Very well! I think that it should be Italian fascism's greatest boast to have arrayed against self so numerous a phalanx of enemies. Fascism must represent an absolutely original element in Italian life, to be made the object of so imposing an hostility . . . of this great, and at bottom grotesque, anti-fascist army." [7]

Mussolini had evidently got over his worst scare and was already becoming reconciled to a parliament which did not " function." He began to think less in terms of collaboration and more in terms of the Revolution. When the Aventine opposition insisted on their cry of " normalization," that only a change of regime would satisfy them, Mussolini began to take the offensive and to plan ways of getting rid of the parliamentary nuisance once and for all.

[6] Mussolini: *La Nuova Politica*, III, pp. 197–200.
[7] Mussolini: *La Nuova Politica*, III, pp. 203–4.

In August the Grand Council of the Fascist Party appointed a Constitutional Commission, which was to go over the whole range of vexing problems and propose a way out. The Commission was composed of fifteen members, "five Senators, five Deputies, and five Scholars." Its chairman was Giovanni Gentile. These "Solons" as they came to be called, outstanding scholars and respected University professors, almost all of them men who enjoyed universal respect and confidence, were charged by Mussolini with the task of studying:

1. Relations between the executive and legislative powers. 2. The State and the press. 3. The State and institutions of credit. 4. The State and secret societies. 5. The State and international parties. 6. The State and syndicates.

As a matter of fact the Commission confined itself to the first and last of these problems. If Mussolini had hopes that this move would help pacify the Aventine opposition, he miscalculated badly. It was the last straw for them: the constitution was being attacked openly. And the mere mention of "press, banks, secret societies, and international parties" in connection with reform was enough to make them suspect the worst. To cap it all, the Commission held its first meeting on October 28, the anniversary of the March on Rome. It was useless for Gentile to explain that the demand for reform was itself traditional and "normal" and that fascism was merely attempting to carry on the work of the *risorgimento*.[8] The attacks grew more violent. Some of the liberals, who remained loyal to the majority bloc, now deserted to the opposition, Salandra, Orlando and Giolitti among them. Giolitti wanted to know: "Whose regime is this, anyway!"

Mussolini put on a bold front. He opened Parliament on schedule time, November 12, and declared the "majority Parliament" could function perfectly well without an opposition. He entered into no discussions or bargains with the Aventine group, told them they could surrender unconditionally whenever they got ready. Meanwhile he carried on with his approximately 300 deputies, plus a handful of communists, who of course always go where they can cause the most disturbance. Before this rump Parliament Mussolini was constitutional in the extreme. He submitted for its ratification all the decree-laws which he had put into effect illegally, he gave it an unusually detailed account of his government, and he allowed it to discuss and approve each minister's budget in detail, a practice which had fallen into disuse for the last twelve years. He introduced an electoral reform bill, which removed the last vestiges of proportional representation, and a b

[8] v. Gentile, *Che cosa è il fascismo*, pp. 199 ff. Also Appendix No. 29.

giving women the vote in local elections. These " olive branches " he
hoped might tempt the Aventine.

But in the meantime the violent press campaign had led to " incidents " on both sides. In September Casalini, a prominent fascist syndicalist, had been murdered by a socialist to avenge the Matteotti murder. Mussolini at the time had given strict orders against reprisals,
and had adopted an attitude of relief, hoping that now " accounts were
square." But he was unable to keep either the opposition or his
own squads in check. Though he preached daily the doctrine that
violence was ended, the papers were full of evidence to the contrary.
On top of it all came the publication on December 27th, of Rossi's
Memorial " [9] which held Mussolini morally responsible for much of
the violence.

The opposition was now irreconcilable, and its struggle became more
desperate as it became more hopeless. Mussolini was forced to give
up attempts at pacification and to declare war. On January 3 he
launched a violent attack on the Aventine, read the list of recent fascist
martyrs " and declared that communism was getting the upper hand
in the opposition. He held up the spectre of the red peril and asserted
that if he should let go of the government, he would undoubtedly have
communist successors.[10] With these weak apologies, he then announced
that within 48 hours the opposition would be crushed by force. From
January 3, 1925, fascism and only fascism would govern Italy!

The immediate measures which followed the declaration of January 3,
1925, were naturally directed against the most conspicuous centers of
opposition, first of all the press. The socialist and communist press
had already been partly muzzled by the decrees of July 1924 which had
given prefects power. But these decrees had not been enforced rigorously. On December 31, that is almost immediately after the publication of the Rossi Memorial, Federzoni sent a circular to all prefects
commanding rigid enforcement. In general the unscrupulous partisan
press, which is ridiculously violent in Italy, naturally fell first and was
not much lamented. In November 1925, after the Zaniboni affair, such
papers as the *Unità, Giustizia, Avanti,* and the *Voce Repubblicana* were
suppressed. Then came the more delicate task of muzzling the big liberal
papers, which not only enjoyed a tremendous prestige but which by
years of persistent effort had built up an unusual independence and
honesty. The muzzling had to be gradual. Only violent attacks were
punished at first. General defenses of " liberty " were still permitted
and Mussolini made it a point to argue that where liberty is still de-

[9] See Appendix No. 19.
[10] v. Mussolini: *La Nuova Politica,* III, pp. 463, 480 ff.

fended, liberty still exists. Then more energetic measures became necessary. Senator Albertini's *Corriere della Sera* of Milan and the *Giornale d'Italia* of Rome had to be suspended for a short time while the editors "reorganized." The *Secolo* was bought outright and its liberal editors, among them Ferrero, were retired. To make censorship more systematic, a body of "competent men" was appointed to approve manuscripts on political issues and still later all "copy" whatsoever on any subject had to be approved by fascist officials. In November 1926 the *Mondo*, the *Stampa* and several other remaining opposition papers were suppressed. But all except the *Mondo* have since then been "fascisticized." Opposition books were suppressed and publishing houses that persisted in publishing them were punished. Of the opposition magazines even the mildest have disappeared, as, for example, the Republican *Critica Politica*. The editor of a leading humorous paper, the *Becco Giallo* (yellow beak), whose political satire was exceptionally keen and influential, was beaten by a band of *fascisti;* whereupon the sheet appeared with a padlock on the beak of the bird on the cover page. The editor's life was then threatened and the paper stopped publication. A limited amount of criticism is still allowed in the press provided it is "loyal" and not directed against Mussolini personally. A critical discussion of the technical merits of a concrete issue is well come, but the democratic luxury, eulogistically called public opinion, is something which fascism thinks it can easily live without. Italy, it claims, is too poor to be able to afford the continual nervous strain and frittering away of energy. The formula is: criticism is allowed, but not opposition.

The Masonic Orders were another serious problem. They were firmly intrenched among the liberal politicians and to all intents and purposes acted like a political club. Being international, they were in a position to bring considerable foreign pressure to bear on the government. In addition to their political activities they were, of course, objectionable because of their internationalism, their strong French influences, and their democratic, agnostic and anti-clerical principles. The problem was somewhat complicated by the fact that a number of prominent *fascisti* were members, and that there was a rivalry between two lodges. The Scottish Rite, with headquarters in the Piazza Gesu, was not condemned as early as the Grand Orient of the Palazzo Giustiniano. Shortly before the Matteotti affair Mussolini had given public recognition to the Grand Master of the Scottish Rite and many *fascisti* wanted to save it for personal reasons. But discrimination was difficult, and finally all secret associations were condemned *en masse.* After the Zaniboni attack on Mussolini, November 4, 1925, in which

General Capello and other Masons were involved, the Grand Master Torrigiani was arrested and later banished for five years.

While these things were transpiring at headquarters, local fascist organizations interpreted the declaration of January 3 as a permission to resume violence. Systematic inquisitions and persecutions of the more violent opposition organizations, especially the *Italia Libera*, were begun. Many opposition leaders were attacked in person or their property destroyed. Nitti, Orlando and a considerable following were forced to flee the country. In Florence and Pisa there were exceptionally violent house cleanings. The Bishop of Pisa telegraphed to Rome as follows: " So last night Pisa was normalized! As a bishop I wept; as an Italian I blushed. . . . Have pity on our country!" In Florence, to take one of the most serious cases, October 2, 1925, long after the worst crisis, the local fascist chief, Liporini, tried by threats of violence to force an old man named Bandinelli, a Freemason, to reveal the names of his Masonic brothers. After some " arguments " and threats, Bandinelli shot the fascist. Thereupon the *fascio* terrorized the whole town for several days and nights, killing seven, among them a socialist ex-deputy, without further provocation and wounding scores in street riots. Each attempt on the life of Mussolini was naturally made the occasion for riots and for violence on whatever prominent opposition members still happened to be available.

A law was passed which deprived anti-fascist lawyers of their licenses to practice. Anti-fascist professors were made subject to dismissal, though very few have actually been dismissed to date. And in general the opposition was deprived of all personal and public rights. The culmination of the movement came in November 1926, after another attempt on Mussolini's life, when the " Law for the Defense of the State " was passed. It provided the institution of the death penalty or attacks on the " life or liberty of King, Queen, Crown Prince, or Prime Minister " (a provision which Farinacci had recommended a year and a half previously and which others wanted to extend to the opposition generally), " purification " of the bureaucracy from anti-fascist elements, and abolition of all parties and journals which " menaced the public order."

The *Italia Libera* and Socialist Party had already been abolished, and the others had been reduced to inaction. The abolition of all parties at this time was therefore largely formal, as was also the definite ending of the Aventine Secession. On January 16, 1926, profiting by the memorial session following on the death of the Queen Mother, a number of populist deputies of the Aventine had tried to return to the Chamber. They had been forcibly expelled, and the next day Mussolini had justified the expulsion. Only an absolute surrender to fascism, he said, could make re-entry possible for any member of the Aventine. In November Bocconi, a socialist deputy, who had remained in Parliament, was confronted in one of the lobbies by a fascist deputy and told " not to allow himself to be seen around the Chamber again." In December, even before voting the new Law for the Defense of the State, the Chamber formally deprived the 125 remaining members of the Aventine of their seats.

A thoroughgoing, rather than judicial imprisonment of suspicious persons now ensued. In the next few months, as Mussolini reported in May, 1500 " ordinary low criminals " and 700 communists and political prisoners were sent to the islands, that is, were exiled. Each of these exiles receives ten *lire* a day toward his support. Many opposition members are faring even worse, for they are not allowed to leave the country and can get no employment inside the country. Filippo Turati and Arturo Labriola have recently escaped to France, but a large number of other opposition leaders are not merely prisoners, continually watched by fascist squads, but practically hostages, held in case anything should happen to Mussolini.

There was now no more trouble with Parliament. Mussolini was delighted with the way in which the Chamber " functioned." At the fascist Congress in June 1925 he boasted: " We have subdued parliamentarianism! The Chamber no longer affords the nauseating spectacle that it had afforded for some time. It discusses, it approves, it legislates which is just what a legislative assembly ought to do."

He was no less delighted with the Senate, whose behavior had been truly exemplary. Discussion was a bit more lively in the Senate and the opposition more evident, but when it came to voting there was alway an overwhelming majority for the government. The Aventine deputies who looked to the Senate as the only remaining champion of liberty and the liberal state, had little ground for their hopes. The Senate had at last come into its own! Mussolini explained: " It is we of the younger generation who have grasped the importance of the Senate and have restored it to its ancient splendor. The Senate will approve fascist laws first of all because the government has a majority in it, secondly because we shall defend it, and thirdly because the Senate with its high sense patriotism will not want to assume the responsibility of a dispute which would lead to a crisis of the most serious consequences." [11]

11 Mussolini: *Discorsi del 1925*, p. 104.

II. Foundations of the Fascist State

The government was now free to carry out those larger reforms which were to lay the basis for the fascist state. Even before the Matteotti affair the beginnings had been made. By the liberal use of decrees, the executive power of the government had obtained considerable freedom. The courts offered some resistance, refusing to sanction over 500 of these decrees. The government evaded this by registering them "temporarily" and then getting busy on "judicial reform."

There was in Italy a supreme court of administrative justice, called the Fourth Session of the Council of State, an institution which had been built up by Crispi and Spaventa and of which Italian liberalism was particularly proud, for it constituted a judicial check even on the administrative acts of the government and was therefore in a sense a sovereign authority superior to the government. Naturally such an institution was inconsistent both with the theory and with the practice of fascist government. In January 1924 the Fourth Session was fused with the Third, "in order to give administrative jurisdiction the efficiency which it lacked and also to give a greater simplification, acceleration and economy to its judgments." [12]

This measure was supplemented by a very genuine unification of the Courts of Cassation (Supreme Court), a reform which had often been attempted but had been blocked by local jealousies in Parliament. A thoroughgoing reform of the various codes is also in process, under the direction of Alfredo Rocco. Its aim is not merely to codify and simplify existing law, and thus to reduce the notoriously enormous complexity and waste in Italian court procedure, but also to introduce fascist principles into the law, especially into the penal codes, marriage and divorce law, collective contracts, etc.

The reform of the bureaucracy had also been undertaken early. Ministries were consolidated where possible and the number of employees reduced (except in the ministries of the Interior and Foreign Affairs!) and an attempt made to define more clearly and to correlate the respective functions of officials. The aim of the reform was to give concrete embodiment to the idea of hierarchy, that organic unity of diverse functions, which according to Mussolini constitutes the very essence of the state.

The more organic constitutional reforms were begun immediately after the declaration of January 3, 1925. The Commission of "Solons" was reorganized at once. It was appointed by Royal Decree, instead

[12] Mussolini: *La Nuova Politica*, II, p. 175.

of by the Party as previously; it was enlarged to 18 members and was encouraged to proceed with its drafting of the reforms necessary to transform Italy into a " corporate state." Of this " corporate " state more in our next chapter. The more immediate parliamentary reforms suggested by the Commission amounted to little more than a learned sanctioning of what had already transpired. The evils of Parliament's supremacy were rehearsed and the " cults and myths of elections and universal suffrage " were exposed.[13] The executive power, it concluded, must be made dependent more on the Crown and less on Parliament and all administrative functions of Parliament must be abolished.

All this had already been done. Nevertheless the Report had its value in encouraging the government to go still further.

A decree was now passed by which the Prime Minister was made responsible solely to the King; the formation of the Cabinet was removed from the squabbles of parliamentary parties (November 1925); the Executive Power was empowered to make decrees with the force of laws (*emanare norme giuridiche*) and in cases of emergency to make laws themselves, (January 31, 1926).

In November 1926, partly as a consequence of the scandals on the French border, partly because of the dictatorial law of National Security which the Minister of the Interior would be called upon to enforce, Federzoni retired to the Ministry of Colonies, and Mussolini himself, assisted by his " private secretary " Suardo, became Minister of the Interior.

The same system was carried into local administration. We have already mentioned some of the problems which had arisen during the war and out of the conflict between the local administrations of the northern cities and the national government. The situation in the south was even worse, where local elections developed into family feuds and where municipal administration was conducted as a private business for private interests. Around Palermo and in other parts of Sicily the Maffia clan reigned supreme. The local fascist forces had changed the personnel but not the system. In some places a fascist *ras* carried on the work of the old boss, and in others the *fascio* as a whole undertook a paternalistic regulation of all the affairs of the community. In small communities especially responsibility was difficult to locate and finances were mal-administered, to say the least. All this was to be changed now. The powers of the prefects were extended. In November 192 centrally appointed *podestà* and *consulte municipali* were substituted for the elective Mayors and municipal councils.

In August 1926, ninety-five sub-prefectures were abolished, both

[13] v. Appendix No. 22.

cause the sub-prefects were difficult to control directly from the central government, and because they were traditionally leaders in local electoral politics. A few months later seventeen new provinces were created, among them the newly "redeemed" territories. The province rather than the municipality now became the chief organ of local government, and provincial administration was controlled directly by Rome. Thus local government was brought under the complete and direct authority of the central government.

The *hierarchy* was now complete. Mussolini became practically dictator and the fascist party the only recognized political body in the land.

Anyone who opposes fascism now is obviously an enemy of his country and to be treated as such. For, so the theory goes, just as the *risorgimento* and the war had transformed the Italian people into a nation, into an indivisible spiritual unity, so fascism has transformed this nation into a state, that is, it has given the inner unity a material embodiment. Hence whoever attacks fascism strikes a blow at the life of the nation. Corradini sums it all up by saying: "Historically speaking there is no opposition, but merely a few left-over parties and politicians who delude themselves into believing that they are opposing fascism." [14]

III. *The Theory of the Fascist State*

The ease with which *fascisti* regard themselves as the true representatives and interpreters of the nation is intelligible only after an examination of the theories and general ideas which accompanied these events, and which dominate the fascist imagination. For though the *fascisti* are professedly men of action, not of thought, their action was facilitated by a philosophy. They were fortunate in not being forced to create a whole philosophy afresh; they were able to pick up congenial ideas from a number of sources.

Anti-democratic theories were to be found in abundance. Democracy in fact was the intellectual scapegoat on which all sins had been loaded. Democratic institutions were a "recent French importation" and had found little real foothold in Italy either in theory or in practice. The great mass of the people had no public political education and had never become interested in elections. A large part of them until recently were prevented by law or by the Pope from participating in politics, but even had they been free to do so, only a small percentage would have made use of the opportunity. At most, they participated in local politics, for to this day among large masses of the peasants, especially in the south, Italy is little more than a geographical expression.

[14] Corradini: *Fascismo Vita d'Italia*, p. 9.

For a brief time during the war, democracy was on everyone's lips. But it was lip service to a temporary foreign idol, Woodrow Wilson; and when he fell, democracy sank to lower estate than ever. Traditionally the Italian democrats were a small bourgeois group. It was this bourgeois minority who led the *risorgimento,* who became republicans, who clamored for a constitution and who founded the liberalistic tradition. The socialists, therefore, began attacking Italian democracy as the most obvious starting point in the class struggle. The nationalists in their turn condemned democracy for its weakness, its stupidities and mediocrities, its enslavement before the unthinking masses, its foreignness, etc. Croce, Gentile and the idealistic school had swept the field of philosophy clean of the remnants of positivism and rationalism with which democracy was affiliated. These idealists opposed it for its individualism, its scepticism, and its materialism. The Catholics did likewise for similar reasons. Political scientists, sociologists and economists expounded the weaknesses and failures of democratic government; at their head was Vilfredo Pareto,[15] a scholar of universal reputation and a man who, by the way, had influenced Mussolini directly during his studies in Switzerland. Lastly the *fascisti* came along with their anti-democracy. In fact they took this stand not so much because democracy was really their prime enemy in practice, for it was not, but because they wanted something unpopular to attack!

The chief sources of anti-democratic theory on which fascism drew were three: the nationalists, the idealists and what for want of a better name we may call the Dante-Machiavelli tradition. These three streams, coming the first from the north, the second from the south and the third from the past, met in fascism and in the " New Rome."

The nationalists, whose chief theorizers are Enrico Corradini, Francesco Coppola, Alfredo Rocco, Federzoni, Forges-Davanzati and Maraviglia, received their inspiration largely from French sources, from Maurras and Sorel, and thus indirectly from De Maistre and De Bonald. We have already discussed in the first chapter the origins and prime motives of the nationalist movement, its preoccupation with foreign policy and with the " greatness " of Italy in the face of other nations. But these interests led the nationalists to a new conception of national politics as well. They were anti-parliament from the start and refused to call themselves a " party "; they were an association.

The notion that a state can build upon a mere aggregate of individuals is the fundamental fallacy of democratic theory, according to the nationalists. Individuals thus atomistically conceived remain atomic individuals.

[15] v. Pareto: *Testamento Politico,* in *Giornale Economico,* 1923.

uals and the state on such a basis must always appear as an artificial construction, an intruder, an enemy to the rights of man. Rousseau's attempt to construct a general will by a mathematical summation of particular wills, together with the whole machinery of elections to which this notion led in practice, perpetuates this fundamental fallacy. It is therefore not surprising that democracy, which at best and in its primary sense is a rule of the majority, has turned out to be a constant bickering of minorities for power. The fictitious people and so-called public opinion turned out to be really a number of parties, each representing certain special interests, bargaining with each other for power, and what was supposed to be a government by *representatives* of the people turned out to be *party* government. Democracy, therefore, is but the organ-✓ ized struggle of particular groups and not a government at all. Or, as Corradini puts it, Parliament ended up by being a synthesis of two corrupting forces; it combined the self-seeking of the bourgeoisie and the class struggle of the socialists into a new profession, that of the parliamentary politician.[16]

The politics of true government, as opposed to this politics of conflict, must be based on a more organic conception of society. This is found in the idea of the nation as a living ideal unity. And it was this unity that the nationalists claimed to represent. The Nationalist "Association" regarded itself as being on an entirely different plane from parliamentary parties, in that it represented no particular clientele nor class, and disbelieved in the whole democratic machinery. It stood for the unity of the nation and for the monarchy as the symbol of that unity. The nationalists believe in popular sovereignty, they say, but in a different sense, that is, in the sovereignty of the people as a collective whole over any individual member or group of members. A people in so far as it regards itself as a unity or a nation, has interests, values and aims which transcend all the particular interests of its individual members or subordinate groups. Therefore its government can not be made up of representatives of particular interests but must be composed of those *élites,* those spiritual leaders of the nation, who are capable of grasping and pursuing the good of the whole. No amount of elections and parties can produce such a government, except by sheer accident. The ever recurring demands by parliamentary governments for extraordinary powers in time of crisis are pointed to as evidence that parliamentary legislation is a luxury which the nation in its normal lethargy is willing to pay for, but which it discards whenever the pinch of necessity demands intelligence and efficiency. An assembly of parties may be a *parla*-ment, but by its very nature

[16] v. E. Corradini: *Fascismo Vita d'Italia.* See Appendix No. 28.

it can never be a government. Government requires unity. A government may not last long, but while it lasts it must have complete power. A series of bosses is preferable to a continual debate!

The crux of the theory, however, in its opposition to democracy concerns not so much the method of conducting a government, as the relations which should obtain between government and citizen. Since the state is but the embodiment of the ideal unity of its members, each citizen must be completely at the disposal of the state. Nothing for the individual; everything for Italy! This implies that the individual citizen should be able to find his own happiness and realization in and through his national state. If he fails it is because he is not really a part of the nation. Duty, discipline and sacrifice must bind the citizen to the state. The state, not its individual citizens, must be free. The state must have rights and the citizen duties. In place of democracy must come "hierarchy" (*gerarchià*), the ordered system of social functions. The democratic representation of classes and class interests must give place to a "popular aristocracy," for the people as an ideal cultural entity is by nature aristocratic.

The old liberal state, they say, might have led to such a conception had it developed its notion of free citizenship as a public duty in pursuit of the general interest; but instead it degenerated into the class rule of private interests, the bourgeoisie hiding under the banner of the *right* or *privilege* of universal suffrage, as the means whereby each citizen can express his own particular interests. The socialist state on the other hand is not only in practice but also in theory opposed to this nationalistic conception, for it is based on internal class struggle and overlooks or even denies the interests of the nation as a whole. Furthermore socialism is materialistic and appeals to the masses on the basis of individual gain, whereas nationalism is idealistic and calls the masses to personal sacrifices for the national interests.

Mussolini personally gave the idea of *hierarchy* a much more prominent rôle than it has among nationalists. He seems to have come by this conception through military channels. His earliest ideas of political reconstruction after the war were all modelled on army patterns. Interventionism had given a military turn to all of Mussolini's thinking and he imagined that the soldiers, to whom he addressed himself first of all would also think in these terms. Gradually, however, as the war receded, he gave the idea a moralistic and idealistic form. For example shortly after his advent to power, he said: "The work of fifty years of history and above all the war have made a nation out of the Italians. The historic task that awaits us is to make this nation into a nation state. This is a moral idea that finds embodiment in a system of respo sible hierarchies, whose members from the highest to the lowest feel the pride and privilege of doing their particular duty. . . . Our one aim must be the erection of this single, unified being, the nation-state, the sole bearer of the whole history, the whole future and the whole power of the Italian people." [17]

The idealists came to much the same conclusion though for different reasons. Politically speaking, Italian idealism represented an attempt to give a spiritual meaning to the secular institutions of the nation. The Catholic tradition regarded Italian politics as the devil incarnate. Gioberti's heroic effort to reconcile church and state failed. But two idealists, Francesco De Sanctis and Silvio Spaventa, gave to secular politics and culture the halo which the church denied them. De Sanctis is significant primarily because he introduced Hegel into Italy and thus laid the foundations for the modern idealistic school. As a political prisoner in the old castle at Naples, he translated Hegel's *Logic,* and then during his exile led the revival of literary criticism on the basis of an idealistic esthetics. During the sixties he took an active part in the politics of the new Italian State. He was one of the first to raise his voice of protest against the cliques of politicians and the maneuvers of special interests, which made their appearance in Parliament. In the interests of more dignified and idealistic politics he joined the struggling Left against the heavily intrenched sordid Right. But later, when he saw that the Left proved to be no better than the old Right, he rejoined the Right and laid the foundations for a new right-wing nucleus of idealistic patriots, who refused to yield to demagogy and corruption, and who continued to uphold the romantic political idealism which the *risorgimento* had inspired in them. This tradition was continued by Silvio Spaventa, who upheld the ideal of the strong, omnicompetent state in the face of both liberals and clericals. [18] His " adoration of the state " became a central theme of debate, and the rallying cry for those forces which wished to strengthen the young and none too strong Italian national government. It was this " noble Right " which is supposed to have passed on the idealism of the *risorgimento* to the *fascisti* and it was this tradition that the fascist Right of the Chamber of Deputies tried to revive.

Benedetto Croce, the greatest exponent of Italian idealism, was never primarily interested in politics and when he did turn to political philosophy he made some innovations in the direction of liberalism and socialism. Of the two great realms of social life which he distinguishes, the economic and the moral, he assigns the state to the former. Not

[17] Mussolini: *Popolo d'Italia,* January 2, 1923.
[18] v. Silvio Spaventa: *Politica della Destra.*

that all states always are merely economic arrangements, but he thinks that under modern conditions of culture, the ideal of the *Kulturstaat* is anachronistic. The modern state is as a matter of fact, he says, largely preoccupied with the material basis of social life, and ideally too it is just as well that the moral realm, that is, science, religion, art, etc., be left free and open. In economic and material affairs order and authority may be necessary, but in the realm of the spirit, freedom must reign. Having revolted against the spiritual authority of the church, Croce is not inclined to submit to a monarchy in morals.

But Giovanni Gentile came to the rescue of the *Kulturstaat*. Reacting against individualistic liberalism, he revived the more orthodox Hegelian conception of the state, the *stato etico*, as he calls it. But he was careful to make it appear to be a strictly Italian doctrine. In his early articles in *Politica* on the subject, he made much of Gioberti, later he seized upon Mazzini, whom he tried to free of his republicanism and positivism and to erect into an idealist. He emphasized especially the Mazzinian notion of the religious unity of the people (*Dio e popolo*) and the close connection between thought and action during the *risorgimento*. This doctrine he preached first as "the new liberalism," and when fascism came along he tried to reconcile liberalism and fascism; but both liberals and fascists were suspicious of this all too Hegelian synthesis and after the Aventine Secession Gentile was forced to abandon the attempted reconciliation and to proclaim himself a straight fascist.

Gentile is now the official fascist apologist for liberty. The more ordinary type of fascist will frankly admit that he does not believe in liberty;[19] that liberty has long since become a meaningless term; and worse, that the goddess of liberty is invoked religiously in order to conceal men's real aims. At least in the present crisis, they say, liberty would be dangerous. Italy has had enough of liberty for a while; what it needs now is law.[20] Or, as Suckert suggests, in Italy liberty had become but one more thing to fight about. Mussolini too had no illusions about the value of freedom of speech. When Parliament was reopened in 1923, he told the Chamber that the increase of violence at that time was directly traceable to the opening of Parliament. Parliamentary speeches excited the people and hence disturbed the peace. The country could never settle down so long as there was boundless liberty to orate in parliament and incessant opportunity to write incendiary editorials in the press. No one is free to think when every one raves about liberty. In his realistic moments Mussolini points out that the mass of the Italian people at this particular time neither need nor want liberty.

[19] v. Farinacci in Appendix No. 20.
[20] v. Massimo Rocca: *Idee sul Fascismo*, pp. 195 ff.

They want peace, work, bread, roads and water, and they are willing to work for these things. It is only certain bourgeois politicians who cry for liberty by profession, and certain socialist politicians who cry liberty in order to stop men from working.

Sometimes he becomes a little more philosophical, and says liberty is a pure abstraction. Only specific liberties exist; and of these some may be granted and others refused, depending on the needs of the moment. The liberty which is being demanded by the politicians of the opposition amounts to little else than the liberty to substitute themselves for the *fascisti* in power, that is, the liberty of revolution. But revolution is a question of power, not of liberty; and fascism will naturally defend its "liberty" to govern as long as it can.

The high-brow *fascisti* on the other hand, have their own doctrine of liberty. Mussolini too ascends to this plane once in a while with his famous: "Liberty is not a right, but a duty." It is not something to be enjoyed but something to be fought for.[21] Gentile with his Hegelian training is the undisputed champion at expounding this doctrine. "A state which presupposes liberty denies it precisely because it presupposes it; for there is no liberty outside the life of the spirit which, unlike natural beings, does not presuppose itself, but creates, conquers and evolves itself. A man *becomes* free; he is not so by nature. And the state is liberal, in fact and not merely verbally, if it promotes the development of liberty considered as an ideal to be attained and not as a natural right to be guaranteed."[22] Only through the state the individual's state (for individual and state exist in each other, not separately), can the individual achieve moral, spiritual liberty, for it is in the state that an individual's moral being becomes objectified. Liberty must be sought in law. "Liberty," says Gentile, "is, to be sure, the supreme end and aim of every human life; but in so far as personal and social education realize it by evoking this common will in the individual, it presents itself as law and hence as the State. And this is not superimposed on individual activity and initiative externally, subjecting them to restrictive compulsion, but is their own very essence. . . . The maximum of liberty always coincides with the maximum strength of the state."[23]

Not any and every state is liberating, of course. The *stato etico*, the liberating state, is one which is in movement, active, creative, giving objective form to the energies of its members. The state whose institutions are rigid, and in which no issues are being raised, no conflicts

---

[21] v. Mussolini: *La Nuova Politica*, I, pp. 23, 222; III, p. 31. Also Appendix No. 27.

[22] Gentile: *Che cosa è il fascismo*, pp. 119–120. Also Appendix No. 29.

[23] Gentile: *Che cosa è il fascismo*, p. 50.

overcome, is deadening to the life of the spirit, is "merely external" to the individual's moral being. Hence conflict, revolution, opposing forces are the very means by which liberty is won, and it is only by identifying himself in all due obedience with one of these objective social moving forces that an individual may win his freedom. The practical moral now becomes obvious. The old so-called liberal state, with its eternal democratic principles and its stagnant parliament was the real enemy of freedom: it was lost in "lifeless abstraction" and inert matter, a foe to the spirit. The new fascist state that is now in process of creating itself is by that very token the home of the spirit and the "*salvezza della nostra libertà.*"

The same sort of analysis applies to justice. Not all law is just, nor all illegality unjust. The *fascisti* do not hesitate to appeal to justice even against the law itself. They speak of their "just violence" and "just reprisals," because such action is more in accordance with their ideas of right than the action, or inaction, of the law. When a people becomes disgusted with its laws, it is sheer academic quibbling to ask whether it has à *right* to revolt. "Devotion to justice does not consist in mere devotion to legality. . . . The respect for law represents but one aspect and not the highest of our human mission; for over and above the legality of today we are required to prepare that of tomorrow. . . . And if ever the struggle for justice requires us in any case to pass beyond the established order, this must never occur . . . out of mere individual interest or judgment, but (for such is the nature of justice) only in obedience to another law, higher and more severe; which we recognize as already operative and whose more serious and onerous duties we accept and undertake. Who says 'justice' says a subordination to a hierarchy of values." [24]

Though idealists and nationalists come to much the same conclusions, they are historically quite distinct theories, especially in Italy. The nationalists have no use for the "German philosophy" and Hegelian dialectic in which the idealists are steeped. The idealists regard the nationalists' uncritical worship of tradition and nationality as devoid of an adequate philosophical basis; or, as they put it, the nationalists have a purely "mechanical and abstract" notion of tradition, nation and state, and fail to select from the mass of custom and convention those traditions which have an inner coherence in action and a spiritual significance in history.[25] Recently Antonio Pagano and other mino-

[24] Giorgio del Vecchio: *La Giustizia*, in *Revista Internazionale di Filosofia de Diritto*, 1926, III, pp. 447–8.

[25] cf. Ercole Reggio: *Fascismo e tradizione*, in *Educazione Fascista*, Februar 1927, pp. 85–92. Also a good statement of the idealistic theory of the nation i

writers have attempted a synthesis of the two doctrines, to accompany the practical political fusion of nationalists and idealists in fascism.[26]

The third element above mentioned which has entered into the theory of the fascist state is the concept of the *stato forte,* the strong state. This idea has its roots back in the Roman Empire, but was revived for modern Italy by Dante and Machiavelli, much as for English speaking people it was revived by Hobbes. The idea is that the fundamental criterion of a good state lies in its strength. The *virtù* of a state is to be able to dominate *fortuna.*[27] By this is meant not so much its physical power or might, as its practical ability to control or govern the various forces which play upon it. And when the *fascisti* say " We have the right to govern Italy because we alone have the strength (*forza*)," [28] they do not mean merely " might makes right "; they mean that in the conflict of forces which characterized the years 1919 to 1922, they, and not the democratic government, proved capable of exercising effective control and reëstablishing some sort of order and authority. And they are well aware that this ability to govern is not merely a matter of " force," but of the interplay of a variety of factors which go to make up the " strength " of a movement. The *fascisti* actually underwent this experience before they theorized about it. It came as an empirical discovery.

Even Mussolini, who claims to be a disciple of Machiavelli and who perhaps has studied him a little more than the average Italian politician, seems to have regarded this as one of the ideas which he got from his own experience rather than from his master. In his essay on " Force and Consent," [29] in which he first formulated the doctrine as a doctrine, he at least gives an original form to the Machiavellian tradition. All government, he maintained, is a combination of force and consent. The two are strictly correlative; " force involves consent, and consent is the very essence of force *per se.*" [30] In the long run the consent which a government enjoys is best measured pragmatically by its force, rather than by election schemes and other devices of so-called public opinion.

Francesco Ercole: *Il carattere morale del nazionalismo,* in *Politica,* February 1922, pp. 193–218.

[26] v. Antonio Pagano: *Idealismo e Nazionalismo,* in *Politica,* August 1926, pp. 201–221; December 1926, pp. 201–221.

[27] On Machiavelli in this connection see Francesco Ercole: *The Politics of Machiavelli;* Gentile: *Che cosa è il fascismo,* pp. 256 ff.; Croce: *On the Conduct of Life, passim.*

[28] v. Corradini: *Fascismo Vita d'Italia,* p. 21. Also Appendix No. 28.

[29] In *Gerarchia,* April 1922. See also Appendix No. 27.

[30] Mussolini: *La Nuova Politica,* I, p. 224.

A government, for example, that relies solely on bayonets and fear is highly unstable and loses its control at the first crisis that comes along. So long as a government can maintain itself without resorting to exceptional and arbitrary violence, liberty is at a maximum, for consent signifies contentment. Hence (and this is where the emphasis falls) liberty is possible only in a *strong* state. Political liberalism may be the worst enemy of liberty. The most common theme, I suppose, on which the *fascisti* harp is that when the liberal democratic state became *weak*, liberty in every real sense of the word was lost in the various tyrannies which anarchy bred. This fact, still fresh in the Italian mind, is, they say, what theoretical considerations ought to lead us to expect. When a nation "loses its head," quite literally it loses its self-control and hence its freedom. To the *fascisti*, who believe in the most literal interpretation of the organic theory of the state, it seems axiomatic that a nation must have a head and a highly centralized organ of control. Self-government ought to be thought of, they say, in terms of "self-control"; if a nation wants to exercise self-control it must be built like the human organism, and must have a central "will" which controls particular organs and their impulses.[31]

This theory is a reaction against pluralistic conceptions of authority. The State ought to be sovereign and the government authoritative. The democratic attempt to govern by checks and balances, to play one authority against another, merely breeds confusion. It is an attempt to govern the government. Ultimately there must be a supreme power. To erect the Law or the Constitution or some other abstract entity into such a power is a mere evasion, for that merely transfers the government to the courts. Law, pragmatically speaking, is lawyers, judges and legislators. The practical problem is simple, *who* shall have the final word in the exercise of the law? Whoever this happens to be is the real governor. Ultimately it is a question of the *classe dirigente*, of certain *persons*, who have power.

The liberals and democrats object to this on the ground that it undermines the whole conception of law. Guglielmo Ferrero, for example, complains that the government is not "legitimate," that "law" must be restored as a prime prerequisite, and that *delegated* authority is the only possible basis of government today.[32] In a similar vein Bonomi, criticising the electoral reform, says: " It reduces the state to the level of our municipalities which are captured in turn by factions that desire nothing better than to undo the work of their predecessors. The munici-

31 v. For example, Roberto Pavese: *Libertà e Autorità*, in *Vita Nova*, Septembe: 1926, p. 12—15.
32 v. Ferrero: *La Democrazia in Italia*.

palities however have a sphere limited by law, and their partisan excesses can be checked by the State. But the State itself, if it be captured by a party, is entirely beyond control." [33] To such criticism the fascist reply is that *of course* the state must be " beyond control," for the state exists to control and not to be controlled. If the state is not sovereign, it is not a genuine state. And to speak of a disembodied *law* or of a principle of legitimacy as controlling forces over and above the state is but a form of idolatry. If, on the other hand, by the term law is meant the sovereignty of parliament, then parliament is "beyond control." Or, if it be insisted that parliament is subject to the sovereign people, then the reply is that there is no government at all. For if the citizens severally expect to govern their government, they ought to say frankly that they do not care to be governed. Self-government is a contradiction in terms, unless it means that the people as a collective whole consents to be governed by a few of its members, and confers authority upon them. But in this sense, the fascist government claims to be a government of the people so long as it enjoys the necessary strength to govern, a strength which only popular consent can give, whether this consent be expressed by elections or in other forms. In short, a government is limited by its power and not by some other authority. Or, if the term law is to be used, the law must be the law *of* the government, not something over and beyond it. For law is itself a variable and is dependent on its ability to retain the moral support and express the political sentiments of those whom it governs.

The immediate aim of any government must therefore be to make itself *strong*, authoritative. The means will naturally vary. Neither Machiavelli's advice to princes, nor any other principles of government, can be followed slavishly. New situations demand new devices, and a government that regards its institutions as ends in themselves and is therefore unwilling to adapt itself to " the whims of Dame Fortune," as Machiavelli said, loses its capacity and hence also its right to govern.

This pragmatic Machiavellian doctrine which has exercised an enormous influence on all political thought in Italy, naturally served the intellectual needs of fascism admirably. For it was evident to the *fascisti*, as it must be to the reader who has followed our story, that fascism was carried along on its career by the force of events and not by any inner aims. The essence of the movement lay not in its programs, which were subject to change without notice, nor in its ideas, which shiftily followed its shifting fortunes, but in its growing power. And by its power, I mean not merely its display of violence and physical force, but its ability to exercise control in a series of practical exigencies. It became

[33] Bonomi: *From Socialism to Fascism*, p. 94.

a sort of universal emergency service for the nation, and the *fascisti* were no more aware than anyone else of where their " services " might be needed next. They naturally pounced on everything that happened to be weak. And their appetite for power grew with their capacity to use it. Their power was a surprise even to themselves, and the directions it took were quite unforeseen.

Once their career was made, however, the " logical necessity " of the events became clear to them. When they finally found themselves fighting Parliament, democracy, liberty and all the institutions of the liberal state, they realized that they had been assigned this historic mission from the first! The era of the French Revolution was over and a new Roman era was dawning. Democracy, liberty and all the sacred principles of the French Revolution were useful expedients at the time they were invented, but society has changed radically within the last century, and nothing ought to seem more natural than that a revolutionary society should need revolutions in government.

Democracy and liberalism were not invented as constructive political reforms, but were used by the new commercial and industrial bourgeoisie to destroy the *ancien régime* in order to give these classes the opportunity to build up a new order of their own, growing out of their industrial revolution. This new order was not the democratic state as is commonly supposed; their new order was economic and not political. It was built up by capital at first, but later labor too built up an order on its side. Science, art, education and religion also were freed to build up their independent contributions to modern society. In all this the democratic state played a decidedly negative rôle, and the real governing forces were non-political. Mussolini, for instance, points out that " The parliamentary system has been seriously, not mortally, wounded by two typical phenomena of our time: on the one hand by syndicalism, on the other by journalism; syndicalism, which gathers into definite associations all those who have special and particular interests to safeguard and who want to remove them from the incompetence shown by political assemblies; and journalism, which is the daily parliament, the daily platform where men from the universities, from the sciences, from the industries, and from daily life thresh out problems with a competence seldom found on the benches of Parliament." [34]

At last, so the *fascisti* believe, the turning point has come. These new and relatively independent orders of modern society are in need of coördination and when coördinated they are able to constitute a new constructive *political* order. The new state is not so much an attempt once more to subject all these forces to an external political control, a

[34] Mussolini's speech to the Senate, July 8, 1923.

it is a political recognition of the fact that new controls have been created. The idea is that if capital, labor, education, church, art, etc., are all incorporated into a cultural whole so that they coöperate, this organic unity of the actual new social forces will itself constitute a new *political* order, a *stato etico, Kulturstaat, stato forte, stato fascista* — call it what you please. The point is that some sort of institutional synthesis is now possible. And it has come first in Italy, they say, because here it is not only possible, but imperative. Italy was forced by its economic and political situation after the war to cut out all internal friction and coördinate all its resources. Though this revolution will no doubt take other forms in other countries, the *fascisti* regard their state as but the beginning of a transformation of European politics; for they regard it as the inevitable consequence of the revolutionary social changes of the nineteenth century. "All over the world," said Mussolini, "there is a feeling that the parliamentary system, a system which lasted for a number of decades in the history of the nineteenth century, has exhausted its usefulness and that today it is insufficient to deal with the growing impetus of the needs and passions of modern civilization. There is a feeling everywhere that in this modern society it is necessary to reëstablish the principles of order, of discipline; of hierarchy, in all their severity, without which human society is headed for chaos and ruin." [35] Modern society, as the *fascisti* are in the habit of saying, demands a modern up-to-date state. When modern society passes, as it no doubt will, the fascist state will pass also; but in the meantime it will have done its work, it will have really governed.

IV. *The Fascisti in Their State*

But who wants to be governed! Last of all the *fascisti*. These knight errants of the new order with difficulty found their places in it. Being aristocrats by profession they naturally gravitated upwards, and, since in a hierarchy there is little room at the top, a high pressure was generated, which threatened to make a volcano out of the social pyramid.

Immediately after its founding in 1921, the Party had begun filling up with a miscellaneous lot of politicians, labor organizers, office seekers, — *affaristi*, as they are called in Italian. For by that time it was clear in which direction the political wind was blowing. The socialists and communists knew they were beaten. Their labor organizations were smashed and their political strength was declining. Their lesser officials

[35] Mussolini: *Discorsi del 1925*, p. 233. Speech in the Chamber of Deputies, November 18, 1925.

and petty politicians were therefore compelled to look elsewhere for careers. By the hundreds such men now knocked at the doors of the Fascist Party, and the *Duce* gave orders to welcome them. He did so not merely because at that time it was important for the party to show voting strength, but also because he took a personal satisfaction in seeing ex-communists and socialists confess their sins and acknowledge the truth. He wanted the masses, the *popolo d'Italia,* to turn to him as their leader, and he hoped that by welcoming these proletarian elements into his ranks, fascism might definitely down its bourgeois reputation. The union early in 1922 of fascism and Rossoni's confederation of patriotic syndicates also encouraged this trend, for these syndicates were many of them bodily taken over from the socialist organizations.

Later in 1922 more reputable politicians began drifting into the Fascist Party and after the March on Rome, naturally, there was a veritable flood of office seekers coming from all parties. To say nothing of those office holders under the old regime, who in order to retain their jobs were suddenly convinced of the truth of fascism. On top of these accretions to the movement came the political trend within the fascist organization itself, which pushed fascist politicians increasingly to the front and fascist fighters increasingly into the background. Membership cards were sold wholesale and having a *tessera* became a common byword, like "I have a pass." In short, within a few months the membership and character of fascism was radically altered.

At first there was loud rejoicing in the camp over this sudden prosperity, but bitter complaints soon made themselves heard. We noted in the preceding chapter that there was strong opposition on the part of the squadrists to the founding of any political party whatsoever. When their worst fears were realized, large numbers protested and not inconsiderable numbers bolted. During the spring of 1922 " autonomous *fasci*" sprang up at Florence, Ferrara and other places. Though most of these were due to personal rivalries (as for example, the case of Pasella at Florence, who was ousted from the Party bureaucracy by his "subordinate" Rossi) nevertheless such conflicts reflected a growing discontent with the Party machine. When the word of the March on Rome began to be passed around, most of these local dissidences were patched up and everybody coöperated in the attack, believing that once fascism came into power, there would be plenty of fat jobs for all.

Hardly had Mussolini's coalition cabinet been announced and the black shirts been demobilized, when fascist dissent reappeared. In Florence the veteran squadrists organized a " Band of Expulsion " which without waiting for further orders began expelling political parvenue and office seekers from the local *fascio*. At Genoa an "Old Guard" was formed for the same purpose, and in the Marches a *fascio di combattimento* ironically revived the original name which Mussolini had given his organization. At Milan the order of *Il 1919* was founded, and a magazine by that name to spread the Old Guard propaganda.

The general tactics of this movement were to swear unflinching loyalty to Mussolini and to the cause, but to attack the party politicians. There was much talk about the Mussolinian doctrine of "fascist aristocracy" and it was carefully pointed out that not only the old bureaucracy, which Mussolini was naturally unable to clean out all at once, but also the official class in the Fascist Party itself needed much "purification." The genuine aristocrats, they claimed, those who had borne the brunt of the fight, and who alone were capable of renewing the energies of the government, had not stooped to party politics and vulgar office seeking; but were waiting in silent discipline for the call of the *Duce!* Etc., etc.

This Mussolinism, as it came to be called, put the *Duce* in a bad predicament. On the one hand it was to his personal interest as well as to that of the government to free himself as much as possible from dependence on his colleagues in the Party and to encourage anything that would give him a reputation as head of a government and not leader of a revolutionary party. On the other hand, he could not afford to defy his own party, for having but a very shaky foothold in Parliament and still less in the bureaucracy and in the army, he would be left high and dry if he should lose the leadership of the Party. Consequently Mussolini's stand was equivocal. He tried to play both sides. He denounced Mussolinism openly, but encouraged Mussolini-worship by his tactics and personal bearing. He repelled all external attacks on the Party, but he scattered the quadrumvirate as much as possible (De Vecchi, for example, was sent as governor to Somaliland!) and decentralized the Party administration. On the other hand he resisted the demand for jobs as much as possible, he announced he would accept no "October *fascisti*," and in June 1923 he requested that out of 250,000 *fascisti* who were members of the Party, but not of the militia, 150,000 be dropped.[36] On the other hand, he denounced all attempts to "judge *fascisti* by their dates" and called The 1919 Movement simply ridiculous.[37] He was very severe on anything that smacked of internal friction and indiscipline; any open acts of insubordination or "autonomy" he suppressed wherever possible.

[36] v. Mussolini: *La Nuova Politica*, I, p. 159.
[37] v. Mussolini: *La Nuova Politica*, II, p. 196.

The truth of the matter was that Mussolini did not care to be bothered with these matters. As a statesman he felt superior to them. Both by temperament and by his nationalist principles he was preoccupied with Italy's international relations and the urgent problems of diplomacy. His notion of the administration of the interior was that it was primarily a negative affair, a police job, which he might safely entrust to Bianchi, while he devoted himself to foreign politics. In his first speech to the Senate he said: "I shall take care of the Ministry of Foreign Affairs; at bottom the Ministry of the Interior is a ministry of police power. I am glad to be at the head of the police force, am certainly not ashamed of it and hope that all Italian citizens will forget certain fruitless atavisms and will recognize the police as one of the forces most necessary for social life. But above all, I intend to conduct foreign policy." [38] Internal disturbances irritated him and he attended to them hastily, impulsively, often violently. For he hated to descend to such petty affairs. After one of his many house cleanings, he told his party leaders brusquely that he did not propose to be disturbed by party incidents while he was busy with high diplomacy.

As a result of this attitude on Mussolini's part, the internal government of the country was practically turned over to the Party politicians, for although a rigid distinction was made in theory between the activities of the Party and those of the government, in practice no such distinction prevailed. Bianchi was both Under-Secretary of the Interior and Secretary General of the Party. He simply transformed the local party politicians into "political commissaries" and gave them extensive authority. Within a few months, however, these commissaries made themselves so obnoxious to the prefects, chiefs of police, mayors and other administrative officers, that Mussolini was forced to intervene and to abolish them. In their stead "provincial *fiduciari*" were created, or, more accurately, the old provincial *fascisti ras* were left intact. Though this relieved the towns and cities of much disorder, it put the burden of responsibility for the conduct of the Party on the provincial heads, who became "little Mussolini's." Hence the administration varied greatly from province to province. Protests against these provincial bosses kept pouring in. Finally, the Grand Council of the Party in the fall of 1923 decided on a further reform. The provincial secretaries were made dependent both on the support of the local *fasci* who from now on nominated them, and on the government, whose approval of the nomination was made obligatory. Also an attempt was made to separate government and Party. Michele Bianchi devoted himself exclusively to the Ministry of the Interior and resigned as head of the Party. I

---

[38] Mussolini: *La Nuova Politica*, I, p. 25–6.

his place came Francesco Giunta, a veteran politician, but with much less personal authority than Bianchi. As a result the various members of the Directorate were practically independent, and they employed their liberty in the lowest sort of grafting and plotting. Besides Giunta, there were in this group Cesare Rossi, director of Mussolini's press and propaganda office, and keeper, as the phrase went, of the keys to Mussolini's heart; Giovanni Marinelli, who had charge of the funds of the Party and who managed them so well that after his arrest for complicity in the Matteotti affair it was found that he had seven million *lire* to his personal credit in various banks; Italo Balbo, who persisted in directing squadrist violence; and a number of other men of the same general calibre. These men were continually sending out orders to the local *fasci*, commanding them "to render life impossible" in their community for anyone they saw fit to persecute; and all this at the same time that Mussolini was promising an end of violence and ordering prefects to enforce the law.

Dissent within the fascist ranks now took on more serious proportions. There were innumerable personal rivalries as in the case of Sala, the fascist mayor of Alessandria, a popular veteran squadrist, who clashed with Eduardo Torre, a politician who was appointed high commissioner of railroads; or the case of Padovani at Naples, who continued to fight the ultra-reactionary nationalist bands. But out of such conflicts arose more general issues. In the south the nationalists flared up when the *fascisti* tried to take over their local organizations. They were willing to fuse, but they did not expect to be forced to surrender. As for the lower classes, they became increasingly hostile after the split with the popularists. The *fascisti*, not having local leaders, or not using them, tried to invade the south with their northern politicians, which only made matters worse.

In the north the first important case to rise to the level of divergence on fundamental principles was that of Misuri. In an earlier chapter we have already given some account of the rivalry between the Deputy Misuri and the squadrist Pighetti. The intricate details of what followed are hardly worth mentioning in themselves, but they may be of interest as a sample of the way in which the Party was functioning. After the Misuri-Pighetti duel in February 1922, the Party sent De Vecchi and Teruzzi to investigate the situation in Perugia. Their report, though it admitted Misuri's hot-headedness, was on the whole favorable to him, and recommended that he be kept at Perugia and that Pighetti be given some other sphere of usefulness. The report was kept secret and buried in the files. Meanwhile Misuri launched several attacks on Bastianini now in the Ministry of Agriculture), then provincial secretary, who was implicated in the rivalry. Receiving no vindication of his conduct from the Party headquarters, he resigned and joined the nationalist group. As he did so he sent a plea for redress to Mussolini, accompanying it with an attack on the bureaucracy. Shortly after, the nationalists fused with the *fascisti*, so that Misuri was faced with the choice of returning to the fold or openly following the opposition. He had some hopes of being able to make a dignified return when the March on Rome was being planned, for De Vecchi wanted to put Misuri, who was a biologist, in charge of the sanitary corps of the militia, but other authorities interfered. In the spring of 1923 a new investigation of the whole case was ordered, and one of Bastianini's friends, Sansanelli, was put on the investigating committee. On the recommendation of Sansanelli Mussolini agreed to transfer Misuri to the Rome *fascio*. But in the meantime Misuri, through De Vecchi had succeeded in getting hold of the first commission's report. He published this in a leading opposition paper, the *Mondo*. Everybody was scandalized. Pighetti challenged De Vecchi and Teruzzi to duels, but was expelled from the Party and locked up for a while under arrest. Three fascist politicians, among them Bastianini, challenged Misuri, but finally the Bastianini-Misuri duel was the only one actually fought. Naturally Misuri, the cause of all this trouble, was expelled from the Party. Shortly after, he told Finzi and Buttafochi, of the Ministry of the Interior, to tell Mussolini that he was planning to make a speech in the Chamber of Deputies for the " fascist opposition " to the Party bureaucracy. He was told that the Prime Minister " ordered " him not to speak. Whereupon Misuri replied that he was not subject to his orders, being expelled from the Party. He was then told that Mussolini said he would arrest him, if he spoke. Whereupon Misuri replied that being a Deputy, he was not subject to arrest. The following day, May 29, 1923, he made his speech. In it he praised Mussolini and his personal work, but he launched a scathing attack on his associates in the Party, from Bianchi down.[39] He urged a clear separation of government and Party, more attention on the part of the government to the voice of the Parliament and less to the bureaucracy, decentralization of the militia and purification of fascism from its recent accretions. The evening following the speech, in an alley behind the House of Parliament, Misuri was stopped by a fascist squad and beaten to unconsciousness. Mussolini ordered the arrest of the squadrists. Bonaccorsi, the leader of the squad, was locked up for a few hours, and then set free to resume fighting the good fight and received the hearty greetings of the *Duce*. Not long after, he was seen among the prominent militia officers gathered around Mussolini on the

[39] v. Misuri: *La Rivolta Morale*, pp. 95–122. Also Appendix No. 17.

speaker's balcony at the Bologna demonstration. Misuri was now cured of his confidence in Mussolini and threatened to speak again in the Chamber. On hearing this, Mussolini was enraged and in violent language ordered his lieutenants to put a stop to him.[40] But instead, the Chamber was " closed for elections " before Misuri had another chance to speak.

Prominent among those *fascisti* who congratulated Misuri after his speech was the Under-Secretary for Agriculture, Corgini. He was also a conservative liberalistic fascist and had openly opposed the syndicalist monopolies which Rossini was trying to establish in agriculture. His getting up from the government benches and shaking hands with Misuri in a very conspicuous manner, was sufficient pretext to cause his expulsion from the Party.

Together Misuri and Corgini now organized a " constitutional association " called *Patria e Libertà*. They explained in their platform that they were " opposed to any form of political or syndical monopoly and proposed to defend the broadest liberty of thought, association, propaganda and press, within the limits of the law." They wanted to prevent the fascist movement, " which was originally a movement of romanticism, of chivalry, of defense for society and civilization," from losing this spirit " among the tortuous subtleties of a party career," or in a " rigid, military, hierarchical " organization. " We want to gather around us," they said, " for a decided stand, that balanced moderate opinion which is forming at the heart of every social class, that is desirous of returning to an enduring normality of life." [41]

The *Patria e Libertà* was applauded by many but followed by few. The opposition liberals and democrats welcomed it as a first sign of returning sobriety among the *fascisti*, but they naturally did not abandon their own old party for this upstart. A number of the dissident *fascisti* adhered to it, but the great majority of them preferred to stay in the party, " boring from within." What practical success it had was local. When the elections came in April, Misuri ran in Perugia as an independent candidate, and thus merely helped to divide the opposition into small groups. He failed of election and the Association practically disappeared from view. Nevertheless it was of considerable significance that it gave initial impetus to a movement which soon overflowed the narrow bounds of Misuri's personal following.

Misuri tried to get a foothold in Florence, but failed because other dissident groups had already established themselves there and in Siena

[40] v. Rossi's Memorandum, in *La Ricostruzione Fascista*, p. 178. Also Appendix No. 19.

[41] v. Misuri: *Rivolta Morale*, pp. 273–4.

and other Tuscan towns. From the platform of these groups, who called themselves *Fasci Nazionali*, I take the following:

" Whereas the wire-pulling and grafting of the politicians, the fiercely autocratic system of the oligarchy on top, the continual superimposition of party machinery on state offices, the harboring of men in the party who are notoriously discredited for their private and political immorality, have brought fascism to a most serious crisis; and whereas in spite of all superficial labels, the conflict and contract between the reconstruction and salutary work of the government and the parasitical demagoguery of the party is becoming steadily more evident, . . . the *fasci nazionali* . . . reconfirm their faith in Benito Mussolini, the head of the fascist government. . . . Though ready to rush to the *Duce's* side at the least indication of a recurrence of bolshevism, the *fasci nazionali* now desire a return to legality, to normality and to a peaceful civil life. They especially condemn unjustified violence, above all when it serves to conceal the protection of certain individual or class interests. . . .

" Every form of syndicalism that is genuinely national must be qualitative, not quantitative; must organize minds, not herd men like cattle. Every kind of monopoly or coercion, the sordid heritage of bolshevist systems, is flatly condemned." [42]

These National *Fasci* obviously differed from Misuri's position in that they explicitly wished to remain within the fascist movement, were loyal to Mussolini and had no desire to upset the fascist regime. They were even unwilling to set up separate candidates for the elections. Their stand was therefore little more than a protest and a temporary secession from the regular *fasci* until these had been " purified." In the meantime, however, Sala and Forni, two *fascisti* who had got into trouble with the party machine, were organizing *fasci nazionali* in Lombardy and the provinces to the north, where they enjoyed a considerable personal following. They felt strong enough to appear as candidates at the elections and they organized an extensive campaign, bringing the Tuscan *fasci nazionali* under their control, giving the dissident movement practical force. Shortly before the election (on March 11, to be exact) the Directorate of the Party sent out orders to various places where these men were campaigning, enjoining the local *fasci* "to render life impossible to the dissenting candidates," and the Provincial Secretary of Novara added his bit to the order, saying, " block the way for Sala and Forni; they must not be allowed to speak." [43] The next day the two men were attacked in the railroad station of Milan, and beaten

[42] From Giacomo Lumbroso: *La crisi del facismo*, pp. 135-6.
[43] v. Appendix No. 18.

severely so that Forni barely escaped with his life. In spite of this persecution, Forni was elected to Parliament. He found himself completely isolated, however, since neither the opposition nor the fascisti trusted him. The *fasci nazionali* were gradually broken up, their officers beaten, and the members expelled from the Party. After the crisis was over, those who had " behaved " during their expulsion and wanted to come back were allowed to reënter, others were to be treated as " traitors."

A milder and more high-brow form of dissent was started by a number of intellectual heretics. After the March on Rome the *Voce* publishing house in Florence began publishing a series of volumes devoted to the intellectual elaboration and *approfondimento* of fascism. The writers connected with the *Voce*, for the most part affiliated with the Gentile school of idealist philosophy (Suckert, Soffici, Volt), were critically minded and fairly independent in their political thinking. Their critical studies naturally led to a certain amount of heresy and to philosophical subtleties which shocked some of the more naïve *fascisti*. Giuseppe Bottai, one of these young idealists, who, by the way, had been a futurist, during the crisis of 1923 founded a journal called *Critica Fascista*. In this journal even more than in the *Voce* books, crucial points were discussed critically. The general point of view represented by these " integralists " was that fascism could neither be dominated by the opportunist politicians who had no constructive ideas at all, nor by the liberals who wanted a return to the constitution, but by a radical reconstruction of the state, wholly in the hands of bona fide *fascisti*. They wanted integrated fascist constitutional reform. They stood for what Mussolini later formulated as " All the power to all of fascism." On the whole the fascist liberals gave them little opposition, and in practice they soon found their only serious opponents to be the old style politicians in the bureaucracy. Hereupon Farinacci and lesser loud-mouthed *fascisti* condemned them for attacking the government and violating discipline. The integralists then assailed not only the bureaucracy but the provincial *ras* as well, and Farinacci and his crowd in particular. These were held up as unworthy of fascism because of their war record and their undue violence, and also because they were uneducated, tainted by agnosticism, and affiliated with Freemasonry. The squadrist journals, like Farinacci's daily *Cremona Nuova*, Settimelli and Carli's daily *l'Impero, La Fiamma Nera, l'Assalto*, and a host of lesser ones, took up the challenge. They styled themselves the champions of *fascismo intransigente*, and dubbed their opponents revisionists, dissidents, *Vocists*, etc. In defense, the *Critica Facista* crowd, and Suckert in his weekly *La Conquista dello Stato*, insisted that their brand of fascism was not a new kind but simply *fascismo integrale,* that is, thoroughgoing, pure, unfaltering. And a serious rivalry ensued between these two kinds of champions of the purest kind of fascism — a rivalry prompted more by personal dislikes and " cultural differences " than by rival political doctrines.

A similar type of criticism was launched against the bureaucracy by a group of writers who frankly called themselves revisionists, and whose chief aim was to encourage democratic control *within* the party and to oppose tendencies toward dictatorship and rigid party cliques. G. Cipriani-Avoglio and other writers in the *Polemica Fascista* carried on this sort of propaganda.

Another distinct aspect of dissidence centered about the case of Massimo Rocca. He was personally in a singular political position. Ever since the beginnings of fascism, Rocca had championed the idea of economic councils of experts. He had succeeded in organizing several of these so-called *gruppi di competenza* and his general idea for the structure of the fascist state seems to have been this: to supplement the ministry and bureaucracy by syndicates on the one hand, and on the other by his councils of the professional and industrial *élite,* and to give both of these economic organizations legislative functions, so that they might introduce technical intelligence into Parliament. It was to be a state modelled on economic rather than on political lines. Being personally intimate with Mussolini and having enjoyed his steady support, he thought he could push his scheme to a speedy realization. But he encountered overwhelming opposition. Rossoni and the syndicalists opposed him because they were trying to get complete control of the whole economic organization for themselves and had no intention of dividing power with Rocca and his *gruppi di competenza.* From the political side, he naturally had the whole hierarchy of politicians on his back, because of his attack on the party, his interference with their machine by his *gruppi di competenza,* and his opposition to political fascism in general. His own *gruppi di competenza* met with little success, since they had influence neither with the syndical confederations nor with the Party. They were forced to be a rather superfluous adjunct to the various national ministries, and a constant source of interference and irritation for the provincial administrations. In this situation, Mussolini's only move was, of course, to abandon Rocca. Hence when Rocca became involved in the general dissident movement, this was quickly seized on by his enemies as an opportunity to get rid of him

Beginning with September 1923 Rocca, a dilettante in philosophy as well as in politics, published a series of articles in the *Critica Fascista* and in the *Nuova Paese,* in which he maintained the apparently innocent thesis that " the revolution was made *by* the *fascisti, for* Italy, but not *for* the *fascisti* themselves." Among other things he wrote: " For some time I have been asking myself whether the Fascist Party represents the necessary support for Benito Mussolini, or whether it is rather a parasitic growth weighing on his shoulders. It now seems to me that this second hypothesis, already true to a certain point, is becoming continually more real in an Italy which is entirely Mussolinian and little fascist; and less fascist every day, and certainly not through the fault either of the *Duce* or of Italy." [44] This was evidently not so innocent. The intransigent journals replied and before long heated polemics ensued. They spread rapidly and became more violent, more personal and more scandalous. All sorts of charges of corruption were made on both sides and the argument descended from the critical and philosophical level in which it had begun to the most violent journalism. Rocca himself, and the *Critica Fascista* too, for that matter, kept in dignified bounds and tried to keep the polemics from becoming personal encounters, but he was caught in the maelstrom and his predicament was exploited by his enemies. The Executive Board of the Party wanted to expel him immediately for indiscipline, but Mussolini objected. The Executive Board then handed in their resignations. The Grand Council of the Party meeting shortly after, January 1924, took up the matter and converted the sentence into four months abstention from political activity, that is, until the elections were over. The Executive Board was replaced by a National Directorate, headed by Giunta, but containing some nationalist members who were favorably disposed toward Rocca. The Directorate's chief concern was to run the election and though their campaign was full of violence and persecution, Rocca was not seriously molested. Though he behaved with a certain show of loyalty, his discipline was by no means exemplary. He made an election speech at Turin on " Moral Reconstruction," which though it displeased the opposition more than it did the fascist authorities, nevertheless smacked too much of " political activity." On the whole he confined himself to writing more serious essays, giving his dissidence a philosophical framework. These were published by the *Voce,* but not until after the elections. Even before the elections, however, seeing that things were going against him, he made a last effort to retrieve his fortunes. He founded the *Corriere Italiano* at Rome, a pretentious daily, and devoted it to a moderate Mussolinism. He attacked such dissidents as Misuri because they had deserted Mussolini, and he adopted a generally middle position, which he hoped might win Mussolini's support. He preached the doctrine of the new legality, a doctrine which Mussolini had preached

[44] v. Massimo Rocca: *Idee sul Fascismo,* p. 64.

all through 1923 in order to retain his parliamentary support. He denounced violence, just as Mussolini did, and he argued that fascism must bend all its efforts to reconstruct the law, to give Italy a "new normalcy," all of which sounded not unlike Mussolini. He called his conception of the fascist state the new liberalism, hoping that this would fit in with Mussolini's coalition politics. But unfortunately he kept at this too long. After the elections the situation had changed and so had Mussolini. Rocca and his newspaper now became a personal embarrassment to Mussolini and a general center of anti-Party polemics. Isolated on all sides, he was expelled from the Party and the *Corriere Italiano* was turned over to Filipelli, of whom we shall say more directly. When Rocca attempted at Genoa to defend himself he was roundly beaten by the local squad. After his expulsion and after the Matteotti affair he continued to hope for a swing in his direction, and he talked much about "my fascism." But after a thoroughgoing attack on De Stefani's budget in 1925, it was no longer possible for him to pose as a fascist of any sort. A little later, ironically enough, he was caught in the maladministration of insurance funds, was forced to flee the country, and was deprived of his citizenship.

The Directorate, which in January Mussolini had announced as a solution for the evils that afflicted the Party, proved but one more stumbling-block. Its conduct of the elections, especially the intrigues of Giunta, were violently attacked by those who had been literally beaten in the elections and by the dissidents to whom it appeared even worse than previous party regimes. The Directorate was asked to resign immediately after the elections, and Mussolini picked a quadrumvirate, which he hoped might prove more acceptable. It consisted of Forges-Davanzati (a nationalist), Marinelli, Rossi and Melchiorri; the last named three being veteran party politicians. The quadrumvirate was not a popular "reform" with anybody, and it was generally understood to be a mere tide-over until the meeting of the Grand Council in June. On all sides the impression persisted that the party was a liability on the hands of the government, and that fascism in general was turning out to be much less of a renovation of Italian politics than the theory of the Revolution claimed.

The various discordant elements which fascism had embraced continued to come to the surface and revealed its lack of genuine unity or constructive program. For example, Rossi and Farinacci, ex-socialists, disapproved radically of De Stefani's *laissez faire* finance. The conservative liberals and the fascist industrialists in turn disapproved of the growing power of fascist syndicalism. The syndicalists were annoyed at the rich men's sons, the students and the bourgeois youths who felt their own importance and made themselves conspicuous in the party and in the militia. The young aristocrats, on the other hand, wanted to expel the fascist labor leaders, who, they said, had merely changed their shirts and not their ideas and standards. The idealistic liberals were opposed to the continuance of violence and shocked by the grafting. Gentile insisted there was a difference between continued ordinary violence and the " divine violence " of the revolution,[45] which latter alone was worthy of true fascists. Filareti, a southern monarchist, said he did not mind revolutionary violence, but " systematic violence " was detestable.[46] There were democratic *fascisti* who expected their regime to invigorate, not to overthrow, democratic institutions. And there were old-fashioned monarchists and anti-democrats who had welcomed fascism as a new aristocracy, but who were now disillusioned by the fascist demagogues.[47] The " 1919ers " looked down on the newcomers, and the newcomers deplored the remnants of squadrism. Many nationalists were worried over tendencies in the party; Corradini, their leader, expressed his worries very frankly. Some of the politicians themselves (for example, Dino Perrone Compagni, leader in Tuscany) sympathized with the dissenters. The dissenters fought not only the intransigents but also each other. In short, all semblance of unity was gone, and fascism threatened to perish not from external persecution but from internal disintegration.

Only one thing kept them together — Mussolini. All were loyal to him. The more *fascisti* disagreed among themselves, the more they exalted Mussolini. Not a little of Mussolini's present prestige is due to this fact. He became the " sad, solitary giant." The Mussolini myth was invented to conceal rebellion, much like the myth of " personal loyalty to King George " of the American Revolutionists. But once established, the myth began to be believed and today practically everybody agrees that Mussolini and he alone had held the Party together. In a sense it is true, just as it is true that God unites his warring children. Mussolini is the symbol for the fact that all kinds of *fascisti* want to join in running the government in spite of their differences.

The strain on Mussolini was considerable. He could be all things to all men, but not all at once. His general policy was to show the utmost loyalty to the Party in his public utterances, but to tinker with the Party machine in quiet. He preached the most rigid discipline, spurned all personal followers, declared himself the most ardent anti-Mussolinian and the most intransigent of the intransigents. But in

[45] See Appendix No. 29.

[46] cf. Filareti: *In Margine del Fascimo*, pp. 207 ff.

[47] v. Filareti: *In Margine del Fascimo*, pp. 390 ff.

practice he acted on the advice of his critics by his "own firm will." In this way he continued to hold universal confidence, but how long could he keep it up?

Such was the inner condition of the *Partito Nazionale Fascista* when on June 11, 1925, the Matteotti murder broke upon it. As regards the Party machine, it caused no great surprise in public opinion, for it was but one more instance of the customary policy of "rendering life impossible" to the adversaries. But on the side of the government, it created an enormous sensation. For it revealed the fact that the contrast which had been established in the public imagination between Party and government was largely a myth. It came out that Finzi, of the Ministry of the Interior, whom Matteotti had intended to expose as a grafter, was one of those principally involved in the murder. Other members of the government immediately came under suspicion. Though the *fascisti,* even the most dissident, did not believe that Mussolini was directly involved, the confidence in his administration and consequently in him was rudely shaken. Mussolini had said to the Chamber of Deputies, some time ago, "In internal affairs whatever happens, happens through my precise and direct volition and on my express order, for which I naturally assume full and personal responsibility. Hence it is idle to argue about the individual members of particular ministries; the orders are mine." [48] Now all sorts of underhand dealings came to light. Something was wrong somewhere. The opposition held Mussolini personally responsible; the *fascisti* maintained he had devoted himself too much to foreign affairs. In either case, the prestige of the government was gone, and it became clear that government and Party were coöperating in this nefarious work.

Mussolini put on sackcloth and ashes. He admitted that he had paid too little attention to internal politics; he decried the few fascist reprobates who were undermining his work and promised vigorous prosecution and complete justice. He would spare no one! Accordingly he sacrificed almost everybody whose name was mentioned in the scandal or who for any reason was unpopular. He jailed not only Dumini and the actual murderers, but also Cesare Rossi and Marinelli (two of the Quadrumvirate), and Filipelli (editor of the *Corriere* Italiano), who with Finzi had carelessly tried to drag Mussolini himself into the affair. Among those who were forced to resign were Bianchi, Finzi, Giunta, General De Bono, — in short, practically all the Party leaders. Mussolini forced the Chamber of Deputies to accept Giunta's resignation a Deputy. The quadrumvirate was supplanted by a "provisional directorate" of eleven members, among them strong provincial leaders

[48] February 10, 1923. v. *La Nuova Politica,* I, p. 61.

nationalists and syndicalists. The August session of the Grand Council established a Directorate of fifteen, among them several Deputies, of which the following five were selected as an executive committee: Farinacci, Felicioni, Forges-Davanzati, Maraviglia and Melchiorri.

Meanwhile Mussolini had completely reorganized his cabinet. He himself withdrew from the Ministry of the Interior, to which he called Federzoni, who enjoyed the confidence both of the nationalists and the liberals. In his place as Minister of Colonies he put the rich agriculturalist, Duca Pietro Lanza di Scalea. Alfredo Rocco, another nationalist, was made Minister of Justice. Carnazza, Minister of Public Works, who was mixed up in the financing of the *Corriere Italiano,* was supplanted by a liberal, Sarrochi. Gentile, who had made himself unpopular by his strenuous school reforms, was succeeded by another liberal, Casati, and he in turn shortly after by Fedele. Acerbo, the hero of the electoral reform, was removed as a sop to the opposition. The only important member whom he retained was De Stefani, who had gained the reputation of having kept the party grafters out of the public treasury.

In addition Mussolini profusely promised law and order, outdoing the dissidents. He appointed a commission for constitutional reform, reformed the militia, flattered Parliament, in fact made every concession possible without weakening the regime. As a result the moderate dissidents or integralists got the impression that Mussolini had really cleaned house thoroughly in the government, and that they had won their point so far as Mussolini and the government were concerned. They were confirmed in this when they discovered that Mussolini was getting opposition from the intransigents. Their leader, Farinacci, who all along had been opposed to a party hierarchy and who wanted fascism to be primarily provincial, governed by the *ras,* but who had now risen to a prominent place in party politics, openly and frankly disapproved of Mussolini's policy of conciliation. He was glad, he said, that he had never " joined the ghostly dance that had been staged around a corpse." [49] " We have merely lost two years by these tactics," he said, and he recommended the most drastic and violent measures against all opposition from without and all indiscipline within the ranks. Some of the extremists lamented the fact that they had ever let themselves in on " electionism," blaming the election for all the evils which had overtaken the party and regretting that they had not cleaned out Parliament completely at the very start. This open divergence between Mussolini and the intransigents emboldened the integralists once more to support Mussolini against the Party, especially against the extremist

[49] v. Appendix No. 20.

faction, and to clamor for further reform and a restriction of the Party's activities.

By December it became evident that Mussolini's policy, though it had enabled him to retrieve his personal reputation a little, had not only failed to bring back the Aventine Secession into the Chamber, but had also stimulated "indiscipline" among the *fascisti*. In January, therefore, as we said above, Mussolini yielded and came out frankly for a policy of forceful repression. The office of Secretary General of the Party was revived, and Farinacci was appointed to it. He went up and down the country preaching his doctrine of discipline and intransigency, weeding out all who did not fall into line with him and superintending the persecution of the opposition parties and press. It was now the intransigents' turn to proclaim the victory. But they overdid it. Farinacci talked too much about himself and not enough about Mussolini. He made it appear that he and his type of fascism had at last proved their supremacy and had even won over the *Duce*. He countermanded Federzoni's orders repeatedly and in general took the attitude that the Party could now run the government. His activity, though it produced the semblance of discipline and unity within the ranks, naturally aroused the most bitter resentment among the opposition. His violent deeds and still more violent language were good ammunition for their guns, and he, rather than Mussolini, became the central object of their scorn and hatred. The culmination came in March 1926 with the trial for the Matteotti murder, at which Farinacci defended the murderers and succeeded in getting such a light sentence for them that it amounted practically to a verdict of not guilty. The trial had been carefully staged in the isolated provincial town of Chieti in the Abruzzi mountains, and all sorts of precautionary measures had been taken, but even at that there was a storm of indignation, and of course it gathered on the head of Farinacci, much to Mussolini's relief. Federzoni now induced Mussolini to ask Farinacci to resign, which he did. It was all done very gracefully. Farinacci was lauded for his noble work and he, in turn, expressed his conviction that his task had been completed and that fascism was now safe and sound.

Nevertheless the significance of the resignation was clear. In the northeast some of Farinacci's fanatic followers threatened insurrection, but he urged them to "discipline" and retired quietly. In his place Mussolini appointed Augusto Turati, the assistant secretary of the Party, and formerly secretary of the Brescia *fascio*. He is a neutral figure, perfectly harmless and very useful in the hands of Mussolini. He uses the same words "discipline and intransigency" that Farinacci used, but he is careful to give them a new meaning. For example:

" If by intransigency is meant the desire to maintain intact the fundamental lines of the fascist idea, to maintain in our actions the original
conception of fascism in its highest, clearest and firmest expression, without intermixture of one's own mind, in thinking of fascism as the will to
work, and the passion to construct, I am agreed; but if by intransigency
is meant sitting down and doing nothing and only congratulating oneself
on being an intransigent fascist or one of the first hour, then I call that
Buddhism and Mahommedanism but not fascism. . . .

" Today more than ever we feel ourselves to be squadrists, not out of
a useless and stupid hankering for breaking heads or burning desks,
but out of a holy pride in defending the purity and beauty of our faith.
And we have never felt more completely than we do today our high
mission, the mission that called us yesterday into the public squares
when they were filled with crowds whom demagogues had intoxicated
with their folly; the mission that drove us, desperate minorities, against
an unfit and timid government; the mission that made us intransigent
champions of the necessity of overthrowing the false idols of an opportunist and corrupt democracy, of an abstract, Pontius Pilate sort of
liberalism, of the popularists who falsely pretended religion. Against
all this, in the realms of faith, of culture, of production, of finance, of
labor, we squadrists are upholding that lively sense of Italian power,
those weighty and systematic works of national reconstruction, willed
and realized by the government of Benito Mussolini. We feel that the
squadrist spirit is more alive than ever, with its fresh new vision of
power and of ideal, not material, violence, and with the activities of a
government which has succeeded in transforming into a real order and
into objective measures the aspirations of our souls and the torments
of our impatience. . . . But for all this, two great forces are necessary:
intellectual discipline and substantial intransigency." [50]

It is not difficult to read between these lines. Turati's job is to lead
fascist energies into constructive forms. He is preaching the " ideal
violence " of political reconstruction. He is preaching " intellectual
intransigency," or as he frequently puts it " intransigency towards
oneself " as opposed to the " formal intransigency " which had come
to mean little more than intellectual irresponsibility. But above all he
is centering all eyes on Mussolini. Unlike Farinacci's his speeches
always close with a peroration for the *Duce*. He seldom speaks long;
he says it is time " to put an end to orators "; he urges fewer ceremonies,
less ritual, more hard work.

His own hard work was to carry out the orders of Mussolini and
Federzoni in the matter of imposing a stricter discipline on the pro-

[50] Augusto Turati: *Ragioni Ideali di Vita Fascista*, pp. 136-8 and 64.

vincial secretaries, who were still a continual source of friction. In October 1926 the Grand Council finally instituted a thoroughgoing reform and passed a new constitution for the Party.[51] The general purpose of the reform was (1) to carry out the idea of hierarchy within the Party and to abolish practically all " electionism "; (2) to define the functions of the Party and subject it to government control. The annual congress at which the officials had heretofore been elected (at least nominally) was abolished. The local *fasci* could not elect their own secretaries. The only concession to democracy was that the Grand Council, not the *Duce,* elects the Secretary of the Party, the Assistant Secretaries and the Directorate. Otherwise authority invariably comes from on top. As the constitution puts it: " The ordinances and hierarchies without which there can be no discipline of energies nor education of the people, must be illuminated and guided from on top where there is a comprehensive view of powers, duties, functions and merits."

The Grand Council, the source of Party authority, is presided over by the *Duce* and contains a liberal admixture of members of the government and senators and other *fascisti* who are not immediately in the party bureaucracy. The Directorate, which is appointed by the Council, consists of the Secretary of the Party and eight others, and meets once a month under the presidency of the *Duce.* It is the administrative body of the Party. The Secretary appoints the provincial secretaries, who constitute the National Council. This National Council, which contains the men who actually carry on the work of the Party in the various provinces and which corresponds roughly to the group that in former years ruled the Party, has very limited powers. The Secretary calls it together to " examine the activities of the life of the Party and to receive general executive orders." Each Federal Secretary appoints the secretaries of the local *fasci* in his province, and the local secretary selects five members as his assistants, constituting the Directorate of the *Fascio.* Provincial councils and directorates are constructed on the same plan. Only those who have been fascists for at least three years are eligible for provincial offices. Party officials are prohibited from holding any other salaried political office.

The duties of the Federal (Provincial) Secretary are defined in detail and are in general non-political, quite distinct from those of the prefect. Friction between prefects and fascist officials had been one of the worst disorders in the regime, and though Mussolini had early [52] and repeatedly announced his unquestioned support of the prefects, this policy was not enforced in practice. Formerly when the prefects and mayors were

[51] v. Appendix No. 21.
[52] v. Mussolini: *La Nuova Politica,* I, p. 151.

left-overs from the old regime there might have been some excuse for their interference, but now that the prefects and *podesta* were picked by Mussolini and directly responsible to him, he said he would tolerate no *ras*ism. Nevertheless friction continued and Mussolini has had to defend his prefects on a number of occasions, notably in January 1927 by his famous " circular to prefects," in which he promised to support the prefects to the limit even against the provincial party secretaries and fascist squadrists. In his speech to the Chamber, May 26, 1927, he reported that the great majority of provinces had been straightened out and that he did not intend to " hand any prefect's scalp to a provincial secretary."

Shortly after the New Constitution was passed, the Grand Council (January) decided to close the doors of the Party absolutely except to the boys as they " graduated " from the Advance Guard, the Junior fascist organization. March 23, the anniversary of the founding of the *fasci*, was established as a sort of commencement day for the new recruits, when they are initiated and given their membership cards and guns. They not only take the oath of loyalty to the King, but they " solemnly swear to follow without question the orders of the *Duce* and to serve the cause of the fascist revolution with all their might and if necessary with their blood." The Party will henceforth be the training school for the *classe dirigente* of the future.

It now seems quite clear that the Party is of dwindling political importance. The Grand Council still duplicates some of the activities of the Council of Ministers of the Government, but it does not interfere. It is an expensive luxury, but no longer a nuisance. There are those who would like to call it an " association," not a party, since " party " implies more than one. But even though it continues to be called a party, it is clear that its functions are to be " cultural " rather than political. It can not be abolished, they say, so long as there is still need of infusing a national consciousness, educating the youth in the principles of duty and sacrifice, and in general " fascisticizing " the country. If it should be a permanent fixture, it would be as a sort of national club for the *classe dirigente*. It is not ever to be an organization of the masses; it is to remain a strictly aristocratic group. Or rather, its chief business is to create a genuine fascist aristocracy.

Whether or not the new Constitution of the Party will do this is a question on which there is much difference of opinion. Farinacci came out openly against the rigid hierarchical organization of the Party, with an argument which smacks of anything but discipline and intransigency. He said: " A dictatorship of the Party over the nation, yes; — but within the Party we are constitutionalists." Camillo Pelizzi, though he is a very different type of intransigent from Farinacci, took much the same attitude.[53] He opposed military discipline and hierarchy within the fascist aristocracy, as undermining the very principles of aristocracy. The aristocrats must govern autocratically, but they themselves must be perfectly free, subjected only to the discipline of their own superior mentalities. On the other hand, while these intransigents defended liberty (!) the liberal group on the whole welcomed the new order, as at least temporarily beneficent. Bottai explained,[54] with more erudition than conviction, that under the present circumstances the Party needed tightening up from above, but he emphasized those passages which hinted at a future day when a more free and pliable organization might prove practicable. He urged also, as did Umberto Guglielmotti [55] even more pointedly, that this " selection from on high " must be a real selection and not merely a confirmation of present cliques. In short, these writers hope that the eventual liberty within the regime for which they have stood all along, may be brought nearer by this temporary suppression of liberty.[56] Other writers in the Critica Fascista, as well as the general run of journalists in the more orthodox papers, heralded the abolition of the last vestiges of " electionism " as an eminently fascist reform, which brought the Party up to the standards of its own doctrine.[57]

Now that the government would seem no longer to need house cleaning Mussolini and others have abandoned the " purification " theory for a " rotation of offices " theory to explain the changes in the government. The idea is that the new classe dirigente can be best educated by a frequent change of personnel, so that as large a number as possible of the young " aristocrats " will have the opportunity of practical lessons in how to govern. The government shake-up of November 1926, occasioned directly by scandals in several departments and by the Law for the Defense of the State, which strengthened the dictatorship and made Mussolini Minister of the Interior, was officially explained on this theory. Though the weeding out of incompetents is no doubt a factor in the

[53] v. His Parlamento fascista, in Critica Fascista, August 1, 1926, and Ordine del Littorio, in the same journal for September 15, 1926.

[54] v. His La Parola ai Giovani, in Critica Fascista of October 15, 1926, and Il Regime: Sistema Chiuso, in the same journal December 1, 1926.

[55] v. His Dopo la soppressione dell'elizionismo interno, in Roma Fascista, October 9, 1926.

[56] v. Also Germano Secreti: Il regime e il partito, editorial in Critica Fascista July 15, 1926.

[57] v. For example, Giacomo Lumbroso: Le nuove funzoni e il nuovo aspetto del P. N. F., in Critica Fascista, October 15, 1926; A. de Marsanich: Governo Partito, in Popolo d'Italia, October 15, 1926; and editorials in the various paper of October 13 — 15, 1926.

process, the shift from "purification" to "rotation" is circumstantial evidence for the fact that there are many more candidates than jobs, and that the pressure on Mussolini for political employment continues to be so enormous that he must make openings occasionally, with or without other excuses.

Both intransigents and revisionists are now perfectly certain that their side has won, but neither knows just why. The intransigents point not merely to the language employed by Turati in his speeches, but to the fact that the Party has withstood all attacks and is now on a firmer basis than ever. They also point out that most of the old-timers, who disappeared for a while after the Matteotti affair, are honorably reinstated, among them Bianchi, Giunta, Marinelli, De Bono, and Balbo. On the other hand, the former dissidents point to the fact that these men no longer have a dominant rôle; that the political activities of the Party have been restricted and subordinated to the government bureaucracy; and that the "purifications" of the government have brought several of the revisionists into power, notably Bottai, who was made Minister of Corporations. There are still smoldering remains of the crisis, occasional sarcastic criticisms in the journals, or personal encounters. (As for instance, the duels recently fought between Suckert and the editors of *l'Impero*, because Suckert called them slackers and they called him a German.) Personal journals still continue to fan personal enmities. The intellectual differences among *fascisti* are as great as ever, and opposed schools insist on approving the government for opposite reasons. But on the whole the battle is over and both sides are reconciled to the way things are going, though they will never be reconciled to each other.

The decision from now on to admit into the Party only the Advance Guardists, brings the junior departments of fascism into prominence and fixes attention on the coming generation. The Balilla, directed by Agnotti of Florence, is the juvenile organization of boys and girls, and the Advance Guard, founded by Luigi Freddi, is the organization of boys 4 to 18, preparatory to their admission into the *fasci*. These organizations are growing rapidly and are really working a revolution. They are very similar to the American Boy Scouts. They have their costumes, takes, drills, sports, etc. Their chief importance lies first in their physical and athletic education, and secondly in their making patriotism attractive and vital. Recently it was decided to put militia officers at the heads of these organizations and to give them a more "serious" character. But the seriousness is ceremonial. Heretofore there was no secular organization which captivated the imaginations and commanded the enthusiasm of the youth of the nation, and what patriotic exercises and studies the public schools afforded were comparatively ineffective in producing national sentiment. Now all this is changed, and the state, as well as the Church, has a means of making itself a dominating force, not merely an abstract conception. In the universities, of course, the fascist organizations are particularly strong and represent the combined force of a fraternity and an athletic club and a so-called literary circle. The shift of relative strength in fascism to these non-political organizations of the younger generation comes out strikingly from a comparison of the figures of October 1926 and those of the previous year.

	1925	1926
No. of *Fasci di Combattimento*	9,000	9,500
No. members in *Fasci di Combattimento* ...	700,000	938,000
No. members in Advance Guard	90,000	211,000
No. members in Balilla	70,000	269,000
No. members in Women's Organizations ...	25,000	53,000

Secretary Turati's report for 1927 shows a continuation of this tendency. Membership in the *fasci* went up about 90,000. Most of these were graduates from the Advance Guard. During the year, 2,000 officers and 30,000 members were expelled from the *fasci* in connection with the " purification " policy. In the meantime the Advance Guard and Balilla had more than doubled, and the feminine branches showed the following registration: Feminine *fasci* — 76,000; Feminine junior organizations — 147,000. The University groups numbered 8,800. On March 23, 1928, 80,000 more young *fascisti* graduated from the Advance Guard into the fasci.

The third great organ of the fascist state, besides the government and the Party, is the Militia. We have already noted that even before the March on Rome the foundations for the militia had been laid. But it was so obviously an armed force in the hands of the Party used as a threat against other parties, that it seemed impossible to embody it permanently into the state. The opposition, of course, hoped Mussolini would dismiss it entirely, after he had dismissed it from Rome; and some of the dissidents, like Misuri, wanted to keep it localized, squads of volunteers for emergencies, as in the early days. But Mussolini put an end to such ideas by his brusque: " Whoever touches the Militia, gets lead." It did not take long for Mussolini to develop the theory that there was room for a third armed force in the state, midway between the police and the army. The army, he said, must devote itself exclusively to the sacred task of carrying on or preparing for war and should never be called on for police duty. The regular police, he said, had their hands full with their regular function of keeping public order. But " by dint of e cumstances, not of will," he said, there was need now for a "political police." He abolished the Royal Guards, which Nitti had created during the bolshevist crisis as a special police, and theoretically substituted the militia which was of course many times larger and more expensive.

The first big job which was found for the "political police" was the policing of the railroads, guarding stations, assisting conductors on the trains, protecting freight from robbers, and weeding out communists and other railroad nuisances. This occupies several tens of thousands of militiamen, practically all of them regular railroad employees. A similar organization was built up for the ports. Two legions were sent to Lybia to fight the African rebels. Since 1926, when serious incidents occurred on the French border, about 3,000 black shirts have been employed as boundary police. But the great bulk of the militia, of course, has no employment and is not mobilized except for review purposes. They have their Sunday morning marches and drills; their holiday celebrations and rituals and their sports.

Every now and then they find or create emergencies and rehearse their squadrists exploits. Though Mussolini had condemned all squadrist violence since the March on Rome with persistence and occasionally with vehemence, he had been either unwilling or unable to put a stop to it in practice. During the first few months of the regime he excused it, saying, "It is impossible in three months' time to take young men who have been accustomed for two years to a very special gymnastics and to make them into lead soldiers. . . . It was impossible to say to these men: 'Go home now, it is all over.' First of all because this would have been an enormous ingratitude, and secondly because it would have been dangerous." [58] Since then, however, Mussolini has been increasingly strict about squadrism, and in January 1927 in his circular to the prefects he went so far as to order the regular police to arrest any fascist squadrists without exception, and he held the police responsible for fascist disorders. The only serious disorders of this kind recently have been reprisals taken after the attempts on Mussolini's life and other anti-fascist acts. But this is due not so much to the fact that the *fascisti* have become orderly as that the opposition has greatly diminished and that there is, is powerless to show itself.

The militia was almost immediately coördinated with the other armed forces, but it was not immediately subjected to the King. Mussolini explained (June 8, 1923) that it seemed unfitting that a volunteer army obviously in the service of a party should be headed by the King, who represented the whole nation. Hence it was merely attached to the Ministry of the Interior. A year later, however, yielding to the opposi-

[58] Mussolini: *La Nuova Politica*, I, pp. 151–2.

tion which demanded the separation of the militia and the Party, the militia took the oath of loyalty to the King and became theoretically one of the regular armed forces of the monarchy. It was to provide pre-military and post-military training for the youth of the nation! Thus it supplemented the work of the army.

The theory was easier than the practice. From the very start there had been friction. General Diaz, Mussolini's first Minister of War, had refused to accept one of the militia generals into the Ministry under him. The regular army officers refused to regard the militia officers as equals, and the militia officers adopted a very superior air. It soon became known that inferior army officers or even men without military training were being given high commissions in the militia. To add insult to injury, medals, crosses and other honors were distributed freely to the officers of the militia for their " services in the revolution." Even Fari-nacci, who had not fought in the War at all, got his *croix de guerre*. Rela-tions between army officers and militia officers became very strained and for a time it looked as though a civil war would break out for fair. The tension was alleviated by a militia reform, which made it impossible for army men to better their rank by joining the militia, and which al-lowed only ex-army officers to have high militia commands. At present relations between army and militia are quite cordial.

Another trouble broke out after the Matteotti affair. In their annual convention at Assisi in July 1924, the War Veterans Associations adopted a resolution, framed by Viola, to the effect that they would continue to coöperate with the *fascisti* " on condition that the government condemn absolutely these mad illegalities and that the state exercise its authority in conformity to the tradition and spirit of the *risorgimento* and with an increased spirit and energy for work in the interests of a regenerated patriotism." This mild rebuke was bitterly resented by the *fascisti*, for they counted on the loyalty of the War Veterans as a matter of course. The split was made worse when in many cities the soldiers absented themselves from the militia parades on October 28, in celebration of the March on Rome. In retaliation the militia broke up a number of soldiers' parades on the national military holiday, November 4. This led to an even stronger protest by the Veterans against fascist violence. A few days later a letter was published, written a year previously by Italo Balbo, Commanding General of the Militia, in which *fascisti* had been ordered outright to commit violences. It caused such a scandal that he was forced to resign. This appeased the general indignation somewhat, but not so much as it might have done had not Mussolini praised Balbo so cordially when he accepted the resignation. Balbo now Minister of Aviation.

There was more or less trouble in the organization of the militia until October 9, 1926, when Mussolini assumed personal command. In doing so he sent one telegram of devotion and submission to the King, and another to his Black Shirts, which read: " Today I assume the command of the Militia. You must certainly understand the import of this deed. The order is: Absolute and unquestioning obedience and be ready always and everywhere to defend our regime which today is our country. . . . Raise your standards and your rifles with the cry of our unconquerable faith: *Viva il Fascismo! A noi!* "

CHAPTER IV

SYNDICALISM AND THE CORPORATE STATE

I. *The Convergence of Syndicalism and Nationalism*

ITALIAN syndicalism is dominated by two disillusionments: the discovery of the increasingly bourgeois character of Italian socialism and the discovery of the growing conflicts between the proletariats of different nations.

In 1903 two Italian professors started the theory that the trouble with Italian socialism was that it contained too many professors and other gentlemen of the lesser bourgeoisie. Take these two for instance: Professor Arturo Labriola was a struggling young tutor at the University of Naples, who, discovering that a socialist had little chance in Naples, moved to Milan, started a weekly, *L'Avanguardia Socialista*, and soon won a large following by preaching war on reformism and the bourgeoisie and back to the good old class war of Karl Marx and Bakunin. Professor Enrico Leone did the same thing at Rome with his bi-weekly *Il Divenire Sociale, Rivista di Socialismo Scientifico*. They soon gained a reputation for being unusually "learned" socialists; they overawed socialistic conventions by their profound discourses, and their books became standard reference works for other professors and for intellectuals in general. Labriola was almost elected to Parliament and one of his colleagues actually was. This was a common occurrence in Italian socialism, as one writer put it, "a bourgeois who is active in the Socialist Party is condemned as an intruder until he becomes a leader."[1] The socialism of such leaders, whether on parliament benches, in editorial offices or in professors' chairs, naturally became so respectable and so "scientific" that it lost its proletarian character completely, for the Italian proletariat in general could not read and the minority who could found it difficult to understand such learned literature. In short, the proletariat was much discussed by its intellectual leaders. The upshot of all this discussion was the scientific discovery that

---

[1] F. S. Merlino: *Collettivismo*, Florence 1901, p. 33.

Italy must be industrialized before it could be socialized and that the industrialization must temporarily be carried on by the capitalist class.[2]

Against all this the above named professors revolted. They wanted to make socialism really proletarian. Accordingly Labriola took as his comrade a genuine son of labor, a pleasant fat ex-lieutenant of the army, named Mocchi. Together they made enough of an impression on the socialist congresses of 1904 at Brescia and Bologna to plan a general strike in September, the first general strike ever called in Italy. Unfortunately, however, Labriola's stalwart comrade, shortly after the Bologna congress and before the strike, married an actress and went on a long honeymoon to North and South America, from which he never returned to Italian politics. Nevertheless the strike was called in Northern Italy and spread rapidly through the east and south, where Leone and his southern co-workers had succeeded in organizing agricultural discontent. The net result of the strike was that the government was frightened, professional classes annoyed by its inconveniences and the merchants and lesser middle class were angered by the financial losses which they more than any one else had suffered. The next elections went against the socialists and the next socialist congress went against Labriola and his "intransigent Marxists." A bitter strife now ensued for leadership within the Party. The Labriola-Leone faction organized their followers into syndicates and with redoubled energy attacked the parliamentarianism and political socialism of the majority faction under Filippo Turati. At this time the writings of Sorel and the French syndicalists were being popularized, so that soon in theory as well as in practice the divergent directions in Italian socialism became evident. In the spring of 1907, the syndicalists openly left the Socialist Party, following the example of the French, and devoted themselves to the General Confederation of Labor, organized in 1906, which soon became powerful, especially in Romagna. In the summer of 1908, under the brilliant leadership of De Ambris, who burst suddenly into prominence, an agrarian strike broke out in and around Padua. The strikers, confronted by a powerful organization of proprietors, and abandoned in the

---

[2] Take for example the following written not by a socialist but by an idealistic nationalist: "Today the socialist party has all the appearance of the liberal party. . . The socialist party and socialism are two distinct things. . . . The socialist party . . . is the liberal party; it holds the place which the latter has ingloriously abandoned in order to serve the industrial and agrarian and bureaucratic bourgeoisies and the clerical peasantry. . . .

"The socialist party is simply the mirror of the Italian bourgeoisie. Who kicked out Mussolini, if not the bourgeoisie of socialism? We have the most stupid socialism of Europe for we know we have the most stupid bourgeoisie." (Prezzolini in *La Voce*, April 13, 1914, p. 56, and October 28, 1914, p. 22.

crisis of the Confederation of Labor itself, were forced to surrender. De Ambris took a trip to America. The Socialist Congress of Florence, shortly after, explicitly denounced syndicalism and expelled the syndicalists from the party. Nevertheless the socialists established cordial relations with the Syndicalist Confederation of Labor; for bourgeois leaders of the two kinds of socialism had discovered that they were no longer rivals for power, there being ample room for both. Soon the theory was elaborately spread by both kinds of professors, that socialism really needed two legs to stand on: the political leg, the Socialist Party, and the economic leg, Syndicalism. And so the two movements peacefully " supplemented " each other until the issue of war and nationalism again divided them.

As early as 1908 a group of nationalists, led by Viana, had attempted to gain labor support in the district of Turin by founding nationalistic syndicates. To their weekly periodical, *Il Tricolore,* some of the ablest nationalist writers contributed. These syndicates were based on (a) class struggle only within the limits allowed by national solidarity, (b) direct action in the economic sphere without any intervention by government organs and without any opposition to the state by the syndicates. But this movement was condemned in 1910 by both the nationalist and the syndicalist organizations. In 1911 however, when the Tripoli War broke out, and to a greater extent during the World War, Italian syndicalism became increasingly nationalistic. The official Socialist Party and many of the older leaders of the Confederation of Labor were against war, but by their negative tactics they attempted to evade the issue. In theory and in practice as well they afforded neither encouragement nor radical opposition to the conduct of the wars. The younger syndicalists on the other hand, with their Sorelian philosophy of direct action and violence, had less trouble in reconciling themselves to war and some of them even became ardent nationalists and imperialists.[3] Labriola himself went so far as to say during the Tripoli War, " Let it be clearly understood that we are fighting not only against the little handful of Turks in Tripoli, nor against the naval clique of the Dardanelles, but that we are fighting against the intrigues, the threats, the

[3] " Revolutionary syndicalism has been well called a form of workers' imperialism, since it reveals the same tendencies of energy and conquest which appear in capitalistic imperialism, the same distrust for sentimental and humanitarian democracy, the same emphasis on the importance of wealth and of the free play of economic force. Its aim lies not in the realization of a fixed type of society, as is the aim of the old fashioned socialisms, but in the ever wider and unrestrained development of the forces which are latent in the heart of the proletariat, in the exercise of those faculties which can increase the proletariat's vigor, vitality, and culture." (Arturo Labriola: *Il Socialismo Contemporaneo.* Naples 1922, p. 344.)

snares, the monies and the arms of plutocratic Europe which will not allow the lesser nations to hazard a single deed or a single word that might jeopardize its iron hegemony." [4] The idea soon took hold that Italy's wars were proletarian wars, that poor Italy must wage a "class struggle" with its richer neighbors. In this spirit many of the syndicalist leaders threw themselves whole-heartedly into the wars, thus isolating themselves completely from the Reformist majority of the Socialist Party as well as from the Confederation of Labor.

The best example of this sort of syndicalist was Filippo Corridoni, who is now hailed as one of the pioneers and martyrs of fascism. He was a feverish, violent soul in a delicate body, with the romantic tragic bearing of Mazzini. His occasional tears and his customary bitter laugh, his fierce hatred and flaming oratory made him a powerful proletarian leader. An admirer of the heroes of the Italian *risorgimento,* he was also profoundly influenced by the writings of Sorel, especially by Sorel's pessimism, his emphasis on the inevitability of violence and suffering, his theory of the moral degradation of the bourgeoisie and of the heroic potentialities in the proletariat. After the war of 1911 he began to develop a new national philosophy for Italian syndicalism, a philosophy which was later revived and expanded by the *fascisti.* According to him it was the moral duty and tragic fate of the Italian proletariat to continue the struggle for liberty which the Italian bourgeoisie had begun in the *risorgimento.* He saw himself as the successor of Mazzini, Pisacane and Garibaldi. In this setting the whole concept of classes and class struggle underwent a transformation. Classes, he maintained, are historic, not primarily economic, and only a historically minded philosophical tradition, such as the Italian, can do justice to the true import of class struggle. The bourgeoisie is a remnant of that degenerate powerful Europe, which for centuries had dominated Italy, and from which the *risorgimento* had only partially freed it. Not merely political liberty, but, what is more, a spontaneous, free national culture is possible in Italy only if the proletariat can assert itself. But the proletariat too, in Corridoni's sense, is not the Marxist, economic proletariat. He had a genuine Sorelian contempt for the masses. The "historic" proletariat is rather that heroic minority, that proletarian aristocracy, that has the sense of its mission and is willing to fight and suffer. He had little confidence in the ability of this small class to gain a really decisive victory over the powerful philistines; but, even as Sorel held up the "myth" of the general strike, so Corridoni preached the myth of the "revolutionary war for liberty" as an ideal which might inspire the true Italian to heroism. The class struggle must be intensely

[4] In *La Scintilla* of Naples, October 11, 1911.

national, waged by a young Italy, conscious of its rich cultural heritage against the international oppression of a more wealthy but more degenerate Europe.

It was in this spirit that he and his syndicalist followers marched through the streets of Milan in June 1914 waving the national tricolor, singing the hymn of the *risorgimento,* crying *Viva l'Italia,* and proclaiming the beginning of Italy's revolutionary war of redemption. Similar insurrections took place in Genoa, Turin and Bologna, and led to seven days of violence and bloodshed. But the grand *risorgimento* went down in history as merely " the red week." A few months later, when the World War broke out, Corridoni immediately accepted it as the continuation of his cause in an unexpected form. He and a large group of his followers joined the Garibaldi brigade on the Argonne front. When Italy entered the war, he returned and fought and died on the Italian front.

Meanwhile a young man named Edmondo Rossoni had returned from the United States where he had been trying to organize the Italian I. W. W. Though he did not return in order to join the army, for he lacked Corridoni's love of physical warfare, he returned to preach nationalism to the Italian worker. He tells of his own disillusionment as follows:

" In 1912 when I was organizing Italian workers in North America, far from my country, I felt that it is absolutely necessary to spread class nationalism, for we must defend not merely workers but Italians. . . . We who for many years have lived in foreign countries and in our long and bitter exile have learned to know and to live the life of an Italian removed from his native land, have begun to understand and feel how the fortunes of Italian workers are indissolubly bound to the fortunes of the Italian nation. . . . We have seen our workers exploited and held in contempt not only by capitalists but even by their revolutionary comrades of other countries. Hence we know by experience that internationalism is but a fiction and hypocrisy. Therefore we must above all work for our country and love our country." [5]

In 1915 he had founded a journal in New York called *L'Italia Nostra* with the motto " Not to deny, but to win our country " (*La Patria non si nega, si conquista*). During the war he served as secretary to the Chambers of Labor in several Italian cities and was active in the *Comitato sindacale italiano,* the successor to Corridoni's organization. In May 1918 this *Comitato* was transformed into the *Unione italiana del lavoro,* and Rossoni immediately became its secretary and his motto became the battle cry.

[5] Rossoni: *Le idee della ricostruzione,* pp. 10, 56, 59.

The aim of this organization was to " unite those workers' syndicates which intend to carry on their action independently of any political party whatsoever," but it was soon evident that most of the leaders and many of the syndicates adhering to it were republican. In fact the Mazzini revolutionary republicans and the nationalistic syndicalists soon became almost indistinguishable. The real aim of the Union was to be revolutionary and its chief opponent, curiously enough, was the great Confederation of Labor itself. For during the war the majority of the Confederation of Labor had failed to espouse the patriotic cause of the Corridoni group, and had affiliated itself with the reformist Socialist Party. And during the economic and political crisis of 1919–20, the *C. G. L.* under Labriola and De Ambris, etc., became one of the mainstays of the government, doing all it could to discourage the communistic revolts of local Chambers of Labor, aiding Giolitti in conciliating the workers who had occupied the factories and in general opposing itself to violence, urging instead democratic and political methods.

Rossoni's *Unione italiana del lavoro* therefore was the champion of the strange combination: patriotism and revolution. Hence it found itself in opposition to both the communist international " reds," and the reformist Socialist Party entrenched in the government, to say nothing of the more conservative parties of the country. It made little progress among the industrial workers, who were dominated by the internationalistic bolshevist group, but found a foothold among rural workers and small proprietors; especially in Romagna and Tuscany, the stronghold of the revolutionary republican patriots, who were in that region the chief political enemies of the socialists.

In its platform we read: " The *Unione italiana del lavoro* wages war against salaried capitalism and against all the institutions which maintain that system, appealing directly to the organized laboring class to take over production and distribution and the exchange of wealth."

" The *Unione italiana del lavoro,* while it carries on its work in harmony with the principle of the international solidarity of laborers of those nations which know how to be friendly and which are not instruments of tyranny over peoples and classes, will never depart from the general conditions necessary for the development and liberty of Italy, whom the working class must not betray but must rather win by radically renewing its institutions."

In March 1919, when Rossoni's *Unione* needed friends badly, it found a new one at Milan. Mussolini, who was then organizing his first *fascio,* and who also needed friends badly, suggested an alliance between fascism and syndicalism. He asked the *Unione* to declare openly against (a) bolshevism, (b) the general strike. If it were willing to do so, he saw no reason why they might not coöperate. On the eve of the National Congress of the *Unione,* Mussolini suggested the following synthesis of the fascist economic program and of syndicalism: "We are opposed to ' merely professional suffrage.' If a representation only of ideas is insufficient, neither is a representation only of interests adequate. Ours is ' integral representation ' in which the citizen not only is not annulled but by a system of national councils enhances his possibilities for action, for initiative, for control in the political and economic management of the nation. I open the discussion. The argument is interesting." [6] But this flirting with the syndicalists received little encouragement at the time; for fascism was then a liability rather than an asset to any kind of labor organization.

After the collapse of the so-called red revolution in the fall of 1920, which left the industrial workers in a bad state of disorganization, patriotic syndicates began to grow rapidly. Despairing of the efficacy of communist leadership, revolutionists of all classes flocked into them. In agriculture, where the distinction between employer and employee is less clear, Rossoni even succeeded in organizing "mixed" syndicates, in which small proprietors and peasants would belong to the same syndicate. In fact, as the peasants flocked into the national syndicates, the proprietors and small tenant farmers became alarmed. They saw the unions which they had believed killed and buried, resurrected almost over night, flying the national tri-color instead of the red flag, and ready once more to offer an almost solid front. In this fearful situation, partly voluntarily, partly by the force of some of the fascist squadrists (in Romagna especially), the landlords suddenly conceived an unheard-of sympathy for their peasants, joined their syndicates and chimed in on the chorus of the "solidarity of producers." Some of these nationalistic syndicates were the direct result of the work of *fasci.* Around Florence and Siena, for example, the fascist peasants formed several such syndicates, under the name of *Fratellanza Colonica.* Usually, however, these were dominated by conservative elements and by the sons of landowners. This was the case in Perugia, for example, where Alfredo Misuri's *Unione sindacale del lavoro* contained few peasants and fewer laborers, but attracted the middle classes in both town and country.

In Romagna and Emilia, however, less conservative squadrists had helped organize the *Confederazione italiana sindacati economici* (the *CISE,* so-called), which was supposed to operate independently of all

[6] *L'Ora del sindacalismo,* in *Popolo d'Italia,* March 27, 1919.

political parties. One of its agents, Pighetti, was sent to Perugia where he soon wrested the control of that syndicate from Misuri's hands and made it more of a laboring-man's organization. The *CISE* soon failed completely, partly because of its attempt to carry on a purely economic non-political policy, partly because it was too proletarian to attract the landed classes and too nationalistic to attract the laborers, and partly because of the prevailing spirit of local autonomy among the various syndicates, whose local leaders were jealous of their independence. Nevertheless nationalist syndicates continued to grow. At first they were predominantly organizations of small farmers and of the lower middle class, but gradually agricultural laborers entered as well. It was not until after 1922 that any considerable number of industrial laborers joined them.

While these developments were transpiring in the labor field, another series of events suddenly added prestige to the syndicates. D'Annunzio and his band had taken Fiume, and had published his constitution for the Fiume district, the *Carta della Reggenza Italiana del Carnaro.* This famous document outlined a system of ten " corporations " into which all the citizens of the state were to be organized, as follows: (1) laborers (industrial and rural), artisans and small farmers; (2) technicians and administrators; (3) merchants; (4) employers (industrial and agricultural); (5) public employees; (6) " the intellectual flower of the people "; (7) professional men; (8) The Coöperative Society; (9) mariners; (10) the " mystic servants of the civic sanctuary." These corporations were explained to be a revival of the medieval Italian institutions by that name. In their hands was the regulation of the whole economic life of the state, of several philanthropic functions and of public ceremonies. The effect of this document on Italian syndicalism can easily be imagined. Nationalism and syndicalism soon joined hands in corporationism. A *Comitato nazionale di azione sindacale dannunziana* was formed, and many of the most important nationalist leaders became converted to national syndicalism. Among these should be mentioned Enrico Corradini, Roberto Forges-Davanzati (who had been a syndicalist before he became a nationalist), Alfredo Rocco and Dino Grandi, all of them now conspicuous fascist leaders. Francesco Coppola continued hostile; he found syndicalism too materialistic.

While the nationalists were thus approaching syndicalism, a large number of old syndicalist leaders were turning toward nationalism. The veteran professors Labriola and Leone returned to the socialist camp, but many of the most active leaders became either *fascisti* or national syndicalists or both, among them, Michele Bianchi, Angelo

Olivieri Olivetti, Guido Pighetti, Sergio Panunzio, Agostino Lanzillo and Paolo Orano.

On the invitation of Rossoni the leaders of these various groups of national syndicalists met together on October 17, 1921, at Ferrara, where Rossoni was secretary of the Confederation of Syndicates. A plan of union of all these groups was discussed and a national congress of syndicates called for Bologna, January 24, 1922. In the meantime, November 1921, at the Fascist Congress an alliance with the syndicalists was discussed and Michele Bianchi, then Secretary General of the newly made Party, was sent to the Bologna Syndicalist Congress to make the offer of union. As a result of these moves the *Unione federale italiana delle corporazioni* was formed, and the Bologna Congress passed the following resolution:

" The Syndicalist Convention of the 24th of January 1922, assembled at Bologna, declares the necessity of organizing all those syndicates whose programs and activities are essentially the same as the program and platform of the National Fascist Party into national corporations headed by a powerful central body, the federal Italian union of Corporations. In order to explain the character and scope of the new syndicalist organization the convention maintains the following chief principles:

" 1. Labor entitles a man to the sovereign and legitimate exercise of a full and useful citizenship in the social order;

" 2. Labor is the result of forces harmoniously united in the process of creating, perfecting and enhancing whatever constitutes the material, moral and spiritual welfare of man;

" 3. All persons irrespectively are to be considered laborers who in any way whatsoever employ or devote their actions to the above-mentioned ends, and accordingly their organization into syndicates should attempt to include all such persons without any of the ostracism employed by demagogues, but with the requisite differentiations and variety of groups;

" 4. The nation, taken as the highest synthesis of all the material and spiritual values of the race, is above individuals, occupations and classes. Individuals, occupations and classes are the instruments which the nation employs to reach its greater glory. The interests of individuals, of professions and of classes acquire the stamp of legitimacy when they come to be embodied in the plan of the higher national interests;

" 5. Syndicalistic organization, which is the instrument of defense and of conquest for labor against all forms of parasitism, must tend to develop within its organization a sense of the willingness on the part of syndicalistic action to fit into the complicated network of social relations, and a wider consciousness of the fact that Country and Society are over and above classes.

"The national corporations headed by the Federal Italian Union of Corporations are the following:

(a) The national corporation of industrial labor.
(b) The national corporation of agricultural labor.
(c) The national corporation of commerce.
(d) The national corporation of the middle and intellectual classes.
(e) The national corporation of seamen."

The name of this consolidated organization, whose secretary Rossoni became, was later changed to the *Confederazione delle Corporazioni sindacali fasciste,* and after the March on Rome it became an integral part of the fascist regime.

Though the majority of the d'Annunzian nationalists followed Rossoni into the fascist camp, some of the most ardent, notably the veteran Alceste De Ambris, maintained their independence, and continued the *Unione italiana del lavoro* as a republican d'Annunzian organization. The national federation of seamen also adhered to d'Annunzio until recently, when they affiliated themselves with Rossoni's fascist Confederation, though they are still in a measure an independent organization.

This in outline is the story of how fascism and syndicalism came to be united. Fascism, as we saw in a previous chapter, needed labor support and syndicalism needed political weapons. It was a forced marriage, and both parties had to, and still have to, make large concessions and adjustments, as a result of which both are being radically transformed. For syndicalism it meant that its leaders had concluded from their brief but turbulent experience that in Italy a purely economic syndicalism is impracticable. Conflicting interests among the various leaders and among the various groups of workers, as well as between leaders and workers, kept the movement in continual turmoil. And even if it were possible to unify Italian labor, its bargaining power is too weak to force capital by purely economic pressure to make perceptible concessions, since labor is the one thing which is always plentiful in Italy. The Italian worker is too near the bare maintenance level and too destitute of funds to be able to wage effective economic warfare. Only by intimidating the government could labor hope to get any power over capital. Hence, if the paradox of a really revolutionary government could be found, syndicalism might succeed. This paradox was found in fascism. Though the syndicalist leaders were at the time very loath to sacrifice their autonomy to a political alliance, they stooped to conquer. After the March on Rome, they not only were reconciled to their political partner, but became the very life and soul of the fascist bureaucracy.

For fascism, on the other hand, this marriage meant that its leanings toward a liberalistic economics and its obligations toward the bourgeoisie would have to sacrificed eventually to a politics of government control over labor organization and thus, indirectly, to a detailed regulation of the economic life of the nation. As we shall see, both parties were soon forced to approach what each had rebelled against — state socialism.

II. The Reconstruction of Syndicalist Theories

Before we can proceed to these later developments, it is necessary to examine more closely the general principles and theories to which the events we have just narrated gave birth. For these theories are not merely rationalizations of facts already accomplished, but also exhibitions of the aims and hopes which became active forces in the years following. Needless to say, events of so revolutionary a character demanded a radical reconstruction of ideas. But the reconstruction of ideas went far beyond what was demanded by the events. We have already noted the elements of this new ideology in Corridoni, in d'Annunzio's Constitution for Fiume and in the Resolution of the Bologna Convention of 1922; we must now follow it into its various ramifications.

The fascist theory of syndical organization is supposed to be thoroughly Italian in origin, but it was really imported directly from the French positivists and French Catholics, who had used it for similar purposes. However, the terms in which it is formulated and the application given it are quite Italian.[7] In general its origins are distinct from the orthodox Sorelian syndicalism.

Of the two great philosophic schools which for a century have been contending in Italy, the positivist and the idealist, the latter had been predominant among the syndicalists. One reason for this, of course, is the hostility between positivism and class syndicalism in France. Another is the fact that nationalism and positivism were conservative allies in the industrial north, while idealism and syndicalism were both movements of revolt, the former more prominent in the north and the latter in the south. Benedetto Croce was a close friend of Sorel and had been a leading writer on syndicalism, while syndicalism was still closely allied with socialism; and more recently Gentile had sponsored syndicalism in his general attempt to establish idealistic nationalism as a rival to the northern, Corradini type of nationalist theory. A group of young idealists, as we saw in an earlier chapter, were among the first interventionists when the war broke out, and many of them espoused

[7] cf. also *Relazione della Commissione Presidenziale*, pp. 106–7.

the cause of national syndicalism. Hence, when nationalism and fascism invaded the syndicalist camp, a considerable mixture of positivism, Marxism, neo-Catholicism, and philosophical idealism resulted. But this mixed philosophical orientation has not entangled syndicalism to any great extent in metaphysical issues. National even more than orthodox syndicalism is decidedly a practical not an intellectual movement. But the practical conflicts within the movement, to which we shall presently proceed, are in no small measure traceable to theoretical confusions. And when these practical issues have been decided, probably the theory will also clear up. Meanwhile, however, the structure of fascist syndicalist theory remains a mixture; its general outlines are positivistic, with an admixture of the idealistic theory of the state and of the Sorelian theory of class organization.

As early as 1910 Sergio Panunzio and several other writers on syndicalist theory had begun to call attention to the theories of Durkheim and Duguit, and to regard them as revivals of medieval economic organization. In " Syndicalism and the Middle Ages " (1910) Panunzio wrote " Duguit has constructed a theory of *general and integral syndicalism,* a syndicalism which extends indiscriminately to all actually existing social classes. Every social class, according to Duguit, should be organized into its own syndicate and *collective agreements* should bind the syndicates together, and at the top of these syndicates should be the state, representing the effective majority of the individuals comprising the various social groups." And later he wrote: " Duguit, the first exponent in France, beside Sorel, of integral syndicalism, had already defined a class in precise terms, as ' a group of individuals among whom there exists an unusually close interdependence because they exercise the same function in the division of social labor.' This is an idea which derives from the sociological theory of Durkheim, . . . a theory which differs, I believe, very little in essence from the organic theory of Plato's *Republic* (*i.e.* of the strong and hierarchical state which is today the aim of fascism). It is obviously but a short step from Plato's *Republic* to the corporationist theory of fascist syndicalism." [8]

Among the nationalists whose vague enthusiasm for syndicalism was due to the intimate connection between Sorel and the Catholic authoritarianism of the *action française,* Enrico Corridini suggested the possibilty of a national syndicalism as early as 1908, but Alfredo Rocco seems to have been the first to revive the term " corporation " and to have robbed syndicalism of its revolutionary implications. In the *Idea Nazionale* of May 23, 1914, shortly before Corridoni's general strike, Rocco wrote: " To us syndicalism appears to be a form of eco-

[8] In *Popolo d'Italia,* May 12, 1923.

nomic organization which, if cut loose from its socialistic trunk and
robbed of the revolutionary and anarchistic tendencies which until now
have characterized it, might be a useful instrument in the service of the
nation.

"We claim that syndicalism can be national, just as it is now anti-
national or Catholic. The form in which a national syndicalism might
be realized would be that of mixed syndicates, a name found in Belgium
and Germany, but an ancient Italian institution, for it is nothing but
our ancient corporationism. And we propose simply to substitute our
name for the foreign one, and to speak simply of Corporations. The
Corporations, which were overthrown by the individualism of the natural rights philosophy and by the equalitarianism of the French Revolution, may well live again in the social ideas of Italian nationalism. . . .
"In the Corporations, we have not an absurd equality, but discipline
and differences. In the corporations all participate in production, being
associated in a genuine and fruitful fraternity of classes."

Again in 1920, at the time of the Fiume Constitution which popularized
corporations, Rocco wrote an article in *Politica*, in which this theory
of integral syndicalism was developed in full. In his later version the
French syndicalists are quite neglected, but the French Revolution
remains as the villain of the historical plot. According to Rocco and
his modified positivism, human history is divided into alternate periods
of organization and of disintegration. In the former the state dominates,
while in the latter individuals or particular groups and associations
assert their independence. In the former, civilizations are cultivated, in
the latter they are destroyed in order to make room for new ones. The
early Middle Ages were a disintegrating period, whereas the 17th and
18th centuries were an organic period when the guilds or corporations,
controlled by strong states, really regulated economic processes and
kept society integrated. But in the French Revolution the bourgeoisie
destroyed these corporations, destroyed the sovereign state as well and
substituted a void of meaningless individual rights and popular sovereignty. The industrial revolution merely accentuated the social dis-
equilibrium thus generated and economic liberalism erected the helpless-
ness of the state into a positive doctrine. Socialism, though it pretended
to establish a new order in place of this anarchy, really exaggerated the evils by pitting ungoverned classes against each other.
Fascism has inaugurated a new organic period not merely by reassert-
ing the sovereign state, but more especially by reviving the medieval
corporate machinery of economic control.

Other nationalists and also syndicalists have discovered in fasci
syndicalism a continuation of the work of Mazzini, Garibaldi, Pisacar

and the patriotic socialism of the *risorgimento*. Panunzio in his recent writings calls Mazzini "our great apostle" and the real founder of integral syndicalism. Sorel, he claims, rediscovered and revealed Mazzini's ethics of "association," his revolt against the materialistic conception of history and his faith in "associations" as the educators and liberators of the common people. Dino Grandi also championed this view in his important speech at the Rome Fascist Congress of 1921.

Other *fascisti*, jealous of their idealistic tradition and aware of Mazzini's close affiliation with positivism, have tried to make an idealist of Mazzini, as does Gentile, for example.[9] Or they show the close similarity between Mazzini's and Hegel's conception of associations. The attempt has even been made to prove that fascist syndicalism is the logical culmination of Italy's dominant idealistic tradition from Vico to Cuoco to Croce.[10] But all this is, of course, mere afterthought. National syndicalism was born of the needs of the moment, and its historical forefathers were discovered later. Nevertheless it is typical of philosophy that as soon as a practical discovery has been made for practical purposes it is immediately made to appear as the logical outcome of history. And the story is already going down in history that the Italians discovered in Sorel an idea which had long had a footing in Italian tradition, that they were therefore able immediately to transcend him by cultivating their own forms of thought, and that because of this traditional historical-mindedness of the Italian, syndicalism has become a political reality in Italy while it remains a philosopher's dream in France.

Dropping these polemics about origins, we may now proceed to outline the theory as it was developed in Italy.

A. O. Olivetti, who has browsed up and down the philosophic field for many years, tries to connect syndicalism with a metaphysical point of view and to make it appear that the universe itself has a syndical structure. He points out how modern science has completely upset the atomic point of view. Matter is not a congeries of atoms, each of which is a simple independent entity. For the atom itself is a very complex organization of electric charges, an organic unity of energies. It is an orderly society, as it were, of forces in equilibrium, a microcosmic transcript of the "associated" bodies which constitute solar systems and constellations. The same may be said of cell structure in living organisms. The atomic concepts of biology have given place to organic ones. In psychology too, thought has been discovered to be a product of "social man"; and in place of the older analysis of simple ideas

---

[9] v. Gentile: *Che cosa è il fascismo*, pp. 43 ff. Also Appendix No. 29.
[10] v. The writings of G. Montemayor.

being mechanically associated, modern psychology has revealed the mind as a function of society, of intercommunication, language, and association. In short, " everything in the universe is association and association implies not the casual agglomeration of entities according to their chance proximities, but a union of entities in a fixed manner, which union determines their state of equilibrium, their forms, and figures, and determines them according to what might be called either Platonic ideas or natural laws, and which are simply the manifestations of reality itself. On the same plan associations of associations take place in ever vaster cycles, but with the same significance. . . .

" . . . We maintain that today it is possible up to a certain point and with the prudence of a critical method to discover the existence of a universal principle which presides over the realm of nature, over the realm of thought and over the realm of society; this principle, according to us, is that of *association*. Association does not mean a blind and casual conglomeration of individuals endowed with a certain degree of liberty and joined together by a fixed order inherent in their nature. . . . Theorists have been preoccupied with the individual and the state and have neglected association, which is not a middle but a higher term and conditions the other two. The ethics of association is still virgin territory to be explored. . . . Only Giuseppe Mazzini grasped the moral and social importance of the fact of association, regarding *association* as an ultimate term of the same nature and substance as the idea of liberty." [11]

How syndicates and their confederations fit into this universe of association is too obvious to demand further exposition. Suffice it to say therefore, that the syndicate state appears no longer as a mere human reform, but as a necessary illustration of a universal natural law.

Leaving these metaphysical flights of Olivetti, we turn to those social and political ideas which are generally shared by all fascist syndicalist. Chief among these is the theory that the struggle between nations more serious and critical than the class struggle, at least for Ital. The conflict of interests between the Italian worker and his neighb in richer countries is much greater than that between him and h Italian employer. For Italy as a whole is a proletarian nation and (the Marxist terminology must be retained) is engaged in a class struggle with its plutocratic oppressors. Really however, it is a Darwini struggle for existence rather than a Marxian class struggle, for on t fate of the Italian nation depends the very life of the Italian work If this was not obvious before the war, when emigration offered (

[11] A. O. Olivetti, *Il sindacalismo come filosofia e come politica: linamenti sintesi universale*, pp. 15, 16, 21, 38.

portunities for a livelihood in foreign lands, certainly now with increased restriction by foreign governments, the Italian laborer must realize that he must stand or fall with his own nation and its government. In the face of ever increasing national competition, both economic and military, Italy least of all can afford the luxury of internal conflict. The Italian had long been accustomed to regard himself as the victim of foreign *political* oppression; now this idea must be transferred bodily into the *economic* field. Some of the jingoists will even have it that bolshevism and capitalism are but two branches of Italy's one great enemy, international-Jewish-finance.[12]

For the socialist formula of " international solidarity and class struggle " fascism substitutes " inter-class solidarity and national struggle." As a consequence of this struggle between poor Italy on the one side and plutocratic Europe and America on the other, the only real interest of the Italian worker can be to stimulate national production. The problem of production, not of distribution, is vital for Italy. " Italy, being a country very poor in raw materials, can not allow itself the luxury of frequent and recurrent interruptions of production, and in the international competitive strife it must seek a compensation for its poverty in a maximum possible utilization of its intelligence and of the energy of its manual labor, combined with the factors of capital and of technical administration." [13]

To all this the socialists, of course, objected. This talk of the " national interest " is a pure abstraction, they said. The *fascisti* merely identify the interests of the bourgeoisie with those of the nation. To this charge the *fascisti* reply that if anything is an " abstraction " it is the Marxist notion of two fixed classes in eternal conflict. As a matter of fact there are an indefinite number of classes or occupational groups, each having its own interests. But in addition there are geographic cultural groups, no less real than purely economic groups, with conflicting interests and aims which imply economic conflicts. Among these groups are nations. Therefore anyone who expects to share in the activities of his national group or " class " must learn to regulate his other group interests accordingly. This is a much more complex affair than the two-class struggle of Marxist theory. It may require a new moral sense, and a severe discipline to apply it intelligently but, though difficult of realization and hence less attractive, such a conception of society is at least more realistic and more honest than the fantastic picture of orthodox socialism. Some fascist writers point out that so-called socialism is really a " pseudo-socialism," which should be called " classism ";

[12] cf. Banchelli, in Appendix No. 13.

[13] Senator Schanzer in speech before the Senate, March 5, 1926.

that instead of really facing the problems of socialization squarely, it abandoned them for its very unsocial tactics of class struggle; that fascism has therefore fallen heir to all the concrete problems which socialism abandoned; and that it is at last attempting a genuinely social solution.

Premising this revision in the theory of classes, few fascist syndicalists deny that there are class conflicts and many of them even admit an organized class struggle within limits. They have no objection to a genuine economic competition and bargaining between capital and labor, but they deprecate the particular forms which the class struggle had taken in Italy. The class conflict may continue, but it need not be violent. As Suckert puts it, " in Italy, class hatred had taken the place of economic class struggle. Herein lay the whole secret of the future of Italian socialism. . . . Class struggle, among us, was understood not in an economic, but in a social sense, and it transformed the instruments of labors into daggers. Industry was like a huge belly to be disembowelled." [14] The strike in Italy, for reasons explained above, was seldom a genuine instrument for gaining advantages for labor; it almost always turned out to be but a violent political protest. It had a political, not an economic function. Consequently this sort of class struggle usually played into the hands of the bourgeoisie. Frequently employers themselves would encourage strikes during dull seasons, in order to escape unemployment charges. In any case, Italian capital was also organized and was generally able to exhibit far greater resources than Italian labor could command. As a result strikes became increasingly violent, wasteful, and embittered, until, as was said above, class conflict degenerated into fruitless class hatred.

There are other contributing factors which made class relations in Italy particularly violent. In Italy, as in Russia, feudal class distinctions and privileges are still widely taken for granted. Employers are frequently brutal and usually excessively overbearing, and the impoverished laborer is both economically and socially in much the same position as the medieval serf. Titles are generously distributed to prosperous factory and land owners, and the recipients usually try to live up to their titles. The middle class is less in evidence than it is in northern European countries, and consequently social extremes meet continually. And in agriculture, which is Italy's chief industry, in spite of the enormous social differences, proprietor and wage laborer, the riches and poorest classes of Italians, come into personal contact. Social intercourse retains its feudal intimacy, while the industrial revolution has created class distinctions and a wage system which makes the intimacy impossible.

[14] Curzio Sucket: *Europa Vivente*, pp. 48, 51.

Rossoni and his colleagues among the practical labor organizers kept more of the spirit of class struggle than did the theorists. He is very conscious of the fact that he is still a labor leader, and regards himself an enemy of the socialists as to means, not as to ends. He thinks the orthodox class struggle to be but another Utopian theory. It is necessary, he says, to proceed pragmatically, starting with the present reality and making of it what we can, leaving the future to whatever may come. His prime effort is therefore to gain for labor whatever he can within the capitalist system, which must at least for the present be the starting point of economic reconstruction. In an early draft of the constitution for the Confederation he came out as follows:

" The Confederation maintains that the dynamic law of social history does not consist in the struggle between classes, that is to say between social functions, much less in the collaboration of classes, that is to say in the confusion of functions; but consists rather in the *struggle of capacities,* that is to say in the struggle of lower class groups who have acquired the capacity appropriate to the functions of the higher classes to take these functions from those higher classes, who have lost the capacities.

" The Confederation maintains that the specific principle of syndicalism, expressed by the formula *struggle of capacities,* does not permit the organizations of citizens in classes or occupations to aim to undermine the very functions which they represent; and moreover it does not permit general strikes, which embrace all the classes and occupations or any of them in the whole national territory.

" The principle of *struggle of capacities* implies the criterion of piecemeal struggles, which may eventually even resort to the strike, but only if this can remain localized and limited to striking a blow at those particular groups which need to be eliminated in the interests of labor and of national production; otherwise the struggle, being impossible in the economic field, comes to be carried into the political field, as in the case of public service employees." [15]

But even this guarded assertion by labor organizers of a modified and mollified class struggle proved to be too strong for their nationalist allies and was omitted in the constitution finally approved. For the nationalists emphasized the " collaboration of classes," what was here dubbed " confusion of classes," and expected the whole nation to be one huge coöperative " corporation." Whereas the practical syndicalists were more conscious of their internal enemies, of the so-called " parasites," *i.e.,* of those employers who refused to " adhere to the corporations " or in some other way proved to belong to that old-fashioned, unproductive, " unfascist " type of capitalist. The syndicalist workers

[15] Pighetti: *Sindacalismo fascista,* p. 25.

even declare frankly that they do not care for large numbers of employers' syndicates in their organization, which is to remain predominantly an organ of the labor movement. They included employers' organizations largely for strategic and political reasons. Wherever the majority of employers as well as of laborers were hostile, they encouraged those who were friendly to organize and " adhere to the corporations," in order to break up the hostile organizations. In practice this meant that the fascist syndicates enlisted the fascist agrarian proprietors to help them against the hostile industrial groups, that is, against both the industrial employers and the socialist labor bosses.

What Rossoni's formula of " struggle of capacities " amounts to is simply that there is no struggle between classes, occupations or functions as such, since they are by nature interdependent, but that there is a struggle between men, especially between ambitious men, who form rival governing classes (*classi dirigenti*). The theory is that both in government and industry the old governors were worn out and that now a fresh, energetic class of intelligent young " aristocrats " has seized control and is revolutionizing production. Accordingly the *fascisti* defend capitalism as an institution but attack the old-fashioned capitalists. Says Rossoni: " We teach workers not to hate factory owners and industrialists. But in their turn the owners must not consider themselves bosses in the old sense of the word. Between Italian and Italian there can no longer be master and slave, but only loyal co-workers for their common interests and for the higher ends of the country. Against the bosses in the old sense of the word, we shall fight inexorably." [16] This is an echo of the difficulties which the *fascisti* had in convincing employers that they would be forced to take the new methods of collective control seriously. In many cases employers had to be literally beaten into recognizing the new labor organs. These recalcitrant proprietors, who thought all restrictions were off after the March on Rome, were the prime object of the militant syndicalists' attacks.

The *fascisti* regard themselves as having vanquished two parasitic classes: the " destructive red " labor organizers and their monopolies, and the " old bourgeoisie." This " old bourgeoisie " is a technical term for: (a) Freemasonry, and its international clique of democratic politicians, who, according to the *fascisti*, sacrificed the interests of Italy to their private social standing among " the brethren "; (b) the official class of the old Italian state in general, whom they regard as a vested interest of aged and infirm pedants, without energy or courage to take any positive steps at all and hence practically parasitic; (c) the leisure class of idle factory owners, absentee landlords, and in general all

16 E. Rossini: *Le idee della ricostruzione*, p. 31.

those who lived wholly on property which the labor of others made fruitful; (d) speculators, investors and managers of foreign capital or interests, manufacturers of goods which had no social value, etc. Over
against these parasitic classes are "all the good Italians" who are
lumped together as simply "producers." The aim of the so-called
"integralist" syndicalists was to organize all these producers into syndicates according to their occupations or "categories," to federate these
into national corporations, or unions of the "industrial" type, and to
make this whole organization, with themselves at its head, an intrinsic
part of the fascist government. This aim, of organization by occupations not by classes, was to be reached not by class coöperation, but by
class "action," that is by competitive struggle, bargaining and the exact-
ing of more favorable labor contracts. All life is struggle, they say, and
struggle must be the means by which harmony may eventually be obtained. Not only is struggle inevitable because of the conflicting interests of these various groups, but within any *one* occupation or category
there is and should be continual struggle of individual against
individual.

Syndicalist writers continually emphasize their individualism. This
is, of course, directed primarily against the communists, for the *fascisti*
frankly defend private property. But they go further than mere objection to communistic ownership. They claim that their whole spirit
is exactly the opposite of the orthodox socialist. Syndicalism is adventurous, combatant, nationalistic, revolutionary, heroic. In a sense,
of course, the syndicate is a collective unit, but it is collective in a realistic sense; it exalts neither the abstract individual nor universal communism, but is based on actual common interests. Moreover the
syndicate is not supposed to be an end in itself but merely an instrument for the education and encouragement of individuals. Just as the
syndicalist leaders themselves have been for the most part violent, independent, rebellious characters, so the aim of syndicalism is to organize a proletarian *élite,* the new aristocracy rather than the masses. To
be sure, even the masses of labor are to be educated, are to be taught
to find satisfaction and self-realization in their work, not to be freed
from it. The socialist's emphasis on shorter hours and more leisure
reveals the fact that he really does not want to work. The syndicalist
on the other hand preaches the possibilities of enjoyment in work:
fatica senza fatica — a formula which tries to convey the idea that work
need not be tedious though it is endless and necessary. But this joy
in work even when immediate results are not visible admittedly implies
a certain nobility of spirit which the masses can attain only by a gradual
process of moral discipline. For the present therefore the syndicates

must concentrate on the superior individuals. The syndicates are to be educational institutions for the development of men of capacity and technical skill. From the syndicates are to come the new captains of industry, who will be far superior to the old, partly because they are schooled in the school of industry and thoroughly familiar with the detailed processes of production and partly because they represent the native vigor and genius of the race which, according to Sorelian theory, the bourgeoisie had lost. The aim is to produce not merely a new class of industrial technicians, but genuine aristocrats, men of culture, individuality and genuis. For the future of Italian culture is to come not merely from the youth, but from the proletariat, from that despised class which the bourgeois philistines of Europe call "*Italia barbara.*" The *popolo d'Italia* is about to come into its own.[17]

Though syndicalism is a revolt against democratic moral ideals and cultural standards, it regards itself as very close to ideal political democracy. As a mode of political organization, syndicalism claims actually to be what democracy merely pretended to be. In the so-called democratic state the people is not really sovereign and the government does not really govern, for neither exercises an effective control over the great technical, industrial and financial interests of the nation. The fundamental economic government of a democratic country is in the hands of a few "interests." Even granted that at one time political parties represented specific interests, they are now becoming representative of little more than rival groups of politicians. At best the various groups which are supposed to be represented by the politicians are not specific interests; Republicans, Radicals, Socialists, Catholics, etc. are becoming continually more hesitant about committing themselves clearly on any specific issue. In short so-called representative government is not representative, and the so-called choice by ballot is not a genuine choice. And the reason for this is not merely the practical difficulties in democratic government, but the theoretic fallacy which pretends that citizens can be represented. Really only interests can be represented.

Hence the French Revolution was democratic on paper only; in practice it was a device of the bourgeoisie to gain complete control. For the notion of the atomic citizen which Rousseau expounded and on which modern democracy is based is purely fictitious. In ancient Greece and Rome (the French Revolution took place in a classicist atmosphere) such citizens really existed, for they had leisure to devote themselves to the *res publica,* while the slaves did the work. The ancient Greeks and Romans really could possess the *virtù* which Montesquieu said was necessary for democratic citizenship. But in modern conditions this is a

---

[17] cf. Also Appendix No. 30.

pure fiction. The reality is not some public-minded, independent citizen, but a *producer,* caught up in a vast net-work of economic interests and associations. The Middle Ages with their guilds and corporations were much more realistic. The French Revolution merely destroyed the genuinely economic associations and government of the Middle Ages, setting up in its place under the banner of an atomic citizenship and a fictitious general will an economic bourgeois monopoly. Real democracy must be economic, a democratic organization of producers. The various particular and conflicting interests must be made explicit. Class coöperation is never the outcome of a supposed public opinion for the public interest, but is possible only if the producers can see that it is to their own private interest to coöperate. Only a sydicalist organization of society can make this community of interests apparent, for it alone creates an orderly hierarchy of organized interests.

Since society is not, as Rousseau preached, a political artifice erected by a political contract, but rather a primary aspect of human life with predominantly economic foundations, political organization must grow gradually out of economic association. Though the state is not based on an original contract, nevertheless contracts mark the essence of the state in the sense that they are the culmination and not the beginning of political organization. The natural forms of association into which men enter become more variegated as civilization proceeds, generating conflicting interests and the necessity of conciliating them. This conciliation can be accomplished only gradually and piecemeal, not by a grandiose Social Contract, but by specific agreements. National syndicalism is the organization of various interests precisely for the purpose of facilitating the drawing up of collective contracts. By means of these contracts a strong and intelligent political order is being evolved.

This machinery of collective conciliation and agreement which is characteristic of fascist syndicalism in practice is fundamental in theory as well. The mere organization of single interests for the sake of class conflict, at which the old syndicalism stopped, is not enough to create a state; old syndicalism was the stronghold of anarchy. Syndicates must be organized for purposes of conciliation and coöperation in order that they may promote the prosperity of the " corporation " and of the nation to which they belong and on which their own prosperity depends. The machinery of coördination (contracts, labor tribunals corporations, ministries, etc.) transforms the syndical organization into a genuine state. Not that the state is a state *of* syndicates, but, as Senator Schanzer put it, " a state *above* syndicates." Or rather in Panunzio's terms, the state is the form and the syndicates the matter, and just as forms are independent of any particular matter, since a given raw material may assume any number of forms, so the state must be strong enough to dominate and give direction to the activities of the syndicates. In other words, when the organized competition of private interests is made to serve national ends, the economic order becomes also a political order. Private interests are never transcended as the idealists say they are, nor are national interests superimposed on them, for that is impossible. The national interests are the private interests coördinated. In this way the syndicates, which according to Croce are not "moral" institutions since they represent merely particular interests, are transformed into factors of the "ethical state." The ethical state is not composed of compounded particulars but is an organic unity of processes, which processes are represented by associations. There are no more particulars to be transcended. This idea is supposed to be suggested by the emphasis on production. A producer cannot be isolated as an individual and he does not merely pursue his own profit; he is a factor in a process and contributes at once to his own profit and to the goods of his nation. But this happy result is not brought about by a natural law or "hidden hand" as the economists believe, nor is every man by nature a producer. It is the product of a conscious, intelligent ordering of society.

Hence production, and production alone, entitles a man to membership in the state and vice versa any one who contributes to the prosperity of the nation is a producer. "Capital, study and work" are thus all placed on the same level. The citizen is replaced by the producer and a man's contribution to the productive activities of his nation is the measure of his worth. Fascism therefore means a revolutionary emphasis on production even to the extent of making this function the very essence of a person's participation in the state. To quote Grandi: "National syndicalism considers the individual not as a subject or a citizen, but as a producer, and sees the syndicates as the cells of a new and greater social organism, a true and genuine 'institutional expression,' destined in this manner to transform the modern and decadent parliamentary state."

A legal theory of the relation between state and syndicates has been worked out more fully by Sergio Panunzio (now professor in the University of Rome) than by any other fascist. According to him fascism represents a synthesis of State and Society. Starting with the St. Simonian distinction between the organic period of history when the state tends to absorb all social functions, and societal periods, when the elementary social functions break the bonds of existing state authorities, he sees in early syndicalism a societal process, destructive, critical, revolutionary, and in early fascism the reassertion of the state authority. With the union of fascism and syndicalism a genuine synthesis has at last been achieved between two tendencies which have been opposites in the past. Fascism is a " revolutionary conservation."

Syndicates, like all forms of association, generate their own norms of control, which have an inner " institutional " juridical validity. Law is not a product of the state, but of any form of association. The origins of law are as pluralistic as societies are. In this Panunzio follows Duguit and the other pluralists. The legislative power is therefore a power of society, *i.e.* of any association, and not exclusively of the state. Hence the contracts and other labor norms which are established by syndicates have a legal validity quite independently of the state. The essential function of the state is not legislative but judicial. The state is the sovereign judge. It applies the laws made by society and as such it is the sovereign authority for the interpretation of law. In a positivistic sense, the state may be said to make law, since a law is really a law only when it is applied or enforced. But strictly speaking society generates the laws which the state puts into operation. The so-called executive power of the state is really identical with its judicial function, since the power to judge implies the power to enforce its decisions. It follows that the courts should be given full power to try labor cases, for by so doing they give political as well as " institutional " validity to labor contracts.

Panunzio accordingly favored a single legally recognized " monopolistic " syndicate for each category, compulsory membership of all citizens, compulsory adjudication of all labor disputes by the courts and the prohibition of strikes and lockouts. The lower house of Parliament, being the legislative chamber, would be syndical; the Senate remaining political. But these latter details of Panunzio's theory must not be taken as typical of the movement in general. He represents one of the extremes of fascist syndicalism. In general Panunzio has been criticized by other fascist syndicalists (*e.g.* Costamagna) for recognizing the independent juridical status of syndicates on the one hand, and on the other trying to evade the pluralistic implications of this doctrine by his doctrine of the judicial sovereignty of the state. Panunzio is evidently much nearer the older syndicalism than are the " corporation " theorists, and has recently come out flatly against " corporationism." Paradoxically enough, though Panunzio's theory is now regarded as obsolete, being superseded by corporationist theory, it really is closer to the present facts of fascist organization than the officially recognized theory is. Though his independent class syndicates and his " monopolies," etc., are being opposed in theory, they are being applied in fact, as we shall see.

On the other extreme, and really quite independent of the syndicalist movement strictly speaking, were the *gruppi di competenza*, or advisory groups of experts. These groups had been proposed in the original fascist program of 1919, as we have seen in a previous chapter, and were modelled on Kurt Eisner's scheme in Germany. At that time, as Mussolini himself said later, " we did not think of founding syndicate organizations." [18]   And even in November 1921, at the founding of the Party, Mussolini and Massimo Rocca still represented this point of view. Several months before the March on Rome, largely through the efforts of Rocca and Giovanni Preziosi, a Neapolitan nationalist, four of these groups were formed: of administration, of schools, of colonies, and of literary affairs. In addition to these national groups, there were also provincial groups attached to the provincial federations and sections of the Fascist Party. They were composed of men within and without the Fascist Party, and began as independent non-political boards of experts, who themselves initiated specific technical reforms or else advised the government when consulted. In November 1923 Rocca induced the Grand Council to transform his organization into the *Segretario Generale dei Consigli Tecnici Nazionali*, to give it official recognition and to make it a sort of go-between between the syndicates and the party, it being independent of both. In practice, these technical councils really accomplished very little. The one on schools, when it proved to be hostile to Senator Gentile's reform, was abolished. Both politicians and syndicalists resented their interference with the more " regular " machinery. And when Rocca was caught in the dissidence movement, was expelled and forced to flee the country, his organization naturally collapsed. But though these groups amounted to little in themselves they paved the way both in theory and practice for more extensive reforms. Rocca himself wanted to make them the basis of a legislative reform, and this idea was championed by others. Govi and other right wing fascists, who were particularly hostile to Parliament, wanted to make them the legislative organs of the government. Govi called his theory of the technical state *epistemarchia,* or the rule of science. The idea was that since parliaments today merely approve laws (most of them highly technical) which they do not make, but which are drafted by committees in consultation with experts, it would make legislation more efficient and intelligent to turn over the whole legislative power to these groups of experts. Acerbo proposed that they be embodied in the Senate and that the Chamber merely act as a check on this new Senate, which would become the real legislative body, thus reversing the functions of the two houses. Others proposed an independent third

18 v. T. Nanni: *Bolscevismo e Fascismo,* p. 277.

Chamber. The Reform Commission of 1925 proposed that the technical councils be embodied in the present Chamber of Deputies. It was generally agreed among syndicalistic fascists that the provincial *gruppi di competenza* would assume judicial functions and act as labor tribunals along with the *collegi dei probiviri*. Pighetti and some of the more aristocratic syndicalists urged that they be attached to the ministries, so that each ministry would have its economic council. If incorporated in this way into the government, they might afford, he thought, a practical means for establishing the much heralded " corporations," those central coördinating agencies between labor, employers and government, which Rossoni's corporations failed to be. As it turned out, of course, nothing had to be done about them in practice, since they died a quiet death; nevertheless the theories and projects to which they gave birth are still living and help to swell the movement for the establishment of the corporate state and economic representation.

We might mention at this place several organizations which are closely associated with fascist syndicalism, but which have played minor rôles in practice and have contributed no new social theories.

The Coöperatives, though of course not fascist institutions either in origin or idea, have been incorporated into fascist syndicalism. Shortly after the accession of the *fascisti* to power a large number of coöperative organizations, especially the rural ones, banded together and formed the *Sindacato Italiano Cooperativo*, under the leadership of Gaetano Postiglione and E. Civelli. This organization tried to bring order out of the chaos into which the coöperatives had fallen as a result of the breaking up of the political parties to which they had been allied, and also in many cases as a result of squadrist ravages. The rural coöperative banks were in an especially serious condition. Under the motto of " freeing the coöperatives from politics " and putting them on a solid economic basis, the above fascist leaders gradually got control of the great majority of coöperatives. They were fairly successful in warding off the hungry politicians, fascist and otherwise, who were rummaging the land for loose funds; in fact, it was precisely the danger from these marauders, who fell upon unprotected coöperatives, which drove many of them into Postiglione's camp. In 1925 after the passage of the syndical law and after Bottai, who had been president of the National Federation of Producers' Coöperatives, became Undersecretary of Corporations, non-fascist organizations were abolished and the organization was transformed into the *Ente Nazionale della Cooperazione* and affiliated in part with Rossoni's Confederation, in part (the coöperatives of Industrial Production) with the Confederation of Industry, and in part with the Confederation of Commerce. The national organization is divided according to the various kinds of coöperatives, into five national federations, and each of these has its provincial federation. There are about 1,800 consumers' Coöperatives, 1,100 labor and producers' Coöperatives, 300 agricultural Coöperatives (*i.e.* "collective renters"), 350 Coöperative Rural Banks, 180 Coöperatives for the building of homes. Altogether they have about 400,000 members. Rossoni is at present attempting to get the whole organization into his confederation, on the ground that all coöperatives, of whatever kind, are agencies of wage control, and wage control ought to be in the hands of the labor organization; but his chances are slight.

A more characteristically fascist institution was the *Commissariati delle opere*. A committee of the *fascio* of Cesena, under the direction of Amedeo Mazzotti, undertook to deal with the unemployment problem. It called together representatives of the public administrations, of banks, merchants associations, industrialists, agriculturalists, workers syndicates, coöperatives, etc., to discover some means of securing additional employment in that province. It was discovered that a number of profitable enterprises might be undertaken if capital could be found. Accordingly this committee of commissaries named commissions of experts to take charge of the enterprises, while the above-named institutions coöperated in furnishing the capital, and thus became the joint owners of the enterprises. The success of this experiment led to its adoption elsewhere. Soon Mazzotti was able to establish various provincial organizations and finally also the National Commissariat of Works (*commissariato nazionale delle opere*), whose director he became. Thus it became a combination national employment bureau and promoter of coöperative enterprises. However, within a year of its nationalization the whole movement collapsed, and its functions were taken over by the syndicalist organizations.

A very important organization is the *Ufficio Centrale* (now *Ente Morale*) *Dopo-lavoro*. This organization started in private factories like the great Fiat works, for instance, who organized recreation centers, sports and entertainments for their employees. It soon became national federation devoted to "the encouragement, through the initiative of the employers concerned, of measures for the sanitary, domestic, physical, cultural, and professional improvement of their employees." Until April 1927 the Duke of Aosta was at the head of the organization when he resigned on account of other duties and Turati, Secretary of the Fascist Party, took his place. It is directly affiliated with the Confederation of Fascist Syndicates, and according to the new law, a percentage of the fees levied by the syndicates goes to its support, as well as to the support of other national philanthropic institutions (*enti morali*).

III. The Crisis

Fascism and syndicalism were much more readily identified in theory than in practice, and the March on Rome, which was supposed to be the final victory for national syndicalism as well as for fascism, really proved to be the beginning of its hardest battle. For since then it has been compelled to fight not other labor organizations but other *fascisti*.

The labor organizations of the other parties had slight chances of offering serious resistance to Rossoni's fascist corporations, after these had achieved the prestige of His Majesty's official syndicates. There was an attempt immediately after the March on Rome to unite all Italian labor into a single solid patriotic organization to be headed by d'Annunzio, but this was promptly suppressed.

Labor leaders of all parties began to get on the fascist band-wagon, just as other politicians did. And Rossoni immediately gave them employment. They were sent all over the country to carry on the accustomed "syndical action." They continued to appeal to the proletariat against the exploiting bourgeoisie with all the demagogy they had been accustomed to practice before their conversion to fascism. In some factories and to a greater extent in the country, they forced surplus labor on the owners, precisely as the socialist monopolies had done before. Here and there strikes were declared, supplemented on occasion by the club of squadrists. In Romagna and Emilia local fascist bosses, like Farinacci, who were favorable to the syndicates, forced employers who "exploited the new patriotic discipline of the workers for their selfish interests" to submit to the fascist syndicates. The success of these activities was due in part to the desperate belief among laborers that their only refuge lay in these syndicates and in part to the system instituted whereby labor organizers were paid by the number of membership cards they were able to sell.

The Catholic Populist Syndicates were the most delicate problem, since their party was a member of the government coalition at the time. But partly under the guise of "fusion" and partly by intimidation, the fascisti undermined the northern populist organizations completely, and the southern they at least robbed of their power of opposition. They were facilitated in this because they already had control of the agricultural proprietors' associations and through these could exercise considerable pressure on the peasants.

More subtle methods were used against the socialists. In August 1923, following upon some suggestions of Mussolini that an independent, non-political labor organization might be encouraged, the congress of socialistic syndicates under d'Aragona renounced their adherence to the

Socialist Party, in the hope that Rossoni's organization would free itself from the Fascist Party. But this merely played into Rossoni's hands, whose corporations took over bodily many of the socialistic syndicates.

Rossoni had also gotten control of the railroad workers and other important groups, and though the industrial employers were more hostile to his mixed syndicates than were the agriculturalists, even several employers' associations adhered to the corporations. In short, it soon began to seem as though the fascist corporations would achieve their aim, would organize all classes of the nation into a single great labor monopoly. In June 1922 they had numbered only 470,000 (277,084 agricultural laborers and proprietors, and only 72,000 industrial workers); in August they reached 800,000; in June 1923, 1,500,000, and in June 1924 about 1,800,000. And in 1925 even the communists admitted that the non-fascist syndicates had lost over three million members of the *fascisti*.

The success of the corporations split the fascist politicians into two groups: one group, which included most of the petty politicians and opportunists, objected to syndicate autonomy and wanted the fascist party to take over the syndicates and embody them into the political machinery of the bureaucracy. The other group, the right wing and liberals, resented syndicate monopoly as a revival of class antagonism and demagogy.

Originally practically all the active syndicalists were opposed to embodying the syndicalist organization into the political machinery of the party. For though they were more than willing to be closely affiliated with the government and to have an official position within the fascist *movement,* they insisted on autonomy, when it came to party politics. The reasons for this were partly personal jealousy, the syndicalist hierarchy being unwilling to subordinate itself to the political hierarchy of the party, partly a well-grounded suspicion that the majority of squadrists and the early crop of fascist politicians were quite ignorant of syndicalist affairs, and some of them even openly hostile. When the intimate alliance between national syndicalism and facism became evident, and syndicalism became well established fascist office seeker poured into the syndicalist ranks by the score, and threatened to corrupt completely an organization which was none too pure to begin with. The syndicalists were apparently flattered at first by their sudden popularity, and opened their door cordially. But they soon realize their mistake and an open clash arose between the party leaders and the syndicalists. The party leaders wanted only registered members of the Fascist Party to be admitted into the syndicates (which would have reduced the syndicate membership enormously). The syndicalists asserted that joining a fascist syndicate was tantamount to becoming a fascist and that therefore membership in the Party itself was to be optional. The Party leaders urged that the syndicates become administrative organs of the government; the syndicalists urged that they could operate more effectively if left autonomous.

The issue then became submerged in the more general one between the "intransigents" and the "revisionists." This circumstance helped to reconcile party and syndicates to each other, for the more prominent dissidents and revisionists belonged to the second group mentioned above, that is, the right wing liberals. But what worried the syndicalists even more than the dissident liberals were the liberals entrenched in the government. In the face of this more serious enemy, the syndicalists made their peace with the Party. The syndicalist leader, Pighetti, for example, wrote in 1924: "To be sure, while admitting the greatest orthodoxy and best relations with the Party, practical and theoretical necessities demand that syndical organization should not be suffocated by the meddling and vigilance of the Party itself. This suffocation can not be said to exist today and certainly syndical organization is aware of the danger and is adopting measures of defense against it. It has to deal with the characters of men rather than written agreements, which may not be perfect either. So also it is engaged in defending itself against the other and greater danger of false *fascisti* (and among the false *fascisti* are those who do not take the facts of syndicalism into account, though it is one of the most vital sources of fascism), who are working against our syndicalism in all possible ways. This danger, I repeat, is much more serious than the other; and it is to be hoped that among all the purifications, about which there is so much talk, those will not be forgotten, by which we shall finally be rid of the anti-syndicalists." [19]

When Mussolini took office, it may be remembered from our previous chapters, he had an over-simplified theory of internal government. Internally the state was to be little more than the old-fashioned liberalistic policeman. If Mussolini was converted to this point of view by reasons of practical and temporary expediency, his first Minister of Finances, Alberto De Stefani, was convinced of it by principle. He was an orthodox individualistic economist, and what is more, a professor of political economy. Hence he set to work not as a practical politician, but as a scientist bent on carrying out his theories in full. Shortly after he took office, Tamorra, the Popularist Minister of the Treasury, died, which enabled him to take over that ministry too, and

[19] Pighetti: *Sindacalismo Fascista*, p. 19.

having been granted extraordinary powers by Parliament, he was thus given ample scope and authority.

The Ministry of Labor was abolished. Telephones were turned over to private companies, and telegraphs, railroads, and post offices would have been also, had they been paying concerns. Most of the socialist land legislation was repealed. Government protection and subsidies for coöperatives were withdrawn. Instead of undertaking extensive public works, he turned the available funds over to private concerns, especially for the big agricultural developments in the south. The inheritance tax was abolished. And of the thirteen direct taxes only three were retained, those on land, buildings and income. The income tax was extended to the salaried class and to small farmers and was made very heavy. The railroad personnel was reduced and rates were raised. Indirect taxes were instituted wherever possible.

In order to offset this burden and to reduce the cost of living, the protective tariff was taken off of flour and was lowered on sugar and other agricultural products. But "the national interests" made it impossible for De Stefani to proceed to a reduction of industrial tariffs, much as he should have liked to on theoretical grounds! In short, his conscious aim and policy was: (a) to reduce the state's budget by reducing its functions; (b) to stimulate saving and the accumulation and circulation of capital; (c) to encourage rigid economy in all branches of the government. He announced that he was making no revolution in finance, but merely "consistent, scientific, technical economies."

His chief success was naturally in the matter of stabilizing finances. He succeeded in balancing the budget, reducing the debt and reducing the circulation of paper. His chief backing, however, came not from the banks who were still a bit skeptical of fascism, but from the industrialists, to whom a new era of *laissez faire* was a veritable God-send. The practical success of his measures increased the general confidence of the business classes in his administration. In addition, he had the good fortune to be opposed by the villains of the hour, Rossoni and Rocca, though for opposite reasons. Hence he was allowed to remain entrenched during the crisis of 1924.

De Stefani's financial policy was, of course, not directly opposed to the syndicalists. They too were individualists in a way. Certainly Rossoni did not object to the abandonment of state ownership and management of business enterprises, for all private business was his prospective prey. But indirectly De Stefani's policy was ruinous for Rossoni, since it gave renewed power and prestige to the industrialists. It became increasingly difficult for him to justify the fascist government to his labor constituency and it became practically impossible for him to make headway against the employers, who were using De Stefani's liberalism as an excuse for disregarding their labor contracts and refusing to deal with labor organizations of any kind.

Worst of all, De Stefani was openly opposed to any form of syndicate monopoly, and was evidently anxious to keep syndicalism within harmless bounds. Just a few days before the March on Rome he had written as follows: "The Fascist Party and the national syndicates are two distinct organizations, the first of which controls the second, in order that syndical activity may develop within the limits of the national and productivistic principle. The political organs of the Party must see to it that the national principle be respected and must employ the work of the *gruppi di competenza* to control the economic action of the syndicates. We must have the strength to go against the national syndicates when they do not respect the conditions which we have laid down for liberty of organization, just as we went against the red and white syndicates. . . . Syndicalism is a mode of procedure for capitalists as well as for laborers, a means for reaching certain conditions of equilibrium which could not be achieved without organization. . . . I should also like to know what the directors of the Party think on the question of unity or plurality of syndicates. I do not believe a forced cultivation of syndical unity to be opportune. . . . We must allow all those organizations to live that obey national principles. Unity favors capitalistic parasitism and also workers' parasitism. The economic situation of the nation does not permit parasitism." [20]

This was a clear threat of opposition to Rossoni's tactics.

Similar opposition kept pouring in upon fascist syndicalism from the right wing of the Party in general, and the internal dualism of fascism was becoming perfectly evident. The "ideal revolt," as several writers put it, "was turning into a 'bourgeois reaction'"; and the left wing was apparently powerless to stop it.

Among the nationalists as well as the liberals there was opposition to syndicalism — opposition on principle. Volt, for example, in his *Programma della destra fascista*, wrote: "To erect, at the foundations of the state and as the sources of its sovereignty, bodies of a technical-administrative nature would give a new and powerful impulse to the current mania for regulating, organizing, fettering, in short of laying hands on that field in which the state should meddle least, the field of national economy. A disastrous tendency, which commonly bears the name of state socialism. The conception of the syndical state leads to analogous consequences. This conception, developed recently by Panunzio, is bound up with the theory of national fascist syndicalism.

[20] De Stefani: *Discorsi*, p. 181–2. See also Appendix No. 14.

But this national syndicalism is an equivocation. Pure syndicalism, as it was conceived by Sorel, is bolshevism. Nationalism excludes syndicalism, for the nation is something much greater and higher and more complex than syndicates. Fascism, when it transferred to the nation that ideal and bellicose fervor with which socialism pretended to permeate the class war, retained the syndicates as technical bodies to be sure, but killed syndicalism as a doctrine. . . . By this we do not mean to deny any and every political function to the syndicates. We deny only that syndical representation can serve as a basis for the modern state." [21]

Some of the revisionists said the same thing. And as for the Old Guard, the squadrists, many of them were violently opposed to any form of labor movement.

More serious opposition came from more practical men of affairs. The agriculturalists had been Rossoni's mainstay throughout the fight on the red leagues. But now when they saw the same old methods creeping in under a different color they became suspicious. They still had a violent repugnance for any form of farming out labor on them (*impostazione di mano d'opera*), and yet that is precisely what Rossoni's syndicates were resorting to in many regions, in order to combat unemployment. And in some regions the provincial *ras* were regulating wages and prices in agriculture, just as formerly the red leagues had done.[22] In short it looked as though the fascist integral corporations were going to turn out to be nothing but labor monopolies under another name. Against this the agrarians tried to revolt, and for a while in 1923 there was an open conflict between the Confederation of Agriculture and the fascist syndicalists, ending in Rossoni's forcing the Confederation to " adhere " to his corporations. Then individual agrarian leaders revolted. Captain Forni attacked the syndicates as a whole, whereupon he was forced out of the Party. Similarly Ottavio Corgini, Undersecretary of Agriculture, set himself against the integral or monopolistic syndicalism of the Rossoni group and at a meeting of the Grand Council spoke his thoughts with the greatest frankness. Even before the March on Rome, he and Rocca had outlined a program for economic reconstruction which was based on liberalistic economics and which had been suppressed by the propaganda office of the Party.[23] Later he ordered an inquiry into the operations of a certain big industrial corporation to which the drainage of the Pontine marshes had been conceded. This

21 Volt: *Programma della destra fascista*, p. 115.
22 cf. *e.g.* Farinacci: *Un periodo aureo del Partito Nazionale Fascista*, p. 344. Se
also Appendix No. 20.
23 v. Volt: *Programma della destra fascista*, p. 81.

incurred the hostility of a powerful industrial group and of a clique of politicians against him, and when his public approval of Misuri's famous speech of protest afforded a pretext, he was expelled from the Party, July 27, 1923. His successor, A. Serpieri, though he reached an understanding with Rossoni on the basis of corporations and class co-operation, continued the policy of opposition to syndical monopoly. He wrote: " We cannot agree to the extreme syndicalist doctrine which is the tendency at present and which tends to coincide in the economic field with state socialism, killing private initiative, undermining free activity by state decisions and judgments in economic affairs. The doctrine, according to the experience of the whole of history, would eventually, if adhered to, lead to a general diminution of wealth to the disadvantage of all; a result all the more serious in a poor country like Italy. The agrarian politics of the fascist government in its early phases was squarely headed in the direction of a recognition of this truth. . . . The national government was firmly bent on allowing the emergence of the clean and efficient machinery of private production based on free individual initiative which, notwithstanding all the ac-cusations of injustice and imperfection hurled against it, had once more proved itself, in the light of experience to be better than governmental or semi-governmental enterprises and all the " rational " regulation and " equitable " distribution imposed by public authorities. . . . To return, though in a different form, by way of a national syndicalism in the sense now given it, to a kind of state socialism or paternalism, to a bureaucratic and even warlike conception of economic life, would be, in my judgment, a grave error." [24]

While such views were being expressed by agriculturalists the in-dustrialists had also let their attitude be known. The Confederation of Industry, which represented industrial employers and which had quietly become the General Fascist Confederation of Industry, proved even more unbending towards the Rossoni corporations than was the Con-federation of Agriculture. There is a curious paradox in the relations between Rossoni's corporations to the agriculturalists on the one hand and to the industrialists on the other. Many agriculturalists welcomed mixed syndicates and the industrialists solidly opposed them, but both attitudes had the same motive, namely, the fear of labor monopolies. The explanation is that in agriculture the mixed corporations were al-ready an effective check on agrarian class domination and seemed to be the only alternative to extreme syndicalism which would have re-established labor monopolies; while in industry, class coöperation and mixed associations were unknown and impracticable and were regarded

[24] A. Serpieri: *La Politica Agraria in Italia,* pp. 215–216. See also pp. 214–226.

by industrialists as a mere phrase on the part of labor leaders by which they tried to conceal their ambition, and as in reality a menace to the independence of employers' organizations. Hence they preferred to deal with organized labor frankly as an enemy instead of welcoming the Trojan horse, the mixed corporations. Accordingly the Confederation of Industry had refused all overtures and had successfully resisted Rossoni's attempts to win over the important industrial associations.

Finally on December 20, 1923, Mussolini called the heads of the rival organizations to a meeting in the Chigi Palace, Rome. He presented a resolution asking the two Confederations in the interests of industrial peace and of promoting more cordial relations between employers and employees and their organizations, (1) to coöperate in organizing, the one the employers, and the other the employees; (2) to name a permanent commission of ten, five from each Confederation, for the purpose of coördinating the activities of the two organizations and resolving any disputes arising between them. After a reply by Benni in behalf of the Confederation of Industry and "several observations" by Rossoni in behalf of the Confederation of Syndicate Corporations, the resolution was adopted. Mussolini took this opportunity to say very frankly: "Rossoni will not be grieved when he sees that the attempt to carry integral syndicalism into the industrial field has not succeeded. Moreover Rossoni has understood perfectly from his very first defeats that what can be done in the field of agriculture, which has its own special economy, can not be done in the field of industry." [25] On February 21, 1924, a similar agreement was made for the rival agricultural confederations (except that the agricultural confederation was willing to continue to adhere to the Corporations) and on the same day also for those of commerce. At this last meeting it was hinted that the economic councils of experts would be given a corporate organization and attached permanently to the government.

Whether Rossoni was grieved or not at these developments, they seemingly marked the definite failure of his deep-laid plans.

Mussolini apparently regarded these agreements between capital and labor as a settlement. Not so Rossoni; he did not surrender so easily. There had been fascist strikes all through 1923. Farinacci had led several demonstrations in his province, notably a strike against the attempt to turn over the railroads to a private concern. And Rossoni had successfully repelled the attacks of the agriculturalists. The signals for a renewal of the fight were given in October. At that time the corporations held their Annual Convention in Turin, the labor stronghold, and it proved to be a genuine stormy labor congress. The cry was raised

[25] v. Benito Mussolini: *La Nuova Politica dell'Italia*, Vol. II, p. 137-8.

with a loud voice that there were traitors in the party and that the employers were trying to undermine fascism. It unanimously accused them of giving vent to their disappointment at discovering that fascism did not intend to betray the workers to the dictatorship of their employers, by trying to detach Mussolini from fascism and to disrupt the regime. Accordingly it declared that fascism would be compelled to remind the employers in their turn of its glorious origins by resorting to force.

In the face of such sentiment the compromises which Mussolini effected in December were evidently to be regarded as but a temporary truce. Rossoni was busy strengthening his position in the Party. He created no further difficulties for the government and even made himself very useful during the spring election campaign in swinging the labor vote. But after the elections he was ready for a different kind of action.

Circumstances favored him, for the Matteotti crisis created an atmosphere in which the stand taken by his labor organizations might settle the fate of the regime. Mussolini was quick to sense this, and was glad of any opportunity to make fascism appear before masses in a more favorable light. With Mussolini the whole *intelligentsià* of the party, the young " aristocrats " took a decided swing to the left. Rocco and Grandi, syndicalistic nationalists, were called to important posts in the cabinet. Panunzio, the most syndicalist of the fascist syndicalists, was put on the National Directorate of the Party. In July Mussolini himself accused the industrialists of granting enormous loans to the government out of their profits, at the same time refusing to raise the wages of their employees; and he even hinted at exorbitant war profits.

Meanwhile the *lira* began falling and prices began rising. This naturally fanned labor sentiment. The fascist syndicates now undertook a series of strikes: August 1924 at Savona, a strike of railroad workers; serious strikes were narrowly averted in the textile industries of Prato by the yielding of the employers; at Turin the fascist syndicates even coöperated with the socialists against the metal industries; in August the Grand Council of Rome decided in favor of the strikers at Valdarno, granting them a subsidy of 50,000 *lire* to carry on their strike; in September at Trieste, fascists forced the workers to declare a strike of protest at the dismissal of several fascist workmen; at Carara in the marble works 30,000 men struck under fascist leadership; and in the spring of 1925 at Brescia and then spreading throughout Lombardy 100,000 workers struck and forced an agreement from the metal industry. In these later strikes Farinacci, then Secretary General of the Party, and his squadrists took a personal hand. Farinacci also repeatedly attacked the banks as unscrupulous manipulators of the national credit.[26] April twenty-first, the anniversary of the founding of Rome, was made a labor holiday, thus anticipating May first, which would otherwise certainly have been a holiday.

In the midst of all this De Stefani committed a blunder. In the spring of 1925 there was apparently a conspiracy in the stock exchange to force the *lira* down still more. Hereupon De Stefani, exasperated to the point of abandoning his *laissez faire* theory, placed severe restrictions on stock brokers and threatened still more drastic actions. The banks launched a vigorous protest and forced the government immediately to define its policy. Mussolini had to step in. He rescinded the De Stefani restrictions and promised to keep hands off the sacred banks. Whether this incident was the cause or the pretext of De Stefani's resignation is hard to tell. To the banks it meant a victory for *laissez faire;* but to labor it symbolized the failure of the bourgeois reaction. For in De Stefani the industrialists lost their staunchest friend. Rossoni was much relieved.

The net result of the whole campaign was that in the fall of 1925 the fascist corporations found themselves in a much more favorable position than they had been a year previously. External circumstances had favored them, to be sure, but in addition their vigorous resumption of class war had demonstrated to the employers that the fighting spirit was still alive even among fascist labor leaders. Rossoni had strengthened his grip on Italian labor enormously. The industrial, socialistic workers began to have a little more respect for him, and the white or Catholic syndicates lost practically all their power, their membership flocking into the fascist organizations. But above all he had forced the *fascisti* themselves to take syndicalism more seriously and to feel the power which the syndicates could wield, for or against the regime.

IV. Reform

In the last chapter we have already described the political conditions by which Mussolini was induced to appoint the Commission of " Solons " in August 1924. The economic crisis, which we have just described, made the proposal for constitutional reform all the more urgent. Under these conditions, the Commission found it more or less futile to discuss strictly parliamentary reforms and instead it devoted most of its attention to the sixth and last problem which Mussolini had assigned it namely, the relation between state and syndicates, with the three subtopics, (a) the state and national economy; (b) legal recognition o

[26] cf. Farinacci: *Un periodo aureo del Partito Nazionale Fascista*, p. 31. Se Appendix No. 20.

syndicates; (c) a body of labor laws and principles for regulating and enforcing labor contracts in industry and the creation of arbitration tribunals. The syndicalist members of the Commission, among whom was Rossoni himself, now took a leading part. They became conscious of the fact that they were designing a new state. The second and greater part of their final report of July 1925 is accordingly a comprehensive analysis of what they called the Corporate State.[27] It recommends the legal recognition of syndicates, and a system of Corporate Chambers to take the place of the provincial chambers of commerce, labor and agriculture, abolished by the fascist revolution. These Chambers were to be constituted as follows: the nation to be divided into three " orders " : (1) professional men, artisans and public employees, (2) agriculture and agricultural industry, (3) industry, commerce, proprietors of buildings and movable property. The members of the various syndicates in each order were to elect representatives to a Provincial Chamber. Each of the three Provincial Chambers to have a council and an assembly. The three Chambers taken together would constitute the Provincial Corporate College. Each Provincial College would have its council and assembly. The Provincial Colleges were to elect their representatives to the National Corporate Council, which would elect its own president. This Council was to be divided into three Committees, corresponding to the three orders. These bodies, both provincial and national, would have complete charge of the administration of economic affairs, the judging of labor disputes, recommending appropriate measures to the government, etc. The government would have the right to interfere at any point of this organization, but if it dissolved any corporate body, a new one would have to be constituted within six months. It was suggested that the National Corporate Council might form a third Chamber of Parliament, but the majority of the Commission favored a scheme whereby one half of the deputies would be elected by the Provincial Corporate Colleges, to sit with the other half elected as at present. The Senate was to remain unchanged.

Such in bare outline was the New Order proposed by the Commission of Eighteen. But there were differences of opinion even within the Commission. Some of the liberals had certain general objections to the scheme as a whole, which they formulated as follows: The system forces the citizen into the narrow confines of his separate economic interests or categories and thus makes impossible any consideration of the general national welfare. The ideal unity and historical continuity of the state is sacrificed to a hierarchy of private interests. The so-called reform is but a " sentimental reaction " toward old-fashioned democracy, except

[27] See Appendix No. 22.

that it robs the sovereign of some of his political functions, and retains some of the "socialistic superstitions" according to which the citizen is merely an economic producer.

Then there were some extreme nationalistic syndicalists who preferred compulsory membership in a single syndicate for each trade. This would make the syndicates direct governmental organs. Instead of labor contracts, there would be "administrative labor decrees and arbitration," and strikes would be crimes prohibited by law. On the other hand, some Sorelian individualistic syndicalists objected to the corporations as subjecting the syndicates, which ought to remain spontaneous and free for "economic action," too much to governmental control. Pighetti, one of the experts consulted by the Commission, welcomed the corporations, but preferred a larger number, affiliated each with one of the Ministries of the government, and acting as advisory bodies, thus carrying on the work of the *gruppi di competenza*. He wanted to put them more directly under the power of the ministers, substituting for elections by the syndicates an outright appointment of one third of the councillors by the ministry and a selection of the other two thirds by the ministry from a list prepared by the National Corporate Council as a whole. In general he emphasized the need of "disciplining the masses" by state-controlled organizations, while the Commission (especially its secretary, Costamagna) emphasized the reform of representation and democratic control. Angelo O. Olivetti, however, emphasized, even more than the general report of the Commission did, the rights of the syndicates to adequate representation. He attempted a more detailed definition of the respective functions of syndicates and corporations, assigning to the syndicates all technical regulation of conditions of labor in any single field, and reserving for the corporations all political functions, *i.e.* those of adjustment, judicial decision, legal recognition of contracts, etc. He was careful to keep all political matters out of the hands of the syndicates, on the ground that it was very important "to prevent the politics of the politician, which is today penetrating and poisoning the whole life of the syndicates, from penetrating also the corporations to make them a matter of political speculation." For this same reason he and others welcomed the Commission's proposal of provincial, in place of the traditional municipal chambers of labor established by the socialists.

The reader will observe that this program is dominated by the ideas of "integral" syndicalism and its Corporations. In fact, though there were a number of syndicalists on the Commission, to say nothing of Rossoni himself, the industrialists' and employers' organizations had no direct representatives at all.

The report immediately caused much excitement. The Confederation of Industry let it be known that serious modifications were necessary; the corporations would have to be " de-integralized " and the syndicates could not be " mixed." Rossoni was reminded that he had been told once before that he and his confederations would not be allowed to have a monopoly over the political organization of Italian economic life. And before Parliament had a chance to take up the reform, the Confederation of Industry forced a compromise.

On October 2, 1925, Farinacci, as Secretary General of the Party, called the heads of the rival confederations together and an agreement was concluded known as The Pact of the Vidoni Palace, which laid the practical foundation for recent labor legislation. In this pact the two confederations not only recognized each other as the official and exclusive representatives, the one of labor, the other of the industrialists, — a recognition which they had already made two years before, — but went on to stipulate that " All contracts between industrialists and labor leaders must be made between dependent organizations of the Confederation of Industry and those dependent on the Confederation of Corporations. Consequently, internal commissions in the factories are abolished and their functions devolve upon the local syndicates, which will exercise them only in connection with the correspondent industrial organizations." A few weeks later this agreement was legalized by Royal Decree, thus giving legal recognition to collective labor contracts even before the syndicates themselves were recognized.

Though superficially this pact may seem to be little more than a confirmation of the agreement of two years previously, since it confirms the supremacy of the Confederation of Industry for employers and of the Confederation of Corporations for labor, it marked a considerable gain for Rossoni. The provisions against factory commissions were in his favor; for though these commissions were a hang-over from the factory occupation movement of 1920 and were supposed to defend labor interests, they had really become pliant instruments in the hands of the employers, especially now that the fascist regime had undermined the old labor organizations with whom the commissions had been affiliated. In their place came the collective contracts negotiated by the national rival confederations and such contracts were not only compulsory but were given legal recognition.

The recognition of collective contracts furthermore marked the beginning of the breakdown of individualism, for it was but a small step from the regulation of labor conditions by the national syndicate confederations of the fascist party, to an outright government control. It was in this spirit that Rossoni accepted the Pact of the Vidoni Palace. For him it was not a settlement, but like the earlier pact one more step in his fight for a corporate state.

Meanwhile the Commission's Report had been taken up by the Grand Council of the Fascist Party and the draft of a bill was sent to the Committee of the Chamber of Deputies which submitted it to Parliament. It is commonly believed that the Commission's Constitutional Reform was in general adopted by Parliament, and certainly Rossoni did not hesitate to claim a victory for fascist labor organizations. But a closer examination of the law which Parliament passed soon reveals that the victory was equivocal.

This law, in view of the developments which grew out of it, has become almost equivalent to a new constitution for the fascist state, though in itself it seems to be little more than the legal recognition of syndicates, a reform which had been carried long ago in other states. It is known as "The Law of April 3, 1926, n. 563, entitled The Legal Discipline of Collective Labor Relations." It consists of twenty-three Articles divided into three Parts. In the first part the fascist syndicates and confederations and their collective contracts are legally recognized; in the second, compulsory labor tribunals are established; and in the third, strikes and lockouts are prohibited. Without attempting to summarize the various provisions we must record the developments which took place during the discussion of critical articles.

a. *Fascist syndicates embodied in the state*

According to Article I, no syndicate can be recognized which does not include at least ten per cent of the members of its category or occupation. The low figure of ten per cent was necessary, not in order to favor fascist organizations in preference to opposition organizations (as the opposition charged), but rather in order to include those provinces, especially in the south, in which *any* labor organization still includes but a small percentage of the workers.

Anti-fascist organizations can easily be excluded under the formula: "the directors must give proof of capacity, morality and unswerving national loyalty." The Reform Commission's formula on this head was more generous, requiring merely that the syndicate must not be contrary to "the general interests, in respect of moral and economic ends." It was of course a foregone conclusion that only fascist organizations would receive recognition, but the *theory* is that hereafter the syndicates must not be the recognized agents of any political party whatsoever.

b. *The end of the Third Order*

Article II authorizes the legal recognition of middle-class syndicates. The Reform Commission had expressly excluded associations of the professional classes, since they were governed by existing laws. It had erected them into one of the three "orders" of the state. But there were also traditional reasons for not recognizing such associations; first, it would raise the whole question of church orders in the state, and secondly, traditional syndicalism had fought shy of "middle-class" syndicates. In the meantime, however, Rossoni had discovered that the "intellectuals" were his allies, and accordingly it was announced that the fascist regime is anxious to organize the professions along with other "producers." More recently, as we shall see, Rossoni succeeded in bringing the "Intellectual Corporations" definitely under his sway.

c. *The end of mixed syndicates*

Article III of the original bill read: "The associations mentioned in the preceding articles may comprise employers alone, or employees alone, or employers and employees together.

"Mixed associations of employers and employees must have special and separate organs for the representation of employers and of employees and, if they comprise several categories of employees, for that of each of these categories; and also common organs for the whole association."

The parliamentary committee amended it by recognizing no mixed syndicates at all and by striking out the second paragraph completely, giving as its reason: "Mixed associations are in practice nothing but coördinating and conciliating bodies, and these can continue to develop their lines of activity very well without legal recognition."

The opposition to the mixed syndicates came both from the employers, as we have seen above, and also from international labor bodies at Geneva, who made trouble for the fascist representatives, because their syndicates contained employers. On this subject Minister Rocco, in introducing the amended bill to the Senate, said: "This does not imply, and I wish to say this explicitly, the exclusion of mixed syndicates. The silence of the law does not mean their prohibition, but merely confirms the present facts, for this type of syndicate is not yet known at present. I know very well that there are prejudices of an international kind against mixed syndicates, but we can not always give such prejudices a favorable hearing. International legislation is dominated by the principles of class struggle, which we are happy to have overcome in Italy. Personally I admit that I am very sympathetically inclined toward mixed syndicates. I believe that they contain no dangers whatever and that they offer many advantages; above all, psychological advantages, notably the possibility of making evident the intimate solidarity by which all the factors of production are bound together.

For we must make everyone understand, industrialists as well as workers, that there is an absolute solidarity between the various factors of that most important of all the aspects of economic life, production." Accordingly Rocco supported Rossoni, who, not willing to see integralism sacrificed entirely, offered an amendment which was carried and which constitutes the second paragraph of Article II. It substituted for mixed syndicates, in seemingly innocent terms, the mixed " central coördinating bodies " which in ordinary syndicalist terminology were known as corporations. In fact this vague little paragraph and a similar one in Article X, slipped in by Rossoni when nobody was looking, later became the chief legal basis for the erection of " the corporate state," as we shall see later. But that at this time there was no clear idea of what these central organs were to be like, is revealed by the questions which Parliament raised: " How will these central bodies of coördination arise? How are they organized? How do they work? " To these questions only the vaguest answers were given and Minister Rocco even suggested: " The members of syndicates who will have the direction of the economic life of the country and will regulate the relations between classes, must constitute an *élite* body of men of capacity and of conviction. When the day comes when all employers and all Italian workmen will have this capacity, this consciousness of the goal to be reached, then and then alone, syndicates will automatically become corporations."

d. *Finances*

In the matter of financing the syndicates, the original draft had attempted to establish a fixed and uniform sum of fees, but the Committee of the Chamber of Deputies changed it to one day's wages, and in the case of employers' associations, one day's wages for each employee employed by each employer. But this was difficult to apply in many cases and regulations adopted by the Grand Council of January 3, 1927, in general used the average wage of the category or occupation as a basis for fixed fees, and established rates well under the maximum allowed by the law. It was also expressly stated that though these fees resembled general taxes, they can be used only for the work of the syndicates and corporations.

e. *Syndical monopoly*

The law recognizes only a single syndicate for any one category. This represents a compromise on a much debated issue. One extreme was represented by the Reform Commission under liberalistic influence which wanted to recognize as many actual syndicates as were able to meet the " moral and economic " qualifications. The other extreme was represented by Sorelian syndicalists, who had reacted strongly in the direction of nationalism (Panunzio, for example), and who wanted compulsory membership of every employer or worker in a single syndicate which thus enjoyed a monopoly for its particular category, prohibiting all others. In the present law the one legally recognized syndicate has theoretically no monopoly since independent syndicates are permitted and no one is forced to join; but practically, since everyone is taxed for the support of the legally recognized syndicate, which is given complete authority to make contracts for both members and non-members, there is every inducement to join and only extreme political hostility could prevent a complete monopoly.

In defending this provision before the Senate Rocco said: "The unlimited liberty of establishing in a single profession an indefinite number of syndical organizations having divergent or antagonistic tendencies is incompatible with the concept of the unity of interest in the profession. With unlimited syndical liberty a syndicate is a weapon of war, not an instrument of social peace. One syndicate competes with another at the expense of the workers collectively. And since there is no public authority to determine which syndicate really represents the workers, the victory goes to the strongest. Especially in our country, as was observed during the discussion in the Chamber of Deputies, the liberty of syndicates led to a multiplication of workers' organizations. Political parties divided the workers into so many groups that they were placed in a very disadvantageous position when they had to face their employers who never had more than one organization. In fact the interests of a single category of workers or of a single profession can not be adequately defended except by a single organization, and the unitary principle of syndicate organization is a logical presupposition of the practical utility of collective labor contracts as well as of the beneficent operation of the labor tribunals." And Senator Schanzer in his report to the Senate said: "It is important above all else that we get rid of the idea that these organizations of the social order should be instruments of political strife and a means whereby politicians and political groups are enabled to put themselves in power. The syndicate recognized by public law is by itself a non-political organ. The men who direct it may have their political opinions, but the syndicate as such has no political function. In short, we must finally establish the separation of syndicalism and politics."

f. *Confederations*

The next issue to be debated was the matter of confederations. The mere mention of only three or four great national confederations, which were reminiscent of the "three orders" of the Reform Commission as well as of Rossoni's corporations, immediately brought down a storm of protest from the existing national confederations. The Maritime Federation, under Giulietti, at the time was still d'Annunzian and has only quite recently been incorporated in the fascist confederation. It refused flatly to renounce its independence. The Federation of Transportation, the Association of Italian Banks, the Confederation of Landed Proprietors, and other powerful organizations feared they were to be wiped out entirely or at least subordinated to the great Confederation of Industry, and accordingly sent in memorials, and proposed amendments guaranteeing their independence. Minister Rocco admitted that the aim was to unify the national organization as much as possible; but agreed that exceptions might be made in certain cases. In any case, he said, the law does not specify and the matter is to be left to the discretion of the government. As we shall see when we examine the "Rules and Regulations," the government decided to yield to the existing confederations.

g. *Liberty and authority*

The president or secretary of any association may be nominated or elected, according to the constitution of the association. But these officers must have the approval of the Ministry of the Interior, which approval may be revoked at any time. The original draft added the approval of the Prefect, but the Committee cut this out on the ground that the syndicates must be safeguarded from local politics. By the Grand Council of June 1926 government intervention was further limited. Minister Rocco explained: "This rigorous control does not infringe on the autonomy of the syndicate nor on the free development of its internal and external activities. In fact, the rules which govern the internal life and external activities of a syndicate are given it by its own constitution, which every association must have and which, though it must be approved by Royal Decree . . . , is framed by the association itself and by it the life of the syndicate is, within the limits of the law, freely regulated." Or, as Senator Schanzer more succinctly said: "They are free to submit themselves to the approval of the competent authority!"

h. *Collective labor contracts*

The Reform Commission had said very little about labor contracts, merely suggesting that contracts entered into by legally recognized syndicates should be enforced by law.

But in the meantime Rossoni's Confederation had been actively engaged in building up a network of collective labor contracts. In fact it was precisely his success in making these contracts which gave his organization its practical power and its hold on the laboring classes. Though private contracts are still being made, the collective contracts are rapidly supplanting them. The system had already been officially recognized by the Pact of the Vidoni Palace at Rome, October 2, 1925, which we discussed above. Now it is given increased scope and authority, and the funds established by Article V guarantee the legal enforcement of the contracts.

The contracts are now really more than contracts, for though they have a private origin they become public norms and are enforced like laws by the labor tribunals. To quote Senator Schanzer: "The fact that the collective contracts are obligatory *erga omnes,* that is, even over those who took no part in the negotiations, as are also obligatory the general regulations for labor and labor conditions, laid down by the central organs of coördination between syndicates, confers on such collective contracts and on such general norms a character which transcends the law of contract and places them on the plane of a special public law. They have an intermediate position between simple contracts and administrative regulations, which fact explains the special forms of publicity required of them."

To the objection raised in the Chamber of Deputies that these contracts would attempt to establish an artificial standardization of working conditions, Belloni replied: " It is always possible in a collective agreement to take account of particular rules and conditions for particular sub-classes of production or for individual firms, as has already been done during the last few years."

By means of the collective contracts Rossoni hopes to realize the " capitalization of labor " which is one of his favorite ideas. By this formula he means a definite system of profit-sharing, which is to be embodied in the new contracts. The dividends and profits which capital is supposed to earn must be calculated, according to him, by adding the labor force to the capital in order to determine the amount invested. Each laborer as well as each dollar is a unit of investment, and this fact must be recognized in the new collective contracts, he says. But this has remained mere theory, though there is a vague reference to it in the Labor Charter.

i. *Public employees excluded*

The original draft recognized certain associations of state employees, but curtailed their rights to such an extent that the Committee thought it simpler not to recognize them at all. Hence the law permits, but does not legalize associations of public employees; except associations of soldiers, police, government officers and professors, which are expressly prohibited.

The practical reasons for this article will be obvious enough to the reader. The theory, however, is a little subtle. Minister Rocco explained to the Chamber of Deputies: "The relations between public political agencies and their employees are by their very nature such that they do not admit of legally recognized syndicate organization, for it is inconceivable that the laws should recognize organs of defense for any categories or classes by whom they would be directed against bodies which represent the general interest. These bodies already have obligations toward their dependents which exclude them from the realm of private contracts. To treat their dependents justly is already an obligation of the state and other public bodies, which they must keep because of their inherently ethical nature."

Associations of professors were put on the prohibited list after the following speech by Mussolini in the Chamber of Deputies:

"Syndicate associations (of state employees) are not recognized by law but they may exist in fact; on the other hand, such associations are expressly forbidden for officials, sub-officials, etc. I believe this list is not complete; I believe we should distinguish among dependents of the state between those who perform their work in an office and those who perform a service, those who fulfil merely economic functions and those who fulfil functions not of an economic nature. . . .

"There are other dependents of the state whose associations should be prohibited. The lists are being completed, and I might as well say it now, they will include professors in intermediate and higher institutions of learning. . . . Let us say it clear and loud! The professor fulfils a function in national life much more delicate than that performed by the official of a public service or by the magistrate. The professor, who molds minds and consciences, and can make of men either heroes or cowards, has an extremely important function in the life of the nation. Hence he must be an atom, not a group or association, in the state."

The following associations of state employees have already been "authorized": railroad workers, postal-telegraph, letter carriers and rural postal agents, state telephones, primary schools, tax collectors, and the General Fascist Association of Public Employees.

j. Labor tribunals

The proposal of a system of labor tribunals, which is established in Part II of this law, did not come from the Reform Commission.

had contented itself with giving the proposed Provincial Chambers certain arbitral powers, analogous to and in fact continuing the functions of the *Collegi dei probiviri;* but it had not intended to throw the whole matter of labor regulation into the courts. This idea came from certain syndicalist quarters, notably from Sergio Panunzio, whose theory of the state is constructed around it. He urged a system of " economic magistrates " similar to the one embodied here. It received the approval of Rossoni's organization and of Mussolini and in this way came to be embodied in the present law.

This provision, as may be imagined from what has been said above, caused a dispute, which brings into relief some of the most serious conflicts of interests and views, which the new legislation had to face. It was hailed by its sponsors as the most revolutionary of all, accomplishing in the field of labor legislation, by putting an end to " the auto-defense of classes," what was accomplished in the field of private law by substituting court procedure for duels or feuds. But the *industrialists* objected. I give the story at length.

Article XIII as first drafted and submitted to the Chamber of Deputies contained the following additional paragraphs:

" The jurisdiction of the Court of Appeals acting as a labor tribunal is obligatory for all controversies relative to the application of contracts or other existing regulations.

" It is also obligatory for all controversies relative to the determination of new labor conditions, when these involve controversies between agricultural employers and employees or between agencies of public services or necessities and their employees.

" When they involve controversies relative to the determination of new labor conditions arising between other categories of employers and employees, the jurisdiction of the Court of Appeals is optional, and in order to establish it the consent of both parties is necessary, but once established it becomes obligatory, as in the previous cases."

In defending this, Rocco said: " It would certainly have been desirable to have made the jurisdiction of the Court of Appeals acting as a labor tribunal absolute, that is to say, that the parties should have been forced to submit to it, so that simply the judicial decision would have constituted a legal judgment as is the case in all civil judgments. However, it was impossible to attain this goal at once. Even stronger than the opposition of genuine interests is that of prejudices and old mental habits, which give rise to fears that the decision of the judge would be disregarded by those employers who may be angered to the point of rebellion, especially those whose work is least appreciated by the populace at large, as for instance the employers of industrial labor.

It is feared that at present, during a period in the life of industry which is still critical, it would be unwise offhand to entrust the terms of labor contracts to a judge. Perhaps this diffidence has been increased by the influence of theoretical preconceptions based on the doctrines of economic liberalism.

"We realize perfectly that the structure of this law departs from the principles of liberalistic economics. But the failure of the liberal economy in this field has been demonstrated so clearly by the facts, that I need not dwell on it. The failure has been total and irremediable, for even while the Liberal regime still flourished, labor conditions were no longer determined by the law of supply and demand, but by the political strength of the organizations. In practice, the law of supply and demand has ceased to operate; in its place there ruled only the will of the stronger. It is undeniable that the necessary equilibrium of economic life can be established much better by the intervention of an impartial judge. All the more since, given a brake on the exercise of private force, the free play of supply and demand can automatically be resumed and in normal cases will reach solutions without hindrance, which cases will furnish the labor tribunals with a sound basis for their decisions. Nor is this the first time in our legislation that the magistrate is asked to determine just prices, or in general to establish the manner in which private employment is to be regulated. . . . The truth is that the magistrate must continually regulate legal relations by his prudent judgment, for the laws can not foresee the particular cases and usually merely give the general lines and principles for the solution of controversies and in most judgments it is the magistrate who creates special norms valid for concrete cases. Experience teaches that the magistrate performs this task excellently, however diversified and difficult it may be, both from a technical point of view and from the point of view of the material submitted to him. . . . In spite of this fact, however, we have been willing to indulge these prejudices, being assured that the experiment of labor jurisdiction which is about to be made will win out by the eloquent testimony of facts."

Belloni, in his report of the House Committee, emphasized the difference between judicial decision involving merely the application of old contracts, and judicial participation in the framing of new ones. The former could be carried on on a legal basis, but the latter entered the field of political and economic administration, in which cases the judge has no law to guide him, but must weigh interests and policies. Then he continued:

"The Minister's speech in which he expounded the design of the law, amply explained the motives which induced the government to take the course it did, in spite of many reasons which militated in favor of an obligatory jurisdiction of the tribunals in all cases. Now we think that the government did very well to adopt the path it did; and this, to be sure, not for the reasons on which the Liberal school bases its objections to the right of state intervention in the economic conflicts between capital and labor, but because the conditions under which industry and commerce are carried on make it very difficult for a judge to fix the norms which ought to govern labor relations with that assurance so essential to a judge, that by his decision he is not doing injustice to one or both parties. These difficulties are of an entirely different order in agriculture and in industry; in the latter the ordering and organization of production and labor are subject to much more complex and delicate rules than in agriculture, and in addition the consequences of an interruption of labor in industry can be offset in whole or in part by a more intensive activity afterward, while the consequences of an interruption of labor in agriculture at certain times of the year may be irreparable and endanger the supply of produce necessary to support the population. Imagine, for example, a strike at harvest time; imagine a strike, one which actually occurred during the times immediately preceding the rise of fascism, of the laborers in charge of cattle and other domestic animals, and you will understand immediately why the state can not afford to remain inactive and indifferent in the face of such collective disputes. Moreover, whereas industrial activity is not limited, at least not up to a certain point, and if one factory closes, the loss can be, and certainly will be, promptly supplied by the greater productivity of other existing firms, or by the founding of new ones, agricultural activity is limited in space and hence the collective whole can not tolerate that a greater or smaller area of soil, the precious gift of nature, be withdrawn from cultivation.

"Hence this great branch of national production, agriculture, is hastening in many ways toward that grand realization of the fascist idea of the state, toward that new political atmosphere which we long for, for that sense of discipline and of order which at last has penetrated the minds of all citizens, especially of the producing classes, thus permitting it to evolve the most favorable conditions and to attain those ends of complete pacification and of social well being which it pursues."

Farinacci made much the same point in his speech, emphasizing agriculture's peculiarly critical position in Italian economy. Hereupon Barbiellini-Amidei, in behalf of the agriculturalists, presented a motion censuring the attitude of the industrialists; and when Benni tried to defend them the syndicalists as well as the agrarians opposed him. At this point Mussolini himself took the floor and said:

" . . . This truly basic law considers two economies, industrial economy and agricultural. . . . I believe a law so constructed remains a mutilated law. I believe that either we are taking a step forward in industrial economy or a step backwards in rural. In short, either option or compulsion for both. For I do not believe that there is a clear separation between the two economies, if it is true as it is that agriculture is being industrialized and if it is true that from the products of the land come the raw materials of several of the greatest industries of our country: the textile and chemical industries. . . .

" I believe we must rather arrive at a unitary conception of material economy. To be sure the grain which is left, or was left standing in the fields, is a net loss, but at times a strike which interrupts production at a critical moment when international competition is unbridled may have even more serious consequences. We need the courage to go ahead in this field as well, a field which is supposed to be unexplored and full of the unforeseen. There are no lions, and in any case the lions are would-be wild beasts! . . .

" Those who hesitate should also consider that in discussing this provision they must take the regime and the government into account. The corporations are fascist in as much as they want to bear the name of fascist corporations and to carry on their work under the shadow of the lictor's rods. They must control their actions and not do anything which may diminish the productive efficiency of the nation or create difficulties for the government.

" Hence besides the work of control which the fascist corporations are themselves conducting, there is the sovereign control of the government. What has taken place during these three years of syndicalist practice? I am not the secretary of the corporations; but there has not been a single great question in industry or commerce involving the syndicates — when the law for private employment was being discussed; when the contract of the seamen was being discussed — I say, there has not been a single question of great importance to the syndicates which I have not examined and sometimes solved.

" This being the case, I believe the Confederation of Industry can take a step forward and will do so, for I also believe firmly that the advantages will far outweigh the inconveniences.

" Honorable colleagues, before closing I wish to give you the reason why I have arrived at this conclusion. I have arrived at this conclusion from a point of departure which is fundamental to my understanding of the Italian situation whenever I examine it. I consider the Italian nation to be in a permanent state of war. I have already said and I repeat that the next five or ten years are decisive for the destiny of our people. They are decisive because the international struggle has widened and will widen still more and we who have come on the stage of the world a little behind time, can not afford to waste our energies."

Hereupon Antonio S. Benni, President of the Confederation of Industry, arose and after giving his reasons for opposing compulsory labor tribunals in industry, said: "As a well disciplined Italian citizen I accept the way which the head of the government points out to me and shall follow it with all the enthusiasm in my power, and with that discipline which the Italian industrial class has always professed towards the government and towards fascism." Whereupon Belloni in behalf of the Parliamentary Committee also expressed his approval of the amendment proposed by Mussolini.

k. *The end of strikes and lockouts*

The prohibition of strikes and lockouts (Article XVIII) also goes much further than the proposals of the Reform Commission; as Rocco explained, it extends the fundamental concept of the prohibition of " auto-defense " to economic groups and issues, a step made possible by the institution of an omnicompetent labor tribunal. The discussion in both Houses made it evident that the government intended to give his the broadest interpretation, practically forbidding any strikes or lockouts whatsoever, certainly those of a political nature.

On the other hand, the first important interpretive decision handed down by the Court of Appeals of Rome, made it clear that the courts would not use the law as a pretext to infringe on the legitimate freedom of individual workers, or small groups. The judgment was in favor of the defendants, a few workmen of Tivoli who near the end of the day had refused to make another trip with their grain carts, when they saw that it would have made them work overtime.[28]

Some doubts were expressed on the ability of the government to enforce the law against huge bodies of strikers. The difficulty was admitted for extreme cases, but it was pointed out that the growing syndicate organization and growing public opinion in favor of the law made enforcement easier. In the case of employers who might close their factories and profit more than their fines cost them, it was maintained that such tactics could be severely punished on the basis of other laws. Also was thought quite possible to force a factory owner to keep his factory open unless the court had made bad blunders in its calculations and had sanctioned conditions which made profits impossible, in which case the judgment of the court could be reviewed.

[28] v. *Lo Stato Corporativo*, February 1927, pp. 9–11.

Strikers among employees of the state or in public service are punished more severely. State employees or those in public services are punished severely if they fail to do all in their power to secure the continual operation of their services during any strike or lockout. Strikes or lockouts having political motives are severely punished. Heavy penalties are imposed on those who fail to abide by a sentence of a labor tribunal.

V. The Corporate State

The twenty-three articles of this Law, which constitutes the economic framework for the new Italian State, really settled less than they started. The need for " interpretation " and detailed regulations had already been expressed. And both sides were decidedly nervous. Many employers refused to have anything to do with the " collective contracts " and had to be threatened into submission by the ever handy fascist officials. The independent and powerful employers' confederations were nervous because of the rumors of consolidation. Neither side was any too confident of the labor tribunals, the employers because they had been forced to yield to political pressure, and to political jurisdiction; the labor leaders because they had preferred to trust their " mixed " syndicates and corporations rather than the courts as the organs of " economic solidarity." Mixed syndicates, however, had been doomed and their surreptitious substitutes, the " central coördinating bodies," were mysterious entities, a vague hope for the integralist labor leaders and a disquieting remnant of sentimentality in the eyes of the supposedly more hard-headed business men.

But there were even more general issues in the air. The law which we have been discussing had embodied but the first part of the Report of the Reform Commission, a part which in the eyes of the reformers was but a preliminary step toward the " corporate organization of the state, and ineffective unless linked to it. As it now stood, it was apparently independent and had passed Parliament, at least in the eyes of the majority, as little more than a thoroughgoing piece of labor organization any question of constitutional reform having been carefully excluded. On the other hand, responsible fascist politicians and publicists began to proclaim the law as revolutionary, the realization of the new fascist state, and the corporate organization of society. Was this to be taken as prophecy or merely as normal newspaper lunacy?

Under these circumstances Rocco and his colleagues set out to draft " rules and regulations," and finally having secured the approval of the Cabinet, presented them to the Grand Council of the Party in June. Rocco, it turned out, had been reconstructing his social philosophy a bit and had arrived at the following already famous formula: "The new organization of labor . . . is developing in a twofold direction: one vertical and the other horizontal. The vertical organization is being realized outside the state but under the control of the state, and comprises syndicates of a single category or trade grouped into superior organizations, federations or confederations. The horizontal organization is being realized within the state, and comprises all the factors of production for each branch of industry. Thus the corporation is being organized within the state, including employers, workers and artisans."

Accordingly his draft proposed:

(1) Three great national "unions," one for employers, one for workers and one for artisans and the professional classes.

(2) Fifteen national confederations: six of employers (in industry, commerce, agriculture, maritime and air transportation, land transportation and inland navigation, banks); six of workers (classified identically); and three of the "middle classes" (one for artisans, one for professional men and one for artists).

(3) A Ministry of Corporations to unite these confederations horizontally into the "central coördinating bodies."

After several nights of lively discussion (the Grand Council does only night work!) the following changes were made in this scheme:

(1) The three unions, obviously reminiscent of the three orders proposed by the Reform Commission, were replaced by two "General Confederations which *may* be recognized."

But the employers, having been delighted with the recognition of the existing plurality of Employers' Confederations, saw no need for a further "union," since each was jealous of its independence and was run by a different group of men. But Rossoni and the labor leaders were equally anxious that their single, powerful organization should in no way lose its unity. Hence, of the two General Confederations which the decree *allows*, the "National Confederation of Fascist Syndicates" was immediately formed; that is to say, Rossoni's organization took the word "corporation" out of its name; while the employers took no notice, nor have they to this day, of their permission to form a single confederation. However, the Confederation of Industry is the natural leader of the group in most labor disputes and in dealings with the government.

The third proposed union or order was now parcelled out among these two, the federation of artisans being subordinated to the Confederation of Industry, and the professional men and artists being combined and placed under the Confederation of Fascist Syndicates. This was the work of Rossoni, who had already gotten control of several organizations of intellectuals and who proceeded as follows. It "happened" that just as the Grand Council was deliberating these matters, a national convention of intellectuals had been called at Rome. At this convention Rossoni had made himself prominent, had emphasized the solidarity between " manual and intellectual workers," and had made it evident to the public and to the Grand Council that the convention was favorable to his organization. Having induced the Grand Council to take this step, he created the Federation of Intellectuals. In this way the professional classes passed bodily into the hands of the Rossoni group, and the " third order " or " middle class " which had played an important rôle in the plans and theories of the Reform Commission, passed out of existence.

(2) The fifteen confederations were thus reduced to thirteen, organized as follows:

A. Employers' Organizations.

 1. National Fascist Confederation of Industry.
 2. National Fascist Confederation of Agriculturalists.
 3. National Fascist Confederation of Merchants.
 4. National Fascist Confederation of Maritime and Aerial Transportation.
 5. National Fascist Confederation of Land Transportation and Inland Navigation.
 6. National Fascist Confederation of Bankers.

B. Labor: The National Confederation of Fascist Syndicates, composed of:

 7. National Federation of Fascist Syndicates in Industry.
 8. National Federation of Fascist Syndicates in Agriculture.
 9. National Federation of Fascist Syndicates in Commerce.
 10. National Federation of Fascist Syndicates in Maritime and Aerial Transportation.
 11. National Federation of Fascist Syndicates in Land Transportation and Inland Navigation.
 12. National Federation of Fascist Syndicates in Banks.
 13. National Federation of Fascist Syndicates of Intellectuals.

One of the most serious disputes concerned lesser federations, but really underlay the issues we have just discussed. Rocco's draft (Article 5), following recommendations made by Senator Schanzer and the Senate Committee,[29] had provided that artisans, small shopkeepers and tradesmen, owners or tenants of small farms which they cultivate them

[29] cf. Also Rocco's remarks on this subject before the Senate.

selves, as well as share holding tenant farmers (*mezzadri, mètayers*) should be organized under employers' organizations, if they employ manual labor and should constitute independent associations if their establishments are exclusively domestic. This was the result of a memorial sent in by the landed proprietors asking for a separate organization. To this Rossoni objected strenuously, not only because it would have broken up many of his rural syndicates and their contracts and thrown small tenant farmers, whose interests are usually those of labor, into the hands of the big agriculturalists, but also because it " split the unity of categories," which was the basis of the whole syndical organization. Finally Mussolini personally worked out a compromise, whereby all artisans, small tradesmen, etc., were to form their own federations subordinated to the employers' Confederation of Industry and all shareholders (*mètayers*) were to be organized into federations subordinate to the labor confederation of agricultural syndicates. When the artisans submitted their constitution for approval, their organization was called the *Ente Nazionale Artigiani* (National Association of Artisans) and it was to all intents and purposes an independent body. But in 1927 its head, Brunati, resigned and it was reorganized as the *Federazione Fascista Autonoma delle Communità Artigiane d'Italia.* This brings it a step nearer to the confederations to which it will no doubt ultimately be subordinated.

(3) The organization of the Corporations and the Ministry of Corporations remains as in the Rocco draft, except that because of the changes just described, the corporate or horizontal organization is confronted by only two great vertical organizations, corresponding roughly to capital and labor, instead of the three of the original draft, in which the " middle class " or " intellectuals " were supposed to form a sort of social balance of power. All that remains of the proposed third order is a number of independent organizations of various kinds which for one reason or another could not be embodied in the double hierarchy scheme, e.g. The Coöperatives, The *Dopo-Lavoro,* the Artisans, etc. These hitherto independent organizations are not being subjected to political pressure, their old directors are being forced out and they are being given " temporary " organizations which look forward to their being definitely incorporated into the hierarchy of fascist syndicates as soon as possible.

As it is, therefore, the government in the form of the Ministry of Corporations, is supposed to synthesize in peaceful coöperative production, two traditional enemies to whom it has given new and powerful weapons and whom it has arrayed more definitely than ever on opposed fronts. The organization of this " horizontal " order is therefore extremely important. To it is devoted one of the eight main divisions of the "Rules and Regulations," which I outline as follows. (Only words in quotation marks are the words of the decree itself.)

Part III. *"Of the Central Organs of Coördination or Corporations"*

Article 42

" The organs of coördination suggested by Article 3 of the Law of April 3, 1926, have a national character. They unite the national syndical organizations of the various factors of production, employers and workers (intellectual and manual) in any given branch of production, or for one or more given categories of industry or trade."

" The organizations thus coördinated constitute a corporation."

" A corporation is constituted by decree of the Minister of Corporations."

Article 43

" A corporation does not possess legal personality, but constitutes an administrative organ of the state."

" The decree which constitutes a corporation also determines its functions and powers. By the same decree its organization is established and the duties and powers of its central and local officials are regulated."

Article 44

" These corporative organs in order that they may serve their purpose have among others the following functions:

" (a) to conciliate the controversies which may arise between the organizations coördinated and to draw up the norms suggested in Article 10 of the Law of April 3, 1926;

" (b) to promote, encourage and sustain all measures intended to coordinate production and improve its organization;

" (c) to establish employment agencies wherever their need is evident; where such offices may be established, a royal decree may prohibit independent mediation and the operation of other employment agencies; . . .

" (d) to regulate training and apprenticeship, drawing up the general norms necessary to this end and to see that they are enforced. Such norms are to be applied to all collective labor contracts."

Article 45

In the making of collective contracts the coördinated organizations are to remain autonomous, except in cases where efforts at conciliation by the corporation are prescribed by the law.

Article 46

" The presidents of the corporate bodies are nominated and recalled by decree of the Minister of Corporations. Every corporation has a council composed of the delegates of the organizations which are co-ordinated by it. In the Council the representation of organizations of employers must equal that of the employees (intellectual and manual taken together)."

" The manner of nomination of such delegates, the functions of the Council and the powers of the president are established by the decree which constitutes the corporate body."

" In any case this must be made to depend directly on the Minister of Corporations."

The decree embodying these rules and regulations (103 Articles) was signed July 1, 1926. The following day another decree created the Ministry of Corporations. Mussolini, in line with his general policy, made himself Minister of Corporations and made Suardo (his right-hand man) Undersecretary. This immediately gave " corporationism " immense popularity and prestige. However Mussolini had already told the Grand Council in very strong language, that he would not stand for an elaborate bureaucracy of politicians in the Ministry, that he proposed to establish corporations only where there was a definite call for them, and that he would put them under the direction of a few competent men, actively engaged in the business which was being corporated.

In November, when other troubles broke over Mussolini's head, he and Suardo were forced to shift their attentions to the department of the interior. He appointed as Undersecretary of Corporations, Giuseppe Bottai, director of the *Critica Fascista,* and formerly one of the leaders of the Fascist Coöperatives, which were closely allied with the syndicalist movement. This brought the Ministry of Corporations much closer in touch with active syndicalists. For Mussolini and Suardo never were syndicalists and though favorable to these developments they really represent a middle ground in the Party and in the government, trying to keep the syndicalistic, the liberalistic, and the nationalistic wings of fascism in a state of equilibrium.

The Ministry of Corporations was immediately given important work to do, such as bringing capital and labor together on specific problems, framing the new Charter of Labor, working out the details of the system of syndicate fees, the examination and registration of the constitutions of new syndicates and confederations, etc., but this work, of course, did not require explicit corporations, as Rossoni wanted them.

A decree of March 17, 1927, definitely established the nature of the corporations. There are to be seven of them, corresponding to the kinds of confederations. The presidency of each corporation is to be assigned to some citizen who has distinguished himself " in production, labor, or in the direction of public offices." He is to serve without salary, but is to be granted fees for specific services. In the various provinces the local functions of the Ministry of Corporations are to be assigned to some official of the prefecture or of the Ministry of National Economy. This means, in short, that the corporations are to have a very limited budget and little independent personnel. The work will be done directly by the Ministry of Corporations and hence these largely nominal bodies will be not merely " organs of the state," as the theory demands, but really mere additional powers for present politicians.

As a result, *not a single corporation has been formally created.* There is some truth in the claim that if the government now tried to form a corporation it would face serious difficulties, since both syndical groups are jealous of each other's power and afraid that a " coördinating body " might upset the present equilibrium. But there is still more truth in the fact that this sort of corporation, except in extreme crises, is at present superfluous; for the negotiating of labor contracts, conciliation by the labor tribunals, and in general all business which arises between the syndicates, can be carried on effectively and directly, without the intervention of the corporation. The corporation thus represents little more than a continual threat which the government can use against refractory confederations. At best it is a name for the implicit coöperation of th various classes in production, which, the more habitual and spontaneou it becomes, the more it automatically transforms Italy into a " corpor ate state." In a sense, almost anything the Minister of Corporation does may be called an act of the corporate state. For instance, ever now and then he calls together the secretaries of the Party, of the Con federations of Industry, and of the Confederation of Syndicates, t examine some problem, *e.g.* industrial policy, wage policy, or high co of living. Such meetings really perform the function of corporation But the corporations have more than a nominal value; their psych logical value is very important. At last the ideal of Rocco, Rossoni a the " integralists " has an official sanction and a legal basis, howev much its practical embodiment may have changed. In fact, the corpo ationists were so encouraged by these developments and their activiti so stimulated that the situation has already been carried beyond t bounds foreseen by either the Law of April 3 or the Decree of July 1.

For in the meantime Rossoni too was working. In Article 10 of t Law of April 3, he had inserted the provision that the corporations " central organs of coördination " establish general principles for lal and labor contracts. These general norms for labor contracts which the decree had entrusted to the corporations now became his own active concern. Not waiting for corporations to do the work, he proceeded to draft the general principles on which future labor legislation was to be based as well as to codify the chief provisions which he was already embodying in current collective contracts. This was to serve as the basis for the government's Labor Charter (*carta di lavoro*), a document widely heralded as a new *magna charta* for labor, a substitute for the "Rights of Man," a genuine "Social Contract" to replace the fictitious one of the French Revolution, and in general as an explicit statement of the constitutional principles of the corporate state.

Rossoni wanted it to be sufficiently detailed in its enumeration of the legal rights of labor to serve as a basis for the decisions of the Labor Tribunals. Hence his draft, published in the *Lavoro d'Italia* and in the *Stirpe* of January 1927, enumerated regulations to govern labor conditions under the following fifteen heads:

(1) Employment and employment bureaus: The offices of the National Confederation of Fascist Syndicates are to keep employment records and statistics and to act as information bureaus and employment bureaus, and all requests for help or for employment are to go to these bureaus.

(2) Discipline: The duties devolving on employers and on employees are to be defined, and penalties fixed for violations.

(3) Hours of work: The eight-hour day is recognized and all departures from it in exceptional cases are subject to detailed regulation.

(4) Trial periods: New employees are to be put on trial for a definite term, under fixed regulations, after which term the employer is not free to discharge at will.

(5) Classification of personnel and minimum wages for each class of workers.

(6) Periodical revision and increase of pay.

(7) Piecework or on contract: Regulations to prevent rates lower than the standard hourly wage.

(8) Vacations: At least one week's vacation for every person employed a year or longer.

(9) Sickness: Provisions for medical care, etc.

(10) Insurance and Benefits.

(11) Military service: Persons called into military service are to be given preference over all other applicants on their return from duty.

(12) Discharge of employees: After the period of trial no employee may be discharged without a fixed indemnity except for disciplinary reasons.

(13) Indemnities for discharged employees, and pensions for dependents in case of death.

(14) Employees' protection in case of closure or change of proprietors.

(15) Labor disputes and contracts must be put in the hands of the syndicates recognized by law for the categories involved.

This draft is evidently a *labor* document, intended as a defense of labor interests and as a legal fortification of the policies of the syndicates. It was presented to the January session of the Grand Council and Rossoni expected it to pass without serious modification. But he was to be disappointed. The Grand Council announced four main heads for the Charter, which, though they corresponded in general to the Rossoni draft, at least indicated that a rearrangement was under way. These heads were: (1) declarations of solidarity between the various factors of production in the supreme interest of the nation; (2) organic coördination of the laws for the insurance and assistance of workers; (3) coordination and formulation of the laws protecting labor; (4) general rules for the conditions governing labor contracts. The actual codification and formulation of labor law seems to have been intended by these resolutions as it was by Rossoni. But shortly after, at the meeting of the heads of the confederations of capital and labor called by the Minister of Corporations to draft the Charter, Bottai emphasized in his opening address that they must guard against the temptation to legislate in these matters, a tendency carried over, he said, from the old democratic mode of thinking; that it was impossible on the basis of the present scant experience of fascism to foresee in detail the conditions and rules under which Italian labor could operate; and that the Charter must aim at expressing general principles rather than at erecting arbitrary norms. The heads of the employers' confederations promptly expressed their hearty approval of this bit of wisdom. The text of the Charter [30] was published on April 21, the fascist Labor Day, but late in the evening, after the big syndicalist celebration was over. It revealed that Rossoni's draft had been considerably modified in the direction of " general principles," and it was expressly stated not to be a legislative document but merely a formal declaration of the fascist labor platform. In presenting the Charter to the Grand Council for publication, Bottai said, without mentioning names of course, but obviously with reference to Rossoni " Many persons spontaneously expected a document of the type of codification of labor law, for the legal habit of mind of the past century turned by preference to codification. . . . In reality, however, the tendency of the Labor Charter proceeds in another direction. Profoundly revolutionary and political, the fascist type of mind could no

[30] See Appendix No. 24.

welcome a technical and legal systematization of the labor regulation which has been practiced during the last decades, under the impulse of extraneous and inorganic motives. It aspired to something more than a legislative document. It wanted to give form to the travail which it has now borne for almost a decade, and to proclaim to the Italian people and to the world the grounds on which it rests, and on which its own historic and political individuality are based. Hence the Labor Charter could not confine itself to accustomed legal procedure, but was destined, without even the appearance or immediate value of a legal document, to express the purpose which animates the new organisms created by the revolution and to establish a foundation not merely for purposes of legislation, but for the whole new mode of being which dominates our national social life. . . . "

The Charter contains thirty articles, grouped under four heads. The first ten, entitled "On the Corporate State and its organization" are a summary exposition of the principles and chief provisions of the legislation which we have outlined above. Numbers 11 to 25 are concerned with "The Collective Labor Contract and labor guarantees." Here the collective contracts are explicitly made obligatory, and each such contract must contain precise regulations on all matters concerning labor. But in place of the minimum wage and eight-hour day provisions in Rossoni's draft the Charter merely lays down the general principle that no fixed rule whatsoever can be prescribed, that salaries must be regulated by the fluctuations in the normal cost of living, in the general condition of production, and in the returns of labor, that "the consequences of financial and economic crises must be borne equally by all the factors of production, and that the responsibility for determining them is to be placed on the Corporations and the Labor Tribunals, on the basis of data furnished by the Central Institute of Statistics and by the various syndical organizations. For, as Bottai explained in his presentation, "the Charter recognizes no limits, either maximum or minimum, to the possibilities of the material and moral well-being of the individual." On the subjects of regulation of piecework production, night work, one day off a week, annual paid vacations, dismissal, death and sickness benefits, military service, change of ownership and such matters the Charter is more definite and follows the lines laid down in Rossoni's draft, though it is less explicit in detailed provisions. In one case it goes beyond the Rossoni draft; it explicitly includes domestic servants among those entitled to collective contracts and to sanitary working conditions.

The subject of Employment Bureaus, Articles 22 to 25, caused the most serious dispute. Rossoni at the very beginning of his draft stipulated that labor distribution and all matters of employment be put (or rather, at least in agriculture, be left) in the hands of the Confederation of Labor Syndicates. This was denied him, and the Charter provided for compulsory government employment bureaus under the Ministry of Corporations. However, the local employment bureaus have their offices in the Labor Syndicate headquarters and are operated by the local officials of the Ministry of National Economy.

Articles 26 to 30 concern " Labor insurance, assistance, education and instruction" which is, if anything, even more explicit than the Rossoni draft, for on these matters there was no serious difference of opinion.

In general, the Charter is rightly and unanimously hailed by the fascist syndicalists as the embodiment of their reforms. It explicitly recognizes the general principles which they laid down, and the particular working out of details would in any case be more a matter of the drawing up of collective contracts than of political legislation. The Labor Confederation now has ample legal sanction for its activities and the real test of its capacity will be in its bargaining power in drawing up the contracts.

Rossoni, of course, championed the Charter immediately as a great achievement of fascist labor organization. It is not without significance, however, that of the two chief speeches made on Labor Day at the publication of the Charter, that by Bottai does not mention Rossoni, and that by Rossoni barely mentions Mussolini. Certainly the corporationism of Rossoni must be distinguished from the Ministry of Corporations. The latter is looked down upon by Rossoni as little more than a politicians' *ufficio*, whereas the fascist politicians regard this Ministry as their opportunity to subordinate syndicalist organizations to government control.

Though there is no serious conflict as yet between Rossoni and Bottai, or rather, between syndicalism and corporationism, there is evidence that they are constantly diverging and that before long the issue may become serious. The revision of the Labor Charter, and the institution of government employment agencies, and of price-regulating committees, are but the first evidence that the syndicates will be increasingly subjected to the political control of the Ministry of Corporations. At present the employers' syndicates feel it more than does Rossoni, but Rossoni's turn may come soon. In fact, recent numbers of Bottai's *Critica Fascista* [31] have come out frankly against those who still think too " syndicalistically " and who seem unwilling to accept corporationism whole heartedly. It is all too plain who is meant, and though "local labor

[31] See Appendix No. 26.

leaders " are the only persons referred to directly, there is evidently friction between the Ministry of Corporations and Rossoni's confederations. In January 1928 the complaints which Rossoni's paper, *Il Lavoro d'Italia,* made concerning the government's negligence in enforcing the Labor Charter, forced Bottai in his report to the Grand Council to admit evasions of the new labor law and to promise more strict enforcement in the future.

The issue became especially delicate when it was linked with the question of electoral reform. The fundamental question was raised: shall the new Parliament be controlled by the syndicate confederations or by the agents of the Ministry of Corporations?

This is the most significant political problem which has arisen out of these developments. Both the corporationist politicians and the syndicalist leaders are now concentrating on the corporate parliament and economic representation. In January Mussolini hastened the issue by announcing the year 1927 as " the corporate year " and even dropped a casual reference to an economic parliament in place of the " worn-out one." Mussolini's words have a thousand echoes; and the slightest mention by him of such a possibility was enough to set the whole scheme on its feet. There was a sudden rush of political job seekers into the syndicates! Mussolini added that the reform of representation could not be carried out all at once, but would begin " at the periphery of the state." This was generally interpreted to mean that *municipal* or *provincial* syndicalistic elections would be widened until finally an economic parliament would be formed. The conservative fascist papers immediately took this hint to dampen any rising suspicions that general elections were imminent. The syndicates, they said, need not expect that the present regime is ready to turn over the government to a new crowd of " electioneers."

Nevertheless, on May 26, the boldest expectations of the corporationists were justified, when Mussolini in his big address to the Chamber definitely announced that in 1929, at the end of the present parliament, the present Chamber would be supplanted by a Corporate Chamber, " elected by the corporate organizations of the state." This phrase was purposely left vague in order to afford an opportunity for further discussion of the manner of electing the Chamber.

The Rossoni group urged this reform not so much as an end in itself, as one last effort to get " integral corporations " syndicalistically organized, *i.e.* in accordance with their original aims. They agreed that the new parliament should be elected by Corporations. For if the syndicates were to elect it, the state would not be a genuinely integrated, corporate state, since parliament would divide immediately into the capital and the labor parties. The genuinely corporate parliament, on the other hand, must represent the specific " horizontal " interests and activities of the nation, not the " vertical " classes. This principle is generally accepted by all *fascisti*. Hence Rossoni urged that a more definite and independent organization of corporations would be a necessary preliminary; for definite organizations would be necessary to carry on the election of representatives and other political functions. Thus Rossoni hoped that by means of the movement for parliamentary reform, he could gain the unified corporate organization of the nation for which he has held out consistently, but in which he has so far been frustrated.

For with the direction which the organization of the Ministry of Corporations has taken, an elaborate " integral " organization merely for election purposes is hardly possible even if the politicians wanted it. At the same time Mussolini announced the new Chamber he also took the trouble to " bury universal suffrage " officially and to attack election machinery in general. And in a circular of July 1927 he explicitly gave the Ministry of Corporations the task of determining the mode of election for the new Chamber.

In November 1927 the general provisions of the new scheme were decided; in February 1928 the Grand Council adopted and published the draft of the new electoral law; and several days later it was enacted into law by parliament, practically without change or debate. The veteran statesman, Giolitti, arose to denounce the reform as unconstitutional, but he was politely ignored.

The law provides that each of the thirteen National Confederations shall nominate its representatives. The total number of nominees is to be 800. This list will go to the Grand Council of the Fascist Party, which, under the guidance of the Ministry of Corporations, selects four hundred of them. These four hundred are then submitted as the official list to the whole body of syndicate members for approval or rejection *en bloc*. A rejection of this official hand-picked list would be tantamount to a general referendum vote of lack of confidence in the government. In such an event the law provides as follows:

" *Article* 8. — In case the designated list of deputies should not be approved, the Court of Appeals of Rome will order a new election by decree, on the basis of competing lists, and will set a date for the voting not earlier than 30 nor later than 45 days after issuing the decree.

" In this new election all associations and organizations numbering 50,000 members regularly registered as electors on the electoral list may present lists of candidates.

" The lists of candidates may not exceed three fourths of the deputie to be elected. Each list must be accompanied by a symbolical figure or design.

" *Article* 9. — The lists of candidates together with the acceptances of the candidates and official documents to prove their regularity, must be presented to the Court of Appeals of Rome, acting as a national central office, 15 days before the day set for the elections. The Court, having verified the regularity of the lists, will submit them to the voters.

" After the voting the reports of the offices of the various electoral districts of the Realm will be transmitted by means of the pretors to the Court of Appeals of Rome.

" The Court of Appeals adds together the number of votes given to each list and publishes the outcome of the balloting.

" All the candidates on that list which receives the largest number of votes will be declared elected.

" The places reserved for the minority are to be divided among the other lists in proportion to the number of votes each receives."

How this reform will work in practice remains to be seen. It is evidently designed to give the Fascist Party politicians practically complete power in picking their advisory parliament. Nevertheless it provides a machinery whereby the members of the syndicates can directly express their disapproval of the government as a whole and can proceed to party tactics and elections of party lists. The parties would presumably form as capital or labor parties, not as anti-fascist parties, and their rivalry would reflect economic rather than political issues. Of course, if the fascist politicians should blunder so completely as to lose the support of both employers' and labor organizations, it would be a simple matter for these syndicalist organizations to combine and elect an opposition parliament. But whether such a parliament would be able to exert any effective control, the government not being responsible to it, is doubtful. In all probability, such evidence of extreme unpopularity of the regime would be sufficient cause to lead the King to demand the Prime Minister's resignation. This might lead to an appeal to force, or to — but why pursue further such purely speculative eventualities!

Sooner or later the issue will have to be faced between authority from below and authority from above, between syndical organization and fascist hierarchy, between some form of democracy and some form of dictatorship.

But this issue will arise within the syndicates as well as between the syndicates and the bureaucracy. For at present it is difficult to tell whether the internal structure of the syndicates is democratic or not. In their origin and general spirit the syndicates are highly bureaucratic. The whole movement was directed from above by a few leaders who imposed their representatives on the local units. The important decisions and contracts are made by the great national confederations, and representation in these is very indirect. As we pointed out above, the national employers' confederations are each autonomous, but the labor confederation of syndicates is highly centralized. The president of the confederation of syndicates is at the same time the president of each of the subordinated national federations, and the president has extensive powers, such as naming his secretaries, appointing labor representatives for political bodies, fixing labor conditions for the employees of the federations, and being responsible for the whole administration of all the federations. This implies a highly centralized administrative bureaucracy, and there is no doubt that Rossoni's aim is to extend his power until he becomes virtually a labor boss.

On the other hand, according to the new constitutions in all the confederations, employers' as well as workers', the president is elected by the Congress (or general council) or the federation, which is composed of representatives of the provincial congresses, which in turn are composed of representatives chosen by the members of the local syndicates. So that on paper, at least, the syndicates have representative government. Also the congress of the federation must approve the budgets and vote on all important issues, financial or others, which concern the federation. The president is appointed for three years (in some cases two years) and the congress must meet at least every two years. In addition the Confederation of Syndicates has a National Council, which includes representatives of the provincial federations and the executive directors, and this must meet at least once a year.

Of course, according to the law, all elections and nominations are subject to the approval of the government (the Minister of Corporations) and the Fascist Party can interfere with syndicalist procedure at any point and at any time. But this is fascist procedure, rather than syndical, and it has already been restricted somewhat by decree and the tendency is certainly not in the direction of arbitrary control by the government over the syndicate organizations. As a matter of fact, the government does not interfere unless there is serious financial disorder or political insubordination among the officers.

At present the Rossoni administration seems to enjoy unquestioned support and prestige, and a real test case of the workings of syndicate government remains for the future. So far as the syndicate constitutions go, the decisive power would rest with the mass of electors in the syndicates, but in practice and under the present regime the Italian government could have its way, if it chooses to interfere. But with the institution of an economic parliament the structure of the fascist government will undergo serious modification and a modification in the direction of syndicate control. However, if the corporations, rather than the syndicates, become the organs of representation, as seems likely, neither the workers nor the employers will have any direct share in the election of parliament.

In any case, it is already evident that the theory which accompanies these constitutional reforms is not democratic. For even those fascists who are most eager in urging a reform of representation do so not in the name of a return to democratic institutions, but in the name of carrying the fascist revolution to completion. Carlo Costamagna [32] for example, one of the ablest of the legal theorists, claims that the fundamental import of these developments is to make the state genuinely sovereign, a true power. *Potenza* is the essence of the state, according to fascist doctrine. These reforms break down the supposed independence of the economic from the political order. The corporate state is simply the synthesis of the productive activities of the nation. He quotes with approval Mussolini's statement to the effect that " with fascism the Italian people, over and above the grotesque lies of the conventional democratic and liberal suffrage, has become an internal part of the state." That is to say, the state is sovereign, not because it *represents* the people, but because it is strong enough to control the whole life of the people. Or, as others put it, there is a vast difference between representation of interests and representation of citizens. The former does not imply a return to " that old electionism which still shows its head in several provinces," but rather a consciousness and intelligent pursuit of interests. Before the talk of economic representation became current this intelligent pursuit of interests was conceived in terms of production. As we pointed out above, mere participation in production constitutes fascist citizenship. But now the theorists have gone further: they insist that the producer must in addition take an active and informed part in the life of his syndicate, and through it in the organized activities of the nation. A *mentalità sindacale* is needed, they say.

Economic representation is therefore not to be conceived too democratically, though it is of course more democratic than the earlier fascist doctrine. It may be that members of syndicates have the vote, but what makes the state really representative, is not this syndical suffrage but the government's capacity to interpret and coördinate the various economic interests in the nation. The fascist doctrine of representation is more like Hobbes' than Rousseau's: the ruler " represents " the people because he, so to speak, stands up for them. On the other hand, the fascist doctrine of sovereignty is more like Rousseau's than like

[32] v. Especially the conclusion of his *Manuale di diritto corporativo italiano*.

Hobbes', for according to the *fascisti* it is the organized people itself, and not their government, that is sovereign. Only it is not the aggregate of atomic citizens of Rousseau, but the hierarchy of associated producers, that constitutes the sovereign state. Or in other words, no man is a member of the state except in so far as he is part of an association which represents one of the interests of the nation.

" No one can fail to see that all this implies a profound change from the traditional basis on which the Italian people used to participate in political elections under the democratic liberal regime. The disrepute into which the ballot had fallen, the conviction that the bickerings and factions of the various political groups in the old Chamber were grotesque, the proven impotence in the face of the great concrete problems manifested by the Chamber elected on the basis of abstract popular will, do not suffice to kill parliamentarianism. Elections on the individualistic basis of the disinterested public have so long represented in Italy a kind of fascinating myth, that it is profitable to substitute for them another system, provided there has first been created in the country, that is, in the masses of voters, a firm consciousness and precise knowledge of the political representation which is embodied in the corporate organization of the state." [33]

" All this may be synthesized in the following political formula: the fascist revolution aims to transform, not to suppress, the basis of popular sovereignty." [34]

In view of these developments it is impossible at present to pass a final judgment on the government of the corporate state. About all that can be said now with any assurance is that the organization has been built up by a bureaucracy and owes its success to autocratic means; that the democratic constitutions were drafted by the bureaucrats themselves and were not won from them by popular pressure; that neither capital nor labor seriously objects to democracy within its own class since democracy, at least in Italy, was objected to by each class as an instrument of domination in the hands of the other; that neither syndicalism nor fascism will change to an inter-class or political democracy overnight; and that there is no urgent call for a change in that direction.

In any case, the *stato fascista* of the Fascist Party is being enlarged into the *stato corporativo*. Though the two are generally and loosely identified, some fascist writers go so far as to say that fascism was merely a violent prelude and necessary means to the introduction of na-

---

[33] *Critica Fascista*, January 15, 1927, pp. 21, 22.

[34] *Critica Fascista*, February 1, 1927, p. 41. Bottai and the *Critica Fascista* have championed this neo-democratic tendency for some time. See for example, the issues of October 15, and November 1 and 15, 1926.

tional syndicalism. At this, other and " purer " fascists are visibly disconcerted. In 1926 Mussolini was willing to say rather timidly to a foreign
correspondent, for foreign consumption, that fascism is a " dictatorship
tending towards democracy." In 1927, however, at the climax of his
speech of May 26, he boldly " announced to the world the creation of
the powerful united state of Italy . . . and this state is expressed in an
accentuated, organized, authoritarian democracy, in which democracy
the people circulate freely." This is, of course, confused language, but
the mere fact that democratic terminology is used, marks a significant
change. Whatever the language employed, however, the fact is clear,
that the emphasis is rapidly shifting from the *fasci*, the militia and the
Party hierarchy, to the national hierarchy of syndicalist associations as
the foundation of the regime and the essence of the fascist revolution.
Back in March 1919, the date of the founding of the *fasci*, Mussolini did
not think of founding syndicate organizations. But now he hails the
new syndicalist law as the *fascistissimo* of all reforms. This implies, of
course, neither a contradiction in theory, nor a violent change in practice. It merely means that fascism is moving, is assuming a positive
direction and laying the foundations of a presumably permanent reform.
But it must be obvious to all that there is a vast difference between the
syndicate confederations and the Fascist Party government, both in their
philosophies and in their practical constitution. They may coexist for
some time, without forcing the issue, but sooner or later these two historically opposed types of government will face each other and a " higher
synthesis " will be difficult.

In the meantime there is already practical evidence that the change
from the fascist to the corporate state is more than a matter of theory.
The all-comprehensive *stato etico* which was little less than a lie and
little more than a boast during the early years of the regime, is now becoming visible in practice. Mussolini's motto: " Everything to the state,
nothing against the state and nothing outside the state," is still a distant
ideal, but it is no longer a mere dream. An account of the practical
achievements of fascism is beyond the scope of this book, but we may at
least mention enough of the facts to illustrate the shift which has taken
place from the individualism of the first year of the regime to the state-
socialism of the present.

In internal affairs Mussolini, in spite of his socialist training, had
apparently never really thought in economic terms. His " battles " were
either military or political or both. His foreign policy was clearly and
predominantly conceived in terms of economic imperialism, economic
treaties and economic rivalries. But, like the nationalists, he seemed
really to believe that there was no economic basis for internal politics.

It was not until the Matteotti crisis that he had taken internal politics seriously at all, and it took him almost a year after that to begin fighting the " economic battle " in earnest.

In the summer of 1925 he discovered that Italy needed foreign loans if it wanted to save the *lira*. De Stefani had tried to get along without resorting to this expedient, for his doctrines told him that Italy's salvation lay in her economic independence. His industrialist supporters were evidently not embarrassed when the *lira* went down still lower and certain speculators were positively pleased. The big financial interests, however, feared further inflation and the consumers feared higher prices. In any case, the government could not avoid responsibility for the situation and was forced to find a way out. Even De Stefani had come to see the *laissez faire* was not the final word. Shortly after De Stefani's resignation, Count Volpi, one of the big men in the Banca Commerciale, and famous as a shrewd bargainer, was appointed Minister of Finances and sent to America to settle the debt question and bring back a loan. This he did very promptly and skillfully. And ever since, with the support of the Italian banking interests and with the occasional aid of Messrs. Mellon and Morgan, he has kept Italian finances well in hand. But in order to do so, the government had to exercise continually wider powers. Mussolini's speech at Pesaro in which he promised to defend the *lira* " to his last breath and to his last drop of blood " was a spectacular symbol of the government's decision to use all available means of control. The tactics of Count Volpi reached their culmination in a series of drastic acts: in a decree regulating certain operations of banks, in the loaning of government funds to hard-hit industries, and in direct intervention by the government in the control of the exchange. The big internal *Littorio* Loan that was floated in 1926 was made practically compulsory by the system of demanding " licenses " from all merchants and requiring a deposit of from five hundred to five thousand *lire* in *Littorio* Loan notes, presumably for " the protection of consumers " against fraudulent merchants. The rapid deflation which followed these measures was carried out in direct opposition to the interests and wishes of the industrialists.

As a consequence of these financial measures the government was forced into price regulation as well. First, in order to keep prices from going up, then in order to force prices down after the deflation. Wages, rents, food prices, restaurant and retail shop prices were all forced down by the direct action of the government; sometimes by decree (as in the case of rents), sometimes by action of party officials and prefects (as in the case of reduction of agricultural wages), and sometimes by decision of the syndicate confederations (as in the case of most retail price regulations and wage reductions). The decree reducing rents was apparently the most drastic, involving in many cases reductions of over fifty per cent; and more than one landlord was sent to the islands for a period of years because he resisted or spoke ill of the decree. The task of such detailed regulation became so overwhelming and its current execution was felt as so chaotic and fragmentary that Mussolini in July 1927 signed a decree instituting a standing " Corporate Committee for action on matters of prices, costs, and salaries," under the Ministry of Corporations, which was charged with the enormous task of going at the whole problem systematically. The committee is largely made up of representatives from the various ministries and is empowered to undertake a " gradual, unitary and methodical " development of " corporate action." If really carried out, this will mean a further, much further, extension of direct government control in matters which the syndical organizations have hitherto regarded as their prerogatives.

Meanwhile the effects of collective labor contracts are making themselves felt. Rossoni had succeeded in getting a decree (January 11, 1927) which permits the nine-hour day (decreed in the summer of 1926 as a temporary emergency measure) only if it is granted by a collective contract made between legally recognized syndicates. This practically restores the eight-hour day, for Rossoni's attitude in its favor is well known and is evident in his draft for the Labor Charter, and though the Charter finally omitted mention of it and other fixed " obsessions," [35] employers will be unable to force a nine-hour concession unless in very exceptional circumstances.

In general, by his collective contracts, Rossoni has been able to gain concessions for labor, which though small are steady and of practical financial value to the workers. Labor has never had much bargaining power in Italy and hitherto local labor contracts have been variable and too dependent on the good will or political power of the local contracting parties. The early collective contracts also suffered from these conditions, but now the majority of contracts, made under the auspices of the Confederation of Syndicates, show a marked improvement. During the inflation they contained provisions for slight wage increases, called " high cost of living compensation," and in the cases of industries which were hard hit by the economic crisis they have at least prevented a wholesale reduction of the wage scale. As a result of deflation the high cost of living compensations have been discontinued and wage reductions accepted. But no reductions can be made until the contracts are revised and Rossoni is holding out as long as possible on his contracts, demanding that prices be reduced first. Meanwhile the government is

[35] v. *Gerarchia*, November 1926, p. 707.

taking various measures to combat the high cost of living, forcing rents and prices down by decree.[36]   Consequently the employers more than labor are feeling the immediate pinch of deflation. Eventually wages will probably drop even more than prices, since deflation has brought on hard times for Italian industry in general.   The Confederation of Industry's demand for wage reductions [37] has been accepted as inevitable; it is certain however that but for Rossoni's organization and the collective contracts, labor would have been exploited ruthlessly by employers.   In general there can be no doubt that within the last year, since Rossoni has made his power felt, Italian workers have been less at the mercy of their employers than they were during the early days of fascism; and it is probable that they are protected more than they would have been by independent labor organizations.   Indeed in the recent economic crisis the protests against the government have come from employers rather than from laborers and the government has gained enormously in the confidence of large groups of formerly hostile labor elements.   It is no longer possible to accuse fascism of being an out and out bourgeois reaction.

No doubt these practical achievements had something to do with the fact that in 1927 Rossoni at last won his seat at the International Bureau of Labor at Geneva, which had hitherto been denied him.

The most significant development of fascist economic organization has taken place in the field of agriculture.   To Mussolini's own mind the building up of agriculture is the key to Italy's economic salvation.   He has become an enthusiast for agriculture in general and is using his personal prestige in every possible way to build up what Turati calls " ruralism " rather than " agrarianism," that is, a passionate love for the land and a scientific devotion to agricultural professions rather than mere interest in making profits off of landed property, which is characteristic of the agrarian capitalists.   Mussolini has moral and political as well as economic reasons for his ruralism, but the economic reasons are fundamental.   He thinks Italy's only chance to make itself economically independent is to increase its agricultural output.   Above all he wants to eliminate as soon as possible all importation of grain. For if Italy could stop importing grain, about half its annual commercial deficit would be overcome.   He restored the protective tariff bars on agricultural importation which De Stefani had let down.   He instituted the " battle of wheat," whose symbol is the reinstitution of war bread

---

[36] In extreme cases the government is even forcing factories to keep on running though at a loss, by the threat to take them over and run them under government management *at the owner's expense.*

[37] See Appendix No. 25.

and which consists in encouraging by all possible pressure a maximum
production per acre and an efficient consumption. Fairs, prizes, competitions, and advertisements have been instituted to stimulate agricultural effort, and numerous decrees have been issued to compel scientific
cultivation — the use of proper machines and manures, rotation of
crops, selection of seeds, etc. Recently Mussolini has even threatened
to cut down the acreage of vineyards in favor of wheat.

Land tenure, too, has been reformed. At first fascist tactics were to
increase small holdings. Big estates were divided and sold on easy
terms to peasants. But it was soon discovered that these peasants were
so thrifty in their effort to pay for their farms, that they threw many
farm laborers out of work. Consequently the outright selling of land
was abandoned in favor of " colonial " share-holding tenant contracts.
Another reason given in favor of the tenant plan is that by keeping
ownership concentrated agricultural savings and capital could be controlled more easily and made more mobile. This is one of the prime
efforts of fascism to encourage agricultural savings and to reinvest
these in agricultural improvements. It is in this way that the government hopes gradually to pay for its huge investments in agricultural
developments. These developments (drainage, aqueducts, etc.) are
being carried on mostly in the south, where there are still extensive lands
to be opened up to cultivation, but they are financed by northern capital.
The general scheme is to build up future agricultural wealth in the south
by investing northern capital, industry and engineering in agricultural
improvement. This is, to be sure, not an original invention of the *fascisti*,
but a policy of long standing. What the *fascisti* invented immediately
after their accession to power was to take the funds which had been
accumulated and appropriated by previous regimes for public works
under government management, and to turn them over to private
companies. This was thought to be both good business and good
politics. The northern industrialists were satisfied by fat contracts
and the southern agriculturalists by the huge appropriations for the
development of the south. Furthermore it was in line with the
fascist theory of " rescuing at least one principle from the general
shipwreck of liberalism — that of individual initiative." But during
the last few years these " individual initiatives " have been increasingly subjected to more careful government supervision until now,
with the new syndicate machinery, it is difficult to find the line between
private and public management.[38] The truth is that here as in other

---

[38] The agricultural reform of 1927, for which Serpieri is largely responsible, is
another step away from individualism and marks the beginnings of a systematic
political control of land tenure, especially of the large southern estates.

fields the government has been forced out of its individualism by the course of events, so that practically all so-called private enterprise is now subject to minute government control.

These are a few illustrations of the revolutionary changes which are under way and which are transforming the fascist state into a single national, centralized workshop. It is idle to argue whether the state has been turned over to economic interests or the interests subjected to the state. The right wing of the Party insists that the corporate state is a glorified individualism; the left wing thinks it to be the triumph of the people "over the threatened capitalist insurrection." The simple fact is that the political and the economic orders are being fused into the corporate state and government is frankly becoming political economy.

The official justification for this kind of a state is not made in terms of these internal class distinctions, but rather in terms of Italy's international relations. The new order is regarded as an iron necessity imposed upon the nation by its poverty. " The economic struggle between nations," said Mussolini, " is becoming more severe and pitiless than the military struggle between these same nations. We dare not believe in an attenuation of this phenomenon. No. We must take cognizance of this fact: that life is becoming harder; it is not more comfortable, not easier for anybody." [39] Especially for Italy the struggle is relentless. Its lack of industrial raw materials and capital must be paid for in terms of hard work and a super-efficient organization of the nation. " Italy is in a permanent state of war," said Mussolini on another occasion; and these " battles " of the *lira* and of wheat are not metaphorical. Hence the appeal for economic organization and discipline to the nth degree is made not in the name of a revolutionary paradise but of national necessity. Imagine a Liberty Loan poster that would read: " Subscribe to the Loan and you and your children will enjoy the serenity of labor! " Yet that is precisely the appeal made during the recent loan drive.[40] The Italian must fight not for happiness, for leisure, for liberty, but for work. Unemployment is not as serious now as it was immediately after the war, but it is still a constant nightmare to the Italian nation. Everybody knows that in some way or other work must be found for four hundred thousand more Italians every year.

" *Fatica senza fatica.*"

The establishment of the corporate state sets the stage for more theories. For now that fascism is taking this positive direction many

[39] Mussolini: speech of July 8, 1926.

[40] One of the official loan movies outdid the irony of the poster just cited. I pictured the sweet fruits of saving by the honey which the bees industriously store up and *which the farmer carried off*.

who formerly saw in it nothing but the devil incarnate are beginning to understand the mysterious ways of Providence. And it is possible that before long both Hegelian and Marxian philosophers will discover that syndicalism is the middle term by which socialism and fascism have been joined in higher dialectic unity. Already certain socialists are revising their philosophy sufficiently to prove that fascism is but a necessary stage in the realization of the socialist state. Perhaps, they are suggesting, fascism is but socialism's logical antithesis, which is soon to be resolved into the higher state in which both will be reconciled.

As early as 1923 the veteran Professor Labriola wrote: " In the abstract, fascism is just as likely to turn into a national socialism as into a system of capitalistic hierarchies and rigid class subordination." [41] And certain socialists began to remark that an intransigent opposition to fascism was too bourgeois, that therefore socialism would do better to encourage fascism to become a higher socialism. D'Aragona and other socialists had made overtures in the early stages of fascist syndicalism, but were repulsed by Farinacci.[42] On February 2, 1927, however, several ex-directors of the reformist C. G. L. published a manifesto in which this theory was outlined, and the proposal was made that they would be glad to develop it still more by means of an independent " associated center of cultural assistance," if the government were willing.

Their thesis is that socialism has at last outgrown its infancy. The early stage of opposition between states and syndicates is a sign of immaturity on the part of socialism and of senility on the part of the bourgeois state. As soon as " the historical process " had given syndicalism sufficient inherent force neither it nor the state could fail to take cognizance of each other. The aged bourgeois state (the legal state) killed itself because it ignored the syndical power (the factual state), but the new state finally embraces the syndicates and the union proves productive. In the meantime syndicalism has outgrown its romantic dream of collectivism and its infantile " a priori, unilateral classism," and is willing to face reality.

" The fascist regime is a reality and this reality is to be taken into account. This reality moreover has taken its rise from our own principles which have imposed themselves upon it. . . . The fascist regime has performed an arduous task in its law disciplining collective labor relations. In this law we see that principles are being acclaimed which

[41] A. Labriola: *Le due politiche: fascismo e riformismo.*
[42] For an account of the attitudes of various parties toward fascist syndicalism in 1925, see V. Ambrosini: *La battaglia per lo stato sindacale.* It also contains interesting evidence showing that the Aventine liberals were much more disconcerted by this trend of fascism than were the socialists.

have always been ours. So long as the liberal state lasted, and on the other hand, so long as the workers remained firm in their misconception of the state, a law like the one now passed was unthinkable. The fascist revolution has cut the Gordian knot, and we must act upon this fact. . . . Therefore, to begin with, no opposition to these reforms."

Accordingly these men declared themselves willing to place at the service of the " national commonality " their " patrimony of experience " in the " workers' militia " by virtue of which they had acquired " special aptitude in understanding social problems and in making them accessible to the masses." At this the fascist labor press, which had in fact extended the invitation, set up a cry of rejoicing, as if the prodigal son had returned, and were to be received with open arms; while the more conservative press (e.g. Forges-Davanzati in the *Tribuna*) said " don't get excited and don't exaggerate." The official bulletin of the fascist party (February 7) called the document a mere confusion of guilt and error, a tardy recognition of what was obvious to the whole world, and hence a declaration of which only anti-fascists need take account.

After the publication of the Labor Charter a number of favorable comments were heard from socialist quarters, notably from Pio Gardenghi, an ex-editor of *Avanti,* who is reported to have said: " Fascism has definitely and victoriously ended the fight which was begun by socialism."

Such ideas will probably grow in the near future, if some of the old professors are spared a while longer. It is therefore by no means impossible that socialism and syndicalism will once more be reconciled to each other and both to the fascist state, but — it is difficult to say which has converted which.

CHAPTER V

FASCIST CULTURE

I. Fascism and Culture

DURING the congress held at Bologna in March 1925, at which the *fascisti* laid the foundations for their National Institute of Culture, an issue arose which puts the whole problem of fascist culture in a clear light. Panunzio, representing the point of view of one large group, said: " We *fascisti* need a definite doctrine," and he proposed that the congress lay the foundations of fascist philosophy, fascist art, fascist morals, in short fascist culture. To this Gentile replied, " No. What we need is not to bring culture into the realm of fascism, but to bring fascism into the realm of culture." [1] This difference in point of view still persists. The *fascisti* are still wondering whether they want to be civilized in their own peculiar way, or whether they are content to be just civilized. Of course, the alternative is not absolute; they may be both. But practically speaking it makes a considerable difference where the emphasis falls. One group of *fascisti* wants to make fascism the final end and subject-matter of its culture, to talk about little else. Another group wants to make fascism a means for promoting culture, universally conceived. Gentile, who is President of the Institute had his way at least on paper, for the organization is called The National Fascist Institute of Culture, and not the National Institute of Fascist Culture, as was first proposed; but whether his point of view has really gained the ascendancy is doubtful. So-called fascist culture is still largely a celebration of fascism. However, now that there is no opposition culture left to stimulate fascist propaganda, the celebration is becoming a bit tedious, and what is more, the books will not sell, presumably because of high prices. Consequently, for economic reasons, if for no others, the intellectually minded *fascisti* must settle down to more serious work.

There seems to be general agreement that fascism must now develop a cultural side. A movement so original, so powerful and so creative, they say, can not possibly remain merely political and economic. It

[1] Gentile: *Che cosa è il fascismo*, pp. 99, 105.

showed its negative side first, to be sure, because it had to. For in order to gain as great a momentum as possible in the negative task of over- throwing a worn-out regime, it had to concentrate on physical problems and on a bare minimum of ideas. The forces of fascism were intellec- tually too heterogeneous to permit any semblance of unity. Even after the March on Rome an over-emphasis on rival doctrines almost ruined the regime. But now that fascism feels secure, it is ready to look after its ideology and its art. Mussolini gave the signal for this cultural phase by his " *libro e moschetto, fascista perfetto.*"

II. Fascist Religion

Culturally, if not politically, fascism's strongest rival is the Catholic Church. No secular force of any kind has ever begun to compete with the Church in controlling the daily life and imagination of the Italian people. For centuries the Church has impinged on every aspect of Italian social and private life. We need say nothing of the long periods during which the Church was also the State in many of the Italian provinces. Its control is much more direct and powerful than any political control can be. The whole intellectual frame-work of life is supplied by the Church. The supernatural world above this perishable material world, the salvation of the soul from the bonds of the flesh, the protection by the saints against disease, misfortune and death, the divine favor and intercession of the Virgin in all the personal issues of domestic and agricultural life, the religious care of the happiness of the members of the family both living and dead, these are the fundamental themes which still dominate the minds of the vast majority of Italians. This theological world dominates not merely in the sense that it is believed implicitly, but in the more practical sense that its moral tech- nique is familiar. Divine protection and punishment are much more real and more conspicuous than their modern political equivalents. For every peasant and every child knows exactly how to govern himself according to divine law. The rather simple, at least intellectually simple, technique of penitence, confession, absolution, alms, indulgences, prayer and worship constitute the moral life of the people.

What is politically even more important is that the Church has organ- ized public life and social functions around this moral world. The cal- endar is made by the Church, and even the daily routine is governed by the ringing of the church bell. The Church takes the place of theatre, opera and city hall. In addition to the imposing gilt, the lights and shadows and the sacred images which fill the churches, and in addition to the daily miracle of the mass, the Church has supplied abundant holi-

days and feasts, when the whole community gathers to celebrate the
season. Cardinals and bishops, gay silks and velvets and brocades, gold
and silver, candles and torches, fireworks and rubber balloons, confec-
tions and drinks! If you can imagine how a combined Christmas, New
Year's Eve, County Fair, and Fourth of July (old style) would affect
an American boy's mind and body, you may approximate a sense of the
power which these celebrations have in an Italian community. And this
happens not once a year, nor for miscellaneous political reasons, but with
every season of the calendar and in celebration of some vital theme in
the moral life of the individual and in the traditions of the Church. Add
to this the treasure of art which centers in the Church, the intellectual and
social prestige which it enjoys, its numerous charitable and educational
institutions, its systematic care of the deceased, and you may understand why the Church has more of a hold on the masses than has the
state.

In comparison the Italian state is hopelessly bare and empty. Being
of recent date, headed by a half French royal house and conducted by
a very prosaic Parliament, having only occasional military celebrations
and still more occasional visits of the King to make it impressive, represented continually by boyish policemen, petty officials and busy tax-
collectors, it is comparatively quite remote and unattractive. Ever since
the invention of expensive armaments, the Church costs less than the
state, and yet offers infinitely more: festivals in this life and salvation
in the next.

Hence the state has no chance whatsoever with the masses. Among
the bourgeoisie, of course, all this is different. Corrupted by rationalism, indifferent to sensual display, or else given over to secular forms of
sensuality and sensuousness, less worried about its sins, more worried
about its prosperity, the bourgeoisie has turned to the state. Religion
for the masses, politics for the rich — that is the traditional compromise.

A Sicilian priest named Don Sturzo upset it. In 1918 he got the idea
of capitalizing the Church for political purposes, or politics for Church
purposes — it is hard to tell which. He met the initial opposition of the
Pope, who saw no reason why he should soil his hands on the state.
But Don Sturzo persisted and soon persuaded the Pope by a few practical experiments. The result was that within two or three years Don
Sturzo and his Popular Party succeeded in completely ruining Italian
politics. All through the spring and summer of 1922, the veteran bourgeois statesmen tried to dislodge the Sicilian priest from his "dictatorship." But it was useless; the old game was up.

At first fascism tried to take the Church by storm. Born in the years
of bolshevist revolt, when even the industrial proletariat had temporarily

turned anti-clerical, fascism hoped to gain general favor by a violent attack. The futurist wing of the movement was naturally a sworn foe to this most "*passé-ist*" of all institutions. The ex-socialists, like Mussolini, were also anti-religious, as well as anti-clerical. The bourgeois liberals and republicans who joined the fascist ranks were the traditional political foes of the Church. Hence during the first year or two of the movement the fascist program was violently anti-clerical. As late as April 3, 1921, Mussolini spoke at Bologna as follows: "Fascism is the strongest of all the heresies that strike at the doors of the churches. Tell the priests, who are more or less whimpering old maids: away with these temples that are doomed to destruction; for our triumphant heresy is destined to illuminate all brains and hearts. Make way for the youth of Italy, whose faith and passion are demanding expression."

Events soon forced fascism out of this position, two events especially: the evident strength of the Popularist Party which no one seemed able to dislodge and the influx into fascism of the nationalists, who were modernist Catholics of the *Action Française* type. Mussolini therefore suddenly turned his back on the futurists and anti-clericals, as he did on the republicans, and made his peace with the Church. He became a defender of the religious exercises of women and children who were being persecuted in their public worship by barbarous bolsheviks. He revived the Mazzinian formula *Dio e popolo*. He preached the doctrine of the synthesis of the two Romes. He supported Rocca's position at the Fascist Congress in November 1921, to the effect that "it is necessary to have a dogma for social life: the dogma, namely, that unity and power lay in Rome, in the Church there is the Catholic God, and in the modern State there is the *Patria*." Thus he finally persuaded the popularists into a coalition.

But when, shortly after his accession to power, the popularists abandoned the regime, it looked as though the *fascisti* would be forced back into their former hostility to the church, and would have to declare open warfare. This would have been disastrous, of course. Instead they played a subtler, safer game.

They came to terms directly with the Church and not *via* the Popular Party. Mussolini promised immediately on his accession to protect the Church and religion and this news was headlined in all the Church papers. The Pope adopted a benevolent attitude toward the "fascist peace" and the "end of civil strife." In December a Papal Encyclical came out as follows: "Though the Church does not condemn the democratic form of government, yet it is a well-known fact that this system of government is especially adapted to party strife." Soon after, by the joint action of the Church and government, Don Sturzo was kicked out of politics, his local organizations and syndicates were destroyed, and in the 1924 elections the clergy were required by the Pope to maintain absolute neutrality. Thus the old compromise was reëstablished: Religion for the people and politics for the bourgeoisie, spiritual authority and temporal authority, a " free church in a free state." The Pope was as content with this arrangement as a " prisoner of the Vatican " might reasonably be expected to be, and was ready to go back to the old status he had enjoyed for several decades before the ambitious Sicilian priest had upset normalcy.

Periodically the Vatican revives the customary pleas for temporal power, which are politely refused. In October 1926 the whole issue was gone over again by the *Popolo d'Italia* and the *Osservatore Romano*, without significant results. Again in March 1928 the Pope's outspoken criticism of fascist education and the pro-fascist Catholic party, seemed to signalize an open breach between Church and state. But both sides immediately drew in their horns and negotiations on the old " Roman Question " were re-opened. Neither side is very optimistic that any definite settlement will be reached shortly; both sides claim they can wait indefinitely. There were rumors that a general basis of accord had been found, involving an extension of the Vatican grounds and payment of a money indemnity (which the Pope has hitherto refused). Some say that the Pope would be satisfied with the temporal possession of enough territory to house himself and cardinals plus " an outlet to the sea " and that he would not insist on this last demand in the bargaining. Others say, and the remarks of Cardinal Merry del Val support this point of view, that the Church would renounce temporal power completely if it were given absolute spiritual power.

This is of course inacceptable to the *fascisti*, for they too have their spiritual ambitions. They pose as the official representatives of the *popolo d'Italia*. They want to have the first place in the affections and imaginations of the people. They want to be the embodiment, not merely of the Italian state, but of Italian culture. They want to be the Church's rival on its own ground. This raises a problem quite different from the old problem of Church and state. It is not primarily a political problem, but a cultural one. At first sight one would no doubt be inclined to regard this ambition of the *fascisti* as sheer folly, doomed to defeat. But the progress which they have already made is remarkable, and Cardinal Gasparri may yet find that friend Mussolini is more than a match for him.

Fascism gained its first victory over the Church by surrendering to Catholicism. Fascism is Catholic, absolutely Catholic; because the Italian nation is Catholic. Whatever is national must be fascist. If it be

objected that the Catholic Church is international; the fascist reply is
that really it is Roman, imperial. Other nations have embraced the
Roman faith when it was brought to them; but Italy has produced it.
It is at home in Italy, an importation elsewhere. The spread of the
Roman Church is, therefore, a phase of Italy's " spiritual imperialism," a
recognition on the part of other peoples of Italy's moral primacy. The
Church is but the organized form of Italian religion. Hence the Italian
state, far from renouncing affiliation with the Church, must recognize
it, protect it, and incorporate it into the organic unity of the nation.
The state itself must be religious, Catholic. This doctrine is two-
edged. The state is spiritualized, but the Church is nationalized. And
here's the rub. The Church is cordially accepting the one half and dogmatically rejecting the other. Fascism insists on the whole of it. Not
that it tries to subordinate spiritual authority to temporal. Never!
It denies the distinction. Church authority is just as ultimate in its
sphere, as medical authority in its. But, since religion is only one
phase of the life of the spirit, according to the idealist-fascist doctrine,
and is really coördinate with science and art, it is not the independent
ultimate good of life which the Church claims it to be; and since the whole
life of the nation must be included in the *stato etico,* it follows that religion must be included as one part or phase of that organic, spiritual
unity which finds its total embodiment in the state. To this the Church
naturally objects. God, not the state, must be ultimate; and, as the
Pope told Mussolini not long ago, the spiritual needs of man reach over
and beyond the state, and hence the Church rejects fascist doctrine,
though it accepts fascist politics.

The idealistic philosophy of the state is naturally not an easy doctrine
to foist upon the Church. Historically it has its roots in the protestant
Hegel and its chief expression in the German *Kultur-staat,* against which
the Church had already waged one *Kulturkampf.* Italian idealism too
was an enemy to the Church from the first. " It was," in the characteristic words of Gentile, " a Catholic movement in a critical way." Its
pantheism and its secular conception of the spirit and of religion itself,
are obviously opposed to Church dogma.

The uncritical Catholicism of the non-Gentilian *fascisti* is not much
better. Their religious enthusiasm is too patriotic. One of them, for
instance, writes: " Our Country and Our Religion are two sentiments
. . . which blend indissolubly. It is impossible to separate them." [2]
From this attitude it is altogether too easy to pass to the idea that
fascism itself is a religion. In fact, precisely this is very generally maintained. Usually not in a sense hostile to the Christian religion or the

[2] Mario Carli: *Fascismo Intransigente,* p. 227.

Catholic Church, but in the sense that fascism takes the old religion into itself, broadens it, vitalizes it, and transforms it into the religion of the future, in which God, Country and *Duce* become practically indistinguishable. Such opportunistic Catholicism deceives neither the Church nor the educated public, but it gives the general impression among the masses that fascism is a defender of the faith, and it has enabled the government to persecute the Popular Party without giving the impression that it was persecuting the Church.

The most serious application of the doctrine of the Catholic state is Gentile's reform of public education. The public schools are to teach religion just as they teach anything else. The regular teachers do the teaching and regular text-books are prescribed. The Church may have the privilege of approving the text books, but otherwise it has no immediate control in the matter. Furthermore, as a symbol of the new order, it is provided that a crucifix must be in every schoolroom as well as a picture of the King. This usually consists of a black and white print of the crucifixion by Raphael, framed in a simple wood frame and hung immediately under an enormous picture of the King.

Religion in the schools was, of course, a severe shock to the anticlericals. Both at home and abroad the general cry was raised that education had been turned over to the Church. But the Church knew better. For the reform put into effective practice precisely what alarmed the Church most, namely, the inclusion of religion into the secular life of the nation. The Church lost its monopoly and religion lost its preeminence. The new generation is growing up learning its religion not from the Church but from the state.

Probably the most serious objection to the reform came from the teachers, who were now compelled to take examinations on the subject of religion, in order to retain their positions. The reader can perhaps imagine how religion is being taught by these overworked teachers. There is no excess of Christian zeal nor of familiarity with the subject-matter! It would be going too far to claim that the introduction of religion into the public schools is a first great step toward the irreligion of the future, but this would be nearer the truth than the current supposition that the Church had been given a new lease on life.

On the other hand, it may be still too early to predict. Gentile's idea is to put religion on a broader, more liberal basis than the Church has been willing to do, and he is trying to induce fascism to be a genuinely religious movement, in his sense of religious — " religious in a critical way." Religion, as he says, is nothing but taking life seriously. He wants to liberate religion from Catholic dogma and Church authority, and expects his educational reform in particular and fascism in general to be a step in this direction. As one of his associates in the reform said: "If we want to teach children religion, we must teach them a real and genuine religion, with its mythology, with its mythical personifications, and with its dogmatic commandments. . . . To restore to the people a sense of the sacredness of life, we must have patience and return to our Christian tradition. . . . Though Christianity at a particular stage in its development has wrapped itself in a rigid theology, it does not cease to represent, to be sure in the form of myths, the essential revelation of the reality of the spirit. . . . We can and we must go beyond the limits of Catholic orthodoxy, but we can not remain absolutely indifferent to a faith and an institution that represents the central nucleus of our national tradition." [3]

But the great majority of the *fascisti* are quite ignorant of and indifferent to this religious philosophy. They are willing to make their peace with the Church for political reasons, but they personally have no interest in giving fascism a religious flavor. Consequently, now that Gentile is no longer in the government, his successors are adopting a more superficial policy. They are catering to the Church not only politically but intellectually as well. For example, at the International Congress of Moral Education, September 1926, Bodrero, formerly rector of the University of Padua, now the Under-secretary of Public Instruction, said: "The Italian national government holds that the only possible form of moral education is that established by the Gospel of Christ in the Catholic interpretation, tradition and teaching, from God's ten commandments to the catechism." The Church is reviving its institutions of higher learning and asserting its doctrines more freely. Recently it has attempted to dictate in matters of educational control, has protested against obnoxious professors, has banished text books (other than religious) from the schools and is regaining a little influence in the universities. Gentile immediately opposed these moves and publicly rebuked the responsible ministers for surrendering part of the authority which rightly belongs to the state. Thus it is possible, if politicians rather than educators should get control of the educational system, that the Church may succeed in reëstablishing its intellectual respectability, and that neo-scholasticism rather than national idealism may become the official theology of the fascist faith. But for the present this hardly seems probable. For the reform of the schools is but one phase of the more general competition between church and state to win the affections of the people.

Less subtle and more generally effective than this reform is the new fascist art of secular celebrations. It is not for nothing that fascism i

[3] v. Balbino Giuliano: *La Politica Scholastica del Governo Nazionale*, pp. 96-8.

so ritualistic. The marches, salutes, yells, songs, uniforms, badges, and what not, are giving a new focus to the imagination of the Italian youth, are linking their social life to political organizations and are filling their minds with political — I will not say ideas, but political — feelings. This is perhaps the greatest of the fascist revolutions. Good Italian youths still go to mass and participate in religious festivities, but their sentiments, their imaginations, their moral ideals are centered elsewhere.

Catholic rites are after all not very well adapted to the emotional needs of a healthy young man. There is little athleticism in the Christian religion. College fraternities and "college life," the American equivalent for youthful religion, are missing in Italy. Hence fascism's inventions in this field have supplied a real demand and captured with ease the enthusiasms of youth, with which the Church had been struggling for generations.

The Church has made counter moves. It has supported its *Gioventù Cattolica*, its young men's organization, with exceptional vigor. During the winter of 1926 it staged a big international Catholic youth convention and celebrated Saint Louis Gonzaga, the patron saint of youth, with great pomp and great display of his sacred skull. There are occasional conflicts between the *Gioventù Cattolica* and the *fasci*. After the 1924 elections and again after the last attempt on Mussolini's life, the *fascisti* destroyed a number of the *Gioventù Cattolica* headquarters. This led to vigorous protests on the part of the Vatican, followed by the Pope's gift of 500,000 *lire* to rebuild the destroyed buildings. Mussolini in turn condemned the attacks. Hereupon the *Azione Cattolica* published a warm praise of Mussolini, coupled with an equally warm expression of the hope and confidence that violence against Catholic organizations would cease.

Fresh trouble, however, arose almost immediately out of the rivalry between the fascist Balilla and the Catholic Scouts. When boy scoutism was first introduced into Italy a few years ago, the Church was hostile. It thought the movement too materialistic; too much attention to the body and too little to the soul. But when the enormous power of the organization became evident, the Church took it under its wing and formed the Catholic Scouts. The movement continued to grow and promised to do precisely what the Church hoped it would, that is, give the Church a new grip on the social activities of the coming generation. When the *fascisti* organized their Balilla and Advance Guard, there was an open rivalry between the two juvenile movements, and consequently between church and state. The Catholic Scouts had been on the ground first and had that initial advantage, but the fascist organizations were more vigorous and more spectacular. In December 1926 the government suddenly ordered the Church to disband its Scouts in all the smaller villages and towns (where there was not room for the two organizations), and in return the *fascisti* agreed to send their own organizations to the priest once a week for religious instruction. The Church complied with the demand, not " wishing to embarrass the regime," but it did so with expressions of severe pain.

In the spring of 1928, when the Church became involved in the German minorities dispute and when the Pope openly censured the pro-fascist Catholic Party, Mussolini in reply abolished the remaining Catholic Scouts, that is, in the cities as well as the villages, and left the fascist *Balilla* and *Avanguardia* supreme. The Church is now left without any independent organizations by which it may lay hold on the future generations of Italy. Here again, the state is winning out; henceforth the Church will have one hour a week, and a comparatively dull hour, in an organization that is molding both the minds and the bodies of future *citizens.*[4]

Public feasts and celebrations play a comparatively large rôle in the social life of the Italian masses, and, as we pointed out above, these have been practically monopolized in the past by the Church. But now the *fascisti* are making serious inroads. The Church gained a big initial lead with its Holy Year in 1925 and the institution of the Feast of Christ the King, which is celebrated in October but which really culminates on December thirty-first, when the Pope celebrates a " royal mass " and the cardinals formally do homage to him. The feast was first fixed in 1925 for the last Sunday in October, on the ground that it ought to come before All Saints' Day. This put it in the midst of the annual fascist celebrations! Then it was changed to October 13, on which day the Pope received the delegates of the First Congress of Catholic Men, an organization which is as nearly political as a Catholic and non-fascist organization may well be.

In 1926 the Church tried the same tactics with the Franciscan Year, celebrating the Seventh Centenary of the death of Saint Francis. But the *fascisti* put their fingers into the pie. It was pointed out loudly and often that Saint Francis is *the* big *Italian* saint — one of the chief glories of Italy. Notice, for instance, the following extracts from an official proclamation of the Centenary in the town of Prato: " . . . and the National Government, strong, free from all prejudices, sustainer of

[4] Here and there the *fascisti* threatened to suppress what little Y. M. C. A. there is in Italy because of its " Protestant and Masonic " character; but after protests by the American Ambassador, it was spared on the ground that it was really an athletic institution.

spiritual values, has done well to decree that the nation shall officially honor and exalt, with civic as well as religious ceremonies, our great Italian saint, perpetual teacher, to peoples and to individuals, of heroic discipline, of fervent toil, of gentle brotherliness. . . . May the saint of humility, and of peace bless our industries and our labors, illumine our minds and convert our hearts. *Pax et bonum."*

In a similar vein throughout the year Saint Francis was capitalized as a *national* figure.[5] It was repeatedly pointed out that though Christ was, of course, the original founder of Christianity and though the Church went back to ancient Rome, really modern Christianity was given its first great impetus in Italy by St. Francis. He is linked with Dante and Giotto as one of the great figures of the Italian Renaissance; not merely because his simple Italian verses became one of the foundations of modern Italian religious literature, but because his anti-intellectualistic, practical Christianity is preëminently Italian, an outgrowth of Italian social and economic conditions as well as an ideal pattern for the religious life of Italy in the future. "And wherever in all the lands of all the continents there is today a splendor or humility of works achieved or suffered in the name of this Saint, there there is a trace of our country." [6]

The climax of the Franciscan celebration came on October 4, Saint Francis Day, with the celebration of a gorgeous pontifical mass at Assisi and a general gathering at the Franciscan shrine of pilgrims from all over Italy. In his address, the cardinal legate, Merry del Val, thanked the local administration for the cordial reception it had given him, said some kind words about the political officials who had coöperated in the celebration, and then spoke of Mussolini as of "him who holds the reins of the Italian government, and who with a clear grasp of the real state of things continues in the resolve that religion be respected, honored, and practised. Visibly protected by God, he has raised again the fortunes of the nation by his wisdom, increasing its prestige before the whole world." This was immediately played up far and wide in the secular press as a step towards the reconciliation of Church and State, and as a tribute by the Pope to fascism.

The crowning stroke of the *fascisti* was to stage a big Mussolini celebration at Perugia (a few miles from Assisi) on the following day, October 5. Public appearances of Mussolini are by this time as great events as public appearances of the Pope. And especially his coming to a hill town like Perugia was an event of extraordinary excitement for the whole of Umbria. The pretext for his appearance at that

---

[5] v. *Critica Politica*, October 1926, p. 362 ff.

[6] Mussolini in his Manifesto for the Franciscan Centenary.

time was that he had been invited to open the summer session for foreigners at the University of Perugia, but being unable to come at the time, he promised to deliver an "academic lecture" some time during the school term. It happened that October 5 was a convenient date for him (the summer session was over by that time and the winter session had not yet begun!) and it happened that the subject of his lecture was "The Maritime Power of Ancient Rome." Though the theme of the lecture created considerable excitement, the reading of it turned out to be a mere incident in an all-day triumph. He harangued "faithful Umbria" in the *piazza*, — bands, parades, long lines of helmeted soldiers, long columns of standard-bearing *fasci*, gay street illuminations and a profusion of flags and banners made the celebration a rival to that of Assisi. The net effect of the whole performance, for the thousands who had gathered in that region from all over Italy, was to make it a two-day celebration — the first at Assisi, the second in Perugia; the first devoted to the great Italian Saint of the Roman church, and the second to the *Duce* of Imperial Rome re-arisen!

This sort of tactics has been continued. It frequently "happens," for instance, that in many of the provincial towns, Turati, the Secretary of the Fascist Party, finds himself scheduled to speak during the celebrations of the patron saint's day, which is usually the biggest day of the year. Pentecost has been made a national "feast of flowers" on which day the anti-tuberculosis society sells poppies. The posters explain that the "flowers symbolize the sacrifice made by the nation in war and disease." The calendar, too, is assuming a secular structure: March 23rd, founding of the *fasci*, the feast of youth; April 21st, the founding of Rome, Labor Day; May 24th, the entry of Italy into the war, Empire Day; September 20th, anniversary of capture of Rome and celebration of Italian unity; October 28th, anniversary of the March on Rome, celebration of the *fascisti's* power by parades of its various organized forces; November 4th, a Victory celebration, and 11th, the King's birthday. These holidays are given elaborate advertisements and long expositions in the daily press. The Church holidays no doubt do not need press notices, but neither do they get them; whereas a political holiday always occupies the chief columns of every paper for several days before and after. Wall posters are an important traditional institution in Italy in this connection; and in this art the *fascisti* are past masters. Their red, white and green posters, with even more flamboyant "messages" printed on them, are a conspicuous feature in the landscape of every Italian town.

Of the tracts, pamphlets and books which carry on this sort of propaganda, no account can be given here. There is an abundance of such literature and it goes to the most ridiculous extreme. There is, for example, a fascist publisher who gets out occasional pamphlets celebrating various aspects of the new harmony between church and state, exalting the Catholic works of fascism and making it particularly plain that fascism and not the Popular Party is the true political champion of the Church. One of these pamphlets contains the parallel lives of Pius XI and Mussolini. Another one draws parallels between St. Francis and Mussolini, emphasizing in particular the Franciscan virtues of the *Duce*, patience in suffering, renunciations, exile, etc.; lastly there is an exposition of their "common love for animals," illustrated very convincingly by a reproduction on the left-hand page of Giotto's St. Francis preaching to the birds, and on the opposite page a photograph of the *Duce* with derby hat and wing collar, laying a gloved hand on the back of his lioness in the zoo.[7]

Recently a belief has grown up about Mussolini personally that represents more than mere propaganda. His spectacular career makes it easy for many pious Italians to believe that he has literally been sent by God to save Italy. And now this belief is not only confirmed but practically established to be true by his miraculous escapes from the assassin's hand. Here is the text of a typical wall poster after the attempt on Mussolini's life in September 1926:

"Italy once more is safe: Mussolini still holds it stronger, more beautiful, more glorious than ever!

"Here is his order to us:

NO REPRISALS

No demonstration either civil or religious!
We must obey!
Who fails to obey offends the *Duce*,
Whom God has given and whom
He now wants definitely to preserve intangible for the safety and the greatness of our Country.

> (signed) The Provincial Political Secretary
> Alezzini-Padua."

On the part of the writer this manifesto is no doubt rhetorical, but on the part of many a poor peasant (and many a city proletarian's *wife*) these sentiments are quite genuine and express literally a religious conviction. And it is by no means impossible, unless relations between church and state become too strained, that the *Duce* will some day figure as an Italian Joan of Arc, and that he will be known to posterity as St.

[7] v. Sac. Paolo Ardali's pamphlets, Edizioni Paladino, Mantova.

Benito. His life, in fact, reads not unlike that of many another saint and of miracles there already is a plenty.

It is more probable, however, that fascism will maintain its own list of martyrs and saints and continue to build up its own mythology. The elements of the new religion are already present in abundance.[8] First of all, the *fascisti* lay much stress on their mysticism. Their political faith, they say, cannot be expressed in a consistent program, because it is mystical. Their love of violence is said to be a mystical devotion to a new faith, and an immediate intuition of a profound truth, which they were unable to define until *after* they had acted upon their vision. Hence they regard themselves as men of faith, spiritual to the core, and it is one of their commonplaces that fascism has reëstablished idealism in a world of skepticism, and has asserted the duty of fighting for transcendent values against the current doctrine of waging class conflicts to protect one's own rights. Furthermore fascism has revived the primitive Christian joy of martyrdom. A true fascist thinks only of his duty, and regards any sacrifice which he may be called upon to make in the performance of it a privilege. This is the inner driving force of the new religion.

Thus fascism represents a religious revival. Not in that it proposes to found a new religion and develop its own theology, but in that it has given to thousands of Italian youths an ideal for which they are ready to sacrifice all. A number of *fascisti* have confessed to me, quite privately, that they would not willingly die for their Christian faith, nor for democracy, nor for socialism, nor even for their King, but for Mussolini? — gladly and unhesitatingly. They claim that fascism represents more than merely one faith among many. They will not admit that the socialist " martyrs " are on an equally ideal plane; for, they say, in the first place, fascism has superseded other faiths, has won the allegiance of the very men who formerly professed less satisfying faiths; and, in the second place, it has made its appeal in the name of sacrifice to a transcendent, non-personal good, not in the name of class interests or salvation of one's soul, or defense of one's rights or any other selfish motive. After all a Christian martyr expected to wake up and " reign forevermore," and a bolshevist hero is driven by an unearthly hatred to seek vengeance on his oppressors, but a fascist asks for nothing more than to be the passing instrument of his nation's greatness.

Then there is the idea of the New Rome, which is supposed to be synthesis of the Roman Empire and the Roman Catholic Church — genuine spiritual synthesis, not a mere coalition. Theologically, c

---

[8] An amusing, sacrilegious and of course unofficial fascist parody on the Creed re-printed in Ludovic Nadeau: *L'Italie fasciste ou l'autre danger*, pp. 132-4.

course, this is quite preposterous; but it is an immediate, mystical union, a harmonizing of Christian and Roman virtues and aspirations. The physical counterpart of this spiritual union is the country of Italy itself, for on Italian soil pagan and Christian Rome have found a common home. There is something supernatural about Italy; it is literally a divine country.[9] Ever since the days of Homer it has been a land to which men have looked forward. The Trojans, the Phœnicians, the Greeks, the Northern savages, all turned toward Italy. Italy has led Europe in the struggle for civilization; first it civilized and Christianized the barbarians, then it led medieval commerce, then the maritime conquests and explorations, then the Renaissance, then modern astronomy and physical science, and now, lastly, it is leading the world to new levels of social and political organization. Obviously Italy is the light of the world. Italy not only enjoys " spiritual autonomy " and cultural primacy more than any other country, but it breaks the way which others follow; it has a world-wide spiritual empire.

This Italian outline of history leads to a spiritualized conception of imperialism, which is something more than either the Catholicism of the Church or the political power of Rome. It is a genuine fusion of the mastering qualities of the race. It surpasses political and economic expansion, for these are merely its material expressions; it is the majestic career of genius, which extends its sway not by physical force, but by the power of its inner superiority, which inevitably commands recognition and admiration. This cult of the New Rome is admittedly a " myth " in the Sorelian sense, whose value lies not in its literal truth, but in its power to command obedience, devotion and sacrifice.

If other nations can command similar disinterested loyalty on the part of their citizens, well and good. Nothing would seem to a fascist more in conformity with the " logic of history " than that other nations should follow in the path which Italy has taken. It is infinitely better that each people should frankly assert its faith, than that they should oppress each other in the name of liberty, impose themselves on each other in the name of equality, and fight each other in the name of international fraternity.

" There is only one internationalism that is morally possible, since it does not exclude but sanctions renunciation and sacrifice, namely that which aims not at happiness on earth but in the beyond: religious internationalism. Hence the only International that has a right and a duty to exist is Catholicism, that is, Christianity. This, in fact, still exists and has endured for so many centuries because in asserting the in-

[9] v. Giacomo Etna: *La divinità d'Italia.* In *Il 1919,* for August 1926, pp. 7-8.

timate brotherhood of all men in charity, in the face of God, it does not
deny but rather it asserts the duty of men in so far as they live on
earth to adhere to and to serve each his own nation; not out of hatred
for the foreigner, for he too is a brother in Christ, but out of a duty
which unites both though on opposite sides in a common holocaust of the
individual, to a cause which transcends him. And so Catholicism in
spite of its intrinsic spiritual universalism is, can be, and must be the
national religion of each Catholic nation.

" For the end of man on earth is not to live blessed and inert in a
paradise of identity of all men, which would make life unworthy of being
lived; rather it is to dedicate himself as an individual to the triumph
of those national values which history entrusts to him for the sake of the
progress of human civilization." [10]

As a symbol of this spiritual synthesis, several months ago a big
wooden cross was restored in the Colosseum. The cross had been
put there after Rome became Christian and had remained there until
the Garibaldists removed it after the capture of Rome in 1870. The
reinstatement took place in the presence of the Queen, of cardinals and
of *fascisti*, and during the ceremony five hundred white doves were
released from the cells in which the Christians had suffered martyrdom.
Perhaps the dove really hovers over the old wooden cross, perhaps the
souls of the martyrs bear willing witness to their modern comrades,
perhaps the black shirts in the Colosseum frighten even the pigeons
and owls that inhabit its crumbling walls, or perhaps the ancient
Roman arena is once more being opened up to religious sport. In any
case a synthesis of cross and Colosseum is not even architecturally possible and time will tell whether the cross has been overshadowed by the
arena or whether the arena has been turned into a Christian cemetery.

III. *Fascist Intellect*

To the common charge, " You have no philosophy," the *fascisti* have
two stock replies: the one, " We are proud of it," and the other, " Our
philosophy can be expressed only by deeds." These two statements are
not mere evasions, but sum up the two fundamental strains of fascist ideology. The former links up fascism with a more general movement of intellectual revolt and the latter indicates fascism's particular brand of
idealism.

Researches on the philosophical forerunners of fascism are still continuing actively, and every now and then Mussolini discovers a new

[10] Francesco Ercole: *Il Carattere morale del Nazionalismo*. In *Politica*, Vol. XI
1922, pp. 193–218.

"teacher" of his. On the list at present are: Machiavelli, Mazzini, Schopenhauer, Nietzsche, Stirner, William James, Georges Sorel, Blanqui, Pareto, Oriani, and perhaps others. This means (and this is about all it means) that Mussolini admires philosophies of revolt and that he regards fascism as the bursting into action of an intellectual ferment of long standing.

The intellectualism against which fascism claims to be a revolt is difficult to define but easy to feel. The combination of French positivism and German Kantianism to say nothing of the Church scholasticism that leaked into the secular universities, had produced a wealth of verbiage and academic intellectual machinery. It was all the more artificial because its problems were frequently as foreign as its terminology. On top of this came the elaborate Marxian ideology, which having become a respectable tradition was worked to death as an intellectual system quite apart from its practical utility. Every event of past or current history had to be worked into the meshes of some grandiose system of " social laws " or " the logic of history." It made little difference whether positivistic, socialistic, or idealistic " laws " were used, the net effect was to rationalize everything. The practical implications of this sort of study seemed to be a disinterested fatalism, an " I told you so " attitude. Whatever happened could easily be explained by every champion of his own neat system. Or as Gentile puts it, scholars were content to stand looking out of their windows, explaining carefully everything they saw, but it never occurred to them to go down into the street and take a hand in anything. The systems were ends in themselves. They led nowhere and could not serve as practical programs. By them everything could be explained but nothing predicted.

Among the early revolters against this type of culture, the case of Oriani may be worth special attention, not because of his importance but because he is probably unknown to the reader. Alfredo Oriani wrote extensively in the decades preceding the war and enjoyed a small circle of admirers in Romagna, but he would no doubt have been buried forever had not Mussolini recently discovered and resurrected him. In 1925 Mussolini made a pilgrimage to the Oriani homestead and in 1926 sponsored a complete edition of his works, and announced him as a leading precursor of fascism. Mussolini said of him: "The politics of materialism and positivism reigned triumphant in lecture room and press; in all parties and minds the Italian spirit was in a state of torpor; it was then that Alfredo Oriani threw at the Italian masses his volume ' The Ideal Revolt,' in which all the problems, the passions, the anxieties and the hopes of our times are set forth, illustrated, in a concise style worthy of Tacitus, which alone would have sufficed to bring greatness to a writer. On these pages we have fed and we regard Alfredo Oriani as a poet who sang of our country, as an anticipator of fascism, as an exalter of Italian energies." [11] This is greatly exaggerated of course. Oriani was one of those typical sad, lonely, looking-for-the-dawn, would-be aristocrats. He revolted against the deadening, levelling tendencies of democracy, socialism and the orthodox church. He had a vague faith in the renewal of the civilizing forces of the family, the state and Christianity and he preached the dawn of a greater Italy. In this he resembled the *fascisti*. On the other hand, he opposed war, imperialism, syndicalism and many of the concrete political tendencies of fascism, and he was a fervent, though confused, champion of liberty and individualism. He has been singled out as a prophet of fascism not for his doctrine, but for his temperament — his note of intellectual revolt.

The same is true of other literary figures whom the *fascisti* claim as progenitors: Missiroli, Papini, the "Vocists," d'Annunzio. There was no unity of purpose nor ideas among these men. In fact, there was frequently bitter hostility, as in the case of Papini and d'Annunzio. But they were all revolters; and though they had no common positive goal, they had two common foes: one, the dominant intellectual conventionality and stagnation of the time, and the other, the foreign, especially German, cultural domination of Italy. Papini, to take but one example, in his disgust with the reigning formalism in philosophy and the lack of originality in literature, roamed all over the world in search of a new gospel. He went to the Encyclopedists, to Nietzsche, to pragmatism, to futurism — until his health broke down. During his convalescence he fell in love with his "own dear Tuscany," settled down to being a Christian and then wrote a life of Christ in the manner and spirit of a good Florentine, who had shaken off all German higher criticism and returned to the classic tradition of Italian art.

The idealist movement in philosophy, which was one of the most important factors in the Germanizing of Italian intellectual life, and which started out as a revolt against Catholic Authoritarianism, has turned into a revolt against German academic systems, and a defense of *italianità*. Croce himself, says Gentile, is a fascist in spite of himself, for in spite of his Hegelian foundations he, more than any other single scholar, has revivified the Italian tradition and contributed by his historical researches to the development of Italian *stoicismo*. So that even in his hands and still more so in the hands of his "Vocist" disciples the idealistic traditionalism has become a movement of revolt against

[11] Mussolini in Preface to Oriani: *Rivolta Ideale*.

the French and German philosophical systems and methods of education which had lodged themselves in the schools and universities.

A much more virulent revolt came from the futurists. Here is a specimen from Marinetti:

" On the façades of museums, academies, libraries, and universities, we ought to read the following infamous principles written with the plaster of imbecility:

You no longer think!

You no longer paint!

You no longer construct!

No one can ever improve on the masters!

All originality whatsoever is forbidden!

Banish follies and extravagances! You must copy, copy, copy!

To win the paradise of art you must imitate the lives of our saints!

And over the doors of academies, museums, libraries and universities we write with the heroic charcoal of office stoves:

TO THE EARTHQUAKE

THEIR ONLY ALLY

THE FUTURISTS DEDICATE

THESE RUINS OF ROME AND ATHENS.

" Poets, painters, sculptors, musicians, you must fight . . . against the principle of inertia and slumber. For the world needs only heroism; pardon, as we do, the bloody and lawless deed of the student of Palermo, Lidonni, who avenged himself contrary to law against a tyrannic professor. The passé-ist professors are the only ones responsible for this murder, those passé-ist professors who seek to suffocate the indomitable energy of Italian youth in fetid subterranean channels. When, oh when, will there be an end of this castrating of the spirits that must create the future! . . . We must hurry to remake everything. We must go against the current. Soon will come the moment when we can no longer be content to defend our ideas with our bare hands and fists, when we must begin the assault in the name of intelligence, the artistic assault, the literary assault on that glorified crust of tyrant professors.

" Our immediate program is a desperate struggle against Italian passé-sm in all its repugnant forms: archeology, academicism, senility, quiet-sm, poltroonery, pacifism, pessimism, nostalgia, sentimentalism, erotic bsession, tourist industry, etc. Our ultra violent nationalism is anti-lerical, anti-socialist, anti-traditional and is based on the inexhaustible igor of Italian blood and wages war on the cult of our ancestors who ar from cementing our race make it anemic and wanton. . . . Futurism . . . is an atmosphere of the vanguard; it is the battle cry of all the innovators, of the intellectual free lances of the world; it is the love of the new; the impassioned art of velocity; the systematic defamation of the antique, the old, the slow, the erudite and the professorial; it is a new way of looking at the world; a new reason for loving life; an enthusiastic glorification of scientific discoveries and modern mechanism, a banner of youth, of strength, of originality, at any cost; . . . it is a box of dynamite for all the venerated ruins. . . . The futurists are ' the mystics of action.' " [12]

Inspired by such preaching, not by their studies or professors, the university students became ardent devotees of the new and higher thought. They joined the free lances and apostles of " mystic action," and in this atmosphere soon found the intellectual life both freer and easier than before. From this point of view the War, " arditism," squadrism and similar forms of " action " took on a profound and beautiful significance in the imaginations of the " actors." They were the embodiments of the new art, expressions of the new spirituality. And when their deeds finally carried them into political power, they were more than ever convinced of the truth of their " thought." The " government of artists " which Marinetti had prophesied was being realized.

Thus emboldened these escaped students and protagonists of the new era turned on the old culture and its academic representatives with a vengeance. They began to expound at length the superiority of their active, anti-intellectualistic culture and to ascribe the most profound meanings to their careless deeds. Gentile and the young idealists, with their philosophy of the pure act, discovered fascism to be the embodiment of the new thought that was too vital, too real to be expressed in " abstract " form. Forges-Davanzati and the national politicians went about preaching the doctrine that real culture must always be closely linked to politics.[13] Mussolini's " Dantesque prose " was held up as a supreme creation of Italian art and intellect. By the futurist *fascisti* all academic discussions of professors as well as the conventional articles in the big liberal dailies, were ridiculed as pathetic performances of a degenerate old age, and fascism was proudly heralded as antiphilosophic in essence. Fascism has no philosophy and wants none. Its inability to formulate its ideas into a coherent system is not lamented as a deficiency, but exalted as the most certain evidence of its creative freshness.[14] Mussolini loses his patience when he is confronted with

[12] F. T. Marinetti: *Futurismo e Fascismo, passim.* v. Also Appendix Nos. and 34.
[13] v. His *Fascismo e Cultura.*
[14] cf. Carli: *Fascismo Intransigente,* pp. 97–9, 42–50.

the conventional labels of political theory. "For me," he said, "all these terminologies of right, left, conservative, aristocracy, democracy, are empty scholastic terminology; sometimes they serve to make distinctions, but more often to make confusion." [15] In short, the *fascisti* claim that they have worked a revolution in intellect as well as in government.

Professor Gentile, however, though he is a leading exponent of this doctrine, is nevertheless still a professor. He has taken the matter more seriously and soberly than most of his colleagues of the revolution, and has tried to lay the practical foundations for the new culture by his educational reform. We have already spoken of his introduction of religious education into the schools. This was a mere incident in a more general and sweeping reform of the whole educational system. The fundamental idea of the reform is summed up in the following words of one of the reformers: "We are beginning to understand that human personality does not consist in matter but in the absolute reality of the mind, as a unified whole, whose being lies in its ability to multiply itself in the process of its own growth. To create this synthesis of human personality it is necessary above all to respect it, and not to plan its disintegration and suffocation in the dead mass of scattered items of knowledge. . . . To teach well is not to pile the baggage of bits of information on to the pupil, and to impose on him the results already given and completed by the thought of another, but above all to promote the activities of the pupil in the conquest of scientific truths, which are valuable only in so far as they are the results of his own work and represent his own conquest. . . . Hence a synthesis in the person being educated is realized spontaneously every time he really educates himself, that is every time he feels the value of his own person in acquiring a new idea, undergoing a new experience, overcoming a limitation, widening the orbit of the life of his imagination. . . . Our mind has a value not for what it knows materially, but for its capacity to win ever new knowledge. And what the mind knows is valuable only as a means to be employed in knowing more. Hence the value of the school consists essentially in its enhancement of the ability to learn." [16]

The practical realization of this program of educating the use of the mind rather than its external accomplishments, is somewhat more modest, of course, but is nevertheless noteworthy. In its main lines it is a continuation on a large scale of the work begun by Gentile's predecessor in the Ministry of Education, Benedetto

[15] *La Nuova Politica*, I, p. 24.
[16] Balbino Giuliano: *La Politica Scolastica del Governo Nazionale*, pp. 84–5.

Croce. The schools are reorganized to fit themselves to the actual practical needs of various types of students. The most radical reorganization was made in the secondary schools, which now consist of five distinct kinds: (1) Regular High Schools (*licei-gimnasii*) which are preparatory to university studies and which have two types of curriculum, the classic and the "modern," each preparing for a different type of university studies; (2) the Professional Schools (*Istituti tecnici*) giving a strictly professional training; (3) Junior High Schools (*scuole complementari*), special sixth, seventh and eighth year work for those who are not going ahead to further studies but need technical education for the skilled trades; (4) Normal Schools (*istituti magistrali*); (5) Girls' Finishing Schools (*licei feminili*). For each of these there is a State entrance examination, which is supposed not so much to measure work already done in the elementary schools, as to measure capacity to go ahead successfully in these various secondary schools. The State examinations not only enforce more uniform and severe standards on the public schools, but make it possible for private schools to send their graduates to these secondary schools on the same basis as the public schools. While the chief aim of the elementary school reform is to standardize it, the universities on the other hand are to be given greater freedom. Smaller, struggling universities are to be abolished and a maximum amount of freedom for research and individual scholarship is to be given to the professors of the big universities.

As far as possible artificial school exercises, compositions and lessons are replaced by more up-to-date methods of helping a child to an intelligent control of his activities. The subject-matter is vitalized, notably by the introduction of practical instruction in religion, fine arts (especially music and drawing) and the mechanical arts. The methods of teaching traditional subject-matters are also revised. Latin and Italian, for instance, are coördinated; history is freed from the old-fashioned chronological exercises and is linked to philosophy, which latter is thereby freed from its former dialectical formalities and given a footing in historical tradition. Perhaps this much of the details of the reform will suffice to give the reader an idea of what the *fascisti* mean by their opposition to academic "intellectualism" in the matter of education.

So radical a reform naturally encountered obstinate resistance. Teachers objected because of the new tasks imposed on them; students because the examinations were too difficult; and parents because their children were excluded from the high schools. To appease this opposition the strict Gentile was retired and he was succeeded by more lenient taskmasters, but on the whole his reforms have been enforced and the most difficult period of readjustment is already passed. In the secondary schools its effects are most marked; in the universities, however, the reform has had but slight success.

The *fascisti* are not mere hard-headed "men of action" who spurn all speculations and attend to business. On the contrary, nothing is more characteristic of a fascist than a passionate devotion to theorizing. Much of it is amateurish, but it is spontaneous.

The flood of fascist journalism is the most conspicuous witness to this fact. The regime is a regime founded by a journalist, carried on by journalists, to the undoing of journalism. Every ambitious young fascist thinks it his duty to have his own journal; and as a matter of fact, the government fills a large percentage of its jobs with journalists who have succeeded in making a loud and loyal noise. There is a saying that the first priniciple of fascist philosophy is not *cognito ergo sum*, but *faccio rumore quindi sono*. The government has suppressed fascist papers by the score, but they still flourish in superabundance and their editors still find themselves in a favorable position when jobs are being distributed. The great bulk of this journalism consists in philosophizing on current events, rationalizing the acts of the government and paraphrasing the words of the *Duce*. It is the sort of stuff that under ordinary competitive conditions would find no market. Of course it has no market even now. It is an expensive luxury, kept up because politically it pays editors and authors to advertise.[17]

The most respectable of the fascist periodicals is no doubt the nationalist *Politica*, of which we have spoken previously. *Gerarchia*, founded by Mussolini and now directed by Margherita Sarfatti, has the most official air but is noted more for the variety than for the distinction of its contents. The official publication of the Fascist Institute of Culture, directed by Gentile, is called *Educazione Fascista,* and publishes some of the better little things by fascist scholars, especially by those of the idealist school. The University organizations have a monthly called *Vita Nova.* The recently established weekly literary review *Fiera Letteraria* is conducted under fascist auspices, but otherwise there is nothing distinctively fascist about it. Of the *Critica Fascista* we have already spoken at length. Then there are small sheets centering about more or less individual points of view, such as Suckert's *Conquisto dello Stato,* Soffici's *l'Italiano,* Gorgolini's *Il Nazionale,* and a number of others.

The stock apology for this literature (and not all of it needs apology) is that it is at least fresh. It is an honest effort of new minds to break

[17] For an idea of the nature and extent of fascist journalism see the bibliography in the Appendix.

new channels, and as such must not be expected to achieve positive results immediately. Or, as it is sometimes put, the mere fact that the foreign domination and foreign patterns which have shaped Italian culture for several generations have been broken, is itself a significant positive achievement. It marks the beginnings of a genuine Italian renaissance, the foundations of Italian " spiritual imperialism."

A few literary expresssions of this confidence in the new Italian culture rise above the level of common journalism. Here we are not thinking of older men like Gentile, whose philosophy was already made before the advent of fascism, but of some of the younger men who have worked directly under the stimulus of fascism.

There is, for example, Curzio Suckert (now Malaparte), an ex-republican, who has been the most ardent defender of the theory that fascism is a renewal of the strictly classic Italian tradition. According to him there is a fundamental conflict in Europe between two cultures: between that of the northwest, Protestant, scientific, critical, modern peoples, and that of the southeast, Catholic, dogmatic, artistic, classic. Ever since the Reformation Italy has tried to imitate its northern modern rivals and has failed. Italians are physically incapable of being critical, scientific, democratic, progressive, " civilized "; they are a classic, static, " barbaric " race. The risorgimento was a first sign of revolt in Italy. It was primarily a reaction against the universalism, democracy and " fraternity " of French Freemasonry. But no sooner had the revolt started than it fell back into the philosophy of the French Revolution, and tried to erect a liberal state on the French model. The liberal politicians were really " intellectual bastards " and their boast that they wanted to " make Italians " was untrue; they wanted to unmake them. At last this has definitely failed. Fascism marks a conscious Italian counter-reformation, a shaking off of modernity, a resurgence of the " barbarian " popolo d'Italia and a resumption of the classic, Catholic, Latin tradition. This fascist Catholicism or neo-Guelfism, as it is called, must not be regarded as a defense of the orthodoxy of the Church. Suckert says himself he is " a good Catholic but fiercely anti-clerical." He regards the Church as but one expression of the essential catholicity of the race. A thoroughgoing Italian is " catholic " regardless of his religion.

Fascism is a fresh embodiment of this native spirit in that it teaches the Italians that they must not look to revolutions or to so-called progress for their salvation; in that it substitutes for free criticism which is foreign, the Italian spirit of artistic intuition, of irony, and of tragedy; in that it offers the people a hero and a myth, to satisfy their need of worship; in that it teaches the " national duty o suffering "; and in that its syndicalism will organize the people as a people and not as classes (for classes are really foreign to Italian society, which is not sufficiently capitalistic to be adapted to socialistic ideology and politics).[18]

In a similar vein the late "Volt" writes: "Unless we want to rob the work of the Italian mind of all ideal significance, we must admit without reserve that fascism has the character of an anti-revolution.

"The March on Rome is to the French Revolution what the Council of Trent was to the Protestant Reformation. Living is reaction. In fascism, Italy has again found itself by reacting. It has found its very self, not as formerly in scattered regional tradition, but in the unity of its new consciousness.

"In the name of Romanity Italy casts off its false prophets, breaks down the profaned altars of golden and silver idols built during the century of perdition. We are at last tired of hearing the text of the Nordic lie. Better for us the pagan orgies than to take lessons in morality from Emerson or Ruskin. . . . Man of the Revolution, abstract man, deified man, a grotesque parody of his Creator, has not succeeded in giving us law. Human will is by nature discordant and can never give birth to a moral order. Order can not rise from disorder nor peace from the conflict of individual wills, truth from discussion, law from free-will, the state from contract, authority from liberty. Peace is possible only there where all bow before the authority of a transcendent power.

"In the face of European civilization, moth-eaten by individualism, imperial Italy solemnly asserts the necessity of a law imposed by God on human minds. The tide of history has turned. From Luther to Lenin, the cycle of the great heresy is closed. The society of the future will not be based on the 'Declaration of the Rights of Man' but on the Syllabus." [19]

Massimo Rocca's theory, while just as Catholic, is conceived less in terms of Italian nationalism and more in terms of a general European crisis. According to him ever since the Protestant Revolt European civilization and thought has been disintegrating, and since the French Revolution this process has rapidly gained momentum. First came the denial of tradition and reliance on historical values, then came materialism both in philosophy and politics, then came the critical spirit (from Kant to Harnack), then came the distrust in reason itself and the "desperation of philosophy." In politics a similar decadence took place

[18] v. Suckert: *Europa Vivente*, and *Italia Barbara*. Also Appendix No. 30.
[19] Volt: *Programme della destra fascista*, pp. 154-5.

under the lead of democracy and liberalism. And in art one tradition after another was overthrown until even Wagner had too much " form and simplicity " to suit the modern school.

The revolt against this degeneration began in France with the anti-intellectualism of Blondel and Bergson. But Blondel's " action " found expression only in a book and Bergson was forced to use intellectual concepts in his attack on intellectualism. In religion, the modernists also tried a revolt in a positive, constructive direction but failed. Sorel tried it with syndicalism. Nationalism had a similar motivation. But none of these movements got beyond the level of the very intellectualistic criticism which they were attacking. In Italy, however, the disintegration became acute, practical and political, menacing the very life of the nation. Hence in Italy the rescue also took practical form, a rescue of deeds not of words. But now that the apparently thoughtless deeds are done, it becomes clear that they were motivated by a general revolt against a general decadence. It represents a synthesis of the positive forces of nationalism, modernism, syndicalism, anti-intellectualism, and futurism. The new " Roman period," prophesied by Spengler, has already begun.[20]

The catholicism of these fascist philosophers reminds one of Gioberti's remark that " everyone has his own." They are " esthetic catholics," homesick souls whom even the Church refuses to shelter. Pretending to be more catholic than the Church itself, they are really an isolated group of individuals, who do not want to be individualists, but who can not make their doctrines prevail. For neither in the church, nor among the *fascisti* have they succeeded in arousing more than a distant and suspicious respect. And in fact they themselves take not a little satisfaction in being the *enfants terribles* of the movement. It is indeed a most enticing heresy, this being catholic in defiance of the Church and being radically conservative in the service of a revolution.

A more orthodox, more romantic note is sounded by such writers as Camillo Pellizzi. He has little use for philosophies of history and for long arguments about the relation of fascism to movements of the past. Philosophical reconstructions of history are but intellectual fads and fashions that come and go like the latest street song. And he answers to all these learned disquisitions: " *Risorgimento?* Anti-*risorgimento?* Oh yes, we have no bananas. . . . " For him it is sufficient to establish the fact that there is a fundamental contrast between " the old bourgeoisie " and the new fascist aristocracy. The contrast is typified to his mind by the two idealists Croce and Gentile. In the former's system everything is closed, neatly arranged and permanently ordered. He

[20] Massimo Rocca: *Il Fascismo nel pensiero moderno*, in *Idee sul Fascismo*.

tells the story of how he and other students of Croce were once listening
to him as he outlined the majestic structure of his system and then
wound up by saying, " And now to you, young men, belongs all the detailed work! " At this Pellizzi rebelled; he was not going to do detail
work in any master's workshop. The big outlines must be left open.
Gentile has left them open, and hence his philosophy still lives. But as
for Croce, he is " the last of the bourgeoisie." He lives in a static world
of everlasting being, just as the old bourgeoisie imagined that its economic and political order must necessarily be the permanent framework
of the universe. This petrified bourgeoisie was rudely thrown out by a
living, young, heroic aristocracy. And like all heroes, these *fascisti* embodied their thoughts in their deeds.

Pellizzi writes as one of the heroes: " Our objectives and aims must
be determined not by the learned, but by the active heads of our
work, day by day. The 'thinker' of fascism is and remains Benito
Mussolini; for he has thought out fascism in the process of making it.
This is the primary, concrete mode of political thinking. But you say,
if fascism can thus be reduced to nothing but action, . . . wherein does
this thing you call fascist thought consist and how can it be distinguished?
The answer is in the question. The kernel of fascist thought is contained in so conceiving fascism. That is, in conceiving politics as creative action and will. And that the thoughts that are being thought, or
the schemes, systems and concepts of social and political life which
fascism is continually establishing and evolving from its own bosom, are
therefore not doctrines premised or facts postulated by fascist action,
but rather are the fruits, products and derivations of the creative action.
. . . We start out with the idea that politics is an original creation of the
spirit and that the spirit realizes itself in politics as an absolute responsibility to itself and to its own action and in politics creates its own moral
personality. It is man creating himself; but also God creating man. By
'willing' in this way, man feels a power within him overflowing into
action to which he can not deny an absolute value, the quality of absolute
reality, and even the quality of a transcendent reality. Not every deed
of man is consequently good, but every deed of man that is inspired by
this total, mystical responsibility." [21]

This is, so to speak, the minimum of fascist philosophy. For a maximum we might mention the work of Pasini, a writer in the newspaper
L'Impero, who has developed a theory of *Sinarchia,* which is supposed
to be, according to him, a *summa politica,* as St. Thomas wrote a
summa theologica. The theory is most briefly expounded diagram-
matically:

[21] Camillo Pellizi: *Fascismo Aristocrazià,* pp. 46–8. v. Also Appendix No. 31.

The Universal Sinarchic State is a fusion of the three aristocracies:

1. The aristocracy of the Will . . . The government . . . The *eagle*, symbol of Empire or of absolute political authority.
2. The aristocracy of feeling or sentiment . . . The Church . . . The *cross*, symbol of divine authority.
3. The aristocracy of intelligence . . . Economic order and science . . . The *bank*, symbol of economic organization.

Each of these three faculties of the spirit is organized as a hierarchy and the three hierarchies are fused into a single " creative synthesis of The Genius of the Race." " *Stato unico in chiesa divina.*"

This gives the bare theme of the rhapsody; the embellishments are equally exalted and yield no end of trinities.[22]

IV. Fascist Art

Of the early political and intellectual affiliations of fascism and futurism we have already spoken. Certainly Marinetti and his associates were among the most active and conspicuous members of the Mussolini group of 1919 and earlier. And these men definitely expected to make fascism the political vehicle of futurism. But as we have seen the early program of the Milan *fascio* failed completely and by 1921 the spirit and membership of fascism was far beyond anything which the futurists could hope to control. In fact the radical anti-clericalism and anti-monarchism of Marinetti became a liability rather than an asset for fascism and when the futurist program was abandoned Marinetti and a few faithful followers abandoned fascism. A large number of the futurists (Settimelli, Carli, Bolzon, E. Rocca, Volt, etc.) abandoned their extreme position and adapted themselves to fascism, whose ideas were less fixed and whose fortunes were better. In this way futurism early lost its grip on the movement, and art of any sort was pushed into the background. Mussolini personally has continued his friendship with Marinetti and his enthusiasm for the new art. The *Rivista del Popolo d'Italia* and *Gerarchia* are full of futurist designs and Mussolini is evidently pleased by the futurist bust and portraits which have been made of him. This suffices to give the movement a limited prestige or at least a toleration which it did not enjoy before. The government has forced the museums and expositions to give space to futurist works and the futurists in turn are making it a point to employ fascist themes and materials in their designs. The " synthetic theatre " and the " theatre of surprise " founded and sponsored by Marinetti have found some foot-

[22] v. Achille Pasini: *Impero Unico.*

hold, though very meagre. The more successful work of Pirandello, though quite independent of either fascism or futurism, has elements which are claimed to be futurist; but in general it is too much infected with "psychologism" to please Marinetti. In this connection Marinetti says: "I believe it is now urgent to combat the psychologism of the theatre in its various forms:

"1. Scientific-documentary psychologism of the *passé*-ist type.

"2. Semi-futurist psychologism *alla* Paris, fragmentary, effeminate, ambiguous (Proust).

"3. Italian psychologism that disguises as futuristic, analyses that are bulky, lawyerish, heavy, funereal, moralistic, professorial, pedantic, with relative decrepit Hamletisms: 'To be or not to be; to live or to dream' and philosophical dialogues without any plastic synthesis.

"These psychologisms are all three of them equally analytic, long and anti-Italian, that is, contrary to the beautiful lyric, spirited, explosive, improvising, winged, colorful qualities of our race.

"Therefore we have created two new forms of theatre (making the round of eighteen Italian cities as The New Futurist Theatre):

"1. An abstract, alogical synthesis of pure elements that portray the living forces of the action to the audience without any psychology. An abstract synthesis is an alogical, surprising combination of blocks of typical sensations.

"2. A tactile, muscular, athletic, mechanical synthesis without psychology." [23]

Whether or not this is fascist art, the government has given it little practical encouragement. Ciarlantini, the politician who is chiefly responsible for promoting art, admitted that the policy of the government was not to encourage "exceptional theatres," not even that of Pirandello, but to subsidize a few regular, standard companies "who know how to follow the way of the Italian tradition with a just sense of modernity." He admitted also that the Italian theatre was not in a flourishing condition but expressed the pious hope that "it is not improbable that out of all the energies being dedicated to the theatre today, a period of some importance for the Italian stage will be born; Italy, it must be remembered, is a land of miracles." [24] In other words the government is playing safe: supporting the big popular theatres and trusting in miracles for a revival of art.

In music the modernists, who are affiliated with the Italian futurist

[23] F. T. Marinetti: *Verso un Teatro Anti-psicologico,* in *Il 1919,* August 1926, p. 44. See also Appendix No. 34.

[24] Franco Ciarlantini: *Imperialismo Spirituale,* pp. 84, 81.

movement, are gradually getting more of a hearing, but they are no more popular among the *fascisti* than among others.

The stronghold of the futurists has been architecture. Marinetti has persistently raged against the Roman and medieval ruins of Rome, Florence and Venice, and the other prize pieces of " *passé*-ism." And he wants the new Italy to be built on an architectural plan suggested by the big industrial centers of Milan and Genoa, " the new Italy " of steel, mechanism, power and velocity. When Mussolini announced his plan of rebuilding and enlarging Rome, the futurists immediately set to work. With Prampolini at their head, they drew up plans for a genuinely new Rome. Their suggestions have met with little general success, and the latest plans published, though they are by no means final, are quite conventional — elaborate but not distinctive. The new building of the Ministry of the Marine has no particular architectural merit, and up to the present at least, as one writer says, " the light is certainly not coming from Rome." [25] The two outstanding contributions toward a new architecture have come from sources not immediately in the government: one, the *Polisportivo* of Bologna, a massive cement stadium, and the other, the new building of the Confederation of Fascist Labor Syndicates at Rome.

Besides futurism there are at least two other major centers of fascist art. One is the idealist Vocist group, primarily interested in literature, in a revival of a free light Italian style. It has made an effort to liberate Italian idealism from the heavy style imposed upon it by its German progenitors, and has also reacted against the heavy Romanism of d'Annunzio. If we omit the pre-fascists like Prezzolini and Papini, the scattered writings of Ardengo Soffici are certainly the most distinguished work of this group. They constitute a vigorous statement of the reactions of an intelligent fascist to the fundamental changes in Italian society produced by the war, without any pretense of philosophic systematization. He is a good example of revolt against revolutionism combined with a militant disdain for democracy and liberalism.[26] He is also a painter of merit.

Lastly there is the d'Annunzian school now on the decline, but nevertheless still very influential. It is sufficiently well known not to need comment here. d'Annunzio, having rebelled against his German master, Nietzsche, and turned to pagan Rome, cultivated a heavy Latin style and an imperial bearing, and, having become the popular idol of the nation by his rescue of Fiume, has now retired to the country and relapsed into humility. In his palatial country " hermitage " he is now

[25] Volt: in *Critica Fascista*, November 1, 1926, p. 399.
[26] v. Soffici: *Battaglie fra due Vittorie*. Also Appendix Nos. 7, 8, 33.

quietly awaiting his end, praising, in the meantime, the simplicity and poverty of his ".Franciscan brethren."

Among these three groups there is an active rivalry, and not a little of the internal political friction of which we spoke in the last chapter is at bottom a product of the antipathies of these groups of artists toward each other.[27] But no one of them or even all three of them have been able to dominate fascist so-called culture. In fact practically all the younger artists of distinction, whether of these groups or not, are fairly disgusted with the present state of fascist art. They blame the government for favoring second-rate conventional talent that is in no sense fascist, and allowing the fresh, original " genius " in the fascist ranks to go neglected.[28] Certainly if the work of Ciarlantini is typical of the fascist government, there is ample ground for complaint. For though he makes a big stir about fascist art and Italy's " spiritual imperialism," he is concerned more with a cheap advertising of Italy's spiritual goods on the foreign market, than with a critical encouragement of a fascist renaissance.[29] But even Ciarlantini's stand seems to be considerably superior to the general apathy among the official classes.

At least this was the general state of affairs until the fall of 1926, when Mussolini caused considerable excitement in the camp. At the inauguration of the new home of the Authors' Association, he spoke as follows: " It is now up to our writers to carry on what may be called ' spiritual imperialism '; in the theatre, in books, in lectures, they must make Italy known not only for its greatness in the past. When I said I had visited only two art galleries, that was not true. I have visited a number. I meant to say that we must not stop at picture galleries, but must work inside ourselves, gnaw at our own vitals, torment ourselves internally, produce something new that will have the stamp of our times." And a few weeks later, during the impressive celebration at Perugia, he paid his formal respects to the Academy of Fine Arts and to art in general, and said: " Now that all the conditions longed for by the great Italians, first and foremost unity, are realized, a great art can develop in our land, embracing and in turn enhancing all phases of life, an art which must be traditionalist and at the same time modern, that must look to the past and at the same time to the future.

" We must not remain mere contemplators, we must not exploit the

---

[27] v. for example, Marinetti: *L'Arte Fascista Futurista*, in *Critica Fascista*, January 1, 1927, p. 3; also Appendix No. 34; and Malaparte (Suckert), in *La Conquista dello Stato*, December 15, 1926, p. 3.

[28] v. for example, Soffici: *Arte Fascista*, in *Critica Fascista*, October 15, 1926, pp. 383-4. Also in Appendix No. 33.

[29] cf. Ciarlantini: *Imperialismo spirituale*.

patrimony of the past. We must create a new patrimony to put beside the ancient one, we must create a new art, an art of our times, a fascist art." [30]

These declarations were immediately given wide publicity and great importance was attached to them. Everyone began talking art. A few months later the Villa Farnesina in Rome was bought by the government as a seat for an Italian Academy, to be established immediately. All this means that the government wants to begin the fascist renaissance in earnest.

There is universal agreement, however, that the government can not make art. The National Academy, and similar institutions are even looked upon suspiciously by some as a sign of a trend toward the conventional patronage and political organization of artists on foreign models and traditional lines. Fascist art, they say, must take its rise from different quarters and under new forms.

Among fascist artists there seems to be agreement on a few general ideas about what fascist art ought to be. Except for those futurists who still hope to be the exclusive representatives of fascist art, there is general agreement that fascism should not attempt to found a distinct school. The movement should be catholic enough to embrace any form of really creative art that is strictly Italian. For fascism aims to be broadly national in this respect as well as in politics.

Secondly, fascist art must not be merely decorative, an artificial embellishment or an independent luxury. It must be a direct and natural expression of fascist life and indistinguishable from fascist activity. Art is not to be a distinct subject-matter or profession, but a quality of life — " art life " is the formula adopted from the d'Annunzians. The traditional dualism between thought and action has been overcome by the fascist conception of art; a conception, they say, really implicit in the philosophy of Croce, had he carried out his method and regarded art as a synthesis of these two realms instead of falling back in his esthetics on the old dualism which he had already transcended in his logic. Art is to life what form is to matter. Hence the *fascisti* are looking not so much toward art institutions like the theatre, the novel, the poem, the statue, the painting, as sources for the new art, but to politics, industry, sport, war, flying, building (of ships, houses, aqueducts, power plants, etc.).

It is, for example, almost a commonplace among fascist " art critics " that the fighting of the war was the first great masterpiece of fascist art — literally a work of art, both in its general conception and in its details. The futurists, of course, are loudest in the praise of military

[30] See Appendix No. 32.

esthetics — not the old-fashioned courage and heroism, but modern fighting — speed, power, huge mechanical, impersonal, dynamic organization of forces. Quite apart from this futurist theoretical prejudice, however, there is a general admiration for the art of war. The same holds true of the art implied in the March on Rome — even finer, they say, than the War for it displayed the same organized energies in a rhythmic way without the bloodshed and it had all the poetic qualities of sacrifice and ideal devotion without the physical torture.

Another chief work of fascist art is the *Duce* himself — a genuinely creative " invention " and a vital synthesis of speech, bearing and deeds. The reader must not take this metaphorically, for the whole point of the fascist doctrine is that genuine art must be expressed literally in the form of practical action and not in so-called works of art; and the whole essence of the fascist faith is this confidence in the esthetic values of their practical achievements.

It follows that if fascist artists want to indulge in any of the more traditional forms of art their works should at least express and interpret the values already embodied in the war, the revolution, and the fascist state. They must be imperial, expansive, synthetic, vigorous, clear, uncompromising, and suggestive of rapid, decisive action. This is the theory. And in theory the *fascisti* can well afford to be unanimous; there will be abundant opportunity for differences when it comes to applying it to particular works of art. But it is idle to anticipate these differences, for as yet there are no particular works of art to speak of.

V. Fascist Morals

In discussing separately fascist politics, religion, philosophy, art and morals, we have, of course, done violence to the essential unity of the fascist spirit, and the reader will no doubt have noticed that these separate discussions are really but variations on a single theme, namely, that fascism is not a doctrine, but a way of life. Strictly speaking this doctrine must be lived in silence, it is mystic; the more it is put into words the further it is removed from reality. Unfortunately, however, Italy has always been a land of language and hence the *italianissimi fascisti* must have their speeches, books and journals! After all, speech, especially Italian speech, is a form of action. Certainly the *fascisti's* accomplishments in this sphere of action are by no means the least of their achievements. For the world of the imagination which has been built upon it already far outshines, both in their own eyes and in those of foreign spectators, their more modest and substantial reforms. The external facts of fascist life really become quite insignificant once the true inwardness and spirituality of the movement is grasped. Fascism's mind, then, is contained in ideal fascist morals and its culture is the character which every fascist thinks he possesses.

The fascist character has been summed up by Mussolini in the Nietzschean slogan " live dangerously." [31] And he explains that by such a mode of life he means " First of all courage, fearlessness, the love of risk, repugnance for a pot-bellied peaceful life, to be ever ready to dare in private as in public life, to abhor all that is sedentary; the greatest clearness in one's dealings, face to face conversations and not clandestine, anonymous and base vociferations; the pride every hour of the day in feeling oneself Italian, discipline in work, respect for authority. The new Italian." [32]

Gentile's version employs a different language but the meaning is much the same: " Fascism means to take life seriously. Life is toil, effort, sacrifice, hard work; a life in which we know very well that there is neither matter nor time for amusement. Before us there always stands an ideal to be realized, an ideal which gives us no respite. We have no time to lose. Even in our sleep we must give account of the talents entrusted to us. . . . Our way of life is the serious way (the religious way, as I call it) of conceiving life and living it. A way which among other things does not allow us to be contented any longer with a show, passably pleasing and even instructive, rich in news and curious enough to stimulate even the most difficult and refined tastes, if in this show along with its delights, instruction, interest, and in its variegated elements, there is no sign of the man himself, and no passion felt — an intense and vigorous passion capable of enfolding the whole of life and of ruling the whole soul by that constant and vehement unity which is one of the most noted characteristics of the religious spirit." [33]

This living religiously and dangerously has several aspects. I would mention first of all that of sport. The interest in sport has grown enormously in Italy during the last few years. Athletic clubs and sporting events are numerous. Everything from soccer to Alpine climbing and from bicycling to flying. The restricted daily press is inadequate to deal with the sporting news and consequently several newspapers devoted exclusively to sport are to be found in every city and their circulation is very large. This is due not merely to the censorship and dullness of political newspapers but to a genuine interest in athletics — not a casual interest in amusement and exercise, but a sporting interest in the American sense, a serious and passionate devotion to athletic conquest.

[31] v. Nuova Politica, III, p. 222.
[32] Mussolini, June 21, 1925. Discorsi del 1925, p. 104.
[33] Gentile: Che cosa è il fascismo, pp. 38 and 167. Also Appendix No. 29.

It is the "moral equivalent" for empire. It exploits even play for purposes of moral discipline and prepares the mind and body for other more serious forms of conflict — not more serious in their inner quality but in their practical consequences.

The government is encouraging sport both directly and indirectly. It was no mere gesture when Mussolini, after outlining the fascist mode of life as quoted above, held up De Pinedo as the "champion new Italian." Flying, of course, has its military side and its heroic appeal, and naturally received recognition. But other important forms of rivalry and sport were also given an exceptional encouragement and official political recognition. In fact, interest in sport among the politicians is nothing short of sensational, for Italian politicians traditionally are not only too old for sport but too dignified.

Vice versa, unfascist forms of amusement are being discouraged. All dance halls and cabarets must be closed at midnight, partly because they are sources of immorality, but chiefly because they are uneconomical, unwholesome and above all un-Italian. There is a censorship of moving pictures and theatres in the interests of morals. In August 1926 a decree was issued obliging moving picture theatres to include an "educative film of propaganda and culture" in their programs, but this has not been enforced as yet, though a private firm has been given the contract to furnish these official educational films. There is an intensive campaign against swearing either in the name of God or Country, and 25,000 of the 187,000 bars and wine rooms, "cheap venders of ruinous felicity," [34] have been closed and more are threatened with the same treatment. In general the government has no hesitation about regulating morals and amusements as it (or perhaps the Church) may deem fit. For there is no aspect of life too private to fall outside the fascist picture. Even play is serious, and even sleep, as Gentile says, is a political function.

One ardent young fascist writes: "Today, as never before, the need is felt not so much of a program as of a practical, severe, Dominican rule of life. May not this be the time to lay down the tables of the fascist law? Laws of daily life, private as well as social or collective?" [35] At this Gentile personally revolted, for though he preaches the *stato etico*, he has an idealist, not a Dominican, conception of the moral law. But among many of the younger *fascisti* there is a veritable passion for obedience — not perhaps for their own obedience: they feel its need in general: when it comes to themselves they usually talk like lawgivers — not in their own name, of course, but as mouthpieces for the *Duce*.

[34] Mussolini, May 26, 1927.
[35] Gioacchino Contri, in *Critica Fascista*, August 15, 1926, p. 305.

Another trait of fascist character is *giovinezza*. This concept has gained a rich emotional " fringe "; it is hard to define but everywhere displayed. It is first of all literally physical youth. Italian politics has not seen so young a breed of politicians for many a generation. The *fascisti* like to point out that Giolitti was the first prime minister since Cavour to achieve that office at the early age of fifty! Depretis was seventy-four years old when he ended his last ministry; Crispi, seventy-seven; Giolitti himself, seventy-nine. Rocco says of the last-named, " he was the head of an old system, a product of an old mentality and of old Italian vices." [36]

Compared with this old type of statesman, the *fascisti* certainly mark a revolution. Settimelli wrote: " It is a real relief to think that Mussolini, the product and leader of this great movement, fascism, is only thirty-seven years old, and loves all the sports." [37]

The juvenile rituals which accompany the movement have turned the whole country into a college fraternity. The fascist anthem, *Giovinezza*, was originally a student song at Turin, popularized during the war. Now that the new recruits of the fascist party are coming almost exclusively from the " graduates " of the *Avanguardia*, the movement is taking on an even more youthful character. " All Italy is but twenty years old today," said Mussolini.

This physical youth implies youthful politics. The main burden of political responsibility is of course not on the shoulders of youths. The mature liberals in the first cabinet were gradually supplanted by mature nationalists, and the government is by no means as young as it sounds. Nevertheless the political atmosphere, the press and platform are dominated by youthful spirits. Early fascism and squadrism was of course full of student pranks and its politics was largely a form of sport. On numerous occasions, for example, communist speakers were captured, their heads shaved, the tricolor painted on their scalps and then they were pushed out on to the platform to speak. The castor oil treatment too was more frequently ludicrous than brutal.

Though fascist politics has sobered down considerably since the days of the revolution, it still retains many of the characteristics of a student movement. Political arguments are more *ad hominem*, political speeches less academic, political tactics less reserved than they used to be. The Chamber of Deputies acts more like a fraternity convention than like a legislative body, especially when Mussolini appears in sight. Politics in general is a form of excitement rather than a field of reflective deliberation.

[36] *Politica*, January 1920, p. 315.
[37] Quoted in Gorgolini: *Il Fascismo bella vita italiana*, p. 20.

But *giovinezza* has also its more positive side: it is exuberance, energy, self-confidence, and optimistic faith. "Today," writes one of these *giovani*, "we can believe with some assurance that we are finding ourselves again, that is, our eternally youthful spirit, which the incrustations of mediocre periods had concealed under a coat of filth and which today can shine more brightly than ever. . . . Now our most diverse capacities and possibilities, from apostolic asceticism to the spirit of adventure, from the *dolce far niente* to the most feverish activity, from the Vesuvian songs to the daring playing of the stock market, from superstition to sport, from impassioned crime to the most perfect industry, must be fused a little, harmonized and encouraged. The true Italian, complete and modern, shares a little in all these qualities; he is a poet, an adventurer, an apostle, a boxer, lover, grandee, leader of masses, warrior and builder. . . . He conquers Fiume and holds it in spite of all the Great Powers. He conquers Rome and establishes there the law of the new youth. . . . This Italian, this extraordinary individual, from a foreigner's point of view, but common enough among us, is naturally hated and besieged by all the weapons which the ' residues of the past ' can command.

"The cornerstone of the nation is the indomitable energy of a man, who impersonates youth, but not that green, thoughtless, light and volatile youth which literary tradition pictures, but the youth full of thought and of fire, supported by an awakened consciousness and power of will, which, having come early into contact with life, having realized at once its dramatic contrasts and painful depths and through the severest of tests having armed itself with optimism and with the faith necessary to meet fate victoriously. This is the youth represented by Mussolini and by the generation which with him waged the war, fought the fight of fascism, and is today preparing itself to realize the imperial destiny of Italy." [38]

Implied in the idea of *giovinezza* is that of the new aristocracy, the genuine *classe dirigente*. The *fascisti* have an unbounded confidence in their capacity to lead the nation politically and culturally as well as physically. They frankly call themselves the best part of the nation, the *élite*. They look down on the masses as incapable of self-government, of ideals, of anything beyond their personal concerns, as so much raw material which must be molded by a superior class. The *fascisti* are the leaders of the people, they say, but they are not *of* it. On the other hand, they are still less *of* the bourgeoisie. Economically speaking they may belong to the lower middle classes, but culturally they are the cream of the nation. They look down on the masses with condescension,

[38] Mario Carli: *Fascismo Intransigente*, pp. 13 and 35.

but on the bourgeoisie with moral indignation. The reign of the middle classes is over, and Italy once more has a genuine nobility, a ruling class composed of that small minority who carry the spiritual burden of the nation. As such the *fascisti* have not only the right but the duty to govern. They have measured up to their tasks, they say, have taken over the most technical and responsible posts of the government, posts which hitherto had been reserved for old age, and have proved their superiority. And as for the " old bourgeoisie " in and out of Parliament, this degenerate class, they say, has been beaten physically and is now being beaten morally and mentally. In place of an egoistic, mate-Italy now has a truly aristocratic government. It is ruled by men of strength, energy and confidence, men who have a genuine interest in the national welfare, who are not tied by profession or tradition to vested interests, but are free to serve the ideal ends which they profess. Pellizzi, one of these young aristocrats, is so enthused over the virtues of this new class that he seriously proposes making it an hereditary aristocracy, for the purpose of breeding " true gentlemen." He addresses his fellow noblemen as follows: " You are aristocrats, I say, because you have strength; and I say you have strength because you have faith. A faith not in any existing human law nor in any established institution of law or politics, but faith in the profound inspiration which comes from your own souls. . . . You are the kind of men who do not take their law from others but who make it themselves. . . . Original makers of history . . . For you are the virtuous, in the classic sense of the term; extremely ingenious and creative and very forceful, the independent molders of a new history." [39]

Another writes: " In us aristocrats, there shines the light of a noble ' myth '; the myth of a race of men no longer men, of a liberated race, without good or evil, without needs, without desire, without passion; a race of conquerors that no longer believes but *is,* in a life of sheer cosmic power, in beings that have a terrifying look, that breathe freely in a world freed of ' providence,' ' aims,' and ' reasons ' — alone, gazing without fear into the shadows where God no longer exists and where they themselves are the creators of God." [40]

This is slightly exaggerated, of course, and tinged with a bit of " unfascist " rhetoric. But the theme it celebrates is an old favorite. The *fascisti* have merely revived the age-old ideal of heroic Italy. Fascist aristocracy is not conceived individualistically; it is not Nietzschean. It is the idea of an aristocratic class leading a heroic nation. The

[39] Camillo Pellizzi: *Fascismo Aristocrazià,* pp. 101-2.
[40] J. Evola, in *Critica Fascista,* October 15, 1926, p. 393.

emphasis is on the ideal unity of the people. The Italians, oppressed for centuries and internally divided for a still longer period, have the heroic, romantic traditon ground into them. And naturally the romance has hitherto been tinged with sadness and pessimism. Italy has fought for generations, not out of hope but out of sheer moral ardor. It has willingly sacrificed itself on the altar of its seemingly impossible aims. Now after a comparatively short struggle, the fight for political liberty and unity has been won. But the larger struggle for economic liberty and national expansion immediately looms up. Liberalism renounced the new struggle and sought to settle down in peace. Fascism, on the other hand, has taken up once more the familiar and hard gospel of the "national duty of suffering," as Suckert calls it. But this time, not without hope. For fascism is confident that Italy's imperial destiny will soon be realized. In the meantime, however, the call is to the old heroic virtues of sacrifice, discipline, duty. Italy's struggle with her richer neighbors and with easy-going liberalism is fundamentally the issue between Stoicism and Epicureanism, or, as one writer expresses it, "the issue between the heroic and the sanitary life." Italy could settle down like some of her neighbors to a peaceful mediocrity. But Italy is Italian and prefers to "live dangerously." Hence the need of a class of conquerors, and the duty of utilizing Italy's natural fund of genius to the utmost.

"Sometimes," said Mussolini, "I play with the idea of a laboratory for making generations: that is, of creating the class of warriors, ever ready to die; the class of inventors, pursuing the secret of mystery; the class of judges, the class of great captains of industry, of great explorers, of great governors. And it is by means of such a methodical selection that the great classes are created which in turn will create the empire. To be sure this is a lofty dream; but I see it being realized little by little. . . . The goal is always — Empire! To build a city, to found a colony, to establish an empire, these are the prodigies of the human spirit. An empire is not merely territorial; it may be political, economic, spiritual. . . . Toward this we must move. And therefore we must resolutely abandon the whole liberal phraseology and way of thinking. The word of command can be none but this: discipline. Discipline at home, in order that abroad we may present the granite block of a single national will." [41]

[41] Mussolini: *Discorsi del 1925*, pp. 105-6.

APPENDIX

Selections from Fascist Literature and Documents of Fascist History

The translation of much of the technical material in this Appendix is literal rather than idiomatic. This has been done partly to preserve the Italian terms for which no English equivalents exist, and partly to give the English reader an impression of the variety of style, or lack of style, which fascist literature presents.

PART I

The War Party

No. 1. *Mussolini Makes a Start*

(The following is taken from Mussolini's editorial in the first number of the *Popolo d'Italia,* November 15, 1914, entitled *Audacia.* It is his challenge to the Socialist Party after his expulsion at the convention of Bologna.)

"On the morrow of the famous œcumenical gathering at Bologna, in which, to speak rather solemnly, I was 'burned but not refuted,' I asked myself the question which I have answered today by founding this journal of ideas and of battle. I asked myself, should I speak or keep silent? Should I retire into the tent like a weary and deluded soldier, or might it not be necessary that by another weapon I resume my fighting post? . . . If it were a matter of secondary importance I would not have felt the need, still less the duty, of founding a journal; but now whatever may be said by the neutralists of conservative socialism, there is a formidable question to be solved: the destinies of European socialism are very closely bound up with the possible results of this war; to be disinterested means to detach oneself from history and life, to work for reaction and not for the social revolution. Ah no! Revolutionary Italian socialists, whether they be guided by reasoning or urged blindly but infallibly by sentimental intuitions, know what the cry is that must be raised by the Italian proletariat. Neutrality can not be a dogma of socialism. For is it only in socialism and more specifically in Italian socialism that 'absolute' truths are to be found that can defy the injuries of time and the limitations of space with impunity, like the indisputable and eternal truths of divine revelation? But absolute truth about which there is no dispute and which can neither be denied nor renounced, is dead truth; worse still it is murderous truth. We are not and do not wish to be mummies, everlastingly immovable with our faces always turned to the same horizon and enclosed in the narrow hedges of subversive hypocrisy, where formulæ are mechanically mumbled like the prayers of ritualist religions; but we are men and live men who wish to give our contribution however modest to historical creation. Inconsistency? Apostasy? Desertion? Nevermore. It remains to be seen on what side the inconsistent, the apostates, and the deserters are to be found. Tomorrow's history will tell it, but our prophetic abilities are able to foresee it.

If there will be a little more liberty in Europe tomorrow, and hence an atmosphere politically better adapted to the development of socialism, to the building up of the capacities of the proletarian class, all those will be deserters and apostates who, when action was demanded, declined and stood aside. . . .

Today, and I shout it loudly, anti-war propaganda is a propaganda of cowardice. It flourishes because it spurs and arouses the instinct of individual self-preservation. But for this very reason it is an anti-revolutionary propaganda. It is carried on by the temporalist priests and the Jesuits who have a material and spiritual interest in the preservation of the Austrian Empire; it is carried on by the bourgeoisie, the more or less smugglers, who, especially in Italy, have proved their lamentable political and moral inadequacy; it is carried on by the monarchists . . . ; this coalition of pacifists knows very well what it wants and we can now easily explain the motives that inspire its attitude. But we socialists, except during the low period of bargaining reformism and of Giolitti, have represented one of the live forces of the new Italy: now do we want to bind our future to these dead forces in the name of a peace that does not save us from the disasters of war today, and that will not save us from the undoubtedly greater dangers of tomorrow, and in any case will not save us from disgrace and from the universal disdain of those peoples who have undergone this great tragedy of history? Do we want to drag out our miserable daily existence blessed by the monarchic and bourgeois *status quo*, or do we rather want to put an end to this sordid and filthy mess of intrigues and baseness? May not this be our day? Instead of preparing ourselves to submit to pre-ordained events, a scandalous alibi, is it not better to try to control them? . . . To cry: 'We want war!' may not this be much more revolutionary under the circumstances than to cry 'down with war'?

These disquieting questions to which I for my part have replied, explain the origins and aims of this paper. What I am doing today is an act of audacity, and I am not unaware of the difficulties in the undertaking. They are many and complex, but I have the firm confidence that I can overcome them. I am not alone. Not all of my friends of yesterday will follow me, but many other rebel spirits will gather around me. I shall conduct an independent paper, exceptionally free, personal, *my own*. It will reflect my mind and mine alone. I have no aggressive intentions against the socialist party, nor against the organs of the party in which I expect to remain; but I have set out to fight all who may try to hinder the free discussion of a position which for various reasons I hold to be basic to the national and international interests of the proletariat.

I care nothing for the malicious and the idiotic. Let the former remain in their mire and the latter go to pieces in their intellectual void.

I shall go ahead! And in resuming the march, after this brief rest, it is to you, youths of Italy, youths of the offices and of athletic contests, youths in years and youths in spirit, youths who belong to the generation to whom destiny has assigned the making of history, it is to you that I raise my cry of greeting, confident that within your ranks it will find a resounding echo and abundant sympathy.

The cry is a word which I would never have pronounced in normal times but which today I raise loudly, with unrestrained voice, without reservations, and with a sure faith: a fearful and fascinating word: War!" (In *Diuturna*, pp. 1-5.)

No. 2. "*Long Live War!*"

"Three cheers for the War! May I be permitted to raise this cry? Even today when so many who willed the War or pretended to will it are obstinately silent, draw in their horns, or worse still, in their baseness and foolishness are chanting hymns in homage to a slimy and plebeian tendency of which they are afraid and in which they miserably join.

Therefore, three cheers for the War, for the irresistible and great act of this glowing young Italy; for the War not wanted by the dark multitude of the overly simple and badly twisted; for the War waged by the prodigious effort of the spirit that revived the profound meaning of our race; and for the War that was won. The War I wanted, waged according to the best of my ability, defended, am defending, and shall defend as long as I live. Three cheers for Italy's War, noble and beautiful above all, with its five thousand dead who are our surest wealth.

And three cheers also for war in general. It is cursed in word and deed by a herd of bastards and fools and infinitely blind and ignorant multitudes, nevertheless the adorable facts will not change their form nor their onward march. War, a physical and spiritual fact combined, cannot fail to exist in a world which has always seen it and always will; and moreover a world in which everything from the act of thought to that of undertaking and accomplishing the slightest deed of free action, is struggle and war against something or somebody.

The instinct of war is in human nature, together with all the other instincts that make up man's specific personality and that determine his every choice, which reason, the most subtle instinct, but sanctions, as everyone knows. And to this fact which might justify war only as a fatality must be added another, which makes us love it, that war is also one of the most fruitful mystic manifestations. Like a storm that relieves and refreshes nature when it is charged with electricity and full of bad vapors, war comes and stirs up in society and in man the putrid sediment of hatreds accumulated by the competitions, the base calculations and the gross and beastly habits of the world. It arouses in the soft and sleepy individual mind those flying energies which without war only the privileged person knows who lives the life of thought and dreams. It is creative of new values, a sower of seeds. War, that brings grief to hearts otherwise closed, that leads to risks and abysses, that puts death before all our eyes, is the great revealer of the most jealously hidden truths. For only at the sight of death does the soul of man go deep and awake in its simplest essence; it is exalted in heroism or it is spent in the ignominy for which it is made and where no one without the irresistible event would have cast it. War is justice, nobility and brotherly pity. This is not to say that it should be waged because of this or that person's will. Like all profound natural phenomena it has its hour and its point; and each people knows this and obeys when the time comes. I say these familiar things which many however would forget, because amid the common abasement I like to uphold a flame of conscience that is not mortified by the wave of vain prattle and drunken threats. Also, if ever the era of a perfectly pacific and idiotic paradise should begin (though this is quite impossible), I wish the illiterate apostles of universal *camaraderie* to know whom they should assassinate.

No. 3. "*Futurism and Fascism*"

(F. T. Marinetti has gathered a number of his writings from the last fifteen years into a volume under the above title. Futurism, of which he is the recognized leader, was a political movement as well as an artistic movement long before fascism and even before the war. In 1919 Marinetti was as prominent in Milan fascism as Mussolini was, but when a year later fascism turned monarchist and Catholic, he withdrew his support temporarily. Most of the futurists, however, continued to be prominent in the fascist ranks though they are much less important today and less representative of the movement than they were originally.)

" The Futurists are the ' mystics of action.' (1909) "

" The cult of the past and mercantilism in art; these are the two terrible plagues that are devastating our country.

In our struggle we systematically scorn every form of obedience, docility, and imitation; we scorn sedentary tastes and prudent sluggishness; we combat the majorities corrupted by power and we spit on current and traditional opinion as on all commonplaces of morals and philosophy.

In the literary field we uphold the ideal of a great and strong scientific literature, which, free from all and every classicism and pedantic purism, will magnify the most recent discoveries, the new intoxication of speed and the celestial life of aviators.

Our poetry is poetry essentially and totally rebelling against all used forms. The tracks of verse must be torn up and the bridges of thing already said must be blasted and the locomotives of our inspiration must be started toward the coming, toward the boundless fields of the New and the Future! Better a splendid disaster than a monotonous race daily re-run! We have already put up too long with the station masters of poetry, the conductors of scanning and the stupidly punctual time-tables of prosody.

In politics, we are as far from internationalist and anti-patriotic socialism, the ignoble upholder of the rights of the belly, as we are from timid and clerical conservatism, symbolized by slippers and bed-warmers.

Every liberty and every progress in the great circle of the nation!

We uphold patriotism and militarism; we sing hymns to war, the world's only hygiene, the superb conflagration of enthusiasm and generosity, the noble bath of heroism without which the races fall asleep in the idle egoism, in the economic urge to ' arrive,' and in niggardliness of mind and will.

We scorn and fight against the tyranny of love which especially among Latin peoples saps the energies of men of action. We fight against rancid sentimentalism, the obsession for adultery and feminine conquests in the novel, the theatre and in life.

All these ardent and dynamic ideas repel and exasperate the public; but we futurists make merry over it, for we fear only the facile approbations and insipid praises of the mediocre.

We are convinced that nothing is more easy and more despicable too than public approval, soliciting coarse and traditional tastes. Hence we seek the approval only of our own great futurist ideal and of the hostile public we ask nothing but to be hissed. . . .

To all our ancient Romans, to all our medieval Florentines, and to all our fallen Venetians, we prefer the inhabitants of Trieste; for their beautiful patriotic impatience will not fail before long, I hope, to set fire to our powder magazine. . . . While the *passé*-ists reprove us for blowing all traditions into the air, the false tomorrow-ists call us reactionaries for our patriotism and for our love of war. To both we reply that it is impossible to make resolute progress in the future without maintaining our personal hygiene of daily strife and our collective hygiene of decennial blood baths. In our blood we nourish the principal hatred that the Italians of the twentieth century feel, hatred for Austria. . . .

When the internationalists exalt peace, it is the worst in their blood (the trembling and decaying part) that speaks in them. To invoke peace among the peoples does not mean to be men of the future but simply to castrate the races and to carry on intensive cultivation of baseness. Who can deny that a strong man breathes much more freely, eats much better and sleeps much more soundly after having slapped and knocked down an enemy? Who can deny that the word man and

the word fighter are synonymous? Hence we conclude that when we
speak of war it is the better part of our blood, the futurist part that speaks
in us.

Futurism is distinctly separate from anarchic ideas. The latter, denying the principle of human evolution, simply ends its parabolic thrust at
the ideal and universal peace and at the stupid paradise made up of
embracings in the open fields and of waving palms. We on the other
hand assert as the absolute principle of futurism the continuous becoming of man. We regard the hypothesis of a friendly fusion of peoples as
overcome and admit but one hygiene for the world — war. The far-off
goal of anarchy, namely, a sweet affectionateness, the sister of baseness,
appears to us as an ugly gangrene leading people toward agony. . . ."

(1910)

" The parliamentary system is almost everywhere a wasted form. It
gave us a few good results; created the illusory participation of the
majority in the government. I say illusory because it is a proven fact
that people cannot and will never be represented by representatives
that they do not know how to select. The people therefore, always
remains outside the government. But on the other hand, it is precisely to
the parliamentary system that the people owes its own existence. The
pride of the masses has been increased by the elective regime. The
individual's stature has been raised by the idea of representation but
this idea has completely falsified the evaluation of intelligence, exaggerating beyond measure the prestige of eloquence. This unhappy result
is being aggravated day by day.

Hence I look forward with pleasure to the aggressive entrance of
women into parliaments. Where could we find a more impatient and
effective dynamite? Almost all the European parliaments are but
noisy henhouses, mangers and gutters. Their essential principles are:
(1) money, the corrupter; and slyness, the ensnarer, which serve to
win a seat in parliament; (2) prattling eloquence, a grandiose falsifica-
tion of ideas, the triumph of high sounding phrases, negro tom-toms
and the deeds of windmills. These gross elements give an absolute
power, through the parliamentary system, to the horde of lawyers. As
you well know, lawyers resemble each other in all countries. They are
beings intimately tied to all that is mean and futile. They are spirits
that see only the little daily fact and that are absolutely incapable of
handling great general ideas, of conceiving the clashes and fusions of
races, and the flaming flight of the ideal over individuals and peoples.
They are merchants of arguments, prostituted brains, shops for subtle
ideas and chiselled syllogisms. As a result of the parliamentary system,
an entire nation is at the mercy of these fabricators of justice, who with
the pliable tool of the law busily set traps for fools.

Hence, let us hasten to give women the right to vote. This is moreover the extreme and absolutely logical conclusion of the ideal of democracy and of universal suffrage as it was conceived by Jean Jacques Rousseau and by the other makers of the French Revolution. Let the women hasten with lightning rapidity to make this grand proof of the total animalization of politics. We who have a profound disgust for professional politicians are happy to abandon the parliamentary system to the artful contrivances of women; for it is for the women that the noble task is reserved of killing it once and for all. No, I am very careful not to be ironical; I am speaking very seriously. Woman, as she has been formed by our contemporary society, cannot help but increase the splendor of the principle of corruption which is inseparable from the principle of the vote. . . .

Very well then, I confess to you that we strong futurists in the face of so intoxicating a spectacle have suddenly felt ourselves detached from women, who have become all at once too terrestrial, or better, have become a symbol of the earth that we must abandon. We have often dreamed of being able some day to create our sons mechanically, as a fruit of pure will, a synthesis of all the laws which science is about to discover."

(Naples — June 26, 1910)

" A Discourse on the Beauty and Necessity of Violence."

" The whole present system of order is absolutely worm-eaten, reactionary, ineffective, blockheaded and often criminal.

Abolish it then as soon as possible.

At best every citizen ought to know how to defend himself. The state ought to intervene only in exceptional cases to defend an individual. The principle of free fist fights, tempered and restricted by fines, already exists in America and England. Seditions and crowd agitations when they are absolutely absurd and without the least bit of real justification should be thwarted, suppressed and extinguished, but without military intervention. A few powerful streams of water by the fire department are sufficient. If the conflagration should take on enormous proportions it means that there is much dry wood to burn and that all of it should burn. The fire departments should then retire with their pumps and leave absolute liberty for the flames. It is absurd that the state should continually intervene to defend the boor, the sluggish and the greedy cretin who allows himself to be caught by the usual tricks of the game. This greedy boor is much more disgusting than the robber himself. We have no compassion for the other classes of sluggish and fat citizens who are lacking in vital agility and whom I would call library baboons. The library baboon and the baboon of the field ought to disappear. To defend them against possible aggression is nothing but immorality. . . .

Courage is the prime and essential matter, in order that, according to the great futurist hope, all authorities, all rights, all powers be brutally stripped from the dead and dying and given to young men between twenty and forty years of age.

I propose the abolition of the present police, and to replace them with a body of picked citizens highly remunerated and not numerous who will intervene only in exceptional cases, using especially the weight of their authority and never that of handcuffs.

I propose, besides, some real schools of physical courage, to enable early adolescents to face with self-reliance and to overcome any danger without ever asking aid and without counting on the public force. Such courage, once become a deep-grained habit, will notably decrease the acts of aggression which inevitably in a country of brave men would tend to disappear.

Our futurist principles are the love of progress, of liberty, of danger, propaganda for courage and daily heroism. . . .

But we artists are not the so-called intellectuals. We are, above all, beating hearts, bundles of vibrant nerves, instinctive beings, governed only by the divine intoxicating intuition and believing ourselves to be as we are all of us, kindled by the so-called sacred fire.

. . . To youth we ascribe all rights and all authority which we deny and seek to wrest brutally from the old, the dying and the dead.

Futurism thus proclaims the necessary intervention of artists in public affairs, *to make governing at last a disinterested art* in place of what it is, a pedantic science of thievery. But I already hear you talking of our technical inexperience. Forget it! Remember that the Italian race is really capable of producing nothing but great artists and great poets, who can certainly very easily instruct themselves rapidly by a few months observation of the parliamentary machinery. I believe that the parliamentary system, a fallacious and faltering political institution, is destined inevitably to perish. I believe that Italian politics will inevitably witness the day of its agony if it does not listen to substituting artists or creative geniuses, for the class of lawyers or disintegrating and mercantile geniuses, that have monopolized it to the present, revealing their own specific function beyond all measure, which consists in thoroughly exploiting and selling their brains and their words. . . .

We have at last reached the profound conviction that everything is becoming more complicated, and that every theoretical, demonstrative and administrative simplification is illusory and that absolute order in political and social matters is absurd. We have reached the necessity of accepting in us and outside us the concomitance of the most contradictory elements.

The people can never renounce the liberties it has won to any force or any will whatsoever. . . . These individual liberties which are rapidly growing and developing into a possible and desirable anarchy must coexist with a principle of authority, which in turn, in order to save liberties severally, tends to destroy all collectively. Hence there is a concomitance as well as a salutary struggle between hostile principles, just as there is among the diverse elements that compose human blood. Thus Italy must always keep alive a double fervor, a possible proletarian revolution and a possible war. . . .

We now believe that the concept of historical evolution in circles is infantile, by which according to the dreams of many myopian imperialists, we are destined to return to a form of tyranny and to a supine slavery. . . . The imperialists seem to ignore, for example, the absolute novelty and exceptional importance which I ascribe to the most important event in the last hundred years. I mean the liberty to strike which the proletariat has mechanically won, a liberty all the stronger because it is not recognized by law, a liberty which no Napoleon can ever abolish. . . .

From all this we obviously conclude that violence has today become the best condition of real health for a people. Order, pacifism, moderation, the diplomatic and reformist spirit, are they not perhaps arteriosclerosis, old age and death? It is only by violence that the idea of justice, now ruined, can be reëstablished not as the fateful principle that consists in the right of the strongest but as that hygienic-sound principle that consists in the right of the most courageous and disinterested. Starting from this principle I may immediately satisfy those among you who are most insistent in the desire and need for dogmatic precision, by establishing the idea that the good is, according to us, everything that encourages and develops the physical, intellectual and instinctive activities of man, urging them to their maximum splendor, while evil is all that diminishes and interferes with the development of these activities.

Just as pacifism and the fear of war have created our painful political slavery, so the horror of violence has made a ridiculous puppet out of the Italian citizen, deformed by the degenerate forms of conflict that reply to a blow with a complaint or a formal satisfaction. . . .

How many times in the last ten years of life at Milan in which I have daily studied the ebb and flow of Italian socialism, attentively reading the reports of all its committees, as the most interesting and painful of books, how many times have I blushed as an Italian, I repeat as an Italian, to see huge masses of workers aroused by the most legitimate grievances and by a magnificent desire for greater liberty, how many times have these huge masses of the people been suddenly seized with the most foolish collective fright, at the sound of the four insolent notes of a policeman's whistle. . . .

But I also hear a formidable cry bursting from this multitude, petrified by courage, replying to the whistle: 'Italians, do not flee! Out of our sublime love of danger we accept a bloody strife under the shining stars of Italy which compel us not to retreat!' . . .

For to the present esthetics of filthy lucre we oppose — and let it come, let it come — an esthetics of violence and of blood!"

(1910)

" On the façades of museums, academies, libraries, and universities, we ought to read the following infamous principles written with the plaster of imbecility:

You no longer think!
You no longer paint!
You no longer construct!
No one can ever improve on the masters!
All originality whatsoever is forbidden!
Banish follies and extravagances! You must copy, copy, copy!
To win the paradise of art you must imitate the lives of our saints!

And over the doors of academies, museums, libraries and universities we write with the heroic charcoal of office stoves:

> TO THE EARTHQUAKE
> THEIR ONLY ALLY
> THE FUTURISTS DEDICATE
> THESE RUINS OF ROME AND ATHENS

Poets, painters, sculptors, musicians, you must fight . . . against the principle of inertia and slumber. For the world needs only heroism; pardon, as we do, the bloody and lawless deed of the student of Palermo, Lidonni, who avenged himself contrary to law against a tyrannic professor. The *passé*-ist professors are the only ones responsible for this murder, those *passé*-ist professors who seek to suffocate the indomitable energy of Italian youth in fetid subterranean channels. When, oh when, will there be an end of this castrating of the spirits that must create the future! . . . We must hurry to re-make everything. We must go against the current. Soon will come the moment when we can no longer be content to defend our ideas with our bare hands and fists, when we must begin the assault in the name of intelligence, the artistic assault, the literary assault on that glorified crust of tyrant professors."

(1911, repeated in 1918)

" They say we are a people superior to all others for our elastic and creative genius and for our resistant muscular youth, but, unfortunately, poverty-stricken.

No. The Italian people is not poor. We futurists assert that the Italian people is the richest in the world, for it possesses incalculable, unutilized capital, made up of the enormous patrimony of ancient works of art piled up in its museums. We propose without further ado that the government sell this patrimony of art, gradually and prudently. Since the Uffizi and the Pitti Galleries alone were evaluated at a billion Italy would in a few years be rich enough:

(1) to have the biggest military fleet in the world; (2) to have an army four times the strength of its present one; (3) to have the first merchant marine in the world; (4) to have a great system of inland navigation; (5) to intensify decidedly all its existing industries and immediately create the missing ones; (6) to develop agriculture to the state of maximum return, and make all the malaria zones sanitary; (7) to wipe out illiteracy completely; (8) to abolish all taxes for at least twenty years.

We foresee all the objections and we can meet them. The sale of our patrimony of art, far from lessening our prestige, will prove to the world that a young people, sure of its own future, is able to face all its problems, transform its dead wealth into living forces and like an aristocratic intelligence deny itself all vain pomp and devote its own gold to industry.

It will also be highly patriotic, this deed by which Italy, bursting traditional and sentimental old chains, will transform her old textiles and marbles into useful, swift and lordly steel. And, on the other hand, our ancient works of art, sold to America, England, Russia and France, will become the most effective advertisements of the creative genius of our race.

An inexhaustible genius this, for it shows itself today in our great and victorious improvised army, in our military mathematics and in our Garibaldist heroism, an army accustomed to war and prepared for it for more than forty years. Our heroes of the Carso, the Isonzo and the Trentino have surpassed a hundred times the greatness of all the Roman heroes. Hence we no longer live in our past; we are no longer merely ' sons of great men '; our present prestige guarantees us an unlimited future greatness.

We are the most artistic people on the earth. No one therefore can doubt that after having won great military power in the world, we shall also win an absolute primacy in art. Our glorious Renaissance will be surpassed by the Italian art of tomorrow."

(November 1914)

" Our immediate program is a desperate struggle against Italian *passé*ism in all its repugnant forms: archeology, academicism, senility, quietism, poltroonery, pacifism, pessimism, nostalgia, sentimentalism, erotic obsession, tourist industry, etc. Our ultra-violent nationalism is anticlerical, anti-socialist, anti-traditional and is based on the inexhaustible vigor of Italian blood and wages war on the cult of our ancestors who, far from cementing our race, make it anemic and wanton. . . . Futurism . . . is an atmosphere of the vanguard; it is the battle cry of all the innovators, of the intellectual free lances of the world; it is the love of the new; the impassioned art of velocity, the systematic defamation of the antique, the old, the slow, the erudite and the professorial; it is a new way of looking at the world, a new reason for loving life, an enthusiastic glorification of scientific discoveries and modern mechanism, a banner of youth, of strength, of originality, at any cost; . . . it is a box of dynamite for all the venerated ruins. . . .

Futurism is the reinforcement and defense of Italian genius (creation, improvization) against cultural obsession (museums, libraries), the solidarity of Italian innovators, against the clique of academics, opportunists, plagiarists, commentators, professors, and hotel keepers, the preparation of an atmosphere favorable to innovators, the temerity to face an infinite Italian progress, heroic disinterestedness in giving Italy more force, courage, light, novelty and elasticity in the world, an order of march and battle plus our arms at our shoulders never to retreat.

Futurism attempts to introduce life brutally into art, to fight the old ideal of the esthetes, static, decorative, effeminate, precious, shy, and hating action. In the last thirty years Europe was taken sick with a ruinous socialistic, anti-patriotic and internationalistic intellectualism which separates body and mind, vaunts a stupid hypertrophy of the brain, teaches pardon for offenses, announces universal peace and the disappearance of war, whose *horrors* would give place to battles of ideas. Against this intellectualism of German origin, futurism rushes in exalting instinct, force, courage, sport and war. Artists, at last alive, no longer seated on the scornful summits of estheticism, want to coöperate as workers and soldiers in world progress. . . .

Dynamic and aggressive futurism is being fully realized today in the great World War which I alone foresaw and glorified before it broke out. The present war is the finest futurist poem that has as yet appeared; futurism meant precisely the breaking in of war upon art, creating such phenomena as futurist evenings, most effective propaganda for courage. Futurism was the militarization of innovating artists. Today we are witnessing an immense futurist explosion of dynamic and aggressive pictures, into which we soon want to enter and display ourselves.

Plastic dynamism, pluritonal music without structure, art of noises and words expressed with freedom, are the most natural artistic expressions of this futurist hour. Bombardments, armored cars, trenches, artillery duels, charges, electrified barb wiring, have nothing to do with *passé*-ist poetry, classicist, traditional, archeological, georgic, nostalgic, and erotic (Baudelaire, Mallarmé, Verlaine, Carducci, Pascoli, d'Annunzio). This pacifist poetry is buried. . . .

The War, intensified futurism, will never kill war as the *passé*-ists hope but will kill *passé*-ism. The war is the culmination and perfect synthesis of progress (aggressive velocity plus violent simplification of efforts toward well-being). War is a lightning stroke of courage, of energy and intelligence, falling on every one. A compulsory school of ambition and heroism; fulness of life and complete freedom in surrender to one's country.

For a poor and prolific nation war is a business proposition; to purchase the needed land by the oversupply of blood. . . . The war will exhaust all the country's enemies: diplomats, professors, philosophers, archeologists, critics, cultural obsessions, Greek, Latin, history, senility, museums, libraries, tourist industry. The war will develop gymnastics, sport, schools of practical agriculture, commerce and industry. The war will rejuvenate Italy, will enrich it with men of action, will force it to live no longer on its past, its ruins, and its gentle climate but on its own national forces."

(December 1915)

" After having seen the Italian people, 'that most mobile of all peoples,' free itself futuristically by a sword stroke from the lurid old armor of Giolitti, we are now seeing how in the busy streets of Milan, the Italian people, that seemed poisoned by pacifism, is able to face with pride this noble, useful and hygienic spilling of Italian blood.

All this confirms us once more in the belief that no people can equal: (1) the creative genius of the Italian people; (2) the improvising elasticity of which the Italians always give proof; (3) the physical force, agility and resistance of the Italians; (4) the impetus, violence and desperateness with which the Italians are able to fight; (5) the patience and methodical calculation of the Italians in making war; (6) the lyricism and moral nobility of the Italian nation in nourishing itself by blood and money.

Italians! You must build *Italian pride* on the indisputable superiority of the Italian people *in everything*. This pride was one of the essential principles of our original futurist manifestations, that is, of six years ago when first and alone (while irredentism was in torment and the nationalist party had not yet been born) we invoked war violently in the theatres and market places, as the only hygiene, the only moral educator, the only swift motor of progress."

(May 1919)

" In the manifesto of the futurist political party I urged: 'the transformation of Parliament by an equal participation of industrialists, agriculturalists, engineers and merchants in the government of the country. The minimum age of eligibility for a deputy should be reduced to twenty-two years. A minimum of lawyer deputies (always opportunists) and a minimum of professor deputies (always reactionaries). A parliament freed of weaklings and rabbles. The abolition of the Senate. If this rational and practical parliament should not give good results, we shall abolish it and put in a technical government without parliament, a government composed of twenty experts. We will replace the Senate with an advisory assembly composed of twenty young men under thirty. In the place of a parliament of incompetent orators and sick scholars, checked by a Senate of dying men, we will have a government of twenty experts stimulated by an assembly of young men under thirty.'

The futurist Volt immediately entered upon the difficulties in the way of realizing a technical government in an article from which I quote: ' We shall abolish Parliament, but many will ask, what will we put in its place? The reply is at hand. We will substitute a parliament based on representatives of agricultural, industrial and workers' syndicates. Syndical representation will be the basis of the futurist technical state.' "

(October 1919, at the fascist congress of Florence.)

" I approve unconditionally, in the name of futurism and the futurist Italians, the whole program of the *Fasci di Combattimento* which has been expounded by my friend Fabbri. However, I find several serious gaps in this program to which I draw your attention.

Fascisti! There is no greater peril for Italy than the black peril. The Italian people that has been able to venture, will, and carry out the immense heroic and victorious effort of the great war, . . . would fail in its mission if it were not able energetically to free this beautiful peninsula, bubbling with life, from the deadly plague of the papacy. We must demand, will, and impose the expulsion of the papacy, or better still to use a more precise expression, its ' devaticanization.'

Continuing in the analysis of the program of the *Fasci di Combattimento*, I find the abolition of the Senate, for which a national technical council is to be substituted. Very well; I maintain that the concept of technicians is very important but it does not suffice. The Senate represents in the history of peoples a constant deference to the wisdom of the aged, summoned to put a brake on the exercise of power, to make the government's proposals mature and direct its decisions. . . .

The technical council that is to replace the Senate must therefore be composed of very young men, not yet thirty. I insist on this, since it has been customary in Italy to call young men to power and to regard a man of fifty-five as very young and virile. Salandra cries: Forward, young men! But with him they all fear young men, and put a forty-year old in quarantine as having cholera, a fifty-year old as a dynamiter, and regard a sixty-year old as a daring fellow almost mature enough to govern Italy. . . .

Italy once freed (by means of the dynamic force of a stimulatorium of really young men, the patriotic flame of the *arditi*, the schools of physical courage and of heroism, the free expositions of creative genius, and the proletariat of genial Italians) will finally give its greatest flood of Italian light to the world."

(November 1919, from an election speech when he and Mussolini were the fascist candidates of Milan.)

" We do not believe that the Italian race should dominate the world by its industrial forces, but we are convinced that it will dominate by the indisputable force of its creative geniuses. Do not forget, O Italians, the great and genial spirits of d'Annunzio and Mussolini, who at this moment synthesize Italy. I vindicate the rights of genius and the rights of intelligence in all its forms against the pretended dictatorship of calloused hands. To speak of a levelling communism to a race full of individuals, to a people full of inventors, is a criminal absurdity.

So they hope to decapitate Italy? It is absurd! Against those who sabotage our great victory, against all who put brakes on the unmeasured future of the most genial people on earth, fascism arises with its revolutionary force, seeking every liberty and every progress, and admitting no glorification of mediocrity and idiocy."

(December 1919, written in a Milan jail where he was imprisoned with Mussolini and several others for leading armed bands against the state just before the elections.)

" Yes! Put the artists in power! The vast proletariat of the genial shall govern. The most sacrificed, the most worthy of proletariats. All are weary and deluded. It does not yield. Its genius will soon explode over Italy and over the world spreading immense red wings of cheering artistic force, purifying and pacifying. The proletariat of the genial, once in the government, will realize a free theatre for all and the great futurist aerial theatre. Music will reign over the world. Every square will have its great instrumental and vocal orchestra. Thus there will be fountains of harmony which day and night will spring from musical genius and will play in the heavens, coloring, sweetening, invigorating, and refreshing the hard, dark, trivial, and hectic rhythm of daily life. In the place of night work we shall have night art. Squads of musicians will take their turns in magnifying a hundredfold the splendor of our days and the sweetness of our nights.

The proletariat of the genial alone will be capable of undertaking the prudent, gradual, and world-wide sale of our patrimony of art, according to the legal draft which we made nine years ago. This spiritual wheat and coal will produce admiration for us even in the rudest peoples. Our museums sold to the world will become a dynamic transoceanic advertisement of genius.

The proletariat of the genial, coöperating with the development of the industrial machinist, will attain that maximum of salary and minimum of manual labor, which without diminishing production will give to all intelligence, liberty to think, create and enjoy artistically.

The futurist revolution that will put artists in power does not promise terrestrial paradises. Certainly it can not suppress the human torment

that marks the rising force of our race. The artists, tireless exponents of
this feverish toil, will succeed in easing the pain. They will solve the
problem of well-being in the only way it can be solved, that is, spiritually. . . .

Every brain ought to have its palette and its musical instrument to
color and give lyric accompaniment to every least and humblest act of
life. Ordinary life is too heavy, austere, monotonous, materialistic,
badly ventilated, and if not strangled at least fettered. In awaiting the
realization of our grandiose aerial futurist theatre, we propose a vast
project of daily free concerts in every quarter of the city, picture theatres,
reading rooms, books and newspapers, absolutely free. We shall develop
the spiritual life of the people and shall magnify a hundredfold its
capacity to dream. Thanks to us the time will come in which life will
no longer be merely a life of bread and work, nor a life of leisure, but a
life in which there will be life-work-of-art. Every man will live his best
possible romance." (*Futurismo e Fascismo:* pages 24–27, 46–49, 56–73,
78–79, 90–97, 99–100, 145–146, 187–189, 195–196, 199–200, 218–220.)

PART II

No. 4. *Mussolini on Imperialism*

"What is happening today is truly fantastic! On all sides they are crying against Italian imperialism. . . . It seems as though the imperialists in this low, sad world are all Italians. All this is an enormous stupidity. Italian imperialism does not exist. Nor does English imperialism exist. Nor French. We must understand each other once for all about this word imperialism. Imperialism is the eternal and immutable law of life. At bottom it is but the need, the desire, and the will for expansion which every living, healthy individual or people has in itself. It is the means by which it is practiced that distinguishes one imperialism from another, both among individuals and among peoples. Imperialism is not necessarily, as is believed, aristocratic and military. It may be democratic, pacific, economic, or spiritual.

In a certain sense President Wilson, and it is not difficult to prove this, is the greatest and most fortunate of all imperialists.

Now I do not cry against French imperialism. . . . The truth is that France not only wants to maintain her position in Europe and in the world, but by the victory wants to utilize and fortify it. She renounces nothing. How silly this democratic ideal, this self-styled Italian democratic ideal, appears in the face of this imperialism of republican France, which does not renounce the famous trinity — liberty, equality, fraternity — but seeks to guarantee for herself the foundations and sources of her life.

I shall not cry against English imperialism. . . against Lloyd George and against his friends who do not want to hear of freedom of the seas in the *Boche* sense, who do not want to hear of restoring the German colonies, who still less intend to renounce English naval supremacy and who are prepared to claim a sizable war indemnity. . . .

Either what the English and French are doing is imperialism and then it is necessary to rise up against theirs as they rise against ours, though it be the least voracious and dangerous of any; or else the French and English politics which at present has the almost unanimous support of the respective nations, is simply and prudently national, and then it is time to stop condemning Italy and only Italy because it is doing what the others are doing. . . .

I hear someone saying to me: and the democratic War? I reply that the War has already attained its democratic and ultra-democratic aims. The central empires which were the bulwark of European reaction have been overthrown and in their place republics are arising. Upheavals more radical and democratic than these were not possible. But I ask myself: will these democracies be pacific? . . .

Those who believe they can win the sympathies of the Croatians by abandoning cities and regions that always have been strictly Italian, are much mistaken. If you yield Dalmatia, the Croatians will be hostile to you because of Fiume. If you yield Fiume they will want Trieste, and if you should be inclined to yield Trieste do not imagine that you will have satisfied that tribe; it wants to come down from the Carso Giulio, camp at Cividale and at Udine, push on to the banks of the Tagliamento, if not to the Piave. It is the fertility of our plains and the blue of our skies that have for centuries aroused the covetousness of barbarians.

League of Nations, disarmament, arbitration, all this is now an ideal patrimony of peoples, but these coming legal institutions must consecrate our rights, not violate them. . . ." (*Popolo d'Italia*, January 1, 1919. In *Diuturna*, pp. 227–232.)

"The bitter bestial wrath of Nitti is provoked by his foolish fear of the Allies. This man presents a base and trembling Italy before the synod of wolves, foxes, and jackals of Paris. And he thinks thus to obtain pity. And he believes by making himself tiny, by diminishing himself and prostrating himself, he will obtain something. The opposite is easier. It is easier to disarm our 'terrible' Allies by showing them our teeth as soon as they laugh at us and do not take us seriously when we whimper." (*Popolo d'Italia*, September 15, 1919. In *Diuturna*, pp. 257–259.)

No. 5. *Mussolini on Internationalism*

"Humanity is still and always an abstraction of time and space; men are still not brothers, do not want to be and evidently can not be. Peace is hence absurd, or rather it is a pause in war. There is something that binds man to his destiny of struggling, either against his fellows or himself. The motives for the struggle may change indefinitely, they may be economic, religious, political, sentimental, but the legend of Cain and Abel seems to be the inescapable reality, while 'brotherhood' is a fable which men listen to during the bivouac and the truce. . . .

Material interests hurl men against each other fiercely, men who claim to be ready to take in the whole human race in the most loving embrace!

But of what avail is it now to enter into the 'merits' of the question? The republicans are right from a legal and moral point of view, but the socialists act *à la* Prussian, that is, they practice the right of the stronger. That zone is entirely theirs. These are the happy (!) countries where all are socialists. In this red desert a republican oasis is intolerable. . . .

Political rivalry is fused with economic interests and men who carry the banner of humanity do not hesitate before civil war.

The ideal is shipwrecked by this contradiction. The Christian and socialist 'men be brothers' is a mask for the eternal and immutable '*homo homini lupus*.' . . . And man will continue to be a wolf among wolves for a bit of land, for a trickle of water, for a crumb of bread, for a woman's kiss, for a necessity or a caprice; he will continue to ignore others and to ignore himself." (*Popolo d'Italia*, March 7, 1920. In *Diuturna*, pp. 279–281.)

"Internationalism is an article of luxury, good for the aristocracies of art, banking, industry, and snobbish imbecility; in short for the bourgeoisie of capitalism and of socialism; but at bottom internationalism is an absurd fable; the great masses do not escape nor can they, and it is the best of fortune that they can not escape, the insuppressible datum of race and nation. 'Go home to your own country!' This is the formula that sums up the workers' internationalism.

The socialist doctrine of workers' internationalism has evaporated into the air or is engraved only on tablets; it does not exist in life. Put workers representing various countries around the same table — witness the Washington Conference — and you will hear the unintelligible clamor of a new Babel; bring laboring masses of different races into forced contact and you will have the story of Upper Silesia or of the Teschen Basin or of Trieste.

Internationalism may be an ideal limit; one of those ideas, that is, which mankind carries in its baggage in view of its long wanderings in remote regions; but to make it an article of faith, an absolute dogma, there is a long distance still to go. And those people who, like slaves, face history for the first time, are the most nationalist and the least internationalist on earth, even when they raise the emblem of the sickle and hammer — which then becomes the emblem of their pan-Slavic nationalism — . . . If those who call themselves communists and internationalists are so fiercely anti-Italian, there is little comfort in trusting in the friendship of other Jugoslavians who openly profess nationalism." (*Popolo d'Italia*, February 1, 1921. In *Diuturna*, pp. 320–324.)

"Under the mask of the noblest ideals, decorated by the 'immortal principles,' covered by the whitest lamb fleece, the fierce hoard of the selfish peoples bursts upon us, of those 'arrived' peoples who chase the proletarian peoples off the prohibited premises of raw materials. O Justice! O Humanity! O Brotherhood! In the committees, assemblies, and speeches at Geneva, yes! but when it is a matter of oil, of coal, of iron, and of territories that contain these indispensable raw materials, justice, humanity and brotherhood come to a sad end like the paper trophies on the last night of carnival.

And so leave us to sow our bit of wind which is our only means of escape from slavishness." (*Popolo d'Italia,* September 27, 1921. In *Diuturna,* pp. 358–361.)

No. 6. *Strife Is the Origin of All Things*

(Excerpts from Mussolini's speech at Trieste, September 20, 1920. This speech marks the transition from the early radical republican platform of 1919 to the more nationalistic program which came to dominate fascism. The passage here cited reflects Mussolini's disillusionment over the Treaty of Versailles and the League of Nations.)

" Strife is the origin of all things, for life is full of contrasts; there is love and hate, white and black, night and day, good and evil, and until these contrasts are reduced to an equilibrium strife will always remain at the root of human nature, like a supreme fatality. And on the whole it is well that it is so. Today strife is possible in war, in economics, in ideas; but the day in which there should be no more strife would be a day of melancholy, of the end of things, of ruin. For the present this day will not come. For history always presents itself like a changing panorama. If one pretends a return to peace, calm and tranquillity, one is refuted by the current tendencies of the present dynamic age. One must be prepared for other surprises and other strifes. There will be no period of peace until the time when the peoples shall have abandoned themselves to a Christian dream of universal brotherhood and can hold out their hands to each other across oceans and mountains. I for my part have little faith in these ideals, but I do not exclude their possibility, for I exclude nothing; all things are possible, even the impossible and absurd. But today, being today, it would be fallacious, perilous, criminal, to build houses on the shifting sand of the Christian-socialist-communist International. These ideals are worthy of respect, but are still very far from reality." (Mussolini: *Discorsi,* first edition, p. 107.)

No. 7. *The Greatest Humiliation (By Ardengo Soffici)*

"The greatest humiliation, after that of having witnessed the vogue of German ware among us, now happily ended, is that of seeing Europe today at the mercy of the Anglo-Saxon race. To see us, the ancient lords of all times, Italy and France (especially Italy) eternal emanators of the sunlight of civilization, creators of ideas, forms and civil customs — of all that is great and glorious in the world, hanging on the lips of big nobodies and of savages hardly civilized: of the English Attorney and the Presbyterian Wilson!

No! Really, for my racial pride this is worse than the toad which Chamfort had to swallow every morning!" (Ardengo Soffici: *Battaglie fra due vittorie,* 1920, p. 44.)

No. 8. *A Notable Service*

"Nothing has given me greater satisfaction since the victorious end of the war than the injustice, ingratitude and spite shown us by our allies. Especially by those whom we helped most. Nothing could contribute more to freeing us once and for all from all the ridiculous illusions to which we clung and which subjected us to them.

Because of these illusions, because of this kind of admiring submission, Italy has never followed directly the path that its genius and its history pointed out for it. It has never carried on the true politics becoming to it. The lesson it has had has been magnificent and salutary.

Italy is now free to choose its own way, to be itself at last; it can coolly look everyone straight in the eye and can achieve its own destiny regardless of others. The selfishness and general roguery with which we have found ourselves face to face has been a veritable lucky number for us." (Ardengo soffici: *Battaglie fra due vittorie,* 1920, p. 78.)

No. 9. *On Disarmament*

(The following is taken from an article by Francesco Coppola in *Politica,* September 1924, re-published in an editorial in *La Tribuna,* March 25, 1927, on the occasion of the last disarmament conference.)

" . . . As regards disarmament, we must immediately and categorically reject the prevalent tendency to a proportional reduction of armaments of the Washington type. According to this tendency the limits allowed for those armaments which are at present still free — that is land, lighter naval and submarine and air armaments — are to be fixed for each power in proportion to its *present* forces and *present* needs, arbitrarily (and that means according to the interest of the stronger) determined by international congresses. Now it is plain that under such a system land forces would be allowed us very much inferior to the French, naval forces very much inferior to the English; air forces inferior to both French and English; in short, a world military power notably inferior both to the French and the English. The consequences which we would derive from this arrangement are very plain:

(1) The humiliation of our prestige and hence of our international standing, because of an *officially* recognized and established inferiority of Italy in the hierarchy of the great powers;

(2) Our manifest definite and permanent military inferiority with its obvious danger for our security and with its obvious lessening of our effective independence and of the weight of our politics not only in all world questions but also in those of Europe and the Mediterranean;

(3) The material, definite and permanent impossibility of modifying

the present world status at any time whatsoever according to our prime historical necessity, and especially the Mediterranean status in which Italy is literally stifled. This would be equivalent to putting a forced end to our necessary historic development, that is, it would be our historical suicide.

Hence what should we do? Demand that eventually armament limits on land, sea, and air be one and the same and perfectly equal for all great powers already officially defined as such. Nobody, in fact, can pretend that a great power can officially recognize and sanction its own inferiority in the face of others, not only at present but perpetually. This does not mean that we must immediately establish an army or an air force equal to the French or a fleet of light cruisers and submarines equal to the English, but it means that we reserve for ourselves the liberty and right of establishing them whenever our economic power permits it or when our historic necessities demand it. It means that we now maintain the right to an equality of position which no one can officially deny us, so that we may realize it in fact whenever we can and must.

The advantages of this system are no less obvious than the disadvantages of the other:

(1) Our prestige of *pares inter pares* is maintained and reasserted;

(2) Our military power, now by right and tomorrow in fact, equal to that of any other state, to guarantee our security, our independence, our standing in international politics;

(3) The possibility of having a force, when the hour sounds, relative and adequate, or at least not too greatly inferior, to the necessities of Italy's standing and growth in the Mediterranean;

(4) Practically speaking, an immediate and effective limitation imposed on the military power of those who are today the stronger, but a purely Platonic one for us who are still far from the eventual relative standing which is really in process of being determined."

No. 10. *American Imperialism*

" Once more in the bright light of noon the falsity of the Wilsonian ideology and European imbecility has been proven, especially the renunciatory and apologetic Italian imbecility. The League of Nations, established by Wilson himself at the same time that he refused a world-wide examination of war debts in order to carry on a financial imperialism over single European debtors, at the same time that he recognized the Monroe Doctrine (Article 21 of the Covenant), was already no longer the League of Nations, but an institution for American intervention in European affairs without a corresponding intervention *vice versa*. A few isolated individuals saw the contradiction, denounced it and were called enemies of the peace by Italian social democracy. And they were merely friends of truth and not enemies of peace, which cannot be served by lies. Their stand was already fascist.

The refusal of the United States, who deny all validity to the signature given to Versailles by their legitimate and highest representative (oh, the guarantees of democratic perfection!), has proved that American imperialism has tried to free itself even from the formal embarrassments of the League of Nations, thus completely robbing Wilson's ideology of all content, though European brains had become generally stuffed with it. Thus the politics of intervention in European affairs has remained intact: witness the Conference and Treaty for naval disarmament at Washington directed to forcing England to naval equality, and to renouncing her naval supremacy and alliance with Japan; the control and patronage of the Dawes plan in regulating German reparations (in relation to the conquered); the systematization of debts with single Allies (in relation to their ex-associates). On the other hand the politics of imperialism on the gigantic American continent is free from any restrictions of diplomatic procedure whatsoever. Today, with American troops landed in Nicaragua, we can estimate the whole unhistorical absurdity and lying falsity of the basic League ideology. . . .

The Nicaraguan intervention following upon the signing of a treaty by which Panama is dependent on the United States, is a typically imperialistic intervention. It is useless to mobilize all the hypocrisies of the customary formulæ against it and the empty indignation of social democracy when it speaks of independence and liberty as *a priori* rights and not as practical concerns and deserts. It is not possible to identify the independence and liberty of states historically with a political void of anarchy, thus withholding vast territories from the needs of organizing and productive civilization. Civilization is imperialistic; it is therefore an international hierarchy composed of great controlling powers who find solutions and do not stop in the face of pretended rights and formal limitations; it is competition and struggle from which alone peoples' rights can be born, for they must always be won and deserved. This imperialistic civilization is European and American and also Asiatic. It is, in other words, world-wide. It is the moving force of all politics; and especially in democratic states which deny the daily contradiction between the facts of their imperialistic action and the labels of the social democratic principles which they flaunt, as do France, England and the United States. Communist Russia herself denies it, which in spite of internal difficulties is feverishly seeking millions of rubles to help the Cantonese armies and to set up their own imperialism against the British, Japanese, and American, even when the latter tend toward a partial reciprocal elimination.

Fascism alone in the world repudiates hypocrisies and lies, asserts their danger, their danger for peace itself, and recognizes the fact that the laws of world affairs are those of imperialistic civilization which has its own reason for being, its own history and its own morality, over against the deceptions of social democracy. Fascism is not surprised at the Panama treaty and the Nicaraguan intervention, nor does it take recourse to that Tartufian surprise shown by the British and

French press, . . . but instead it sees in these two events one of the essential tendencies of United States politics and in its turn reasserts that the turmoils in which we live, the misunderstandings which have afflicted us during the aftermath of the war, the worst threats to European peace and, above all, European civilization itself are caught up in this monstrous equivocation weighing on world politics, by which men try obscenely to preach something different from the facts and therefore allow a festering contradiction to grow, a corrosive of the Protestant Anglo-Saxon type of mind, of the fatuous French oratory and of anarchic Russian universalism, repudiated only by the serious and suffering manliness of fascism." (From R. Forges-Davanzati; in *La Tribuna,* January 2, 1927.)

No. 11. *Life Is Becoming Harder*

"Every day we feel more how the economic problem, and now especially the monetary problem, is dominating the life of every country. . . . Solid metallic money is inexorably destroying poor paper money, just as the great mechanic industry of the first half of the last century hopelessly destroyed small domestic industry. . . . Now the good money concentrated in the Anglo-Saxon world, the dollar and the pound sterling, are asserting themselves and dominating over the monies of all other countries, thereby gaining both an economic and a political position of international command, against which countries of poor exchanges will continually have less sure defense. A slow pressure from America and England is now directed toward suppressing the disparity of the various national monies which has led to incidental advantages for the poor money countries by their low cost of production and hence their ability to compete, and toward imposing on all of them a general adoption of the gold standard which, by levelling the value of money, will also level the cost of production and will restore to the rich countries their possibility of fully enjoying in foreign markets all the technical economic and financial superiority of their industries, which is now neutralized by this unsolved problem of exchanges. Hence we must count on an inexorable Anglo-Saxon pressure. . . .

What weapon of defense has Italy against this advance of foreign economic tendencies, which is being encountered by her commerce in all the world markets? One only, and entirely a matter of will: saving. I mean here not only the more usual and classic Italian form of saving by the patient and faithful accumulation of small salaries, made possible by the daily sacrifices of workers, but in its more modern and wider technical form of a reduction of the costs of production and of a maximum utilization of all its raw materials and combustibles, to be obtained by an application of all the most progressive technical and economic systems of production and distribution. It is a singular spectacle, the state of this poor Italy that keeps up old and very wasteful habits of work, instead of zealously launching out into a thoroughgoing renovation of its principles of production. Up to the eve of the new regime the liberalist idea, century-old and by this time antiquated in almost all industrial countries of the world, maintained itself in Italy, expecting to find the solution of the problem of minimum costs in an unlimited application of the principle of free competition and perfected individualism, whereas it really lies in another direction: in a technical economic and capitalistic association of all its energies and cycles of production. . . . Strength and progress lie in the great co-ordinated unities: science has the victory.

'Life is becoming harder, not softer, or easier for everyone,' said Mussolini. Hard for men and hard for their work. But we may add that it is also becoming more elaborate, more ingenious. . . . Thus the close competition of world commerce is also becoming an intensive elaboration of industry and production. Woe to those countries that do not grasp this inexorable law of productive evolution. The technique of military war is developing toward new arms and new scientific elaborations. . . . For the principle of extensiveness is being substituted that of intensity. Aerial and vertical arms are being added to the horizontal lines of battle, and are displacing the latter. No less revolutionary is the evolution of the technique of economic war, for the production of every country is turning not merely to satisfying needs but to beating competition and conquering new markets. Hence Italy must face this problem, which I would call the struggle for saving the *centime*. To solve this problem of the infinitesimal we need a vast transformation of mentality, uses, means and functions." (Virginio Gayda: *La Lotta per il Centesimo*. In *Gerarchia*, July 1926, pp. 451–459.)

No. 12. *The New Empire*

(The following selections are taken from articles written by Mario Carli, one of the editors of *L'Impero*, the leading paper of the intransigent faction. Carli was one of the most prominent futurists and is noted for his verbal violence and exuberance.)

"When Italy came into the hands of the fascist government, not only the political conditions of our country were changed, but the whole mechanism of politics took on a radically different aspect. The new man who is at the head of the government has stamped his style and his rhythm, his style of energy and the rhythm of velocity, on every expression of political life. The very atmosphere in which men move and in which political phenomena take shape is flooded by a new color, by a sense of nobility and of force which it had not before. Let us admit it: until today a militant politics was impossible. The best men remained outside this vast field of action; the true geniuses entered it with repugnance only to leave it immediately with disgust. The reason for this incompatibility that for so many years excluded men like Carducci and Alfredo Oriani from public life and that still keeps out d'Annunzio, Marinetti, Vilfredo Pareto, almost all men of strife besides being powerful geniuses, is only this: the impossibility of using an exceptionally endowed brain in this field.

Evidently in the democratic regime political genius was useless. The levelling tendency of democracy, the state of hidden slavery in which Italy found itself, the debility by which state action was oppressed, which in turn forcibly debilitated the action of the national parties while the subversive parties buoyant and apparently creative were coming into the foreground, the extinguisher-silencer which was clamped on to every cry, every act of will and every forward-looking effort, all this discouraged even the slightest desire on the part of the higher and more far-sighted minds to devote themselves completely to politics.

Politics therefore remained the crucible of mediocrity, the stage of buffoons, the arena in which fools and rogues displayed themselves, the ship whose rudder was held by the hands of the flabby and the vile. And since a ruinous and automatic selection took place, which definitely rejected the few courageous men who had dared to face this base kind of life, a governing class inevitably resulted composed of men without backbone, courage, or genius.

One who looks to the bottom of this phenomenon will tend to judge more leniently those men of the liberal state who preceded and involuntarily favored the present state of things. They were but the products of a ruinous selection; they were the necessary refuse of a nation that, not yet in entire possession of its own forces and of its own independence, could not press into the government any but trembling and powerless men. . . .

Today a return is possible for those 'magnanimous spirits that had disappeared from the sky of the country,' and even a poet can practice politics, and even a 'visionary' has his rôle in the concerted action of operating forces. When we hear a head of the government, who for the first time is worthy of the name, speaking with so much virility and so much nobility, of his country, with so much pride in the present and with such faith in the future, we feel that finally we can approach this field without mortification and without shuddering; not, to be sure, in order to carry out all that our imagination and our burning impatience would like to, but without doubt infinitely more than would have been permitted us heretofore.

We are moving in a different historic clime, no longer dominated by fear and doubt, no longer contaminated by baseness, fraud and compromise. Today, with all the evils and deficiencies that still afflict us (fie! we are hardly born to our true political life!), we are a people of strong and conscious men, a people burning and active, moulding its own future with virile hands and sound heart.

We feel an infinite emotion when the Head of the Government, who once used to be regularly employed to stifle the generous voices that were raised in the interests of the future, speaks in a dominating manner and with a high resounding voice of an 'immortal Italian people that always finds a springtime for its hopes, its passion and its greatness.'

We feel a magic impulse course through our veins when this Head, this thirty-nine year old President of the Council of Ministers, sprung from the vigorous soil of Romagna, distilled from the soundest and boldest soul of our adventurous people, asserts that we are too 'squeezed into this narrow and adorable peninsula' and that 'the problem of Italian emigration in the world is a problem of life and death for the Italian race.'

We cry with joy intoxicated and exuberant when this Man sings us the hymn of Italian youth, 'keen, fearless, restless, but mighty,' whose 'powerful ferment agitating its life' he feels.

At last! It has been centuries since a similar language was heard and we needed it badly. Glory to him who first was able to talk this language after so much debasement! Fate, that gave Italy a man like Benito Mussolini, demands this prodigy also: that the elect spirits and outstanding geniuses, encouraged by the new situation, gather round him to coöperate in building up the prosperity and greatness of our country.

The Triumphant Beast has been overthrown forever, and politics, no longer an arena of the mediocre and the knaves, is being reëstablished by the return of the strong, the impassioned and the faithful. . . .

It is time to eradicate from the minds of the many the idea that imperialism is a prerogative of the few, an aristocratic conception that cannot and should not interest the laboring people. . . . This laboring people must be freed from this last illusion. Imperialism is not a dream, more or less mad, of a handful of seers; it is a hard and fatal necessity for all growing races, a duty imposed by history on ourselves, on our own generation and on those to come. Much more than the rich classes, much more than the intellectuals, the low and obscure masses have an interest in imperialism since they aspire to wealth, and will never, never, never have it unless they become able to grasp the necessity of expansion beyond their paternal boundaries, wheresoever and howsoever, by means of peace or of war, but with the spirit of a dominating not a slavish people; for only thus can wealth be acquired, that wealth which we do not have and which we need at all costs. . . .

Now given a nation like Italy in which there is a greater wealth of impatient energies, of imagination, of the ability to desire and to possess, than elsewhere, and no gold, no iron, no coal, no oil, one cannot understand how there can be so much incomprehension and indifference toward the imperialistic problem — or expansionistic, if the word is offensive — which is primarily a problem of economic and only secondarily of political conquest. Why do our peasants feel forced to cross the oceans in search of work and comfort? Because there are too many of us in Italy, because our land has no mines, because our feet get in our way, and we cannot breathe for the crowd that stifles the peninsula, because in the primitive mind of the people there is the unnoticed but clear instinct, that the strength and breath of Italy must be carried over the seas, must be imposed on people of inferior civilization, inferior genius, inferior birth-rate, and inferior capacity to work; and these are not merely the negroes.

I repeat we must popularize imperialism. This we propose to do, and this we are doing every day until we shall have succeeded in giving Italians of every class and culture an imperial consciousness, freeing the field of the turgid rhetoric which has been abused hitherto and erecting a series of practical postulates that will inject this formidable problem of life into the consciousness of the masses. . . .

It is impossible today to cultivate a Napoleonic conception in Europe; conquest by force of arms over nations on our continent in 1923 is an absurd dream which no power, be it France, England or Italy, may attempt with impunity. . . . Hence we must conceive European politics as a rivalry of diplomatic influences and nothing more; Italy can teach them all in this sense, and whoever is preoccupied with peace would do well to listen to its advice and imitate its actions.

However these diplomatic influences may have more or less reason for existing; they may be more or less justified. The preponderant domination of one nation over others cannot be tolerated if it is not based on an authentic moral, spiritual and physical superiority of the race.

We can never allow states like Jugoslavia and Russia even though more powerful and ordered than they are now, to impose themselves on other states, whatever be their military and political power. But often the absurd state of affairs is seen where a less civilized nation enjoys greater credit and arouses more sympathy among the leading nations of civilization, only because it is better armed and more warlike.

Today genuine superiority, that is so-called hegemony, can be acquired by a complex of qualities and means which we shall not discuss here. The 'primacy,' in order to be maintained in practice, must be total; only that people can wield the sceptre (and I do not mean over adjoining territory), which displays a greater amount of physical and moral energy and prevails over others in every department of life. Now Italy, even though it has not yet the wealth that constitutes other nations' single pretext for predominance, is nevertheless so endowed with every other gift, physiological health, prolificacy, genius, sobriety, capacity for work, courage, energy and adventurous spirit, that in a not distant tomorrow it may well aspire to this Primacy. . . .

Very well then; if it is incontestable that our people finds itself in this period of total resurrection and gradual rise in the world, then its Primacy, which is being integrated day by day, will automatically lead it to Empire. But let us be understood: an extra-European Empire over peoples not yet capable of self-government, over lands whose mineral products can give a nation like ours not only wealth but, by their raw materials which we lack, commercial independence.

The Latin Primacy in the hands of Italy implies a pacific, radiant, civilized, Mediterranean Empire. Not the hypocritic pretences of Albion, nor the brutal cynicism of the German blonds, nor the trembling despotism of a dissolving France; but the balanced wisdom inherited from the Romans, the sense of human justice which the Catholic Church has instilled in us during twenty centuries of her civilization, the good sense that does not lack the irony given by true intelligence and by the consciousness of one's own strength.

This will be our Empire and the world need but hasten its coming if it really aspires to peace. . . .

We, fascist Italy, feel that our loins are directly descended from Roman fierceness, nor are we displeased that a little barbarian influx has added to us that migratory impulse that may be considered as the patient period of waiting for the inevitable expansionist movement of peoples destined for Empire. The warlike spirit is the fundamental character of Italians; it is not a fascist invention nor a post-bellum attitude. Find me a single moment of history in which we have not fought — for whom and for what little matters. . . .

A century of democratic dysentery was needed to submerge the individual valor of Italians in the equalitarian and humanitarian soup. But today it is re-arising. The Great War put us on our feet and fascism has revealed us. Italians, mindful of themselves, want to return and be the indomitable warriors that they were, and outdo themselves. Our stupendous youth is weary of theories and philosophies; it loves and wants war. The cultural corrosive is a terrible snare for the energies of a healthy organism; it hampers, deforms, bends and scatters these energies, poisons them with doubt, and embitters them with irony. A people of warm vitality and sound muscles like ours must energetically reject all doctrines that do not lead it immediately to a satisfaction of its thirst for power. This explains fascism. The rediscovery of the warlike spirit of a race that has always been at war with the universe. . . .

Mussolini, Minister of War! This is what seems to me the supreme and most splendid incarnation of the Mussolinian spirit. His work, though it has been magnificently many-sided, lacked this essential side: it lacked the leadership of the military organization. And now comes this too. Who can any longer doubt that Mussolini is the most complete man of our times, the magic guide of the nation's fortunes, whom God has generously conceded to Italy?

Fascism will never be able to fulfil its tremendous task on a strictly political plane. Fascism issued from the War and in war it must find its outlet. Our country can conclude nothing except by a great war which we will neither provoke nor seek, but which we shall confront with the serene courage of peoples predestined to dominate the world. If the last war was one of liberation, the next one will place us in power.
. . . And we will not find ourselves facing an atrocious war like that in

which we paid for all the anti-militarism of the preceding twenty years, together with the widest liberty and indulgence for those who carried on sabotage, defeatism, treason, and spying for the enemy.

If an iron government had been given Italy during and previous to the War, how many disasters and how many ruins, how many misfortunes we would have escaped!

But let the past warn us for the future and make us more severe and warlike, give us the consciousness of what war really is, make us more conscious of our valor, and of our enormous possibilities. We who for fifteen years have invoked the advent of more virile generations, more dynamic, more bellicose, are happy to state that there are indubitable symptoms of this advent. The Italian people, in its overwhelming masses, is no longer a soft moonlight serenader, but, without forgetting its prodigious artistic imagination, it is a people of soldiers ready for every risk and every sacrifice. It is a people of religious, rhapsodic warriors who will conquer the future with the mystic fire of their own faith, interwoven with songs and with flourishes and thrusts of the sword. Thus we look down almost with a feeling of sorrowful pity on the ideas and sentiments that inspired the wars of liberation, though holy and worthy of benediction in so far as they unified us and gave us our strong natural boundaries. The war of the future will be . . . a futuristic war. It will be a conscious, proud, optimistic, voluntary effort, anxious for dominating expansion, breaking forth, strong in its higher and divine right, not to burst chains, but to win breathing space. It will be less sentimental, democratic, and humanitarian, and more ' sacred egoism '; more a spirit of greatness and a physiological instinct than a romantic conspiracy. We will not march against oppressors, but towards a life that awaits us in its fulness and of which we are becoming daily more worthy by our ardor, our genius, our numbers, and our energy. . . .

We may hope that many equivocations towards us will be cleared up, and that Italy will be regarded as a powerful nation, vigorous, wilful, intent on its tomorrow, re-awakened to a destiny of power and hence of dominion, by which all the old humanitarian and equalitarian doctrines . . . have been dispersed like unwholesome fogs in the fascist sun.

We are not weak and hence we do not know how to wail and cry for help. But America must . . . not exploit this fact to close the access to its lands for our emigrants, who . . . overflow the soil of our country. And America must also unburden itself a little of its indigestion of gold which like good King Midas isolates it from the sympathies of the world.

Real friendship is possible only on the basis of absolute parity. Now you have health and we have it; you have muscles and we have them, you have freed yourselves from the disintegrating doctrines of Wilson and we have banished forever all defeatist theory. But there are other things in which we differ. We must seek to suppress these differences as far as possible. We are sure that if there are a hundred intelligent and sincere men in America, . . . Italian-American coöperation will no longer be a dream. America has every interest in encouraging in every manner the development of a nation like Italy, for the sake of the equilibrium of races and of civilized nations.

And we who for fifteen years have championed the doctrine and the practice of energy, of the fist, of the racing pace, of the death leap, now that fascism has largely realized all this, now that the Italian youth is dedicated to physical exercises as is the American youth (the athletes of Italy, Mussolini said yesterday, are innumerable legions), we are convinced that we will easily understand each other.

For our imperialism, which is an imperialism of rich blood, of heavy muscles, and strong stomachs, can be understood by no one better than the American people that has founded an Empire between two oceans, by miracles of courage and energy. . . .   (Mario Carli: *Fascismo Intransigente,* pp. 15–22, 28–31, 68–69, 89–91, 215–217.)

FASCIST REVOLUTION AND GOVERNMENT

No. 13. *From the Memoirs of a Squadrist*

(Umberto F. Banchelli was one of Dumini's closest associates in one of the most famous and notorious of all the squads. In 1922 he was expelled from the Party for "conduct unbecoming a fascist." This circumstance should be borne in mind by the reader in connection with Banchelli's judgments on party politicians. He was sentenced for being implicated in a petty swindle, trying to export straw hats to South America.)

Beginnings of Florentine Fascism.

" In the first months of 1919 Fascism began in Italy; in Florence, the Alliance of Civic Defense (*Alleanza di Difesa Cittadina*). It arose through the will of several scoundrels aided in its arduous military tasks by several ex-combatants who acted in good faith. In the first class was the lawyer, Terzaghi, later deputy of Parma, whose boast, nevertheless, it can always be to have first publicly raised the standard of revolt against the outrageous conduct of the reds. In the second class were the lawyer, Carlo Marini, Umberto Banchelli, centurions, . . . and Amerigo Dumini, . . . etc., the tiny remaining percentage of the bourgeoisie and aristocracy which was still alive and red-blooded. Terzaghi and the Directorate made a large collection of money, about a million *lire*. They filled the city with wall posters and handbills and the rooms of the Bastogi palace were not large enough to hold all who joined, amounting to 25,000, both men and women. The odor of powder pervaded the city. The reds were seized with such trembling that on the eighteenth day of the month of August, the day set for the Revolution, everything passed off quietly.

It may not be amiss to glance at the manner in which some of the members of the Civic Alliance contributed to its merits. For example, they had printed 10,000 wall posters and 50,000 handbills, which they put into the hands of a crippled veteran and well-known crook. He gathered a number of associates, and took a number of carriages for a pleasant ride, during which 1,000 of the posters were pasted up. Then they sold the rest of them for paper by the pound. There were also the picked squads, with their innumerable bills for carriages, meals and travelling expenses. There were those who stole the keys to the armory from me while I was asleep, and appropriated ten or twelve of the finest pistols. But, thanks to the five hundred *lire* I gave to an expert, they were recovered. Of the higher degrees of dictatorial power I know nothing, for they were not in my field. I do know, however, that of the million *lire* there remained not one penny. Later a co-operative was established, but a very fat mouse made enormous holes in the cheese — and the treasury. Soon, however, the political elections approached and then the Civic Alliance was transformed into a mosaic of candidates. The military group and their leaders immediately retired, and ex-captain Francesco Giunta, now fascist deputy of Trieste, was made their commander-in-chief. The Alliance for Civic Defense made of itself a little theatre of comedies and smirches, featuring both men and women, who entertained themselves with all sorts of graceful indoor gymnastics. There was a lot of small talk, but after the departure of the stage-manager, Terzaghi, the comedy lost the last trace of intellectual vigor. The Alliance for Civic Defense, transformed into a political body, lost in the public eye the reputation for forceful action which the needs of the moment had at first conferred upon it. . . .

Umberto Pasella, the Political Secretary General,[1] with the aid of several volunteers, tried to establish *fasci* in Florence and the rest of Tuscany. But the wind being very unpropitious in those times, he did not dare insist nor come out into the open. As soon as Amerigo Dumini and the writer returned from Albania (where we had gone to avenge the assassination of Lieutenant Dumini by the Albanians), Florentine fascism began to take root. Amerigo Dumini, a genuine soldier, wounded in the War, and decorated with three medals for bravery in the face of the enemy, may regard himself as the real founder of Tuscan fascism. . . .

After a series of street fights and general beatings in Florence, came the first expedition, that of Montespertoli, which sounded the trumpet of resurrection for all the discouraged and dormant patriots. The members of this small and dangerous expedition (among whom was Dumini) were all in danger of being massacred by the red drunken mob, but by their courage they succeeded in winning the fray and only one of them, Cuesta, was lightly wounded. Two months later Montespertoli was friendly to fascism.

It is well to understand how beautiful the idea was for which these men, after three years of dangers in the war, did not hesitate to risk their lives to rescue a friend or to assert an ideal."

Enter, the Sons of Grey-beards.

" The election of Zamboni [2] . . . proved to be the glowing crucible from which emerged both the most beautiful and the most abstruse

[1] He was sent by the Milan *fascio* to organize and " discipline " Tuscany.

[2] The *fascisti* in October 1920 were already about 600 strong, and elected as their new director an ex-captain, Zamboni.

forms of Tuscan fascism. It must be remembered that in the case of the Alliance for Civic Defense, the party of grey-beards, those who for fifty years have governed Italy, had made ample representation for itself in the *fasci* by their clients, by their sons. But though they had entered *en masse* into the first organization, they stayed out of the second, for the report of firearms was something which disagreed both with their positive principles and with their practice. . . . Florentine fascism was duped from the beginning by the sons and clients of the grey-beards, who though they attended the meetings in great numbers never went on dangerous expeditions. We had thus two different policies among us: the politics of assemblies,[3] and the politics of expeditions. The true ex-combatants followed the example of Dumini and with their squads dealt out strong blows, not occupying themselves overmuch with the petty politics of meetings, being tired of small talk.

It is necessary to remember that the grey-beards and their clients had entered the *fascio* with their particular aims. One of them was to exercise class justice, that is, to inflict punishment, not as *fascisti*, but as sons of lawyers, or of doctors or of dry-goods merchants, etc. And so for a long time whenever a troop of these agents of justice met somebody dressed as a laborer, they laid about them in holy ardor. They had a conception no better than that of the communists who had beaten and assassinated anybody *well-clad*.

As soon as a few of these grey-beards and their clients and sons found themselves face to face with force they acted like their big brothers at the front: they withdrew shouting: '*Viva Italia! Viva Fiume!*' In such circumstances the combatants offered real resistance, but somebody tried to harangue the mob, and then all was useless. Discouragement took the upper hand."

Punitive Expeditions.

"There was the expedition of S. Piero a Sieve, in which Chiostri, Capanni (now Honorable Capanni), and Zamboni himself and Frullini participated — an expedition badly conceived and badly executed. The *fascisti* fell into an ambush of peasants, white bolsheviks. Bruno Frullini, giving the account of the expedition, tells how Zamboni and the other two fired like devils at a closed window and did not stop until it was completely shattered. From this it can be inferred that it was untrue that the *fascisti* killed that peasant who was found dead behind a doorway. . . .

In Tuscany our expeditions had spread terror in the camp of the subversives. The Florentine *fascio* had gone as far north as Carrara and as far south as Chiusi. Our squads were still invincible even for the greatest vigilance of the reds.

[3] The "grey-beard" element formed the *Unione Poltica Nazionale* and set up a bloc of candidates for election.

The Hall of so-called Labor and the *Fiom* [4] had been entered, their papers burned, and their banners taken. Red flags were displayed by the hundreds in the museum of the *fascio*. Communism among the railroad workers received a mortal blow when Lavaguini, its leader and perhaps the only one of all the red leaders who was bonafide, was killed by an unknown person. The places in town where railroad communists were well known to be in the habit of meeting, were deserted *en masse* by these fathers of the revolution. For a long time there was no more talk of strikes. . . .

The countryside was searched daily: Empoli, Santa Croce sull' Arno, Fucecchio, San Miniato; then Perugia and the valley of Chiana. In that place there had been a communists' ambush, where several Aretine and two Florentine fascists were killed . . . barbarously assassinated but afterwards very fully avenged. It was a triumph of energy, though lacking the necessary discipline."

The Economic Question.

" The more intelligent began to realize that the economic question was becoming more serious every day, and that the hour had come for launching labor syndicates. Fascism at that time was almost entirely unprovided with men competent in the field of economics; those whom they had, came from socialism and were caught in the general uncertainty. A few were not listened to. Others did not make themselves heard, because though being in evidence in fascist circles, they could not make up their minds to come out in the open and declare decisively what they thought. The cry went up that the worker must be befriended. Now at last they discovered how unfortunate had been the work of the young goody-goodies (*figli di papà*) who had erected an insurmountable wall over against the working classes. Perrone outdid himself in his efforts to succeed, but either because he lacked the necessary qualities or the suitable means, he could do little.

Now came a moment which was undoubtedly one of the most critical for our *fascio*. Caught between the duty of being the friend of the people, as had been said and re-said thousands of times, and the lamentable tears of the merchants, business men, and industrialists, from whom they had received money, our *fascio* preferred to do the noble thing and defend the people. However, the Directorate was not unanimous. The entire responsibility and direction of the hard work was entrusted to Banchelli in his capacity of Commissioner of Vigilance; the official rôle was entrusted to Pirelli. . . .

The desire of the Central Committee of *Fasci* was to defend the consumer and I observed this scrupulously. The campaign found me perfectly prepared. Scarcely had I been nominated Commissioner of Vigilance in the interests of civic police, when I had created a corps of

[4] *Federazione Italiana di Operai Mettallurgici.*

70 inspectors with about 1,200 men under them. To their previous duties was added that of reducing prices by the measures established. In a room in the *fascio's* office, I put a special tribunal and from it proceeded orders, inspectors, squads, punishments and praises. In order to avoid misunderstandings, before beginning the agitation and the cudgellings, I went out one day with a *centuria* of men, who carried large cards on which was written, 'You have two days within which to reduce prices.' We marched through the whole city amid the acclamations of citizens of all classes. In San Frediano (the poor district) the people wanted to carry us on their shoulders in triumph. Both out of political tact and in order to get closer to the mass of workers, we kept to the streets in which the people were thickest. Two days later, as predicted, the cudgellings began and prices were reduced in the just proportions, from fifteen to twenty-five per cent, established by the *fascio*. The cudgellings were innumerable, equal to the innumerable petty thefts on the part of the merchants. Whole squads, trembling from the blows received, were brought by the inspectors into the room of the tribunal to receive a little lecture of admonition, without partiality from all classes alike, from the currier to the wine merchant, from the clothing merchant to the broker. . . .

The egregious merchants of the town, instead of hating me, should have thanked me, for with the prices reduced they began to sell the merchandise which had been unsold on their shelves for three months. . . .

In those days the *fascio* became a sore spot for the profiteers. Among those beaten up and afterwards brought to the court by me, there were very many business men of the communist faith who were selling at higher prices than their democratic colleagues. Then for the first time I had a glimpse of the number of rascals and speculators who live like parasites on the shoulders of the consumer. I had a chance to see how the necessities of life pass through the hands of numerous grabbers and robbers before they arrive at one's table. I was assailed continually by brokers, merchants and business men, all of them asking for guards for their stores, having naturally acceded to the rules of the provisory committee. I had six secretaries to take care of the correspondence, but they were not enough.

Several merchants were found repeatedly violating the agreements made, and accordingly by order of the *fascio*, their stores were closed for two or three days, and on the doors were posted cards reading, 'Closed for continued robbery.' I had to occupy myself personally with the central market, and especially the market of vegetables at Sant'Ambrogio. At four in the morning, I took twenty young *fascisti*, one of whom carried a tri-color flag, and we mingled with the peasants and among the retailers to control the prices for the day. I found a valuable aid in Signor Fusi, city counsellor assigned as director to that market. He explained to me the whole mechanism of the vegetable market, which through the imbecility of the various authorities had become more and more complicated, and always at the expense of the consumer in the town.

The traditional democratic-bourgeois mentality was the cause of all the evil. And the tri-color among the vegetables, carried by men of honor and accompanied by young men of confidence, had a more quieting effect than any club. The peasants were found to be disposed to lower their prices. Their president, a keen peasant, told me that he was happy over what the *fascio* was doing, that he was very well satisfied indeed over the concession which had been made to the peasants by the Paszrowsky brewery. It had reduced by thirty per cent the price of the malt residue which the peasants use extensively. The general secretary of the brewery, Signor Polli, was extraordinarily accommodating in arriving at this agreement.

Pirelli, on the other hand, in conjunction with the authorities of the prefecture and municipality and the representatives of merchants and business men, nominated various commissions, a large number of them, and tied himself up in interminable councils in which agreement was always reached with difficulty.

What purpose was served by these commissions of the prefecture and commune we soon discovered. The creaking old bureaucracy was given a new lease on life, and hardly had the work of the squads and their inspectors ceased, when these commissions permitted prices to return to their former level. I am certain that if the Directorate had coöperated with me in the practical offensive, we would have left more permanent traces. As it was, action was diminished and there were finally two commissaries of the Directorate, one of finances and one of syndicates, who set themselves to work transporting poultry in trucks from Sesto to the central market, and this without my knowledge. Another sent a truck to take some wine casks. Pirelli himself, with the advice and aid of an inspector, had a whole avalanche of shoes arrive which he gave to a dealer on Borgo San Lorenzo to be retailed. Of this also I was not informed at the time. Producers of wine, oil, milk, dry goods, made attractive offers to the *fascio*. I wanted to make sales direct to the consumer, but was given no support in this matter. However, I should say that even had I succeeded in this intention, the benefits would have been of short duration, since I had at my disposal volunteer elements who were little suited to the task. I began to see weariness around me, even as I myself was becoming weary. We were not the kind of people who can by profession keep peace and exercise control. At last the cudgellers were getting tired!

Our fight touched intimately not only the economic system of the city, but also of the nation as well. We butted up against a wall centuries old, which, though indeed it bent a little, did not break, for it was sustained by too many interests genuinely and artificially created, hidden and open. I realized this after three days of the struggle, and told my colleagues of the Directorate that I could keep up the agitation for perhaps only three weeks more. And so in order not to lose the sympathy which we had gained among the people, I beat a slow retreat. But the interference which came from those famous commissions in the service of legality, increased the confusion. I have the impression that our work was more than a little profitable to someone, but I do not know to whom, certainly to the immediate political and economic interests, perhaps of a group of financiers of grey-beards."

Politics.

" After the political elections a number of types joined the fascist movement — bankrupts, malcontents, communist spies, office seekers. Mussolini announced the unfortunate phrase about the 'republican tendency,' which, though not bad as an honest idea, did damage here and there in the ranks of the *fascisti*, which were a mosaic of political principles. It was premature by at least six months. The fascist deputies, each still standing alone out of surprise at the unexpected and bewildering honor which had come to him in being seated at Montecitorio, were the first to rebel against the *Duce*. All forgot that they owed what they were to him alone, and that but for him they would not have been lifted out of the political obscurity in which they would have lived forever. Some wrote to the newspapers that they were democrats, others liberal monarchists. There was a shameful competition among inferiors who were unwilling to admit that Mussolini had created for them an unpolluted fresh start in politics which they did not know how to use profitably."

The Sarzana Expedition.

" The Caporetto of Fascism."

" About five hundred Tuscan *fascisti*, among them several fine excombatant figures, set out for Sarzana. Some of them were commanders of squads, but they were easily overruled by the undisciplined mob when the tragedy broke upon them.

The rendezvous was held in the country near the Avenza, and the march was started about two o'clock of the night of July 21st, under the light of a magnificent moon. In the minds of the *fascisti* there seemed to be something both mystic and grand about this column marching across the countryside! But an evil prophet thought it looked like a funeral march. This unfortunately proved to be true. As for tactics, we departed unorganized and unprepared for an emergency. The plan of action could not be read nor explained to the captains of squads, who moreover worried little about it, since in the matter of tactics almost all expected to use their own.

The idea was simple: to march upon Sarzana openly with one half of the force and in an orderly manner make the authorities surrender the nine prisoners; with the other half, if provoked, to ferret out thoroughly the squads of communists that were stationed in the environs of the city. . . .

Dumini, the leader, and his general staff had no choice but to march at the head of the enormous column marching single file, and to be the first to confront the communist ambush which reliable information gave us to understand was a certainty. The guides marched behind us. The march of sixteen kilometres carried us through the shadows and between farms and then along the railroad track. As a train was passing on its way to Sarzana undisciplined spirit made headway, and several shots were fired to halt the train. The leaders suppressed this impulsive conduct, but it was too late, for the railroad men spread the alarm at Sarzana.

The expedition was isolated from any friendly contacts. The few shots fired announced our march in advance, the aim of which could easily be imagined, and they proved a large factor in the staging of that tragedy.

At the inside gate of the Sarzana Station, two policemen begged the *fascisti* not to pass beyond them if they wanted to avoid being punished, and then as a compromise, we were told to pass by the side entrances, but the noisy mob broke out in undisciplined spirit, and insisted on doing the contrary. And so having passed on, about 200 of the *fascisti* reached a place where a police captain was stationed, one of Bonomi's hired assassins, together with eight policemen with their rifles in hand. They began a parley with Dumini and Santini, the captain of the Pisa squad. The parley was naturally interrupted by more than one of the *fascisti* present who also wanted to take part in it, until finally two pistol shots coming from the direction of the policemen immediately provoked a volley from the policemen's guns. It is worth noting that there were then two pistol shots, and also that the police captain suddenly raised his arm, with a stick in his hand, — a gesture which is commonly that of the commander of an executioner's squad. From the captain's manner of talking and his sarcastic smile at first quite indefinable, it was evident that he realized that we had witnessed something serious.

In fact the tragedy broke upon us unforeseen and like lightning. Our men had previously had strict orders that whatever happened at Sarzana no one was ever to fire at soldiers or at policemen or at Royal Guards, if there were any; so that very few of the *fascisti* answered the fire of the assassin policemen. What then took place was pitiful. Among the shots, the groans, the falling of the dead and wounded, there arose a general cry of indignation from many of those present. . . . The lack of moral and tactical unity provoked most of them to flight. In others it provoked bewilderment though they remained at their post under fire. A few retaliated. Among the many who fled into the countryside about thirty were wounded or killed in a truly barbaric fashion.

One need not go to Lybia to seek ferocity; the peasants of Sarzana gave such horrible evidence of their bloodthirsty rage that no revenge in the world could suffice to punish them adequately.

A platoon of Royal Guards endeavored hard to fire at our flank, but their Captain remembered in time that he was an Italian and at the risk of his own life made his soldiers, many of whom were Reds, lower their arms. Those *fascisti* who did not flee across the fields took refuge inside the station; others remained to help the wounded and then to carry them to the hospital. The disgraceful conduct of the Sarzanese continued to vent itself even against the wounded who had recovered in the hospital. These poor friends of ours were treated not as men needing aid, but as beings unworthy of care or compassion. The siren of alarm against *fascisti* incursions had been sounded by persons in the hospital and offices of public charities, who were always among the first to take on themselves the burden of defending Sarzanese *pussism*.[5] The physicians either out of fear of their patients, or out of congenital meanness, received the wounded in the most careless manner. The women of Sarzana were busy boiling oil and water to throw down on the *fascisti*. One comrade who was accompanying a wounded friend, was killed by the communists only a few steps from a squad of Royal Guards, without their taking the trouble to defend him or to arrest the assassins.

Among the *fascisti* there were many who had come to pursue their class interests. Several of these I found hidden under the beds and divans in the house of the Station-master. Several others had disappeared.

With the first train that passed in the direction of Carrara, a large crowd of them took their departure, leaving their friends in the dark and in the lurch, and all the energy of the head of the general staff was required to regulate the retreat. Dumini succeeded in about an hour's time in having the prisoners freed who had been locked up in the Sarzana jail. The personal work of Dumini always measured up to the most extreme demands of the tragic situation. If he committed a mistake it was in leading men who were morally and militarily inferior to the type needed. . . .

Sarzana demonstrated that in active organizations the person who makes speeches to incite others to battles should himself take part in the battles, in order that he may know what he is talking about. The most odious and injurious diatribes were heaped on the unfortunate leaders of the expedition. 'Crooks' brought confusion into the meetings, secured the expulsion of several of these leaders and assumed the places of command left vacant. The big electors and protectors of the Florentine *fascio,* eternally involved in fascist battles, made use of the fact of Sarzana to carry their inner electoral organization to that level of baseness which finally ended in the autonomist movement of the Pasella faction. . . .

[5] A fascist term for the *Partito Ufficiale Socialista.*

Sarzana, however, was a terrible warning for fascism. Military organization took more definite shape, and with the tangible signs of a better understanding among *fascisti,* discipline began to take on a wholesome and strong form.

After Sarzana many of Dumini's and my personal enemies made our dead a pretext for proclaiming benefit celebrations and subscriptions for both dead and living. The demagogues who aspired to public offices did not hesitate in their conclaves to recall with rhetorical phrases the sacrifice of our friends."

Towards the End.

"Towards the end of September 1921, the directors of the *fascio* published the bombastic and rhetorical manifesto announcing that the *fascio* would retire from the struggle since the bourgeoisie was no longer giving it aid. It explained that fascism was being persecuted by the authorities with the consent of the democracy, and hence, its dignity being offended it would retire. . . . Really it was the directors [6] who were undergoing a crisis, for their personal ambitions had not been entirely satisfied! . . .

It is certain that the *fascio* of Florence for its own reasons did not want to be subordinated to any superior control. The crisis had its origins far back in the very founding of the *fascio,* and all this because of the work of the moss-backed, slippered grey-beards. For from the beginning there were two policies and divergent aims: the market-place policy and the assembly policy, which together produced the book-keeping policy. This was the logical consequence, and perhaps the only one, of Mussolini's giving fascism to Pasella to be wet-nursed.

It appeared at that time that between the *fascisti* of the *Partito Nazionale Fascista* and several autonomists, there would have to be some duels, but because of the gravity of the situation the disputes were pacified. Pasella and his Directorate continued to promote numerous subscriptions for all sorts of things, ever new sources of money. The expenses were always very heavy! — the rent of the new headquarters in Piazza Mentana is 18,000 *lire* annually. There were also, I believe, some lotteries and benefit entertainments, for the purpose of erecting marble memorial tablets. In a restaurant of the city, amid spaghetti and beefsteaks, they decorated with a gold medal one Mario Pelagatti, the friend from Spezia.

Pasella tried feverishly to win the sympathies of the workers and of the professional classes, in order to enlarge the little syndicates created by him and employed all the malcontents to swell the numbers.

According to my judgment, instead of democratic duels, which never really settle any question, *fascisti* ought to wage duels *all'Americana,* or armed only with sticks. This latter is a better way also for the reason

[6] Rovello, Pelagratti, Pirelli.

that the life of a fascist belongs entirely to fascism until the day of its complete triumph."

(*At the very close elections of 1921, Agnoletti assembled the fascio in the Piazza, ready to storm the Palazzo Vecchio, in case the vote should be adverse. The vote favored them, consequently it was the communists who began rioting.* — Ed.) "And when the bomb exploded in Piazza Antinori and with it the civil war, Agnoletti immediately gave orders to a few men of action to strike a blow at the *head* instead of at the *body* of Leninism, and so it was done."

The Peroration.

"Ah, miserable rogues! Legality! That painted slave of yours and docile pimp for your evil dreams! Do you think you can give her as a companion to an able-bodied legionary? We too shall stand by legality, but our own, which can never be yours. Give thanks to your gods, o you worshippers of the golden calf, which for the moment is helpless because the fruit is not quite ripe. But you will soon meet us again at the new battle ground. We shall see if your traditions, which go back but to 1848, will give you the courage to wage battle with the legionary, who has re-arisen stronger than ever!

Fascism, the resurrection of our race, will assimilate those national forces that are still capable of coöperating with it and for it. Its path is marked out for it, splendid and sure, and speedier than we would have believed six months ago. No one any longer believes in the present institutions and in the representative men in power. The state is but a mint, and until now its money was believed to be real gold. Now the state with its democracies is counterfeit and is no longer trusted. Fascism will not limit itself to substituting new men in the public offices, but will clean out thoroughly all the organs of the state and of society. Over and above the incidents of battle, for a considerable period of years, there will remain in the arena on the one side fascism and our country, and on the other side there will be communism dressed up in various colors, but ever a foreign invasion. In time Catholicism will absorb into a single ideal both country and fascism, and then its single adversary will be the Jewish international capitalism with all its negative men and tendencies. Between Catholicism, which is Rome, and Hebraism, which is New York and London, the victory can not be doubted: *Rome*." (Umberto F. Banchelli: *Le Memorie di un Fascista,* 1919–1922. Florence 1922.)

No. 14. *Fascist Individualism*

(The following excerpts from the speeches of Alberto De Stefani indicate his position on some of the major issues within fascism. They were written in 1921–1922, when the position of the fascist deputies in the Chamber was being debated, when the national syndicates were incor-

porated into the fascist ranks and when the general economic platform
of fascism was being determined. De Stefani was a professor of political economy in a technical school near Venice. He took a prominent
part in the activities of the *fascisti* in Venetia and especially at Trieste
and Fiume. He was one of the first fascist deputies to Parliament.)

" If we look closely into our history from its very origins we shall find
that fascism in its most fundamental signification has always existed
and has always operated in the most serious crises of the nation. Moreover there have always existed two opposed conceptions of history:
the individualistic and heroic conception of our Latin race, and the
socialistic gregarian conception which is Teutonic and characteristic of
current socialism. So-called scientific socialism is a foreign product, a
product exported by a German Jew.

Solidly opposed to socialism stands the individualistic conception
that we have inherited from liberalism, from our own forefathers of the
risorgimento, who had the assurance of their own convictions and who
continued to sit on the benches of the glorious national right wing even
when its fortunes had declined. The liberals of today have migrated in
a body towards the center, for liberalism is being submerged in democratic ideas. Fascism reëstablished the tradition of the national right
and when the issue was being discussed where our parliamentary group
ought to be seated, I claimed energetically that it ought to sit on the
extreme right.

The historical function of fascism is very clear today and does not
lend itself to equivocation: fascism is an aristocratic and individualistic
movement." (*Discorsi,* pp. 96–97.)

" Democracy is a concrete reality that we accept, that we recognize as
an insuperable condition of life today. But for us democracy is not an
end, it is a means, a field in which we can work to the advantage of the
nation. We were and are opposed to those interpretations of present
democracy that tend to subject the nation to the will of the majority.
Even a handful of men has the right and the duty to set its own ideal
vision and its own line of action against an erring and ignorant majority.
Look closely into history and you will become aware that history is not
only and perhaps not mainly a democratic product but an aristocratic
product. I heard very well how the Head of the Government told us in
the Chamber how necessary it is that the authority of the state be re-
established in Italy. Now I do not understand these abstract phrases:
the authority of the state is nothing but the authoritative force of men.
It rests in and is entrusted to the concrete energy and power to rule
which one man has over others. This power of ruling you feel when
you look into the eyes of the man who commands you, it is transformed
in you, by his look, his actions, and his words, into necessary obedience,
into a spontaneous recognition of his force, into a dedication of your

own forces to his, and in your being inflamed by his passion and his ideas. Thus gentlemen, the superiority of a man makes itself felt." (*Discorsi*, pp. 112–113.)

" The predominant characteristic of the present crisis is to be found in the increasing disparity between population and the material means of production, due on the one hand to the natural increase of the people, and on the other to the slower rate of increase of capital, which latter is the consequence of war and of the destruction of wealth resulting from the preponderance of socialistic politics. The pressure of population is great and today constitutes one of our weaknesses but tomorrow may constitute our strength. The greatest task for fascism's political economy today is the reduction of this pressure. There are two ways: emigration and speeding up the process of the saving and the formation of capital. It is needless to speak of a Malthusian policy.

Two means have been used for regaining an equilibrium between population and capital: public works and the imposition of a definite quota of laborers on employers. Illusory tactics. The employment of laborers is determined and limited by the amount of instrumental capital available both mobile and immobile. At any moment this quantity is whatever it may be. Public works and the imposition of a quota of laborers cannot increase it. Instead they coöperate in many cases to retard the accumulation of capital. . . .

We must face the facts without taking recourse to deceptive means that almost always end in decreasing production. Let us open our eyes. Italy is a small country both as to its agricultural area and as to its raw materials, relatively to its population. It must send its own human surplus beyond its boundaries. The peace treaties have not changed this tremendous fact. England and France have kept the German colonial empire for themselves; the Asiatic and African policies of England and France are anti-Italian. In supplying ourselves with raw materials we must first of all undergo the economic and political monopolies of producing countries. The protectionist immigration policies of those states to which our emigration is directed is becoming more accentuated and is receiving the support also of the workers in those states. Hence in the face of our population pressure there exists the pressure of the bonds by which our country is encased and which prevent it from regaining an equilibrium between capital and population. Unless we accept the facts of hunger, we are compelled to resort either to pacific means, persuading the world of our necessities, or to violence on the supreme ground of self-preservation.

The foreign policy of fascism is dominated by the internal population pressure. It is clear, precise, and outlined by the most definite projects. There are states that must choose between coming to agreements and being forced into them. Ours is a small country that holds a large people. We have overcome socialistic pacifism. The necessities of emigration may, if they should not be recognized, give way to phenomena of an entirely different character." (*Discorsi*, pp. 177–179.)

"Our *fasci*, having risen so rapidly and having such a burning faith that they are too impatient to solve their economic and technical problems laboriously and systematically, have now and then adopted methods that lead to a destruction of wealth and to retarding the growth of capital. Those who have assumed the direction of syndical organizations have a tremendous responsibility on their shoulders, increased by the power of choice which the organizers have conferred on them.

The Fascist Party and the national syndicates are two distinct organizations, the former controls the latter in order that syndical activity may proceed within limits of national and productivistic principles. The political organs of the Party must see to it that the national principle be respected and must avail themselves of the work of the *gruppi di competenza* to control the economic activities of the syndicates. We must have the energy to act against the national syndicates when they do not respect the conditions which we have laid down for liberty of organization, just as we acted against the red and the white syndicates. . . . I do not believe a forced cultivation of syndical unity to be opportune. The political organizations of the party must not be brought into play to suppress those competing syndicates that accept our nationalist and productivist postulates. We must let live all those organizations that obey these principles. Unity favors both capitalistic and labor parasitism. The economic situation of the nation does not permit parasitism." (*Discorsi*, pp. 180–182.)

"A political economy that frees the mechanisms of production and exchange from all incumbrances is more effective in producing income than increased tax rates and new taxes can possibly be for an organism that is fettered in its initiatives and movements. We shall therefore follow this indirect financial criterion according to which the interests of private economy are reconciled with the interests of the state and of public finance. Let me tell you plainly a financial policy based on the persecution of capital is a mad policy. The economic straits of a nation demand a continual influx of capital in order that it may be preserved and may make progress. Rather than prevent the extinction of capital by bringing pressure to bear on reinvested savings that have been robbed by the state from private enterprise, it is desirable to bring pressure to bear on consumption and that too in the true and definite interests of the poorest classes of the population. The struggle against the accumulation of private capital falls back on the shoulders of the laborers.

We shall welcome instead, in so far as present conditions allow it, the accumulation of saving." (*Discorsi*, pp. 190–191.)

No. 15. *The Proclamation of the Quadrumvirate*

October 29, 1922.

"*Fascisti!* Italians!

The hour of decisive battle has sounded. Four years ago, at this time, the national army started the supreme offensive that led to victory; today, the army of black shirts reasserts this mutilated victory and, desperately pushing on Rome, is leading it to the glory of the Campidoglio. From today on the *Principi* and *Triari* are mobilized. The marshal law of fascism goes into full force. Under the order of the *Duce* the military, political, and administrative powers of the Party leaders are being assumed by a secret quadrumvirate of action with dictatorial powers.

The army, the reserve and supreme safeguard of the nation, must not take part in the struggle. Fascism renews its highest esteem for the army of Vittorio Venito. Nor is fascism marching against the officers of public order; but against a political class of imbeciles and delinquents who for four long years have not been able to give the nation a government. The classes that compose the productive bourgeoisie know that fascism wants to impose a single discipline on the nation and to aid all those forces that augment its economic expansion and welfare.

The laboring people, in fields and offices, on railroads, and in factories, have nothing to fear from fascist power. Their just rights will be loyally safeguarded. We shall be generous with harmless opponents; inexorable towards others.

Fascism draws its sword to cut the too many Gordian knots that bind and depress Italian life. We call God on high and the spirit of our five hundred thousand dead to witness that a single impulse drives us, a single will unites us, a single passion inflames us, to contribute to the salvation and greatness of our country.

Fascisti of the whole of Italy!

Apply your minds and forces like Romans. We must win. We shall win.

Viva l'Italia! Viva il Fascismo!

The Quadrumvirate."

No. 16. *Mussolini Introduces Himself to Parliament*

(To the Chamber of Deputies, November 16, 1922.)

"Gentlemen, what I am doing now in this hall is an act of formal deference towards you for which I ask no special sign of recognition.

For many years, too many, government crises were made and solved by the Chamber by means of more or less tortuous maneuvers and machinations, so much so that a crisis was regularly called an attack and a ministry was represented by a tottering stagecoach. This is the second time within a decade that it has happened that the Italian people, in its better elements, has overthrown a ministry and has given itself a government over and above and against all parliamentary designations. The decade of which I speak stands between May 1915 and October 1922. To the melancholy zealots of super-constitutionalism I leave the task of making their more or less pitiful lamentations on recent events. I maintain that revolution has its rights. I add in order that all may know it, that I am here to defend and enforce in the highest degree the revolution of the black shirts, injecting them intimately into the history of the nation as a force of development, progress and equilibrium. I refused to outdo the victory though I could have. I set myself limits. I told myself that the best wisdom is the wisdom that does not abandon one after the victory. With three thousand youths fully armed, fully determined and almost mystically ready to act on any command of mine, I could have chastised all those who have defamed and tried to harm fascism. I could have made of this sordid grey assembly hall a bivouac of squads; I could have kicked out Parliament and constructed a government exclusively of *fascisti*. I could have, but I did not want to, at least not for the present. . . .

I have formed a coalition government not with the intention of having a parliamentary majority, which I can now do very well without, but in order to call to the aid of the gasping nation as many as are willing to save the nation itself over and above all smoke of parties. I am deeply grateful to my associates, ministers and undersecretaries; I am grateful to my colleagues in the government who have been willing to assume the heavy responsibilities of this hour with me; and I cannot help recalling with pleasure the attitude of the laboring masses of Italians who have strengthened the fascist motto by their active and passive solidarity. I believe that I also interpret the thought of this whole assembly and certainly of the majority of the Italian people in expressing warm devotion to the Sovereign, who refused to listen to the uselessly reactionary and last minute attempts, and avoided civil war, allowing the new impetuous fascist current risen from the War and exalted by the victory to be injected into the fatigued arteries of the parliamentary state.

Before attaining this post I was asked on all sides for a program. Alas! it is not programs that are wanting in Italy; it is the men and the willingness to apply the programs. All the problems of Italian life, all of them I say, have been solved on paper; but the will has been lacking to translate them into fact. The government today represents this firm and decisive will. . . .

The state is strong and will prove its strength against all, even against any eventual fascist illegalism, for this would be an unenlightened and impure illegalism without the least justification. However, I must add that almost all the *fascisti* have given perfect support to the new order of things. The state does not intend to abdicate in favour of anyone at all. Whoever rises against the state will be punished. This clear call goes out to all citizens and I know that it must sound particularly welcome in the ears of the *fascisti* who have fought and won in order to have a state that would dominate all, all I say, with the necessary inexorable energy. You must not forget that outside the minorities that carry on militant politics, there are forty millions of first-rate Italians who work, reproduce, perpetuate the deep bases of the race, and demand and have a right to demand that they be not thrown into chronic disorder, the sure prelude to general ruin. . . .

As far as possible, I do not want to govern against the Chamber; but the Chamber must feel its particular situation which makes it subject to being dissolved within two days or two years. We demand full powers because we want to assume full responsibility. Without full power you know very well that it would be impossible to make a single *lira*, I repeat a single *lira* of economy. Hereby I do not intend to exclude voluntary coöperation which we shall accept cordially whether it comes from deputies, senators, or competent private citizens. All of us have a religious sense of our difficult task. The country encourages us and waits. Let us not give it mere words but deeds. We formally and solemnly assume the task of balancing the budget and we shall balance it. We want a foreign policy of peace but at the same time of dignity and firmness; and we shall have it. We have proposed to give the nation discipline and we shall give it. Let no one of our opponents of yesterday, today or tomorrow be under illusions about the briefness of our stay in power. Puerile and foolish illusions like those of yesterday. Our government has formidable bases in the consciousness of the nation and is sustained by the best and freshest Italian generations. There is no doubt that in these last days an enormous step has been made toward the unification of their minds. Our country of Italy has once more found itself, from the North to the South, from the continent to our numerous islands which will never again be forgotten, from the metropolis to the busy colonies of the Mediterranean and the Atlantic. Gentlemen, do not throw any more vain prattle at the nation. Fifty-two members scheduled to speak on my remarks are too many. Rather let us get to work with clean hearts and alert minds to bring prosperity and greatness to our country.

And God help me to bring this my arduous task to a victorious end."

(To the Senate, November 16, 1922.)

" Honorable Senators: the whole first part of the declarations I read recently in the Chamber of Deputies does not concern the Senate in the least. I must not use the necessarily severe language before the

Senate which I had to use before the Honorable Deputies. Not only today but for several years, I can safely say, I regard the Senate as one of the fixed points of the nation. I regard the Senate not as a superfluous institution, according to certain fantastic views of a small democracy; I regard the Senate instead as a form of the state, as a reserve of the state, as a necessary organ for the just and sagacious administration of the state.

The last years of parliamentary history have given a character that might be called plastic and dramatic to the conflict between the two chambers. Italian youth, whom I interpret and represent, and whom I intend to represent, looks to the Senate with great lively and patriotic sympathy.

I repeat that the first part of my speech was directed only to the Chamber of Deputies." (Benito Mussolini: In *La Nuova Politica dell'Italia,* Volume I, pp. 9–17.)

No. 17. *The "Moral Revolt"*

(The following selections are taken from Alfredo Misuri's famous speech in the Chamber of Deputies, May 29, 1923. It was the first major symptom of revolt within the ranks. Misuri was severely beaten after his speech and later expelled from the Party.)

" It has certainly not escaped the perspicacity of the Honorable President of the Council that the popular favor, which still follows him and his work, is beginning to assume a certain amount of reserve as regards fascism.

The country was not greatly scandalized when it saw him, wreathed in laurels, with his triumphal quadriga pass over the already decayed body of the goddess Liberty. The demagogic governments that preceded him had reduced the goddess to the state of a common harlot, and it was not worth the trouble to mourn. The country has faith in him, a faith made up of recognition and of fervor, of expectation and of devotion.

The opponents themselves, who recognize his conqueror's magnanimity, though with natural reserve, hope that God will preserve him to Italy, because they feel the helm of the ship of state to be in good hands, while the last waves break on the sides of the ship. But friends, both among his sympathizers and among the opposition, have an aversion for his imitators great and small. They will not tolerate the oligarchies that are being created around his great and small imitators. . . .

The Party and the State must no longer be identified.

The generality of good citizens does not believe, nor do the sincere friends of the government, that it is in the interest of national reconstruction to have government powers and party hierarchies continually and reciprocally insinuating themselves and superimposing themselves on each other; they do not believe that the national government is helped by being entitled, according to some, 'a fascist government.' The authority of the government must mount to higher levels. . . .

The public does not contest the government's right to choose its principal agents, entrusted with great responsibilities, so that they enjoy its absolute confidence. It is a legitimate reaction against the ultra-liberal democratic system which allowed agents of the state to be members of subversive parties and to carry on a subversive work against the powers of the state itself.

The so-called 'injection of fascist blood into the veins of the state organism,' and especially the nomination of several fascist prefects and police chiefs, though it followed on a rather hasty sifting, has in fact scandalized no one, as a matter of practical principle.

It is logical that a strong government should be able to count on the execution of its orders on its circumference, by means of its agents, who should not only possess the technical capacity for their office but should have the same type of mind as those who govern.

In practice things have gone very differently, but all this can be corrected so that the roads of invasion into the prefectures and police offices of the realm be not opened to schemers and favorites; or to the improvisations and returns of civil and military agents who had been ousted and are being readmitted by means of the baptismal font of some complacent *fascio* or other. . . .

And more, I believe that free spirits still have before their eyes the sorry spectacle that the public offices offered on the morrow of the March on Rome. . . .

Ordinary employees, still pallid from the unaccustomed event, superintendents of public services with their round Nittian bellies, general directors, full of insults, all of them displayed the lictors' *fascio* in their buttonholes, like lightning rods, and all over the steps and halls they began whistling the first notes of *Giovinezza!*

In fact one had to ask oneself how it was possible that with so many *fascisti* already incognito in the capital, it had ever been necessary for four years to sow corpses along the road from Milan to Rome. . . .

Ever since the moment in which the National Fascist Party and the government became interlaced to the extent of being confused and interchanged in the Grand Council, even when coming from minor organs and institutions, it has been evident that, to grasp the actual situation of the country, one must not overlook the fact that every action of that Party is reflected in the government and that every action of the government is reflected or should be reflected in the Party. The facts prove daily that the former relation exists in greater measure and to a greater extent than the latter. Nor can the eye of an intelligent observer have failed to notice the general dismay, created by the fact that the decisions made at the first meetings of the Grand Council were followed by decisions made by the sessions of the Council of Ministers, which coincided with them. It was the Party that outlined policies for the government. . . .

Following upon the handful of heterogeneous elements that began the reaction gathering around a single man, a newspaper, and a black flag, with a few simple schematic postulates, there gravitated toward them and was absorbed by them a little of everything from all directions. Fascism's travail lies precisely here.

The sound nucleus remains but it is submerged beneath the scum of present errors. The grafters by the strength of their numbers have outweighed the zeal of the Templars. The few rebels of the dawn are now flanked by myriads of converted opponents, no one knows whether in good or in bad faith.

An entire party of more than a hundred thousand men has been enslaved rather than absorbed, and the passions are raging of all those whose dignity was not sufficiently safeguarded. . . .

The vague consciousness of their own unpreparedness exaggerates the boldness manifested by the youngest; embitters their intransigence against the more experienced, who were first held as critics and then changed to advisors, who were first obnoxious pedants and then willing participators in the work of civic reconstruction. And as the circle of intransigence narrowed, everything that did not fit in with the lively improvisations of the most recent Chrysostoms, great and small, who grow in swarms from the Viminal Palace to the *Fascio* of Vattelapesca, was taken as an anti-fascist manifestation, as perhaps this my conversation with the government under the public gaze may be classified by some (certainly by the *Popolo d'Italia*) as anti-fascist, when it is intended to be, and is, fervently inspired by the desire to coöperate in inserting a restored and healthy fascism more deeply into the national life.

This mania for creating taboos, this dread of everything and everybody, is a symptom of weakness and fear in weak oligarchies when they appear most formidable.

The Honorable President of the Council, who is a strong man, does not share these dreads and wisely holds his course among honest agreements. The loyal coöperation which has been solemnly reaffirmed toward him by the Liberals in these days, is not without significance. Also in respect to certain democratic factions such agreements can be greatly strengthened and eventually extended to all men of good will, who put the salvation of the public affairs before the narrow selfishness of their party. But all this is due to his own action and personal prestige, to the confidence that he inspires personally. . . .

The mind of the *Duce*, though weighty, is too much preoccupied with the serious problems of foreign policy to be able to follow the many-sided internal life of the country by a daily report and a few telephonic communications from the Viminal Palace; all the more so since he cannot even have an objective view of the situation from the newspapers because of the one-sided activity of the Press Office and because of the padded opposition of non-official opposition organs.

Italy demands the coördination of internal politics. Whether the nomination of a Minister of the Interior is needed, or whether it is preferable to let a group of under-secretaries rule, either must be solely responsible under the *Duce*, for the conduct of internal politics. But too often, beside him, and often even with those functions usurped by the super-minister, the dominant party has set up as a general secretary, its ineffable Secretary General,[7] . . . a person not nominated by the people or the Crown, who by the influence of a party, even though it be the strongest and most meritorious, acquires a supernatural power, and brings his own pleasantries and bad taste into the very serious concern that modern public life is, invading everybody's field and superimposing himself on everybody, — the people does not understand him and will not tolerate him. Absolutely. The system in actual use is that of discounting those who are chosen by the people even when *fascisti*. I believe that, except a few members of the government, more or less all the members of the parliamentary fascist group, who were certainly the most legitimate representatives of early fascism and of the sound part of the nation that allied itself with fascism, are forced to move on a ground that has been undermined by the invasion of local bureaucrats and by the subjection of the will of the masses to the oligarchy; it is the directors who are substituting themselves for electoral bodies.

Remember the first moral defeat of a party once fortunate and powerful, went back to the well-known cases of invasion of a personnel not elected by the people, who made themselves felt by their vetos and impositions with which they obstructed the will of the people's representatives in a critical moment.

A similar substitution of will and action is not necessary to the work of restoration which has been begun so energetically and under such favorable auspices.

When the interferences by the action of the Secretary General and his followers in the central powers of the state will be eliminated, there will also be eliminated, as a matter of consequence, the interferences of political secretaries in the work of prefects and other local authorities. The organs of the state will reassume their whole vigor and will obey the head of the government, and him only.

A clarification, a simplification is necessary.

Gentlemen of the Government, tell the Honorable President of the Council: Bonaparte overthrew the unfit directory." (*Rivolta Morale:* pp. 102–121.)

No. 18. *Election Incidents*

(The following documents are taken from the election campaign which preceded the fascist elections of April 1924. The dissident *fascisti*, Corgini, Misuri, Forni and Sala were particular objects of fascist wrath because they were waging an independent and hostile campaign.)

[7] Michele Bianchi.

A Telegram to the Prefects of the Kingdom:

March 1924.

" Organization fascist dissident elements by work of Honorable Corgini and Misuri is confirmed by the General Secretariat of the P. N. F. Please exercise very active watchfulness reporting urgently every emergency and above all the possible presence in your territory of above-named deputies.

Minister Mussolini."

A Telegram:

Rome, March 11, 1924.

To the Provincial Fascist Federations of Alessandria, Cuneo, Novara, Milan, Pavia, Turin.

" Following orders given by the President of the Council and leader of fascism with the approval of the National Directory, the Provincial Secretaries should consider Messrs. Sala and Cesari Forni as the enemies of fascism most to be feared.

Consequently and parallel with instructions given by the Head of the Government to the Prefects of the Provinces, life must be made ' impossible ' for the above-mentioned men in those provinces where they have an interest in creating major schisms for the purpose of electoral exploitation.

They must not be permitted in committees or lectures; in whatever place they may appear they should be attacked ' violently ' by ' all the *fascisti.*'

The attention of the *Fascio* of Biella should be particularly called to this, which did not react ' as is proper ' to individuals declared to be enemies of fascism and the government. I await telegraphic reply with a report, data, and character of this circular, in order to communicate to the *Duce* that the orders will be executed.

The Secretary General, Francesco Giunta."

A Telegram:

Novara, March 12, 1924.

" I transmit the orders from Rome. I intend that they be ' very rigidly ' applied. Sala and Forni must not speak in the Province, it is necessary that ' they be barred.' I await assurances. Fascist greetings.

The Political Provincial Secretary, Amedeo Belloni."

From the Stampa of Turin, April 6, 1924.

" The *Stampa* hears from Alessandria of a curious travelling incident occurred to Honorable Ottavio Corgini, ex-Undersecretary of State, who with his friends Maricanola, a candidate on the Piedmont list of National *Fasci*, Revelli, Pagliani, and Balzani, all of them dissident *fascisti*, was going in an automobile from Valenza to Turin.

Toward midnight yesterday the group arrived near the crossroads of Ponte Tanaro, . . . and was stopped by a group of fascist sentinels stationed there. The travellers were made to get out and were accompanied in three other automobiles to the police headquarters, where they kept Pagliani and Balzani as a measure of public safety because they were not provided with personal documents. Honorable Corgini, Revelli and Maricanola were this morning accompanied to the Central Railroad station and made to leave.

Corgini's chauffeur, who had remained at the Hotel Europa, returned that night to the crossroads of Tanaro to take his automobile which belonged to a private Turin garage, but found only a heap of wreckage. During his absence it had been consigned to the flames."

No. 19. *Confessions of a Scapegoat*

(On December 27, 1924, the newspaper *Il Mondo* published a "memorandum" by Cesare Rossi from which the following extracts are taken. Rossi was at the time in jail accused of complicity in the Matteotti murder. The publication of this memorandum was the immediate occasion for a violent renewal of the Aventine opposition, which in turn led to Mussolini's decision to stamp it out by force, January 3, 1925.)

". . . Let me say immediately that all that happened, happened always through the direct volition, or with the approval, or with the complicity of the *Duce*. I allude to the beating of Amendola, the orders for which were given by Mussolini without my knowledge to De Bono, and which was organized by Candelori; to the beating of Misuri, organized by Balbo on the suggestion of Mussolini; to the attack on Forni, the orders for which were excitedly given by Mussolini to me personally and which was organized with the help of Giunta; to the demonstration against Nitti's villa, to the recent demonstrations against members of the opposition, orders for which were given by Mussolini to Foschi; to Mussolini's proposal given to the Quadrumvirate that Honorable Ravazzolo be given the lesson which his indiscipline merited; to the destruction of the Catholic clubs in Brianza, orders for which were given by Mussolini to Honorable Maggi and repeated to me with approval.

I add that daily Fasciolo had the orders, on Mussolini's suggestion, to send to the local *fasci* the names of those who subscribed to the *Voce Repubblicana*, to the *Avanti!*, to *Justizia*, to *Unita*, to *Italia Libera*, etc., in order that they might be purged and beaten. I allude also to sending Dumini, Volpe, Putato, etc., to France with falsified passports issued by De Bono, and with money furnished by Finzi in the presence of Hon. Bastianini, in order to avenge the fascist Geri who was killed in Paris. I add that Dumini, Putato, and Volpe possessed a pass for free transportation, issued by the general director of public safety to the director of railroads.

Besides all these episodes, . . . added proof of such state illegalities is given by the menacing speeches of the *Duce* and by some of his remarks in letters. I recall the most recent: a letter to Giampaoli, Secretary of the Milan *fascio*. Among the most suggestive threats, I recall the one issued to the Florentine *fascisti* after the killing of Nenciolini in a disagreement among *fascisti* at Lastra a Signa. In it he said that lead should be reserved only for adversaries.

Other concrete evidences of the polemic activity of the President are the notes to the Volta Agency. The most violent were written in his hand. Some of the originals must still be traceable, for hardly had Mussolini given me an original than I passed it on to Fasciolo who had it typed and then destroyed the manuscript. But a group of journalists who would gather the Volta notes could easily recognize among the calm and sober notes of the Volta Director, the sharp and threatening ones of Mussolini. But Mussolini did not limit himself to the Volta: the most notable polemic attacks of the *Popolo d'Italia* after the March on Rome, issued from his pen and can be gathered because they were given the place of honor. Moreover, the paper *l'Impero* several times published violent attacks in which one can obviously see the Mussolinian prose; one of these against the *Giornale d'Italia* was also somewhat vulgar. All this perfectly agrees with Mussolini's temperament, violent and diplomatic at the same time, always very changeable. . . .

The better to illustrate the state of alarm in which the President lived, and made us live, I recall that one morning, having read an intercepted telegram from a Cremona family which had been sent to d'Annunzio with expressions of hearty support, he ordered that Farinacci should be telegraphed in order that the persons who had signed it might be purged and beaten.

In this atmosphere of hatred and of fear, the sequestration of Matteotti, which then degenerated into his suppression, was germinated. Hence we are facing a political crime, naturally of the state. As to the case of Matteotti there is no direct and concrete responsibility of mine, in that over forty days before, I had broken all relations with Dumini following upon an indiscretion committed by him at my expense. . . . Is it possible that I would have organized an attack on Matteotti through a man with whom I was not on speaking terms? . . . Sometimes, but very seldom, I had given Dumini some hundreds of *lire,* for I did not ignore the fact that he was at the disposition of the Party for many investigations and above all at the disposition of Bastianini (for *fasci* in foreign countries); not however as direct payment, for that was not my business, but because he often served me on various commissions. . . .

While I share the responsibility for the attacks on Misuri and Forni, always under orders, I know nothing of that on Amendola. I read the news in the paper . . . and then telephoned from my office to De

Bono, asking for information. By the ambiguous manner in which he replied I understood that it was state aggression, manufactured in the family. In the afternoon, my curiosity aroused, I went to De Bono's room. He told me that those —— (an indecent term) had committed a bunch of nuisances. Later I learned that the organizer had been Candelori, Consul of the Legion of Rome. Then I asked for the impression of the President, who was at Milan spending Christmas with his family. De Bono replied as follows: ' At first over the telephone he made a show of anger evidently having some people around him. However a little later, he called me over a direct wire, and after he had asked me particulars, closed the conversation saying that he had eaten his lunch with more appetite.' . . .

After the killing of the fascist Geri at Paris, Honorable Bastianini after he had talked with Mussolini sent Dumini, Volpe, and Putato to Paris. False passports were given all three by De Bono. Finzi on Mussolini's orders in my presence gave ten thousand *lire* to Bastianini. I believe that on their return some more was handed over to them. According to the reports which Dumini sent me and which were read to the President and then passed on to De Bono, the work of revenge and inquisition in France had been successful. Mussolini sometimes praised the reports, sometimes remained sceptical about their contents. On his return from Paris Dumini, wounded, met the President and was affectionately congratulated by him. The Secretary of the Foreign *Fasci* had a cigarette case engraved and given to Dumini.

After Misuri's speech in the Chamber I met the President who was irritated, and he told me that fascism could not tolerate such an insulting attitude and that it was necessary to punish Misuri immediately and inexorably. Honorable Balbo carried out his wishes with the help of Bonaccorsi and Consul Candelori. On this occasion Mussolini next day exhibited his extraordinary satisfaction, and made an insignificant reply by means of Acerbo. Naturally Misuri might have died.

Later on, one morning when De Bono informed the President that Misuri continued to insist that the judge should issue orders of arrest against the known authors of the aggression, someone said that Misuri would make another fierce speech. At this the President interjected: ' But this time that bullhead is surely going to be killed.' De Bono replied smiling: ' But let us be agreed; if we must kill him, we had better do it before the speech, and then we shall not incur harmful and hostile speculations.'

Among Misuri's aggressors there was also, as is known, Arconovaldo Bonaccorsi, to whom shortly afterward Mussolini . . . gave an affectionate embrace. The motion may be found easily, introduced by Mussolini and voted by the Grand Council the day after the attack on Forni, in which it is asserted that traitors are to be treated as such. As regards the attack on Forni, the very evening on which the above-mentioned order was voted by the Grand Council, De Bono and I informed him that no incident had taken place at Mortara. To which he replied, smiling: 'Go on. Go on. When one takes the lead and takes it decidedly, one is always right."

The attack on Forni had the following origin: One morning I was called urgently to the Palazzo Chigi by telephone from Mussolini; I found the President in a really furious state of excitement against Forni because of his speech at Biella. He was irritated also at Gasti, because in the name of their committee he had sent an idyllic sort of telegram while Forni was attacking the Party and the government.

He cried repeatedly to me that fascism had no defensive sensibilities whatsoever and that it was always up to him to take the brunt. At one point he said: 'What is Dumini doing? Is he —— (an indecent term)?' For Dumini was the man suited for punitive deeds and he knew that he was at the disposal of the Party and of the government for these deeds. I tried to calm him, explaining to him that dissidence was an isolated phenomenon; but finally I too was impressed and then I promised that I would immediately go to Giunta's office to send somebody to Milan or Pavia.

Giunta and I sent a friend, who was ordered to get in touch with the *Arditi di Guerra* to give Forni a lesson. However, bearing in mind Forni's past, I recommended that they limit themselves to a clubbing, although I had not received any orders to temper the revenge."

No. 20. *Intransigent Fascism*

(The following selections are taken from the speeches of Roberto Farinacci, who was called to the head of the Fascist Party after the decision was made to crush the parliamentary opposition by force, and who remained in office over a year until after he had defended the Matteotti murderers at their trial. He was the recognized leader of the so-called intransigent faction and is still the best example of a fascist local boss, or *ras*. Among the squadrists, especially in the lower valley of the Po, he rivalled in popularity Mussolini himself. He has been one of the most independent and violent of the fascist leaders.)

(*February 17, 1925.*)

" If the Party has today expressed its recognition of me, it is because you, *fascisti* of the province of Cremona, have faithfully and enthusiastically followed me. I like to recall that when many municipal and provincial administrations hastened to vote resolutions in connection with the killing of the socialist deputy, the Provincial Council of Cremona, in a resolution reconfirming its unconditional solidarity with the *Duce*, refused all signs of reaction and all association with the chorus of lamentations. If the government and the Party, after the obvious bad faith of our adversaries, had done the same we would certainly not have witnessed the funereal dance that was staged around a corpse. . . .

Today our adversaries have a single hope: the Matteotti trial. Very well, we do not hesitate to declare that the Matteotti trial will be a trial of the oppositions and that fascism has been so much preoccupied with it that perhaps it will choose this very Matteotti trial as its electoral platform. We must not be too severe towards the oppositions; they have done fascism a service, for by calling me as Secretary General fascism decided the other day to assert its intransigence against everybody and everything.

It marks the triumph of a thesis which I have maintained for months: fascism must utterly disregard all conditional support, as the fascism of Cremona has done in disregarding democrats, liberals, and veterans of the type of Viola and company, and must rely solely on the forces of its own ranks. Had the opposition followed other tactics, had they tried to wrest Mussolini from us as if to divide fascism, disintegrate it, they would doubtless have obtained what they desired. But no. The opposition pretended that the whole of fascism must present itself before the royal courts. What do they intend to do, and how can they undertake an effective governmental action; with what program do they come before the nation, being so diverse in the ideas and parties which constitute them? Really we do not know. Only this is clear, that the aim of all their action is simply negative: to overthrow fascism and Mussolini. But we will never permit it, never! . . .

Perhaps the opposition thinks that we intend to carry on our future action by means of the black-jack and of violence. No. The first appeal that I shall make within a few days to the *fascisti* of Italy will be to the highest discipline. The squadrist element ought to be the best interpreter of my will. All ought to remain spiritually mobilized to follow the orders which will be given by us. In calling me to this burdensome task, Mussolini clearly outlined a precise program for me and the party. He said: we have won a battle. Now we must win the war! I am convinced that only by an act of force can fascism assure that tranquillity and prosperity to the nation which will render its internal enemies innocuous. But in order that the victory may be assured us, the nation must retain its full efficiency, and leave to us, and we are willing to assume it, the entire responsibility in the face of history, a unity of command and a faithful interpretation of the *Duce's* thought.

Already I foresee that my reference to an act of force will give the opposition papers an argument for reopening their talk tomorrow about a second wave and another night of St. Bartholomew. No. We merely claim that fascism cannot renounce extreme measures of defense if it finds its way blocked toward carrying out its precise aim, namely, to insert fascism into the state."

(February 25, 1925.)

" On October 28, 1922, we said: we are making a revolution on the basis of this program, to change the present social order. We have lost two years; this is the error, the greatest error of fascism. And in confessing it we must look to its remedy. What have we done? We have allowed Giolitti to fiddle for us, we have been moved to tears by Orlando and have been seduced by the paternal affections of Salandra.

We, however, to tell the truth, have always opposed this for we knew that these gentlemen were steeped in their past. In fact all our reforms have found an obstacle in their old ideas and in the word liberty. But they have never explained to us what liberty is. I picture liberty as a beautiful woman who has been taken ill and to whom the doctor has prescribed an absolute fast, but who wants, none the less, to eat. To prohibit this woman from eating what may do her harm, is this perhaps a lack of liberty? To seek to establish tranquillity in the nation, is this perhaps to deprive her of liberty? Is it a lack of liberty to prevent political strikes? Is it a lack of liberty to prevent demagogues from going into the offices and fields and preaching that the land belongs to the peasants and the factories to the workers? Is it a lack of liberty to prevent Italy's being discredited abroad to the ruin of her finances? . . .

No. Fascism's kind of liberty is that of allowing the country to work, to prosper and to make a bigger imprint on the world. Let us talk a little about this liberty that our adversaries invoke so much. Have you been aware, *fascisti,* that thirty-five million inhabitants rose up against us when we suppressed the *Avanti,* the *Mondo* and the *Voce Repubblicana?* I observed at Milan that when the *Corriere della Sera* was being seized no one was grieved. The fascist government has been too indulgent and has allowed too long the publication of unfounded alarmist news. Do you remember what was published? When the Matteotti affair sees the light, when we can bring certain men to trial, some of whom even belong to fascism, we shall see what a difference there is between the true outcome of this trial and what has been printed by many papers. The Italian people has the bad defect of forgetting too easily. It ought to recall how they printed that a fascist column was seen marching that night toward the Polyclinic Hospital where it burned Matteotti's corpse; it ought to recall how the *Popolo* of the moralists, related how the testicles of Matteotti were served on Filippelli's table. A little later they said that the corpse had been dissected. Then when the body was found intact, they said that it was not Matteotti's corpse, but that of a woman with one man's leg and one woman's, and that it had been put there forty-eight hours previously, and other similar enormities. The clear results of expert inquiry have finally denied such fantastic nonsense.

Fascism did not know at that moment what to do. It had lost its bearings. It was faced by two alternatives: either to abandon the position it had won by blood or to make a stand and face the enemy. I was for the second alternative. In fact after the Matteotti crime I said one day that I would assume Dumini's defense, for if they were going to strike a blow at our Party and government by means of that crime, we must defend ourselves to the limit. . . .

The government wanted to make the experiment and to see if the Italian people would follow the gentlemen on the Aventine who claimed to be the interpreters of the thought of all Italians, or whether it would follow us. An opposition paper said one day that if we adopted restrictive measures, the whole people would rise up and overthrow us. The Decree on the Press took place, and the people accepted this necessity with discipline. Finally came the President's speech on the third of January and following on it the nomination of the author as head of the Fascist Party. The Italian people approved. . . .

We have a very clear program. We wish to insert the fascist revolution into the state. What does it mean to insert the fascist revolution into the state? It means to legalize fascist illegalism. Separate incidents cannot help our cause. Our strength lies in organization, our doctrinary violence must be the strength of our Party, since it alienates the timid and the traitors.

Therefore let our adversaries and false friends take notice of what we think about these problems and what I now say.

The Press. The press, hostile or friendly, must be at the service of the nation, for the nation must be defended by all Italians without distinction.

The Banks. It must no longer be possible for the banks to cause fair or foul weather in Italy. The government must see to it that it controls the financial activity of the nation as France has recently done. We want to control, for what has already happened too often must not happen again tomorrow. One of our largest banking institutions, the *Commerciale,* to mention no names, when the rumor was spread abroad that Mussolini had been assassinated, did not feel obliged to deny this rumor in order to defend the national economy. Hence we shall exercise control, in order to protect our savings.

The Bureaucracy. We must accept the bureaucracy, though we must mend many errors. When we went to Rome, all these bureaucrats in the various ministries, thoroughly frightened, gave us the Roman salute as soon as they saw us. We youngsters, somewhat ingenuous and inexpert, believed that these gentlemen were sincere, and now we are taking the consequences. Today we see that the bureaucracy serves the opposition more than the fascist government, and this because in it are various protégés of Nitti, Bonomi, Giolitti, Orlando, and Salandra. We are convinced that the fascist government, in order really to insert the revolution into the state, must accept the state's executive organs after having thoroughly purified them.

I remember that after the Matteotti crime, when some of us, not all, however, gathered around these gentlemen, their shoulders were seen to turn. Now that the government has given proof of its great energy they are again beginning to give the Roman salute. But we no longer

believe them.   The bureaucracy must be purified, but not suppressed.
The bureaucracy is indispensable and remarkable, but whoever of its
members does not feel able to serve the fascist cause must leave."

(June 21, 1925.)

"We have always been on our guard against great erudition and
against so-called very intellectual men, being certain that a firm faith and
simple and impassioned intelligence, lively ideas clearly and deeply felt
will conquer erudition and faithless intellectualism, for these are truly
fruitful and creative.   It is only too logical that many of the intellectuals are enemies of the regime.   They are the Pharisees and Doctors
of the old law; they are the hypocritical commentators of old customs;
they are those who find a justification for every shame.   Their power
is at an end and young men, capable of sacrifice, have dislodged and
humiliated them.   But faith out of itself creates its culture which
consists in a clear consciousness of what it must do.

The new ruling class has been ripened by the battles of life; thousands
of squadrists are today honest, serious and capable administrators and
our parliamentary majority has revealed well prepared and valiant men.
In general, we prefer the rough, honest activity of a humble mayor who
makes a budget balance that had been shattered by erudition, to the
fruitless presumptions and the pompous and grotesque gravity of our
most erudite adversaries; and we are sure that faith, discipline, and labor
are the forces that are sufficient and necessary to make our country
great."   (*Un Periodo aureo del Partito Nazionale Fascista:* pp. 17–19,
28–32, 104–112, 154–155.)

No. 21. *The New Constitution of the Fascist Party*

(Passed in September 1926.)

"*Declarations of Faith.*"

"Fascism is a militia at the service of the nation.   Its aim: to achieve
the greatness of the Italian people.   From its origins, which are fused
with the rebirth of Italian consciousness and with the will to victory,
until now, fascism has always regarded itself as in a state of war; first to
defeat those who oppressed the will of the nation, and today and always
to defend and develop the power of the Italian people.   Fascism is not
merely a grouping of Italians on a definite program realized or to be
realized, but above all a faith which has its confessors and in whose
orders the new Italians work as soldiers, offspring of the energies of the
victorious War and of the ensuing struggle between the nation and the
anti-nation.

The Party is the essential part of this order, and the function of the
Party is fundamentally indispensable to the vitality of the regime.

In the dark hours before the dawn this order was determined by the necessities of battle and the people recognized the *Duce* by the signs of his will power, his force and his achievements.

In the ardor of the struggle, acts always precede rules. Every step was marked by a conquest and our assemblies were but the gatherings of commanders and rank and file under the memory of their fallen.

Averse to dogmatic formulas and rigid schemes, fascism feels that victory lies in the possibilities of continually renewing itself.

Fascism is today living for the future and is watching over the new generation as the force destined to attain all the aims set up by our will.

The order and hierarchies without which there can be no discipline of force nor education of the people, must receive their light and rules from the head, where a complete view of the powers and tasks, of functions and merits is centered.

The Most Important Articles.

" Fascism is politically organized in the P. N. F. (*Partito Nazionale Fascista*) formed by the *fasci di combattimento* organized into provincial federations. The P. N. F. carries on its activities under the supreme guidance of the leader of fascism and according to the program determined by the Grand Fascist Council.

The hierarchies of the P. N. F. are: (1) the *Duce*, (2) the Secretary General of the P. N. F., (3) the Secretaries General of the provincial federations, (4) the Secretaries of the *Fasci di Combattimento*.

The organs of the P. N. F. are: (1) the Grand Council, (2) the National Directorate, (3) the National Council.

The Grand Council is the highest organ of fascism. It determines the program of action which the Party must undertake in all fields of the national life.

The Grand Council is composed of: (a) the *Duce* of Fascism (President); (b) the Ministers; (c) the Undersecretaries of the Presidency of Council, the Minister of the Interior and the Minister of Foreign Affairs; (d) representatives of Fascist Senators named by the *Duce*; (e) the Quadrumvirate of the March on Rome; (f) the members of the National Directorate of the Party; (g) the President of the National Fascist Institute of Culture; (h) the President of the General Confederation of *Enti Autarchici;* (i) the Secretary General of the Foreign *Fasci;* (j) the General Commander of the Militia or Chief of Staff; (k) the President of the Fascist Confederation of Laborers; (l) the Presidents of the Italian Syndicate of Coöperatives; (m) one of the presidents of the employers confederations; (n) men who may be called by the President who have given proof of their great devotion to fascism and of their noble earnestness in practical achievements.

The Grand Council is called by the President. The Grand Council nominates the Secretary General of the Party, and Assistant Secretaries and members of the Directorate, and determines the general lines of the work to be carried on.

The Directorate is composed of eight members besides the general administrative secretary.

The Secretary General determines the rules of action in the Directorate and in the various offices, nominating their subordinate assistants and employees. The offices are: administration, *Enti Autarchici*, the press, propaganda, juvenile organizations, feminine *fasci*, Association of the Families of Fallen *Fascisti*, Association of University Students.

The political secretariat operates by the functioning of the Party by means of its peripheral organs and sees to it that every activity of the Party corresponds to the spirit of fascism. The political secretariat controls the activities of the following associations: (1) fascist teachers, (2) fascist railroad men, (3) fascist post office and telegraph employees; and works in coöperation with: (1) the Commander of the Voluntary Militia of National Safety, (2) the Fascist Secretary General in Foreign Countries, (3) the Presidents of the Confederations of Employers and Employees, (4) the Presidents of the National Organizations of Coöperatives.

The National Directorate of the Party meets once a month under the *Duce* and whenever the Secretary General thinks it necessary. The general administrative secretary administers the patrimony of the Party.

The General Administrative Secretary is responsible for the order and discipline of the whole personnel.

The National Council of the Party is composed of the Federal secretaries.

The National Council is called by the National Directorate to examine the activities of the life of the Party and to receive general executive orders. Whenever the Directorate demands it, regional meetings may be called.

The General Secretary nominates the Federal Secretaries, who must carry out the will and orders of the Grand Council and of the National Directorate.

Each Federal Secretary must choose among the *fascisti* of his province seven associates who, ratified by the General Secretary, constitute the Provincial Directorate.

The Federal Secretary is also the Secretary of fascism for the provincial capital. The Provincial Directorate must guide and promote the life of the Party in the whole province and see to the execution of the orders of the National Directorate.

The Provincial Secretary must also supervise the following organizations: (1) the Federation of *Enti Autarchici*, (2) the Federation of the Party, (3) Juvenile organizations, (4) Feminine *Fasci*. He must also, by means of trustworthy agents, watch over the various cultural, economic and athletic activities of the province.

The Federal Secretary must keep in touch with (1) fascist senators and deputies, (2) the commander of the fascist militia of the province, (3) the syndical organizations, (4) the coöperative organizations, (5) associations headed by the Party.

The Federal Secretary must call the Provincial Directorate at least once a month, and every six months the secretaries of the *fasci* of the whole province, to examine and discuss the problems of the life of the Party.

The Federal Secretary nominates the secretary of each *fascio di combattimento* in the province, seeing to it that the rules which come from on top constitute a uniform discipline for the whole rank and file. Each secretary of a *fascio* will call five comrades as associates, who will be subject to ratification by the Federal Secretary and who will constitute the Directorate of the *fascio*. One of the associates will be charged with administrative functions.

Every secretary of a *fascio* must know the moral qualifications of every member of the rank and file and his means of livelihood.

Whenever a fascist falls short of his duty by breach of discipline or by deficiency in those qualities that constitute the *fascist* spirit — faith, courage, industry, and honesty — he should be subjected to an investigation by the Directorate. Disciplinary punishments are: (1) deploring the faults, (2) suspension for a determinate or indeterminate period, (3) expulsion. No punishment may be inflicted until after the guilt of the person has been ascertained and he has been given an opportunity to defend himself. Every punishment must be reported to the higher officials up to the Secretary General and is not official unless ratified. A fascist expelled from the ranks of the Party is a traitor to the cause and must be banished from political life. No *fascio* can be dissolved without authority from the General Secretary of the Party.

No fascist who has not been a member of the Party for at least two years can hold provincial office. No provincial director can take on or hold remunerative offices in public bodies, institutions affiliated with the state, and economic bodies dependent on local administrations.

No fascist, even in carrying on his professional activity, can fail to direct his work according to the spirit and discipline of fascism.

The Federal Secretaries are entrusted with establishing the rules for the conduct of the various subordinate organizations in the Party."

PART IV

FASCIST SYNDICALISM AND THE CORPORATE STATE

No. 22. *The Judgment of the "Solons"*

(The Commission for Constitutional Reform, composed first of fifteen and then of eighteen members, appointed first by Mussolini as Head of the Party, and later by Royal Decree, marked the official beginning of the conscious effort to construct what has come to be called the Fascist State. It was presided over by Senator Gentile and was composed for the most part of distinguished scholars. Its primary purpose was to study the parliamentary problem forced on the *fascisti* by the Aventine Secession, but events compelled it to undertake a comprehensive reconstruction of the whole constitution. It laid the theoretical and schematic basis for the "Corporate State," and though its specific proposals have been seriously modified, it served to give an appearance of profound political wisdom to fascism's emergency measures. The following are selections from the official report of the Commission.)

"The parliamentary system is the gravest and most dangerous degeneration of political custom. It constitutes a complex deviation and usurpation of powers. It is not in harmony with the origins and historic bases of parliaments. It is evidently opposed to the logical demands of the constitutional and representative regime. And what is more important, it is an obstacle to the attainment of the higher ends of the state.

In the parliamentary regime, above all as it had been understood in recent times, the Chambers exercise faculties that belong to the executive power and supplant the most essential prerogatives of the Crown. The government, in its turn, usurps the functions of Parliament and it too imposes itself on the Crown, denying it the exercise of that supreme directive and integrative function that is indispensable for the harmonious coördination of the major powers of the state. The body of elected representatives is being distorted and deprived of true liberty in the exercise of its mandates. It is natural that under the pressure of needs created by parliamentary exigencies, there should be frequent infractions of the executive power in its judicial function.

Historically, since the executive power grew out of the royal power with the change from absolute to constitutional government, it was reserved for the Crown, of which the executive is an emanation, to set rules and limits for the executive itself. Parliament, which is characteristic of the representative system, arose and displaced the ancient sovereign body that embraced the whole population of free men in order to assure a continual agreement between the laws and social aspirations and to carry on a function of financial control for keeping the action of the government within due limits, by deliberating on the laws that it must observe and acting like a political accounting body in controlling its actions. The progressive growth of its powers was intended to limit those of the Crown at a time when the Crown had the character of an absolute government, but it exceeded all logical bounds; having robbed the monarchy of the direct exercise of executive power, it also invaded the Crown's own field, substituting itself for the Crown in the nomination and recall of ministers and thus preventing such powers from being exercised in view of the higher needs of the country, which must certainly not be confused with those transient and contingent needs of the prevailing political parties.

Thus the principle of the separation of powers, which is the essence of constitutional government and is certainly not to be applied in a rigid and mechanical way, is being destroyed.

But even independently of all this, the parliamentary system must be condemned, because it prevents the executive power from carrying out its own activities in a durable, careful and coherent manner, in view of the higher ends which it serves. The executive power's general interest is not the sum of particular interests and hence cannot be adequately represented by a fluctuating majority, determined by the half-plus-one rule, of the political forces they represent.

The state needs continuity and readiness in action, in its international no less than in its internal relations. This necessity is being felt more and more under present conditions of life. The complexities of international relations have a variety of influences on all fields of activity and sometimes (as for example in the highly important game of determining the rapid oscillations in exchange rates) they operate so suddenly that they must be watched and confronted almost hour by hour, which requires a strong government, free, independent, and permanent, such as the parliamentary system certainly cannot guarantee.

The coördination of the infinite internal needs of the country, arranging them in an orderly scheme based on the possibility of satisfying them, and determining which matters and functions should be emphasized, remembering that, though their present utility may not be noticeable, they may nevertheless serve distant and higher ends, — all this pre-supposes a government above parties, not continually threatened by their possible snares.

When extraordinary events like war or a public calamity occurred, and it was felt that the future of the country in whole or in part was at stake, the directive activities continually exercised by Parliament were always recognized as embarrassing and superfluous, and it was thought necessary to reinforce the ministerial body and keep it whole. These extraordinary events are daily facts for those who fully grasp the tasks and difficulties arising in the modern life of states. The complexity of state functions and responsibilities is such today that in the face of it the tasks the state once had resemble little more than those of a modern large private firm. Hence if the state of today wants to make its way in the world confidently, it must allow itself to be guided by a strong and vigorous government that is not based on the instability or predominance of this or that party.

The principle of universal suffrage, according to which all citizens legally qualified participate with equal rights of voting in the political life of the country, is bound up with the idea that this is or should be the best means of adequately satisfying the majority of individual interests, an idea which is now opposed and supplanted by the idea that the state is a self-sufficient principle, that it is not a sum but a synthesis of individual interests and hence has its own higher and permanent ends to follow, that it is of a moral and ideal nature rather than economic and material. The almost indefinite extension of the suffrage, coupled with the fact that the numerical size of the population has reached proportions not even suspected formerly, and the fact that the functions of the state have been so intensified as to make it more than difficult to understand the essence of a political mandate, raises the doubt, the certainty, that the system of direct election of deputies to Parliament and the modest, but nevertheless discernible tendency to reject even a plurality of votes, make vain any direct effort to improve the mechanism of electoral procedure. Certainly the abolition of proportional representation, to which the most deplorable exhibitions of the parliamentary system were due, has indicated progress in this direction. Then the return to the single list (*collegio uninominale*) marked still further progress; for without doubt, where the undermined bases of the present order still hold firm, this system among all the systems so far developed, and in view of the political evolution of our country, offers the greatest number of advantages. But if anyone should claim that we could today be satisfied with this relative and very modest progress, he would close his eyes to the facts.

It is above all in this field that the common fallacy clearly appears of those who fall back on the constitutional order formed more than a century ago under conditions of social and political life radically different from the present. It suffices to recall that while it is becoming evidently more impossible for the greater part of voters really to know the persons for whom they have voted, and that therefore the whole illusion of free individual choice is gone, nothing has been substituted for it that in any manner guarantees that the choice fall on the most deserving and suitable. . . .

Of the powers among which the acts and the explicit sovereignty of the state is divided, the greatest importance must be given now as always to the executive. It is above all in its action, whether it be in its internal or foreign relations, that the responsibility of the state shows itself. And it is above all the need for action that gives the state its continuous coherence.

The legislative power, which determines the limits between the action of the state and that of individuals, and the judicial power that enforces these limits, integrate and in a sense reinforce the executive power, but it is in this latter that the whole life of the state, by the logical demands of things, is summed up. However, in legislation actually the initiative for the most part can come only from the executive power; and this implies that the function of legislative organs really reduces itself to that of prevision, of holding to account and of approval. When the executive power becomes weakened, the action of the state is depressed, for initiative and decision in daily affairs can no longer be demanded of it. The decline of the executive power therefore means the decline of the state. And hence it is of the greatest importance to the public interest to keep the executive power high and strong, a need which is always recognized in the times of greatest cohesion, as in war, and which it would be foolish to deny in more normal times. The exercise of the executive power can only take place under the direction of a limited number of persons who constitute an organic unity, for its action must be ready, sure, unanimous, fully conscious and responsible. It is neither logical nor useful to seek the coöperation of many irresponsibles in the action of a few responsibles. Assemblies can give general norms and directions for action to which the government is committed, they may approve and disapprove its action, but they cannot and should not take part in it. Such a participation weakens its action at the expense of the state. The executive power, synthesizing the life of the state, must be committted to those who are above contingent individual interests and who by their position are always able to have an integrated view of all the various complicated problems, seeing them in their traditional, historical and ideal relations to the higher ends of the state. Therefore it can only come from on top. Even when a written constitution expressly ordains it, the executive power can only be headed by the King, that is, by the head of the state.

Without discussing thoroughly the admissibility of the principle of popular sovereignty, it is undeniable that when it is broken up and distributed among tens of millions of citizens each in turn preoccupied with the necessity of satisfying his own personal needs, sovereignty is corrupted and cannot in fact be the expression of the organic strength of the state. To seek somehow by means of the exercise of popular sovereignty to participate in the selection of those to whom the exercise of the executive power must really be entrusted, is a pretense that is contrary to good sense and the public interest.

Political assemblies by their origin and aim, must not participate in the executive power, either by directly coöperating in it or by contributing to the selection of those to whom it is entrusted. . . .

The relations between the government and the Chambers must be dominated by the principle that the former is an organ of the Crown and not of Parliament and that in regard to its action the latter has the power of prescribing the general limits within which the government may act, approving its budgets and proposed laws and exercising a check that culminates in votes of confidence. But no more direct participation can be in order in the exercise of the functions that belong to the scope of the executive power and to the formation of the cabinet. . . .

The principle that really as well as constitutionally the government is an organ of the Crown, by means of which and under whose responsibility the Crown exercises executive power, and that it must in no sense be regarded as an emanation of Parliament, implies that the government itself may presume to be legitimately invested with power as long as it has the confidence of the King. The necessity, however, of enjoying the confidence of the Chambers and of keeping a continuous and effective initiative and freedom of action, further implies that the Cabinet may, whenever it pleases and on whatever provocation, demand a showing in one or both branches of Parliament with respect to itself. . . .

The judge of the situation is always in any case the Crown, to whom alone the recall and the nomination of ministers must belong, in fact as well as in theory. A vote, though it is not sufficient to make the Cabinet lose the confidence of the Chamber, may, in view of the particular circumstances, induce the sovereign to recall the mandate it enjoys. In any case the vote may be renewed without necessarily postponing it to the next day when the vote of lack of confidence is an order of the day, and without allowing the government to demand its postponement. But the King too, may invite the government to demand an expression of its attitude in the other House of Parliament. This provision is linked up both with the principle of the equality of the two Houses of Parliament and the other principle that, in deciding a crisis, the sovereign has a real power of initiative, direction, and decision.". . .

" Proposed Law for the Corporate Ordering of the State "

" Division I. Of the Orders.
Article 2. By the present law, all the social activities of the citizens (professions, industries, arts, trades, etc.) are divided into three orders: (1) of the free professions, arts and public services; (2) of agriculture and agricultural industry; (3) of industry, commerce and ownership of real estate and movable capital.

Within the orders, these activities are then subdivided into categories where such exist and into sub-groups. The categories may be grouped into sections. . . .

Division II.

Article 7. In every community the citizens may be registered according to their categories or sub-groups. . . .

Article 11. In every province there will be three chambers corresponding to the three orders of activity indicated in Article 2. . . .

Article 12. The chambers will be composed of representatives of registered citizens according to their categories of activity.

The representatives in the chambers will be elected by the citizens by the categories and sub-groups according to which they are registered in their communal registers. . . .

Article 13. The number of these representatives will be proportional to the citizens registered in their categories. The percentage quota for the first chamber will be greater than for the others, so as to guarantee to it a number of representatives not less than one fourth of the total number of representatives of the three chambers of the province. . . .

Article 14. In the first chamber one half of the representatives will be distributed by equal quotas to all the categories represented by it and the other half will be distributed according to the number registered in these same categories.

Article 15. In the second chamber, the representatives will be divided among the various categories and sub-groups existing in the province so that the various orders of interests represented will be kept within the limits demanded by the general needs of agriculture. . . .

Day laborers and salaried employees will have their special representation where they constitute a continuous and essential element in agricultural enterprise. However, the number of representatives given them will never exceed that of the representatives assigned to the noncultivating landowners, employers and large tenants.

Article 16. In the third chamber the representatives will be distributed among the three sections of industry, commerce and proprietors in proportion to the double criterion of the number registered in each category and the fiscal taxes levied on these various activities.

Within each category of the industrial section, where the structure of the various firms demands it, a further subdivision will be made among them so that two fifths of the representatives go to the employers, one fifth to the technical and administrative employees and two fifths to the laborers. This last quota may be further divided into two equal parts, one for the skilled laborers and one for the non-skilled. . . .

Division III. Of the Organs of the Corporate Organization.

Article 18. Every chamber will have a council and a general assembly, composed of a number of members to be determined in relation to the number of members of the chamber. It will also have a president elected by the council. . . .

Article 19. The three chambers in each province will constitute the Provincial Corporate College, which also will have a council and assembly. . . .

Article 20. The Provincial Corporate Colleges will elect representatives to participate in the National Corporate Council, which will meet at Rome. Members of Parliament will not be eligible to this office.

The National Corporate Council will be divided into three committees corresponding to the three orders of activity which are represented by the three chambers in each province. Each of said committees will have its own assembly. . . .

The president of the National Corporate Council will be elected by the council itself. A three-fourths vote will be necessary to elect him. His election will be subject to the approval of the government. . . .

Article 32. When the corporate organization has been put into effect political representation will take place on it as a basis, assigning one half the number of deputies to the institutional colleges to be formed." (*Relazione e Proposte della Commissione Presidenziale per lo Studio delle Riforme Costituzionali:* pp. 33–35, 53–54, 73–77, 147–154.)

No. 23. *"The Transformation of the State"*

(The following is taken from the first chapter of Alfredo Rocco's book by the above title, a chapter first published in *Politica,* October 1926. Rocco, the fascist Minister of Justice since the Matteotti crisis, and a leader of the nationalists, is perhaps the most intimately connnected with the supposedly constructive reforms of fascism of all the fascist politicians. The brief survey of these reforms given below supplements some of his earlier expositions of the fascist state (v. Appendix Nos. 55 and 59 of this volume), especially his important speech on Fascist Political Doctrine, delivered at Perugia on August 30, 1925, and translated into English by Professor Dino Bigongiari and published in the pamphlets of the International Conciliation series of the Carnegie Endowment for International Peace, October 1926, No. 223.)

" From the legal point of view there is no doubt that the years 1925 and 1926 mark a decisive step towards the transformation of the state. Undoubtedly also January 3, 1925, marks a principal date in this field. . . . The anti-national reaction of the second semester of 1924 gave fascism the clear feeling that the time had come for it to govern alone and to transform the state or to accept the failure of the revolution. Given this alternative, there could be no doubt of the choice, and Mussolini, with the infallible intuition which comes to his aid in the most critical moments, in his speech of the third of January, which was the necessary complement to the March on Rome and was therefore eminently revolutionary, opened the new phase of the revolution, the phase of fascism's realization and its creation of the fascist state. . . .

Nevertheless the historic value attributable to the third of January, 1925, as decisive in the realization of the fascist state, does not rob the preceding period of change and collaboration of its important reforms. Especially in 1923 a notable work of revision of the legislative order of the state was carried out by the government on the strength of the full powers obtained from Parliament. . . .

From this point of view the first place undoubtedly belongs to the reform of the schools prepared and carried out with rigid coherence and indomitable energy by Giovanni Gentile, which radically changed the whole school system, from the primary schools to the universities and which was not merely a reform of organization and routine but of spirit and method. From the agnostic school, which the liberal democratic state had created, devoid of moral content, without ideal scope, a mere supply store of opinions, arose the school that educates not merely the intellect but the soul, a school with a religious and national content, worthy of the new history of Italy, which is capable of understanding and realizing it. . . .

Beside Honorable Gentile's school reform stand the financial reforms of Honorable De Stefani; technical reforms, to be sure, but contributing powerfully to the financial order of the state, and leading to the rehabitation of the budget, the indispensable preliminary of Italian financial and economic reconstruction. Suffice it to recall the revision of taxes, which at last have a definite and organic order, the revision of the law for the general state accounts, which has established an iron control over the expenditures of a government which has come out of the revolution a most cautious and orderly administrator; and finally the reform of the organization of the bureaucratic hierarchy, which gave Italian administration an order perhaps not flawless, but at least an order in a field which for some time had become the favorite field for the activities of private interests and demagogic pretenses.

Lastly we must not overlook the reforms carried out in the administration of justice, among which the most important are those in the organization of the judiciary, especially the unification of the Courts of Cassation, a long-standing aspiration, but never realized because of the insuperable opposition of local interests which the parliamentary regime could not and would not resist.

But after these technical reforms come the political ones. . . . The conquest of the state by fascism necessarily led to its transformation. Gradually but incessantly . . . first in fact and then in law, the fascist state is being formed, totally different in form and content from the liberal state.

I say fascist state and not national state, as some do, for this term is more comprehensive and exact. The fascist state is the state that brings the legal organization of society to its maximum of power and coherence. And society according to the fascist idea is not a mere sum of individuals, but an organism having its own life, its own ends, transcending those of individuals, and its own spiritual and historic value. The state too, the legal organization of society, is, according to fascism, an organism distinct from the citizens who at any given time compose it, and has its own life and its ends higher than those of individuals, to which those of individuals must be subordinated. The fascist state is therefore the truly social state. . . . When one says the fascist state is the national state, one tells the truth about present Italy, which is a national type of society, but not about the Italy of tomorrow nor about present England, France, Japan, and United States of America, for in these cases a fascist state would be an imperial state. . . .

The fascist state has its own morals, religion, its own mission in the world, its own function of social justice and lastly its own economic tasks. Hence the fascist state must defend and diffuse morality among the people; must occupy itself with religious problems and hence profess and safeguard true religion, that is, the Catholic religion. It must live up to the world-civilizing mission entrusted to peoples of high culture and great traditions, which means using all the means of political, economic and intellectual expansion beyond its boundaries. It must enforce justice among classes, prohibiting the unlimited self-defense of classes. Finally it must promote the increase of production and wealth, using, where it is expedient, the powerful spring of individual interests, but also intervening, when it is expedient, with its own initiative. . . .

The fascist state is the truly sovereign state, dominating all the forces existing in the country and subjecting all to its discipline. . . . This theory of the sovereign state is really not new, for the whole legal school of public law professes it. This school has always taught that sovereignty is not of the people but of the state, a principle asserted in all the writings of all the teachers of public law, foreign and Italian, and also of our jurists, who then called themselves liberals or democrats in politics, without really raising the doubts implied by the patent contradiction in which they became involved. . . . Superiority of ends, supremacy of force: these two terms sum up the idea of the fascist state. The whole new fascist legislation tends to realize this conception of the state. . . .

The legislative reforms carried out during the first four years of the fascist government have had a great importance on this internal transformation of the state. I have already noted the decisive value of the school reform from this point of view. In creating a school that educates character, propagates religious sentiment, forms the national consciousness, the state has undertaken tasks which formerly it regarded as extraneous. But no less important are the laws protecting maternity and infancy, and above all the National Work of the Balilla. This great institution is preparing to give a military and national education to our youth, from seven to eighteen years of age, by means of an uninterrupted work carried on in and out of school, which in a short time will radically transform the spirit and character of the Italian people. Thus Italy, by virtue of the War and of fascism, after centuries of indiscipline and indolence, is becoming a great military and warlike people.

The reform of the legal codes, already authorized by Parliament, and at last on the way to realization, will also contribute to giving the state that concrete content which it has hitherto lacked. In the civil and penal codes the state will assert itself as the guardian of morals and of the family. Again in the civil code and in the commercial code the protection of private property, the indispensable instrument for building up savings and the regulation of credit will be regarded as essential state functions. In the civil, commercial and penal codes the political and economic interests of the nations will be strongly guaranteed, as is the duty of the state. In the penal code, the code of criminal law procedure as well as in the law for public safety, the necessity of the repressive and preventive defense of society and the state against crime will find a prominent place and adequate treatment. Lastly, in the code of civil procedure the administration of justice will no longer be considered as a passive function of exclusively private interest, but as one of the highest activities of the state, having the eminently political aim of guaranteeing social peace and of rendering to each his due.

But the reform which in my opinion has most contributed to giving the fascist state its physiognomy and fascist action its concrete social content, is and will remain the reform embodied in the Law on the Legal Discipline of Collective Labor Relations and its related legislative regulations. This law puts an end to the traditional state agnosticism in matters of conflicts between groups and classes, and regards the enforcement of social justice as a problem, which it must resolve in its own realm and by its own forces. By this law the state finally gives a stable order to the relations between groups and classes, facing them in the position of judge and arbitrator, thus preventing one from oppressing another and their struggles from leading to the anarchy, poverty and slavery of the citizens. But besides solving the problem of substituting justice for class self-defense, the new syndical legislation also solves the problem of the organization of Italian society on an occupational basis. The democratic system of atomistic suffrage, ignoring the producer and recognizing only the citizen, though it was able to be of service in destroying the social and political organization of the eighteenth century, which had been surpassed by the social and economic evolution of the times, had no reconstructive virtue whatsoever. . . . When the system had been carried to its extreme consequences and had done its worst damage, threatening to overturn the whole of modern civilization into a universal anarchy, the problem of a reorganization of society, no longer on the basis of the individualistic atomism of the French Revolution, but on the basis of an organic view of society, became imperative. The solution of this problem is one of the most important tasks of the fascist state, and by the Law of April 3, 1926, and the regulations of July first of the same year, it has been resolutely faced, for they organically regulate the whole institution of syndicalism. . . .

And in this connection . . . we must not forget the law instituting provincial economic councils, by which the state is supplied with an adequate means for exercising its economic functions, which it has hitherto lacked, since in the provinces the state was represented by many organs, but was absent precisely in the economic field. . . .

To restore to the state the full exercise of its sovereignty means above all to reënforce the executive power. The executive power in fact is the most genuine expression of the state, the essential and supreme organ for its activity. . . . By a series of legislative provisions the powers of the government are being directly reënforced. To this group of laws belong: the law on the powers and prerogatives of the Head of the Government, Prime Minister, and Secretary of State; the law on the extension of the powers of prefects; and lastly, the law on the institution of *podestà* in municipalities and the substitution of appointive for elective municipal councils. The law permitting the executive power to issue legal norms, thus bridging a gap in the constitution of the Kingdom which was made for a small state in a historic period of slow evolution of economic and social life, gives the possibility of exercising the legislative power in certain cases, even in the field normally reserved for Parliament, to the government, the permanent and supreme organ of sovereignty. . . . By giving the government the power in cases of necessity of issuing norms having the force of laws, the approval of laws is made possible which would never be passed by ordinary parliamentary procedure, on account of the opposition of particular hostile interests. . . . The deepest significance of the law on the powers of the Head of the Government is that it freed the government, by a formal legal provision, from its dependence on Parliament, reconsecrating the principle, already contained in the Constitution but by long traditions neglected, that the Government of the King is derived from the regal power and not from Parliament, and must enjoy the confidence of the King, the faithful interpreter of the needs of the nation.

Thus the elective Chamber becomes what it is, *viz.*, only one of the modes by which the needs and sentiments of the country are made manifest, and not the only and decisive one. In a period when the life of a great people has become highly complex, it is no longer possible to give to electoral representation, based on an atomistic suffrage, an absolute value in the government of the nation. . . .

The fascist state has worked this transformation; it has asserted its own dominion over all the forces existing in the country, coördinating them all, incorporating all and directing all of them to the higher ends of national life. A series of laws reasserts this necessary superiority of the state. To this series belongs the law on secret associations which aims to put under the control of the state all associations that exist in the land, and which aims to be a general regulation, in the most limited and moderate form, of all associations as such, . . . though it has hit especially a particular association, the Masonic orders, which had taken root in the state and which in a thousand ways held fast and dominated it.

To the same class of provisions belongs the law on the press, which aims to restrain one of the saddest spectacles in recent Italian life. In fact an immense force such as the press is, had been built up in Italy claiming the right to remain beyond the law and irresponsible. . . . The press has a high and noble function, but the establishment in the state of a force above the state, uncontrolled and irresponsible, could no longer be tolerated.

And the same thing may be said in connection with the Law on the Legal Regulation of Collective Labor Relations. . . . The phenomenon of syndicalism is an insuppressible aspect of modern life; the state can not ignore it, but must know it, regulate it and dominate it, dominate it with that spirit of absolute impartiality which is characteristic of it, thus being the guardian of the general and supreme interests of the nation and not, as it is regarded by Marxist materialism, the representative of an oppressive class.

Lastly, to this cycle of laws restoring the sovereignty of the state over minor groups, belongs also the law on the legal profession. . . . The professions, even the noblest and traditionally greatest, like that of the lawyers, are but parts of the state organism, have public functions which they exercise in the name of the state, and hence can not be independent of its control. Precisely such a control, within the most careful and discreet limits, has been established by the recent reform of the legal profession.

Thus is being realized Mussolini's formula: 'Everything for the state, nothing outside the state, nothing against the state.' This does not mean, as some claim to believe, the constitution of an all-powerful state, that absorbs and oppresses everything. No, our conception of the state is rather that of a sovereign state above individuals, groups and classes; but with the clear and explicit presupposition that the state must use this sovereignty not to carry on a work of oppression but rather to realize higher ends. In the superiority of its ends, in the fulfilment of its mission of perfecting men morally and civilly, at home and abroad, rests the reason for its superior powers. Thus the power of the state, far from oppressing citizens, is reflected on them beneficently. Citizens were never happy in a weak and miserable state. On the contrary, only by means of the state can a citizen find the paths of his own welfare and fortune."

No. 24. *The Labor Charter.*

(This document which is commonly supposed to supplant the Rights of Man of the French Revolution, to be a genuine Social Contract, and to mark the last word in labor legislation, was published on the fascist Labor Day, April 21, 1927. It had been championed for some time previously by Rossoni and a tentative draft for it was drawn up by him in December. Rossoni's draft was more specific and was conceived more as a concrete codification of fundamental labor conditions to be applied to the collective contracts. But as it got into the hands of the Ministry of Corporations and received the criticism of the politicians and the employers, it was modified into a general statement of principles having a moral and constitutional rather than a strictly legal value.)

Of the Corporate State and its Organization.

(1) The Italian nation is an organism having ends, life, and means of action superior to those of the separate individuals or groups of individuals which compose it. It is a moral, political and economic unity that is integrally realized in the fascist state.

(2) Labor in all its forms, intellectual, technical and manual, is a social duty. As such and only as such it is safeguarded by the state. The complex process of production is unitary from the national point of view; its aims are unitary and may be summed up in the welfare of the producers and in the growth of the national power.

(3) Professional or syndical organization is free, but only those syndicates regularly recognized and subjected to the control of the state have the right to represent legally the whole class of employers or employees for which they are established; to pursue their interests in their relations with the state and with other professional associations; to draw up collective labor contracts obligatory on all those who belong to that class; to impose their taxes and to exercise the functions of delegates of the public interest with respect to them.

(4) In the collective labor contract the solidarity between the various factors of production finds its concrete expression, by means of the conciliation of the opposed interests of employers and employees and their subordination to the higher interests of production.

(5) Labor tribunals are the organ by which the state intervenes to regulate labor disputes, whether they arise from the application of existing contracts or other rules or whether they arise in the determination of new labor conditions.

(6) The legally recognized professional associations assure legal equality between employers and employees, maintain the discipline of production and labor and promote their increasing perfection. The corporations constitute the unitary organization of the forces of production and integrally represent its interests. In virtue of this integral representation, the interests of production being national interests, the corporations are recognized by law as organs of the state.

(7) The corporate state regards private initiative in the field of production as the most effective and useful instrument of the national interest. Since the private organization of production is a function of national interest, the organizer of an enterprise is responsible to the state for the directions its production takes. From the coöperation of the productive forces it follows that they have mutual rights and duties. The employee, whether a technical expert, clerk, or laborer, is an active coöperator in the economic enterprise, the direction of which belongs to the employer who is responsible for it.

(8) The professional associations of employers are obliged to promote in every way the increase and perfection of their products and the reduction of costs. The representatives of those who exercise a free profession or art, and the association of public employees coöperate in protecting the interests of art, science, and literature, in perfecting its production and in following the moral ends of the corporate order.

(9) The intervention of the state in economic production takes place only when private initiative is lacking or insufficient, or when the political interests of the state are at stake. Such intervention may assume the form of control, encouragement or direct management.

(10) In collective labor disputes judicial action cannot be attempted if the corporate organ has not first made an attempt at conciliation. In individual disputes concerning the interpretation and application of collective labor contracts, professional associations have the power of offering their offices towards a conciliation. Competence to handle such disputes devolves on the ordinary magistrates with the addition of assistants named by the interested professional associations.

Of Collective Labor Contracts and Labor Guarantees.

(11) Professional associations are obliged to regulate by collective contracts the labor relations between the groups of employers and laborers whom they represent. A collective labor contract is made between associations of the first rank, under the guidance and control of central organizations, except for the power of substitution granted to the associations of higher rank by laws and statutes. Every collective labor contract, under penalty of being null and void, must contain precise rules on disciplinary measures, trial periods, the amount and payment of compensation, and the hours of labor.

(12) The action of syndicates, the conciliatory work of corporate organs and the sentences of labor tribunals guarantee an agreement between wages and the normal needs of life, the possibilities of production and the labor return. The determination of wages is freed of all general rules whatsoever and is entrusted to agreements between the collective contracting parties.

(13) The consequences of crises in production and financial phenomena must be equally borne by all factors of production. The data published by the public administrations, by the central institute of statistics and by the professional organizations legally recognized on conditions of production and labor, market and financial conditions, and on variations in the standard of living of employees, coördinated and elaborated by the Ministry of Corporations, will yield a criterion by which the interests of the various groups and classes may be adjusted to each other and to the higher interest.

(14) When remuneration is based on piece work and the accounting of the piece work is made over periods longer than two weeks, adequate bi-weekly or weekly accounts are required. Night labor not included in regular periodical shifts, is to be compensated by a percentage in addition to the rate for day labor. When labor is paid on a piece-work basis, the piece-work rates must be constructed in such a way that an industrious worker of normal working capacity is able to make a minimum gain over and above the rate basis.

(15) An employee has the right to a weekly rest on Sunday. Collective contracts will apply this principle, taking account of existing legal rules, of the technical demands of the business, and within the limits of such demands will provide otherwise that civil and religious solemnities be respected according to local traditions. The hours of labor must be scrupulously and intensively observed by the employee.

(16) After a year of uninterrupted service, an employee of a steadily working firm has the right to an annual paid vacation.

(17) In steadily working firms the laborer has the right, in the case of an interruption in labor relations by dismissal without his fault, to an indemnity proportional to his years of service. Such an indemnity must be paid also in the case of the death of the laborer.

(18) In steadily working firms a change of owners does not abolish the labor contract and the personnel employed retains its rights toward the new employer. Similarly, sickness of an employee which does not exceed a determined duration does not break the labor contract. Being called to arms or service in the militia is no cause for dismissal.

(19) Infractions of discipline and acts which disturb the normal run of a firm committed by employees are punished, according to their seriousness, by a fine, suspension from work, and in serious cases by immediate dismissal without indemnity. The cases in which the employer can impose fines, suspension or immediate dismissal without indemnity will be specified.

(20) A new employee is subject to a trial period during which the breaking of the contract by either party can take place with mere payment of wages for the time in which the employee was actually engaged in work.

(21) Collective labor contracts extend their benefits and discipline also to domestic workers. Special rules will be given by the state to assure cleanliness and wholesomeness of domestic labor.

Of Employment Offices.

(22) Only the state can ascertain and control matters of the employment and unemployment of laborers, and of the complex index of conditions of production and labor.

(23) Employment offices on an equal basis are under the control of

the corporate bodies. Employers are obliged to employ laborers registered at these offices and have the privilege of selecting from the list of those registered, giving preference to members of the Party of Fascist Syndicates in order of the length of their membership.

(24) Professional associations of laborers are obliged to exercise a selective activity among laborers, intended to raise continually their technical capacity and moral standing.

Of Insurance, Aid, Education and Instruction.

(25) The corporate organs must see to it that the laws on the prevention of accidents be observed by single members of the federated associations.

(26) Emergency benefits are another instance of the principle of cooperation. Employers and employees must coöperate proportionately in assuming this task. The state by means of its corporate bodies and professional associations will undertake to coördinate and unify as much as possible the system and institutions of benefits.

(27) The fascist state proposes: (1) the perfecting of accident insurance; (2) the improvement and extension of maternity insurance; (3) insurance against industrial diseases, and tuberculosis, as an approach to a general insurance against all sickness; (4) the perfecting of insurance for the involuntarily unemployed; (5) the adoption of special forms of endowment insurance for young laborers.

(28) The administrative and judicial representatives of employees' associations are charged with overseeing accident insurance and social insurance. In collective labor contracts provision will be made as far as technically possible for the formation of mutual sickness funds, contributed to both by employees and by employers and administered by representatives of both sides under the supervision of the corporate bodies.

(29) Aid for those they represent, whether members or not, is a right and duty of professional associations. They must directly exercise their mutual aid functions by their own organizations and can not delegate them to other associations or institutions except for general reasons surpassing the interests of any single group of producers.

(30) Education and instruction, especially the professional instruction of those they represent, members and non-members, is one of the principal duties of professional associations. They must aid the work of the national organization of *Dopolavoro* and other educational movements."

No. 25. *Loyal Industrialists.*

(The following is taken from a manifesto issued by A. S. Benni, the President of the General Fascist Confederation of Industry, on May

16, 1927, on the occasion of the government's pressure to reduce prices because of the deflation. The Confederation of Industry is the official organization and mouthpiece of Italian industrial employers.)

" The Head of the Government is today outlining his program for the internal increased value of the *lira,* which must increase its purchasing power even for the whole of strictly Italian production.

The General Fascist Confederation of Industry wants all industrialists to direct all their actions to this most noble end. Several industrialists, in fact, have already diminished their profits in these last months, others have abolished them and still others have sold below cost, and of this the noticeable reduction of wholesale prices and export prices even at a material loss is eloquent proof. But this is not enough: it is passive resistance, not positive effort.

Costs must now be reduced. The decided rapidity and intensity of the process makes it indispensable above all to take recourse to a reduction of salaries, since they represent one of the most important elements in the cost of manufacture and the one on which material action can be taken now that an immediate reduction of costs is urgently demanded.

Naturally it is indispensable that the reduction be kept within strictly necessary limits, taking account of all factors of a social, physiological and human nature to which salaries are related.

Italian workers have with a praiseworthy spirit of discipline always proved and will again prove their ability to take account of the needs of production, to the fate of which their own fates are indissolubly bound. And the example set by state employees is certainly not in vain.

In other words, the workers understand that the sacrifice that is being demanded of them today, besides being absolutely inevitable, will immediately and mediately turn to the advantage of the laboring classes, immediately because it will permit keeping unemployment and reduced hours of labor and their consequences within the most narrow limits, thus allowing a greater daily return than would be possible with reduced labor and the maintenance of present uniform salaries; mediately, because it will permit industry to pass the crisis and regain as soon as possible the growing rhythm on which the economic welfare of the whole country depends and that of the laboring classes in particular.

At this time the responsibilities and tasks of industrialists are more important than ever; they must take the greatest pains in reducing the other factors in the cost of production which are susceptible to variation by the influence of producers' efforts. Avoiding waste of raw materials, inventing the most suitable means for increasing the return from human effort, decreasing fatigue and eliminating all waste of energy, utilizing capital and credit most efficiently, applying the technical improvements suggested by science and practical experience, and reducing the various steps in production to a minimum — these constitute a series of formidable problems to which Italian industrialists should bend their whole creative activity. It is not sufficient that they should carry production to the level of technical and economic efficiency of which the country may justly be proud at present. There is an urgent need to do something more and better in order to face the needs of the present situation.

The part which they contribute to the internal rise of the value of the *lira* will re-echo in those factors of the cost of production as well as the cost of money and other factors that are beyond their direct influence. It is the higher interest of the country that requires industrialists to make every effort that their positions in internal and world markets be maintained. The industrialists know that these positions, laboriously won by years of patient preparation, by overcoming infinite difficulties set up by foreign commercial competition, intensified and favored by varying factors, will be reconquered with difficulty if they are lost today, and that it would be an incalculable harm to themselves and to the laboring masses as well as to the economic standing of the country. They will link their own sacrifice to that of the workers and will carry on a work worthy of our country's future."

No. 26. *Syndicalism* versus *Corporationism*

(The following editorials from *Critica Fascista* were among the first open expressions of the gradual divergence between syndicalist leaders and corporationist politicians. Since the corporations were turned over into the hands of the politicians — the Ministry and prefects — some of the syndicalist leaders, the very ones who had first championed the corporations, feared that their syndicalist activity would be subjected to arbitrary political control under the thin veneer of nominal corporations. Apparently both labor and employers' syndicates were alarmed.)

"We need not be under the illusion that we have already entirely conquered the traditional and characteristic defects of the Italians, those defects that for centuries have prevented the formation of an organic national will and consciousness. . . . Now that it is impossible to carry on political defeatism in the face of concrete facts and the persuasive energy of the government, some of these champions of national knavery are today turning toward syndicalist defeatism. Here and there we have had indications of the existence of these idiotic and harmful persons; there is grumbling, for instance, to the effect that fascist collaboration is turning out to be entirely at the expense of the working classes, the shadow of discredit is cast on the new syndical laws, they say that the means of repression and prevention will not be efficacious, they declare themselves sceptical about the attainment of the ends set up by syndicalism, they exploit the necessarily slow, difficult and methodical procedure of corporate organization by asserting that an organic and functional order is impossible in the new state, they try to make light of the concrete value and the efficacy of the provisions of the Labor Charter, pretending that they can already see today what the natural effects in the future will be. . . ." (*Disfattismo Sindacale*, in *Critica Fascista*, June 15, 1927, p. 229.)

"The posthumous syndical survivals, and above all the conviction that syndicates have rights over and above the state, are now evident in current terminology. Too many continue to talk of syndical law, the syndical order, syndical functions, and they persist in using this adjective in a critical, polemic and anti-state sense, which the Labor Charter has sought to exclude, by declaring definitely that the bases of the corporate order consist in the *inseparable unity of production and labor,* and in the organizing and *disciplining* function of legally recognized professional associations. Thus, excessively independent attitudes are not wanting among certain syndical directors towards the state and towards the authorities which represent it; and there is a neglect of coöperation even in details and an exaggerated regard for the vindication of particular interests. Those who govern the associations of employers and workers in the provinces do not always observe with the proper solicitude and intelligence the politics which the Head of the Government and Minister of Corporations has established by means of the corresponding ministry and by the confederate and federate bodies and which tend to constitute the solid skeleton of the regime and ought to transmit that marvellous governing will that is the supreme virtue of the regime itself to all spheres of the nation. Moreover, some of them even present themselves as the nearest heirs of the old parliamentary privileges and pretend to exercise in the life of the state, on the periphery as well as at the center, the traditional influences of 'Member of Parliament,' without taking into account that whatever be the solution that will be given to the problem of the legislative bodies of the fascist state, the position of syndical representative can never approach, not even formally, that fiction of representative sovereignty which veiled the exorbitant political and administrative claims of the parliamentary system. The breaking up of certain productive forces, which took place in connection with the present efforts at price systematization, is the most evident proof of this state of things.

That the corporate fascist system is a system of duties and not of rights, that the syndical representative is an instrument of the state and not of separate parties, that class interests have no emphasis nor claim because they are outside the corporate unity, these are three given facts that it still behooves us to engrave deeply into the minds of many syndicate organizers in the corporate state. And it may be opportune and preferable that the energies of the fascist party in which the predominance of spiritual motives is most active, be dedicated to this work.

Corporate representation, destined to so important a place in the life of the nation, can not and must not in any way revive the reproduction, under a new terminology, of political liberalism, made worse by being given a syndical content. . . .

The reform embodied in the law on the legal regulation of collective labor relations and in the Labor Charter is often treated in bureaucratic practice as a partial, limited and incidental reform in the face of which the continuance of the old democratic machinery of public administration is excused. Occasionally they even refer to the attempt to *devancer* the corporate reform, by putting improvised bodies and complicated systems into operation, that are destined to create situations of increasing conflict with the bodies of the corporate order and in general represent a waste of energy and of means.

Let us speak clearly: *the law on the attributes and prerogatives of the Prime Minister is the premise to which the present and coming rules of the corporate order are the conclusion.* To imagine today, after similar fundamental acts, that the structure of the separate administrations can remain unchanged, is equivalent to refusing the principle of the revolution; a refusal all the more reprehensible and dangerous because the executive power is by force of circumstances called to take the first place in the new state.

It is not merely a matter of 'substituting men.' It is a matter of 'renovating systems.' Or better: it is a matter of doing both these things at once, which is more difficult and more decisive.

To sum up, political syndicalism and bureaucratic democracy, the two causes of state dissolution in the pre-fascist period, still persist here and there, among the increasingly few remains. Against these it is truly necessary that the revolution concentrate its forces." (*In Fondo alla Rivoluzione.* In *Critica Fascista,* July 15, 1927, pp. 261–263.)

PART V

Fascist Theory and Culture

No 27. "*Force and Consent*"

(This article of Mussolini's was the first outspoken challenge to the liberals after his accession to power, and served as a philosophic basis and rationalization of subsequent policy.)

"A certain Italian liberalism that claims to be the only representative of the authoritative immortal principles, extraordinarily resembles socialism now half defunct, since it too like the latter, believes it possesses an indisputable " scientific " truth, good for all times, places and situations. Here is the absurdity. Liberalism is not the ultimate word nor does it represent a final formula in the matter of the art of government. In this difficult and delicate art, which works on the most refractory of materials and in a constant state of movement, since it works with the living and not with the dead, — in the political art there is no Aristotelian unity of time, place and action. Men have been more or less fortunately governed in a thousand different ways. Liberalism is the contribution and the method of the nineteenth century, and is not stupid as Daudet believes, for there are no stupid centuries and intelligent centuries, but intelligence and stupidity alternate in greater or less proportions in every century. It does not follow that liberalism, which was a good method of government for the nineteenth century, that is for a century dominated by two such essential phenomena as the development of capitalism and the rise of the sentiment of nationality, must necessarily be adapted to the twentieth century, which is already assuming characteristics very different from those which distinguished the preceding century. Facts are worth more than books and experience more than doctrine. Now the greatest experiences since the War, those which are in continual movement before our eyes, indicate liberalism's defeat. In Russia and in Italy it has been demonstrated that it is possible to govern irrespective of and contrary to the whole liberal ideology. Communism and fascism are outside of liberalism.

But wherein does this liberalism essentially consist, with which all the enemies of fascism are today more or less directly inflamed? Does liberalism mean universal suffrage and related things? Does it mean keeping the Chamber of Deputies open permanently because it affords the indecent spectacle which had been generally nauseating? Does it mean to allow to a few in the name of liberty the liberty of killing the liberty of all? Does it mean to open the door wide to those who declare their hostility to the state and who are actively working at its destruction? Is this liberalism? Very well, if this is liberalism, it is a theory and practice of abnegation and of ruin. Liberty is not an end but a means. As a means it must be controlled and dominated. And this raises the theme of " force."

The honorable liberals are begged to tell me if there ever was a government in history that was based exclusively on the consent of the people and renounced any and every use of force. A government so constituted there never was and there never will be. Consent is as changeable as the formations in the sands of the seashore. We cannot have it always. Nor can it ever be total. No government has ever existed that made all its subjects happy. Whatever solution you happen to give to any problem whatsoever, even though you share the Divine wisdom, you would inevitably create a class of malcontents. If in geometry so far it has been impossible to square the circle, it has been even more so in politics. Given as axiomatic that any provision of the government whatsoever creates some malcontents, how are you going to avoid that this discontent spread and constitute a danger for the solidarity of the state? You avoid it with force; by bringing a maximum force to bear; by employing this force inexorably whenever it is rendered necessary. Rob any government of force — and I mean physical, armed force — and leave it with only its immortal principles, and that government will be at the mercy of the first group that is organized and intent on overthrowing it. Now fascism throws these lifeless theories on the dump heap. When a group or a party is in power it has the obligation of fortifying itself and defending itself against all. The plain truth that must stare into the eyes of anyone not blinded by dogmatism, is that men are perhaps tired of liberty. They have had an orgy of it. Today liberty is no longer the chaste stern virgin for whom the generations of the first half of the last century fought and died. For the youth that is intrepid, restless and hard, that faces the dawn of the new history, there are other words of much greater power, and they are: order, hierarchy, discipline. This poor Italian liberalism that is groaning and battling for a wider liberty is singularly behind the times. It is completely incomprehensible and impossible. They talk of the seeds that will bring back the spring. Jesting! Some seeds die under the shroud of winter. Fascism that was not afraid of being called reactionary while many of today's liberals lay prone before the triumphant beast, has no hesitation today in calling itself illiberal and anti-liberal. Fascism will not fall victim to this kind of vulgar play.

Let it be known therefore once and for all that fascism knows no idols and worships no fetishes; it has already passed over and if necessary will turn once more and quietly pass over the more or less decayed corpse of the Goddess Liberty." (Benito Mussolini: *Forza e Consenso*. In *Gerarchia*, March 1923, pp. 801–803.)

No. 28. *Liberty and Liberalism*

(Enrico Corradini is the veteran leader of the nationalists and has carried on an intensive propaganda ever since 1909. He delivered the speech from which the following selections are taken on February 8, 1925, in defense of fascism's decision to crush the parliamentary opposition.)

"When were we free? During the times in which we had freedom of the press, did we really have that other more precious liberty, the liberty of citizens? During the times in which the socialists had liberty, was there a real liberty of the laws of life, the laws of labor and of national production? During the times in which we had the liberty of socialism and anarchy and of every sort of subversion, did we really have the liberty which belongs to citizens, classes, national society, our eternal country, that is to say, liberty for the state?

When were we free? For a long time (I speak of that normal and too often forgotten pre-war age and not of the post-war and bolshevik period, which alone our intelligent and good bourgeoisie is accustomed to recall), for a long historical period the liberal regime was nothing but a regime of oppression of private and public rights.

When were we free? Years and years passed during which you were citizens of the bourgeoisie and as such suffered humiliations and offenses, were persecuted as a class to be destroyed. Years and years passed in which you were owners of property by heredity or by the fruit of your labor, and as such suffered humiliations and offenses and were persecuted as usurpers to be plundered. . . .

The liberal state was in itself without liberty both in peace and in war. It was without liberty and in its organs and functions lived under condemnation. It was without liberty to defend itself and to defend order when it was besieged and stormed in open day. It was without liberty in its international action and foreign policy. . . . After the War the state was without liberty to defend itself and to defend the victory and its fruits, I need not say in the face of foreign competitions but in the face of its own subjects who betrayed it. The state in Italy, for a quarter of a century, in peace and in war, from the defeat at Adua to the victory of Vittorio Veneto, was without liberty; the state, the organic nation itself in its historic life, was under the suggestion of its own subjects who come and go day by day. And such a regime was called liberalism and democracy. And the old parties and old men in Parliament and government accompanied it to its ruin — until the salvation of the state by the grace of God and the will of the nation was assumed by fascism and attained by the March on Rome. . . .

Fascism has the right to govern Italy, because only it has the strength, because only it is strength, and the rest is weakness and the residuum of weakness, dissolution and the residuum of dissolution, pushing the nation and the state towards dissolution.

Fascism has the right to govern Italy because it alone is a product of the new Italy, of the victory, and the rest is pre-war residuum.

Fascism has the right to govern Italy because it alone has a program for the future of Italy, and the rest has exhausted itself in the past.

And I add that fascism, since it has the right to govern Italy, has the right, when the opposition of old parties and old men is raised against it, to use force in repressing them proportionate to the force of their attack, in the interest of its sacrosanct right, which all revolutions undertaken to renew the life of peoples and states have, of freeing itself from the incumbrances of the past.

For the sake of Italy, fascism has the right to go its way and live its life, to be secure in order to carry out the program committed to it, which program does not consist in robbing Italians of their liberty or democracy, but consists precisely and above all in giving liberty to the Italian state, fortifying it by new laws and new institutions, in order that it may defend its own free sovereignty in the nation and its own free activity in the world." (*Fascismo vita d'Italia*, pp. 18–22.)

No. 29. *Gentile's Version of Fascism*

(Gentile and his disciples are the most conspicuous and the most distinguished group of fascist thinkers and have succeeded in giving the impression very widely that their particular brand of idealist philosophy is also the official philosophy of fascism. Though this is not true and though fascism has no single philosophic content, the idealists are certainly predominant and far above any other philosophical group, both in their numbers and in philosophic erudition. Gentile is no longer a member of the government, but his former activities are still very influential. His educational reform and the work of the commission for constitutional reform, of which he was chairman, are among the most constructive and far-reaching of the works of the fascist government. Gentile is at present director of the Fascist Institute of Culture.)

" We see two Italies before us — one old and one new, the Italy of centuries, which is our glory as well as our sad heritage, weighing on our shoulders and spirits, and which is also, we may say it frankly, a shame from which we seek to hide and for which we must make amends. . . . For us this Italy is dead; but thanks to heaven, there is another. And one may say in a certain sense, as I shall now explain, that the first Italy has been dead for two hundred years. But it is not so dead that from time to time we do not find it before our eyes even today in this year of grace 1925. There are still too many people in Italy who believe in nothing and laugh at everything, who sigh for Arcadia and other academic visions and who turn bitterly on anyone who disturbs their digestion. . . . But this old-style type of spiritual temperament, that does not dare because it does not believe, that flees from enthusiasm because it sees no advantage in sacrifice, that measures national fortunes by individual well-being, that always loves to walk on the ground, never to compromise itself, never to get heated, that leaves ideals to poets, to women or even to philosophers, and that willingly lays aside any question that might endanger the peace and quiet of life, that likes to joke about everything and everybody, that always throws the cold water of prose on the enthusiasms of poetry and advises moderation at all costs and shows a holy horror of polemics and violence, that harbors closely all the maxims of egoism, reflects on them, studies and understands them, and takes them bodily as the quintessence of foresight and wisdom; is not all this for too many persons still the *non plus ultra* of the refinement characteristic of Italians? There are Masons who, as we know, ran their notorious lay principles into the ground, being neither for religion nor against it; but also outside the Masons, how many Italians are there who still prefer to be silent on religious matters and who are reticent and ashamed at revealing and defending their own convictions when they have any? All this is the old Italy, the Italy of individualism, the Italy of the Renaissance. . . .

The personification of Italian patriotism that has given us a country, the person to whom we always turn with reverent and grateful minds, because he was the highest and most genuine prophet of the *risorgimento,* the Ezekiel of the new Italy, which thanks to him has finally arisen among the nations and now stands on its feet and knows and asserts that it too is in the world, with its duties but also with its rights, and that it will not fall, will no longer lie low, — for the old Italy of which we have spoken, if it is not yet entirely dead, must die — this man was Giuseppe Mazzini.

Fascism has returned to the spirit of the *risorgimento* with the greater vigor which it derived from its fresh consciousness of the great trial borne so honorably by the Italian people and of their certainty in their capacity to fight and win and really to amount to something in the history of the world. It has returned with an impulse that tolerates no frivolity and no baseness, with an irrepressible ardor for arousing the nation from its recent, and to be sure momentary, mental darkness and brutishness, in order that the fruit of the immense sacrifice might not be lost, in order that the place, finally deserved and already almost reached, of a great power or of a nation that has its own will, might not be lost from view but might become the object of this will, to be one and to be maintained intact.

The story is really too simple that explains the origin of a political and moral or, in general, a spiritual movement, as a simple contrast or negation of a preceding movement. . . . From nothing nothing comes; and from the democratic mire in which no germ was hidden, it would never be possible to see any plant sprout and grow, nor any vital germ of political renovation. The origins of fascism are different and much more complex than this schematic explanation of contrast to so-called bolshevism that spread through the political and social corruption of the aftermath of the War. . . .

I have heard it said that fascism is not a doctrine and has no philosophy, that in opposing itself to the disintegrating forces of socialistic demagogy and mass rule, with the energy of a moral force whose large merit is being recognized and which all in fact seem disposed to admit, fascism is returning to the liberal doctrine, to the liberal sane concept of the state strong and ready to subordinate all particular interests to the general interest and to oppose the inviolable rule of law to the free will of individuals. I am not of this opinion, for above all I beware of confusing doctrine and philosophy with the systematic expositions that can be made verbally in well constructed treatises; and I am convinced that the true doctrine is that which is expressed in action rather than in words or books, in the personality of men and in the attitudes which they assume in the face of problems; and this is a much more serious solution to problems than that of abstract dissertations, sermons and theories. A false theory. The true theory is always a practice, a form of life; it is the man himself involved not by a blind fatality of instinct, but by the conscious convictions and mature proposals coming from a sure intuition of the end he must follow; it is the man involved in a yes or no who is much more effective and of a much clearer affirmation or negation than speculative philosophy. What more decisive negation of the value of life could there be than suicide, and what more energetic affirmation of its value than the voluntary sacrifice of the citizen who dies for his country, which is the perpetuation of a concrete ideal of life. Hence let us leave books aside and let us look at the animating ideas and the consequent significance of the facts that are before us in the great book of history which is much more imposing than even the most elaborate doctrinary exposition; and first of all let us exclude the possibility that of all doctrines the fascist doctrine of the state coincides with the liberal doctrine. . . .

Of which liberalism do we speak? I distinguish two principal forms of this doctrine: for one of which — I wish to use the very words used by Honorable Mussolini in his speech in the Costanzi Theatre — liberty is a right, and for the other it is a duty; for the one it is something to lean on, and for the other it is something to be won; for the one it is equality, for the other it is privilege and a hierarchy of values. One liberalism locates the root of liberty in the individual and hence opposes the individual to the state, which latter no longer has an intrinsic value but serves the welfare and perfection of the individual; a means and not an end. It limits itself to the maintaining of public order, thus remaining entirely outside the realm of spiritual life, which latter is enclosed in the inner realm of the individual consciousness. This liberalism is historically classical liberalism, of English origin, and I add immediately it is false liberalism, or contains only a half truth. It was opposed among us by Mazzini by a criticism which I hold immortal.

But there is another liberalism developed by Italian thought and by German, which declares this antagonism between state and individual absurd, observing how everything that has value in the individual and can pretend to be guaranteed and promoted, by the very fact that it stands as a right, has a universal bearing and expresses a higher will and interest than the will and interest of the single individual; it implies a common will and personality, which becomes the ethical substance of the individual. For this liberalism, liberty is to be sure the supreme end and rule of every human life; but in so far as individual and social education bring about its realization, actualizing this common will in the individual, it manifests itself as law and hence as state. Which is moreover not a super-structure that is externally imposed on individual activity and initiative, subjecting it to a restrictive coercion, but is its very essence, manifesting itself at the head of a continual process of formation and development; just as everything that is part of the greatness and glory of man is never a natural and immediate quality, but is the result of persevering effort whereby the individual, conquering his natural inclinations that drag him down, raises himself to the levels of his proper dignity. State and individual from this point of view are one and the same; and the art of governing is the art of reconciling and identifying these two terms so that the maximum of liberty agrees with the maximum of public order, not merely externally but also and above all in the sovereignty assigned to law and to its necessary organs. For always the maximum of liberty coincides with the maximum force of the state.

Which force? Distinctions in this field are dear to those who do not welcome this concept of force, which is nevertheless essential to the state, and hence to liberty. And they distinguish moral from material force: the force of law freely voted and accepted from the force of violence which is rigidly opposed to the will of the citizen. Ingenuous distinctions, if made in good faith! Every force is a moral force, for it is always an expression of will; and whatever be the argument used — preaching or black-jacking — its efficacy can be none other than its ability finally to receive the inner support of a man and to persuade him to agree to it. . . . The material force to which I attribute a moral value — the context is clear — is not that of a private person but of the state. . . . The black-jack of fascist squadrism was intended to be, and actually was, the vindicating force of a state whose constitutional powers were renounced and denied by its own central organs. It was therefore the necessary surrogate of the force of the state itself during a revolutionary period, when, according to the logic of all revolutions, the state was in crisis, its force was being gradually shifted from its fictitious and legal organs to its real organs, which, though illegal, tended toward legality. . . .

There is violence and violence, and no fascist worthy of marching under our banners has ever confused the two. And whoever has confused them is unworthy of staying with us and will be expelled as soon as discovered. There is private violence, which is free will, anarchy, social disintegration; and unless fascism is a word without meaning, which not even our adversaries would admit, such violence has never found a more resolute, clear-cut and formidable enemy than fascism. But there is another violence, willed by God and by all men who believe in God, in order and in the law which God certainly wills for the world: the violence for which there is no equality between the law and the criminal, and which does not admit the latter freely to choose or accept or rather demand the punishment which, as a great philosopher has justly observed, is his right. The will of the law annuls the will of the criminal; that is, it is a holy violence. And, from Jesus down, men have always had recourse to acts of violence which they firmly regarded as representing law, or a higher and universal interest. . . . When a state was in crisis, there were always at hand men of the revolution who installed a new state. Fascism is a revolution. . . .

We reached the point in Italy where even the etymology of 'state' was forgotten in the general disappearance of the state. At least in relation to individual free will, the state must stand, must rule, as something firm, solid, unshakable. Law and force: law that makes itself prevail and does not yield every time an individual does not like it, and that does not turn to favor this or that particular group. And in order that the state may be this force, it must be power, internal and external, capable of realizing its own will — a rational or reasonable will, as are all those wills which can not remain on the level of mere wishing, but transform themselves into act and triumph; but also a will which can not admit others as limiting it; hence, sovereign, absolute will. The legitimate will of citizens is that which coincides with the will of the state, organized and made manifest by its central organs. In respect to international relations and foreign affairs, war, as a last resort, tests and guarantees the sovereignty of a single state in the system of history, to which all states belong. And in war a state proves its own power, that is to say its own independence.

This state that seeks to be and actually is the only concrete will — for all others can be called wills only abstractly in so far as one overlooks the indissoluble ties by which each individual is bound to society, breathing as it were its atmosphere of language, custom, thought, interests and aspirations, — this state, I say, would not be a will, if it were not a person. For in order to will one must have the consciousness of what one wants, of the ends and means; and to have this consciousness one must first have self-consciousness, being distinguished from others and asserting one's own independence as a center of conscious activity; in short, one must be a person.

But to be a person is to be a moral activity, an activity that wills and must will according to some ideal. And the state, which is the national consciousness and the will of this consciousness, derives from this consciousness the ideal at which it aims and toward which it directs all its activities. Hence the state must inevitably be an ethical substance. Permit me this philosophical terminology. Its meaning will be transparent, if each of you will appeal to his own consciousness and feel the sacredness of the country which commands you to serve it, by indisputable orders, without hesitation, without exception, even unto death. The state has an absolute moral value for us, as being the person by whose functions all others have a value, which in coinciding with that of the state also becomes absolute. Bear in mind: human life is sacred. Why? Because man is spirit, and as such has an absolute value. Things are instruments; men are ends. However, the life of a citizen must be sacrificed when the laws of the country demand it. Without these evident truths, which are imbedded in the hearts of all civilized men, there can be no social or human life.

An ethical state? The liberals object. . . . They claim that morality is to be attributed to the concrete individual, who is the only true will, the only personality in the true sense of the word; and the state is but an external limit on free individual personalities and reconciles their several activities so as to prevent any one of them from being carried out at the expense of others. This negative and empty conception of the state is decidedly rejected by fascism; not so much because it pretends to impose the state on the individual but because, according to Mazzini's teaching, it is impossible to conceive individuals in atomistic abstraction and then to expect the state to mold them into an impossible synthesis. We regard the state as the very personality of individuals themselves, robbed of their accidental differences, removed from those abstract preoccupations with their particular interests which see and evaluate them independently of the general system in which their reality and the possibility of their actual effectiveness consists; a personality rooted in the deepest parts of its consciousness, where the individual feels the general interest as his and hence wills as with a general will. This consciousness which is realized and should be realized deep down in each one of us as a national consciousness in all its power, its legal forms and its political activities, this basis of our own personality, this is the state. And to conceive it as outside of the moral life is to deprive the individual himself of his moral substance. The ethical state of fascism is, of course, no longer the agnostic state of old-fashioned liberalism. Its ethical nature is spirituality, a conscious personality, a systematic will. . . . What else is the state but the reconciliation and unity of will and law? Will is will when it is law, just as law is law only when it is will. Hence the individual realizes his own nature in so far as he forms a state and feels in the bottom of his own consciousness the incessant pulse of a universal ethical reality that transcends the boundaries of his abstract particular personality and just as it makes him face death when his country is in extreme danger, as if to make him find his own true self by losing his illusory being, so it makes him recognize every moment the powerful force of a law to which his lower instincts and passional nature bow. . . .

The state is the great will of the nation and hence its great intelligence. It ignores nothing and keeps aloof from nothing which touches the citizen's interest which is its own interest, neither in economics nor in morals. *Nihil humani a se alienum putat.* The state is neither a grand façade nor an empty building: it is man himself, the house, built, inhabited, and enlivened by human joys, pains, and labors, by the whole life of the human spirit.

Is this state-worship? It is the religion of the spirit that has not been plunged into the abject blindness of materialism. It is the torch raised high by youthful fascist hands to kindle a great spiritual conflagration in this Italy, which, I repeat, has rescued itself and is fighting for its own redemption. But it can not redeem itself unless it restores its inner moral forces; unless it becomes accustomed to conceiving all of life religiously; unless it revives the sound and manly simplicity of citizens ever ready without hesitation to serve the ideal, to work, live and die for their country, uppermost in their thoughts, venerated and sacred; unless it loves the militia and the school, which make a people powerful, and labor, the source of all national and private prosperity, the arena of will and character. . . .

Fascism was the most uncompromising rebel against the myths and lies of internationalistic socialism, of those who were without country and without duties, who offended the sense of right and hence of individuality in the name of an abstract and empty ideal of human brotherhood. . . . Fascism fought the abstract, Marxian class conception of society, and tore down the antithesis by which the artificial myth of the class struggle was supported. . . . Then too, fascism fought Marxism in what Mazzini with apostolic ardor had already fought — Mazzini, the prophet of our *risorgimento* and in many aspects of his doctrine, the teacher of current fascism, — namely, the utilitarian, materialistic and hence egoistic conception of life, understood as a realm of rights to be vindicated, instead of as an arena of duties to be performed by sacrificing oneself to an ideal. . . . The fascist doctrine has the merit of fighting it precisely by Giuseppe Mazzini's method: not by words and abstract theoretic arguments, but by deeds, by the ideal which is actualized and inculcated in youthful hearts.

We *fascisti* remember and should remember Giuseppe Mazzini as our predecessor and as one of our forefathers. . . . His thought has a pure breath of religious feeling. His ' people ' is a term of an inseparable binomial: God and people; his ' people ' is bound in his mind to that absolute from which it is impossible to escape, through which politics becomes, as he said, a mission, that is, a religious life. Hence we *fascisti*, turning back to find our model in the history of the Italy to which we are so passionately devoted, feel that in coming upon the austere figure of Giuseppe Mazzini we find the purest and brightest form of

our faith and of our ideal. He was destined to arouse in the breast
of Italians that young Italy which has arisen with fascism and which
sings with us the hymn to eternal youth, to the springtime of life blos-
soming in faith and hope.

Gentlemen, fascism is a party and a political doctrine. But above
all . . . it is a total conception of life. It is impossible to be a fascist
in politics and not in the school, not in one's own family or office. . . .
Thus fascism embodies what may be called its own characteristic,
namely, taking life seriously. Life is toil, effort, sacrifice, and hard work;
a life in which we know perfectly well there is neither matter nor time
for amusement. Before us there always stands an ideal to be realized;
an ideal which gives us no respite. We have no time to lose. Even in
our sleep we must give account of the talents entrusted to us. We must
make them yield fruit, not for us who are nothing, but for our land and
country, for this Italy that fills our hearts with her memories and aspirations, with her joys and labors, that rebukes us for the centuries our
fathers lost, but that comforts us by recent events when Italian effort
produced a miracle, when Italy united in a single thought, a single sentiment, a single desire for sacrifice. And it was precisely the young men,
the young Italy of our prophet, that were ready, that ran to the sacrifice
and died for the country. To die for that ideal by which alone men can
live and by which men may feel the seriousness of life. . . .

Modern man is at the cross-roads. On the one hand is the liberty
of the egoists that leads to anarchy and the ruin of those ideals in which
man may find himself; on the other, the liberty of men who over and
above their particular egos feel the power of the ideal, of country and
family, of the state and law, of liberty not as an inherited privilege or
free gift of the gods, but as something to be won by our efforts, out of
which family, state and a higher law are created, and in which resides
the world's worth and the reward for our work. On the one hand,
rights for those who have nothing to give to the world; on the other,
duty for those who ask nothing of it. . . .

Fascism is war on intellectualism. The fascist spirit is will, not
intellect; and I hope I will not be misunderstood. Fascist intellectuals
must not be *intellectuals*. Fascism is and should be an enemy without
truce or pity, not against intelligence, but against intellectualism which is
a disease of intelligence . . . for intelligence too is will, and fascism at
least feels this, disdaining the culture that is an ornament or adornment
of the brain and longing for a culture by which the spirit is armed and
fortified for winning ever new battles. And this may be, this should be
our barbarity, a barbarity moreover of intellectuals! Against science
and above all against philosophy; but, of course, against the science and
philosophy of decadents, of the spineless, of those who always stand at
the window and are satisfied to criticize as if it were no affair of theirs!
. . . One of the major merits of fascism is this, to have obliged little by
little all those who once stood at the window to come down into the

streets, to practice fascism even against fascism. And when all Italians will have come down into the streets, and will think and reflect without any longer feeling the temptation to turn to the window, the Italian people will begin to be the great people that it should be. . . .

Fascism is art, for it too is an original movement of the spirit and is not a deduction but a creation; and even in action it relies on a genial inspiration rather than on conclusions closely drawn by reasoning. Certainly because of its spontaneity and originality fascism is art. But I should like to complete this definition. The artist himself is in fact a spirit, seeking and finding its liberty beyond this real world, where toil and pain exist, where an iron law binds the individual, and where a force weighs upon man which is ultimately superior to every natural or human force, which is called God or Fate, and which no will and no science can conquer. . . . Life is art, to be sure, but it is also religion. It is the exaltation of our creative powers, but also the sense of our limitations and of the existence of something which we are not and which does not depend on us, something that besieges and impinges on us, that presses on us and that demands an account of what we are doing and what we are. . . . This is the great force of religion, and hence fascism has instinctively welcomed religion, whose neglect in the past was but one among the many other signs of decadence in the old Italy. . . . Fascism . . . is a religion. Therefore it has been able to reconsecrate in the hearts of Italians the war and the victory, though they had been vilely vituperated; therefore it has reëstablished a love of martyrdom for the ideal of our country; and therefore it stands invincible in the field while its unfit and base adversaries abuse it. . . .

The school must be agnostic neither in religion nor in philosophy, for it dare not be agnostic in morals. Hence neither can it be agnostic in politics. Agnosticism is a suspension of judgment and a consequent refusal to take sides actively with any party. It is the separation of one's personality from life. . . . Now it is evident that a school which takes this attitude instead of performing its essential function as an instrument and constructive activity of moral life, becomes instead a fatal organ of disintegration and destruction of all the fundamental energies of a people's spiritual life. . . .

Therefore we are fighting as we must, this other sort of secular education that seeks to banish politics from the school. . . . To be sure, politics divides and the school should unite; it unites by nourishing that common humanity by which men understand each other and coöperate in building up those spiritual structures by which civilization is being realized. . . . The school cannot participate in the daily battle of life, in the life of ever fresh conflicts. But the school must prepare for this life; and first the child, and later still more the youth, must be accustomed to giving an ear to the noise of the battle, that is being waged outside the closed walls in which he is still permitted to grow, and that awaits him with its problems, its diverse and conflicting interests, destined however to be reconciled; he must occupy himself with these problems and must develop a firm will to solve them. . . .

Hence the school cannot be confined to grammar, to mathematics, or to any other material that is a mere ornament or adornment of the intellect. The intellect can be developed only by developing personality. Hence we must seek to understand all things and to love all things so far as it is true that to understand is to love. But love must always set out from a center and return to it; a center that is a point of view, a faith, a pillar on which the conscience may safely lean. . . . For this reason we need today a national Italian school, governed by a lively conception not so much of the rights as of the duties of the Italian people, and that is of every Italian. A conception not strictly and foolishly chauvinistic. But nevertheless firm and religious. And this is politics, a holy politics, and we intend that those who deny it be considered not as champions of broadmindedness and liberal-mindedness, but as vulgar and miserable profaners of that temple which we must jealously guard.

Liberty? Yes, she is the very goddess of the temple of which we speak; but liberty, as you know, is no one's natural prerogative, but an ideal to be realized, a duty to be performed, the highest conquest to which man can aspire by means of self-abnegation and sacrifice." (Giovanni Gentile: *Che cosa è il fascismo,* pp. 14–17, 29, 46–51, 31–32, 34–36, 121, 37, 43–44, 114–116, 38–39, 93–94, 98, 107–108, 163–166.)

No. 30. *Fascism as a Counter-Reformation and Anti-Risorgimento*

(Curzio Suckert (Malaparte) is the leader of a small group of *fascisti* who are attempting to give fascist ideology a Catholic form; not Catholic in a Church sense, for they are anti-clericals, but Catholic in the sense that they regard fascism as a revival of a long-established Latin tradition which had been temporarily submerged by northern movements from the Reformation to the *risorgimento*.)

" We know our people and the people has known us for almost ten centuries. For our spirit is that ancient, classic, traditional, legitimist and Catholic, essentially Italian spirit on which those *personæ* and minorities, who in a thousand ways have guided our people along the way of Catholic Rome, have always based their own justification from the most distant centuries of our national history until today. . . .

We are not afraid to go counter to the common opinion in asserting that fascism was at first profoundly Sorelian; its justification for its violence is historical, not political, and lies in the Sorelian ethics which assigns to the proletariat the function of creating a modern myth and a fabulous atmosphere to aid and hasten the ripening of a new society according to the natural order of the first Ionian and Asiatic cities. The new fascist ethics was born from that of Sorel, but in time detached it-

self by transforming the concept of social classes into that of national
classes and economic presuppositions into historical ones. . . . Fascist
syndicalism differs from the Sorelian in distinguishing society and
civilization, and hence does not assume the task of establishing a new
proletarian civilization on the ruins of bourgeois civilization . . . but of
preparing and performing a return to the national civilization, strictly
Italian, thoroughly historic, on the ruins of modern, anti-national, class-
ist, originally Anglo-Saxon civilization, which from the Reformation on
has suppressed all our native and natural forces and recently triumphed
with democratic liberalism and socialism. . . . From the Reformation
on, the manifestations of the Italian spirit have not been the product
of a free natural activity, of an independent, instinctive, almost physical
need of creating, but have obeyed a higher and continual necessity for
reaction. The rise of the Reformation signifies the end of our creative
liberty. From the second half of the sixteenth century, we have always
been obliged to defend ourselves against the same enemy; the barbarian
spirit which then became the modern, would have gained the victory over
us and over our nature and civilization, had it not been for our vindication and defense. . . . We represent in Europe . . . a living element
of opposition to the triumphant spirit of the northern nations; we have
to defend a very ancient civilization, strengthened by all the spiritual
values, against a new heretical and false civilization that is strengthened
by all the physical, material and mechanical values. This is our function. The first mode of defense was the same as our own last mode of
the present, and we are not afraid to claim that powerful spirit of
the Counter-Reformation, historically re-arisen in its own manner in
fascism. . . .

We have faith in the people, in its strength, in its instinctive wisdom,
in its destiny, even more than in its forms of economic defense and offense. We have faith in the spirit of syndicalism, in its violence, in its
continuous revolutionary toil, even more than in its daily practice; we
have faith above all in its fundamentally ethical and religious value.
We believe as did Sorel, though still too socialistic, in a *social* mission of
syndicalism. . . . And we believe, as did Corridoni, in its mission not
economic but historic, not social but national. We firmly believe that
syndicalism will kill social classes and will lead to the rise of a single
class, of a *new nation*, of a new *gens*, including in it as in a new race,
born of a mysterious fusion of diverse and conflicting races (the classes),
all the forms and all the ethnic, political and economic valor of our race.
We do not believe in the advent of a new society, but of a new civilization, and we are sure that it will be neither bourgeois nor proletarian.
We hate both equally. The experience of the last years supports our
certainty. We have seen how Italian syndicalism took the class myth
of the general strike from Sorel and transformed it into that of a revolutionary war for Italian liberty, for us an historic concept; and today we
see how fascism has made use of its own revolutionary spirit of syndi-

calist violence in order to complete that profound transformation of the modern social order . . . from which will rise a single powerfully organized national class. Fascism already represents this new class." (*L'Europa Vivente,* pp. 109, 112–116.)

"That ancient, traditional, historic, popular and ingenuous Italian that still lives, notwithstanding decrees and ordinances, in a very 'civilized,' bourgeois and proprietary Europe is supposed to be a residue of olden times, which modern Italians should bury as soon as possible if they wish to retain their title of a civilized people; it is supposed to be a residue of barbarism that shows itself beneath the disgust of the triumphant nations of the northwest. The actual state of inferiority of the Italian mind, our very civilized fellows tell us, in comparison with that of modern or rather Anglo-Saxon Europe, comes from this, that we have not yet succeeded in assimilating the spirit of modern civilization. Our historic *morale,* which still constitutes the basis of our civil life, has now been banished by the new European *morale,* sprung from several centuries of travail of that first modern revolution, the Reformation, a real and genuine revolution against the spirit of Italian civilization.

It is not enough to be Italian, today, to be civilized, so our champions of modernity tell us: one must be European. When they talk of the years '21 and '48, it would seem that the *risorgimento* on their premises was nothing but a kind of providential foreign invasion whose ostensible agents and justifiers were romanticism and liberalism. Modern Italy is the daughter of the *risorgimento,* they say, and to those who reply that the *risorgimento* was rather an aspect produced by that authentic traditional, historical, ancient, popular, and ingenuous Italy which they would have dead for some time, those very civilized Italians of D'Azeglio answer that 'the *risorgimento* is civilized Europe against barbarian Italy.' To those who protest that the *risorgimento* was a spontaneous and original movement of reaction against the invading encyclopedist, Jacobin romantic and liberal . . . spirit of the French and Anglo-Saxon, the bastards of D'Azeglio reply that it was rather the struggle of European progress against Italian obscurantism. . . .

The pretense of remaking Italians on the model of modern, that is 'civilized' French, German and English, is common to all the bastards of D'Azeglio. 'Now that Italy is made, we must make Italians.' . . . This pretense of remaking Italians is based above all on the presumption that our people is retarded and barbarian, closed to the new times and an enemy of progress, and that they, the bastards of D'Azeglio, are the living examples of what other Italians should become when they finally decide to enjoy the modern experiences of northwestern peoples. In order that Italians become civilized, modern, European, and not merely Italian . . . it is necessary, they say, that Italy too should undergo the experience of that revolution which opened the new age of modern civilization in Europe. But they do not know, or pretend not to know, that Italians are by nature unfit to become modern, and that if there is need of a revolution in Italy it is of that one which will make us return to our own natural and historic modes of civilization. . . .

We are the defenders of liberty, the liberals announced, and on our banners is not written ' *Christus imperat* ' but ' *Populus imperat.*' But in its good common sense the people, who by long experience knows how to read the Latin on banners, past ' *Regna chi può.*' We are the champions of liberty and of progress in a barbarian and retarded country, announced the patriots, as they set out to remake Italians. But when the people raised their voices demanding that the promises be kept, the liberals and patriots immediately hit them over the head in the name of the rights of civilization and, recalling that they were themselves proprietors and bourgeois, they resorted to the usual instruments of usual justice, to spies and policemen now become liberals. . . .

How good it is to feel oneself a barbarian in a country where the champions of civilization smell like foreigners and policemen. How good it is, when all are calling themselves brothers in the name of a free and united Italy, to feel oneself a mortal enemy of civilized Italians. . . . It is finally time to praise them, these barbarian Italians, ingenuous and free spirits who remained rooted in the traditions and customs of their country and always reappear taciturn and obstinate whenever there are ancient liberties to defend or injuries to avenge. These barbarian Italians are suspicious of those who talk to them about justice in their name; for they trust no one and ask no one to assume the risk of doing justice for them. They do not believe in liberty, but they will not suffer slavery; they know how to be free men without fearing laws which they do not know and in which they do not trust. . . . They know how to choose at pleasure between hell and paradise, and they have each his own saint who protects him from being harmed against his will. They go to jail without blushing, they respect friendships and alliances. They rob the robber . . . and they repay the suspicion that civilized people have for them by an ingenuous and timid gentleness of manner. From the foreign lands to which they emigrate through necessity and often through greed and avarice, they return with the bitter experience of the mortifications to which they are condemned by the scorn and hatred of civilized nations. They know that the Italian people is the most admired, scorned and hated in the world. They return with bitterness in their blood. Some day they will avenge themselves on the modern, civilized, patriotic, liberal Italians for the wrongs they have suffered in foreign lands. They will avenge themselves for the rhetoric of patriots and their deceptions. This modern, mediocre, false Italy has little longer to live; it will not live." (*Italia Barbara:* pp. 20–23, 32, 38–40.)

No. 31. *"Fascist Thought"*

(From Camillo Pellizzi: *Fascismo-Aristocrazia*.)

"Is there a fascist thought? . . .

We recognize only one system of dogmas, that of the Roman Church. These dogmas are more necessary to life than life itself; but life, being entirely and always spiritual life, goes on every day remaking and adding to the infinite web of its values, its faiths and its principles. Now fascism is above all and must become still more a ' mode of living.' To fix a dogma for it, in whatever sense this word be understood, means to bind it with a chain which, if it be not immediately burst in the process of action, could not help but coerce and perhaps kill all its major future developments.

The doubt, which without a written doctrine fixed once and for all falls into uncertainty and indiscipline, has now been eliminated by the experience we have gained. Fascism has always obeyed its leaders even when it did not understand them; and its leaders have always guided its actions towards the noblest and remotest heights, even when they themselves were unable to define the nature and meaning of their undertakings in an explicit and simple form. It seems that God Himself, and we must be understood with discretion, is promoting and hiddenly directing this great movement of minds and wills.

Our champions, and first and greatest the *Duce,* have been urged and inspired from on high — from these heights which are in every man and from which springs the creative flood of will. There is no need of dogma; discipline suffices. This is fascism's only dogma.

And this also explains why the dogmatics of fascism can not be forthcoming, in any case, from a congress of thinkers and scholars. We are no academy, but a voluntary movement; the problem is not before us, but in us; there is no puzzle to be solved, but a reality to be constructed. It is not the business of the learned, but of the practical leaders of our work to determine, hour by hour, what are the objectives and the goals. The ' Thinker ' of fascism is and remains Benito Mussolini; for he has been thinking out fascism by making it. And this is the first and concrete mode of political thinking.

But you say: if fascism can thus be reduced entirely to action, and to action inspired by its heads and its disciplined ranks, wherein does this thing consist that you call fascist thought, and how can it be distinguished? The answer lies in the question: the kernel of fascist thought is contained in understanding fascism in this way. That is, in understanding that politics is creative action and will. And that the thoughts thought, or the schemes, systems and concepts of social and political life which fascism is laying down and developing in its own bosom, are therefore not premises presupposed for the facts of fascist action, but rather fruits, products derived from its creative action. . . .

We take as our principle that politics is an original creation of the spirit, being realized in it as absolute responsibility towards itself and its own action, and in it creating its own ethical personality.

It is man who creates himself, but also God who creates man. By willing in this manner, man feels a power welling up in him and realizing itself, to which he can never deny an absolute value and a quality of absolute reality, and also a quality of a transcendent reality. Hence not every work of man is good, but only the work of man that is inspired by this total and mystic responsibility.

These truths have always been true, and will always be true, but fascism first recognized their value not only in morals and religion, but also in politics, and fought under their banner. . . . It is here that Italian idealism, reviving its most ancient and pure tradition, has carried us to a full consciousness of the religious problem; and here and in this sense it is that Giovanni Gentile may and should regard himself as the first philosopher of fascism. He has definitely disentangled the dialectics of the concrete from the dialectics of the abstract, and action from objective logical reflection, and thus has placed the true life of the spirit in the sphere of action, understood as a conscious process and hence responsible and moral. It is not an accidental difference between Croce and Gentile that made them evaluate fascism differently. Croce, 'the last of the bourgeoisie' completing the cycle of the liberal and bourgeois type of mind in the modern period, shut himself up in that cycle and could not gain a sense of the new times, sprung from a renewed and reanimated faith. It is not accidental that Gentile's idealism finds so many echoes and moral affinities in the fascist action of today," (*Fascismo-Aristocrazia:* pp. 45–49.)

No. 32. *Il Duce on Art*

(By the following words Mussolini started much talk about fascist art.)

"Without art there is no civilization. I believe that art marks the dawn of every civilization. When Italy was still divided, its unity was expressed by the rebirth of art. Italy appeared in the world with the glory of the Renaissance. Today Italy is a people of great possibilities and those conditions have been realized which all her great men awaited, from Machiavelli to Mazzini. Today there is even more: we are also being united morally.

Now on a ground thus prepared a great art can arise which can be traditionalistic and at the same time modern. We must create, otherwise we shall be the exploiters of an old patrimony; we must create the new art of our times, fascist art." (Mussolini, in the *Accademia delle belle Arti*, Perugia, October 5, 1926.)

No. 33. *Waiting for Fascist Art*

(This is taken from the first of a series of articles in *Critica Fascista* discussing fascist art. The author, Ardengo Soffici, is one of the pioneers

and most distinguished of the fascist artists. The discussion was stimulated by Mussolini's statements that fascism must create a serious and
original movement in art.)

" I do not believe that I am making an extraordinary revelation when
I say that knavery, ignorance, and wire-pulling, rather than their con-
traries, have been encouraged in these years; that the, most stupid
representatives of the official art of pre-fascism have been decidedly
reconfirmed by the new authorities and by the so-called new journalism; that worse still, fascism has always selected its men from those
whose type of mind, esthetics, and forms of artistic expression were in essence and origin not merely foreign but clearly barbarous and anti-
Italian: liberal, Jewish, Masonic, democratic, in a word, anti-fascist *par
excellence.*

I mention no names for it seems superfluous, nor do I cite old and
recent examples; but is it not perhaps a well-known fact for anyone
who is competent to judge in such matters, that among base academic
vulgarities, dilettant imitations of the primitive, archaic, romantic
and anarchic futurism, imitating German and American models, artistic
internationalism everywhere discredited and re-arising among the die-
hards of artistic liberal democracy, fascism has never been able to find
its own way, to establish the elements of its own proper character analogous to those that constitute the living nucleus of its political structure?

I have said more than once lately and I now repeat it, that it is really
a curious thing to see how the high officials of fascism who know beauti-
fully how to refute and reject the opponents of fascist ideas, and who
would laugh at the idea of readmitting Facta to the government, Treves
to the Ministry of Foreign Affairs, Misiano to that of War, Bombacci
to the Interior, etc., do not hesitate to make *exactly* this type of selection as soon as they cross over into the field of intellectual, literary or
artistic matters.

This being the case, I was inclined to think that the best policy would
be to stand apart and see how the story would end; and this not out of
disdain or despair but only because, being a realist to the core in this
too, I hold that a movement like fascism can not immediately orient itself in the forest of errors and stupidities which it came to destroy, that
it is therefore expedient and beneficent for it to stand alone and make its
own experiences and overcome all sorts of difficulties that stand in its
way, and that in any case 'time is a gentleman,' — the more so since
by a fatal law of history a movement like ours, being Italian, is bound
to triumph and is hence necessarily forced to annihilate and expel
whatever is not ours, not Italian, and to burn the refuse of all that is of
foreign or impure brand, the deposit of whole decades of our life. . . .

I believe that the literature and art which fascism should and must
patronize are those which, precisely because they participate in its
spiritual essence, least lend themselves to a simple definition and the
excellence of whose character least appears in the present general con-

fusion. It is the literature and art that can not be said to be either reactionary or revolutionary because it embodies the experience of the past and the promise of the future; it is the literature and art of equilibrium and honesty; it is the literature and art that may be called both materialistic and idealistic, since matter and spirit both have their share in it as ultimate categories of life; which, neither new nor traditionalistic, neither romantic nor classic, neither heavy nor light, neither cultural nor entirely instinctive, tempers the extremes of every experience and thus tends to the sincere expression of the mind of the creator, that is, to a good style and to perfection. I would say that it is a realistic literature and art, meaning by this term what it means when applied to the poetry of Alceus and Sappho or the sculpture of Phidias and Praxiteles. . . .

I would now add the adjective synthetic. And I would say that by this I mean to indicate an art not objectively veridical, but one that in its representation of truth also reveals the lyric spirit and independent style of the author; an art that does not abstract from visible reality, perceptible to the senses, as do all the decadent schools of an idealistic romantic origin from cubism to Dadaism via neo-classicism and futurism, but takes its inspiration and its elements from an observation and study of living, present, working reality, elaborating them until they reconstitute a higher synthesis, a creation evoking the poetry of nature, the variety and beauty of the beings and things among which we live. . . .

Thus there remains nothing for us to do but to wait and see how the *Duce*'s words are put into practice. I do not conceal that this waiting is in my case at least combined with a certain perplexity and apprehension. Has it not been proved perhaps that many of the best ideas expressed by our Head have found stumbling-blocks and have been deformed in every way as soon as they descended among those who had to translate them into practical reality and make them bear fruit?

Let us hope, however, that in this case it will be different." (Ardengo Soffici: In *Critica Fascista,* October 15, 1926, pp. 383–385.)

No. 34. *Fascist Futurist Art*

(This article, which Marinetti contributed to the *Critica Fascista* series on fascist art, shows his defiance toward the idealist school of art and indicates the chief rivalries within the fascist camp.)

" . . . In the question of fascist art, it is first of all necessary to decide who has and who has not the right to talk.

Benedetto Croce and the Crocians have no right to talk. Benedetto Croce was the creator of a disastrous type of mind, skeptical, pessimistic, denying all the spiritual values of our race and subjecting them to an idiotic idolatry of German thought. Benedetto Croce, far from having any intuition of the formidable power of development that was fermenting in Italian youth twenty years ago, foresaw nothing, hoped for nothing, and tried to belittle and castrate everything. The daring and innovating were denied by him in the name of the pretended divinity of history. Naturally his merits as a historian leave us very cold. . . . Benedetto Croce was a Germanophile neutralist, and dedicated some pompous useless articles to Goethe while we were fighting on the front against the Germans. He was, and remains, the discordant philosopher, without smell, heavy with books and poor in ideas.

The Vocians, almost all sons or disciples of Croce, have no right to intervene in the question of fascist art. Like their teacher they were the implacable defamers of the creative temper of our race. Implacably they yelped against us futurists when we, first of all, asserted Italian literary, artistic and political pride in the theatres and squares, confronting jeers and mockery and arguing with blows and beatings. The Vocians, in ecstasy before all foreign spiritual values, dreamed of augmenting the cultural labor and cultured class of our Italy, which all along has had marvellous creative forces to sustain and glorify. They were the critics and pedantic hurlers and pharmacists of thought, worshippers of blending colors and of idiotic semi-expressions. They hated the impetuous burst of Italian youth, they showed their disapproval of our first holy futurist fights, they vilified the army and our first colonial attempts. One must not confuse the cultural neutralist, pacifistic, friend-of-the-foreign *Voce,* with *Lácerba,* inflated with Italian futurism, in which Papini displayed his improvised and ephemeral futurist soul, and Ardengo Soffici, the author of a magnificent eulogy of futurism, carried on some genuine Italian futurism.

The present anti-fascists have almost all of them (for example, Salvemini) the typical Crocian and Vocian type of mind. Who then has a right to talk in the discussion of fascist art?

First of all, the futurists.

The futurists, eighteen years ago, foresaw all this. Into a soft Italy, undone by socialism and foreign culturalism, they injected a renewing Italian pride by their fights and beatings. They were the first interventionists and were imprisoned for their love of the great renewing War. They fought the War with terrible Italian pride . . . and were the first to coöperate with Mussolini in public squares, in gatherings and in prison in founding the *fasci di combattimento.*

Between battles they were able with their futurist elasticity to carry on the great literary revolution of free words. They opened infinite vistas for the theatre by their destruction of all technique, by the concept of surprise synthesis, café-concert, moving picture art, and created the esthetics of the machine and plastic dynamism, which has generated the new schools of painting. They renovated the art staging and scenery throughout the world. . . . They are modifying all the cities of the world by the architecture invented by S. Elia.

Futurist art is thoroughly Italian, for it is virile, warlike, merry, optimistic, dynamic, synthetic, simultaneous and colorful. . . . This is fascist futurist art in perfect harmony with the typically improvising and anti-cultural, anti-Crocian, anti-Vocian, temperament of Benito Mussolini." (In *Critica Fascista*, January 1, 1927, p. 3.)

No. 35. *On Fascist Art*

(The following is taken from the editorial in *Critica Fascista* which gave the " results " of its series of articles on the subject, written by various prominent fascist intellectuals. The comments on the Academy are prompted by the recent formation of an Italian Academy presumably closely modelled on French lines, and hence criticized as apt to be a conventional rather than a fascist institution.)

" . . . In the fascist state, in the state, mind you, the problem of art can be solved by leaving art to free creation. . . . What can the state do for art? . . . Agnosticism in these matters is a democratic-liberal product and belongs to that thoroughly superseded social doctrine that left everything to individual decision. . . .

First of all an immediate, necessary and very useful kind of public intervention should be exercised by the various fascist organizations, the Party and the syndicates. All the headquarters of *fasci*, of municipal governments, of associations and syndicates, are loaded with horrible pseudo-artistic objects, and similarly all the cultural expositions of the above-named bodies in their celebrations and propaganda are thick with the display of materials that indicate the most undisguised bad taste. Incredible pictorial decorations on the walls, horrible busts of colored plaster on every side, emblems and standards in glaring colors, lictors' rods in gilded stucco that look like bundles of firewood, chromo-lithographs of the *Duce* in impossible postures. . . . Enough of all this. We need to clean up our cities of these circulating monuments to bad taste, and to disqualify all those visiting-card publishers and all the false artists who sold or donated them, in either case exploiting the inexperience of the local directors.

This much said, we regard the intervention of the state in favor of art as something to be carried on very thoughtfully and prudently. First of all the economic interests of artists must be looked after, be they good or mediocre artists, and this the state is doing through the artists' syndicates. . . .

Today the bohemian artist of the good and bad old anarchic times no longer exists, living by his own moral law contrary to the ordinary laws. Every period of civilization has an art corresponding to its own moral substance, and fascist civilization will not admit that artists form a group morally separate from the complex of national society. . . . They need the state, now that the times of patronage and bohemianism are gone forever, for an artistic, moral and spiritual guidance, which should be exercised, especially in regard to the choicest artists, on the basis of precise and particular judgments, a very difficult thing in practice. And here is where the necessity is seen for creating an adequate body for this task, within the Italian Academy. . . .

The Italian Academy must be an anti-academy; must be anti-parasitic, anti-static, dynamic, operating, creative. In short, we believe that the Italian Academy must be the organ of the fascist revolution in the field of art. . . . This must be understood in the sense of a prudent, spiritual and material conservation of the artistic patrimony of our race. . . . Every form of intellectual and artistic expression should be favored which, in the judgment of the Academy, is in perfect harmony with the historic and immutable Italian temper and capable of reporting and asserting this temper by a style which is its own, distinct from that of every other people. . . .

In short the Italian Academy should be a kind of Ministry of Italian Culture. . . . Of course the members of the Academy will be chosen among the live, illustrious, Italian and fascist artistic personalities of the nation. . . . The spiritual empire of fascist Italy should be founded by artists who are clearly and traditionally Italian, that is fascist. The *Duce* announced some time ago his intention of making Rome a great modern metropolis, not unworthy of her formidable traditions. Now what state body could better indicate the way to be followed to achieve this aim than the Italian Academy? . . . The Italian Academy, the ideal, artistic and intellectual synthesis of fascist Italy, would impress its Italian character, its unity of style, its traditional and modern imprint, on everything that the new Italy is endeavoring to create. . . ." (In *Critica Fascista*, February 15, 1927, pp. 61–64.)

BIBLIOGRAPHY

This bibliography is by no means complete. A fairly comprehensive one is: *Guida Bibliografica di Cultura Fascista,* published by Berlutti and listed below. (v. *Bibliografia Fascista.*) The books and journals given below deal for the most part with the general political history and theory of fascism, not with technical details. Occasional comments are made to indicate the general point of view or subject-matter of a book, or to identify the author.

I. BOOKS AND ARTICLES

Acerbo, Giacomo: *Il Fascismo nel primo anno di Governo.* 40 pp. Berlutti. Rome. 1923. (By a prominent agriculturalist and Fascist politician.)

Acito, Alfredo: *Corporazioni e sindacati nella storia, nello Stato, e nei partiti politici.* 232 pp. Trasi. Milan. 1925.

Agnesi, Giovanni: *I nostri orientamenti.* 43 pp. Cazzamalli. Crema. 1921. (A statement of the 1921 platform.)

Alazard, Jean: *Communisme et Fascisme en Italie.* 118 pp. Bossard. Paris. 1922. (Slight, but impartially informed.)

Ambrosiani, G.: *Sindacati, Consigli Tecnici e Parlamento politico.* 167 pp. A. R. E. Rome. 1925.

Ambrosini, Vittorio: *La Battaglia per Lo Stato Sindacale.* 156 pp. A. R. E. Rome. 1925.

Amendola, Giovanni: *Una Battaglia liberale.* 233 pp. Gobetti. Turin. 1924.

—— : *La democrazia dopo il 6 aprile 1924.* 169 pp. Corbaccio. Milan. 1924.

Antologia della Nuova Italia. 342 pp. Voghera. Rome. 1923.

Ardali, Paolo: *Pio XI e Mussolini.* 35 pp. Paladino. Mantua. 1926. (Amusing pamphlets — propaganda against the popularists.)

——: *San Francesco e Mussolini.* 41 pp. Paladino. Mantua. 1926.

Arias, Gino: *La Riforma dello Stato.* Chapter in *Mussolini e il suo Fascismo.* Edited by Curt Gutkind. Monnier. Florence. 1927. (A good discussion of constitutional reform by a prominent authority — member of Commission of " Solons.")

Arnaldi, Ulrico: *Rossi-Bianchi e tricolori.* 194 pp. Vallecchi. Florence. 1920. (For early Florentine history.)

Baciocchi De Peon, M.: *Manuale del Fascista*. 74 pp. Bemporad. Florence. 1923. ("Spiritual regulations of discipline.")

Balabanoff, Angelica: in *La France de Nice et du Sud-Est*. February 25, 1927. (A character sketch of Mussolini by a Russian communist associate of his during his youthful exile in Switzerland and his revolutionary journalism before the war.)

Balbo, Italo: *Lavoro e milizia per la nuova Italia*. 48 pp. Berlutti. Rome. 1923. (By the former head of the Militia.)

Baldesi, Gino: *Dalle antiche corporazioni al moderno sindacalismo*. 62 pp. Alpes. Milan. 1924. (By an ex-director of the C. G. L., now favorably inclined toward fascism.)

——: *Sindacalismo fascista*. 48 pp. Botta. Turin. 1924.

Banchelli, Umberto: *Le Memorie di un fascista, 1919–1922*. 230 pp. Florence. 1922. (Very entertaining account of the life of a prominent squadrist and associate of Dumini, expelled from the Party in 1922 for misbehavior.)

Barbarie rosse, Le. Edited by the *Fascio Italiano di Combattimento*. 110 pp. Rome. 1921. (Chronological account by *fascisti* of deeds of socialists since 1919.)

Barnes, J. S.: *The Universal Aspects of Fascism*. 247 pp. Williams and Norgate. London. 1928.

Bastianini, Giuseppe: *Rivoluzione*. 130 pp. Berlutti. Rome. 1923. (By a prominent fascist organizer now head of the *fasci* in foreign countries.)

Bergamo, G., with G. De Falco and G. Zibordi: *Il fascismo visto da repubblicani e socialisti*. 130 pp. Cappelli. Bologna. 1922. (Lively polemics.)

Bernard, Ludwig: *Das System Mussolini*. 143 pp. Berlin. 1924.

Bibliografia Fascista. Berlutti. Rome. (Berlutti Publishing House has organized the *Libreria del Littorio* and is headquarters for fascist books. It gets out a periodical by the above title and also a volume, *Guida Bibliografica di Cultura Fascista*. The first edition of the volume is 1925; the second and greatly enlarged edition is 1927.)

Bodrero, Emilio: *Presagi d'Impero*. Alpes. Milan. 1925. (By the Under-secretary of Public Instruction, an ex-professor.)

——: *Vittorie dottrinali del Fascismo*. 38 pp. Bemporad. Florence. 1927. (A popular and exceedingly superficial exposition of fascist doctrine.)

Boffi, Ferruccio E.: *La Riforma Scolastica e l'Ufficio Stampa del Gabinetto Gentile*. 182 pp. Sandron. Rome. 1925.

Bolzon, Piero: *Le verghe e la scure*. Vol. I. *Roveto Ardente*. 226 pp. *La Voce*. Florence. 1923. (Futurist-fascist literature. He is now an Under-secretary in the government.)

——: *Le verghe e la scure*. Vol. II. *Il Dado Gettato*. 270 pp. *La Voce*. Florence. 1923.

Bolitho, William: *Italy under Mussolini*. 129 pp. Macmillan. New

York. 1926. (Collection of anti-fascist articles published in the New York *World;* lively account of fascist scandals, but now quite out of date.)

Bonomi, Ivanoe: *From Socialism to Fascism. A Study of Contemporary Italy.* 147 pp. Martin Hopkinson. London. 1924. (By an ex-Prime Minister. Good survey of origins of fascism.)

Bottai, Giuseppe: *Il Fascismo e l'Italia Nuova.* 74 pp. Berlutti. Rome. 1923. (Formerly a futurist, now editor of *Critica Fascista,* and Minister of Corporations. See his numerous articles in *Critica Fascista,* especially on the Party, the bureaucracy and the syndicates, and in *Il Diritto del Lavoro,* on his activities as Minister of Corporations.)

Brescia: Quaderno sull'attività sindacale di Brescia. Apollonio. Brescia. 1926. (An account of early fascist syndicalism in Brescia, one of the centers of violence, the *fascio* of Augusto Turati, now Secretary of the Party.)

Cambò, Francesco: *Il Fascismo Italiano.* Translated from the Spanish by G. Giardini. 177 pp. Alpes. Milan. 1925. (Good account of the state of fascism immediately after the Matteotti crisis. Also a good critique of parliamentarianism. By a Spanish reporter.)

Campogrande, Valerio: *Le recenti leggi fasciste.* Lattes. Turin. 1926.

Cantalupo, Roberto: *Fatti Europei e politica Italiana (1922–1924).* 196 pp. Imperia. Milan. 1924. (By a prominent nationalist writer. See also his numerous articles in *Gerarchia and Politica.*)

——: *La classe dirigente.* Alpes. Milan. 1926.

Carli, Mario: *Fascismo Intransigente.* 271 pp. Bemporad. Florence. 1926. (A collection of polemics by one of the editors of *l'Impero.* He is one of the most prominent of the early futurists in fascism and one of the most violent of the Intransigents. He is a continual source of embarrassment to more sober *fascisti.*)

La Carta del Lavoro. Edited by Giuseppe Bottai. *Ministero delle Corporazione.* Rome. 1927. (Contains text of Labor Charter and some related documents and is being translated into several languages.)

Carta del Lavoro. Series of articles in *Gerarchia,* May 1927. (The papers and journals are full of comments on the Labor Charter during the weeks following April 21, 1927.)

Casalini, Armando: *Scritti Sindacali.* 31 pp. Imperia. Genoa. 1925. (A pamphlet by the fascist syndicalist who was murdered in September 1924 to avenge the death of Matteotti. He had a number of articles in Rossoni's magazine, *La Stirpe.*)

Chiurco, Giorgio Alberto: *Fascismo Senese: martiriologio toscano dalla nascita alla Gloria di Roma.* 253 pp. *Combattenti.* Siena. 1923. (A typical martyrology.)

Christo, Homem: *Mussolini, Bâtisseur d'Avenir. Harangue aux*

Foules Latines. 329 pp. *Editions Fast.* Paris. 1923. (A harangue by an enthusiast for a Latin confederation under fascist hegemony.)

Church and State. Series of discussions between Arnaldo Mussolini in *Il Popolo d'Italia,* and the *Osservatore Romano.* September to October 1926.

Ciarlantini, Franco: *Imperialismo spirituale.* 192 pp. Alpes. Milan. 1925. (An outline of the fascist budget for art and the advertising of Italian art abroad.)

Ciccotti, Ettore: *Cronache quadriennali di politica Italiana ed estera (1919–1923).* 2 vols. 898 pp. Unitas. Milan. 1924. (By a socialist.)

——:*Il Fascismo e le sue fasi.* 456 pp. Unitas. Milan. 1925.

Cippico, Antonio: *Italy, the Central Problem of the Mediterranean.* 101 pp. Yale Univ. Press. New Haven. 1926. (Typical general statement of fascism by a fascist.)

Cipriani-Avolio, Giacomo: *Da una Rivoluzione ad un colpo di Stato.* 86 pp. *Polemica Fascista.* Rome. 1924. (A leading " revisionist.")

Codignola, Ernesto: *Il problema dell'educazione nazionale in Italia.* Florence. 1926. (By a leader in the educational reform.)

——: *La Riforma Scolastica.* Chapter in *Mussolini e il suo Fascismo.* Edited by Curt Gutkind. Monnier. Florence. 1927. (A good outline of the reform.)

Contri, Gioacchino: See his articles in *Gerarchia* and *Critica Fascista.* (Prominent among the younger polemic writers and theorists.)

Coppola, Francesco: *La Rivoluzione Fascista e la politica mondiale.* 96 pp. *Politica.* Rome. 1924. (He is the most prominent and voluminous of the nationalist writers, the mouthpiece of Federzoni; also an ex-delegate to the League of Nations, and its bitter opponent.)

——: See his articles in *Politica.*

Corradini, Enrico: *Il Nazionalismo Italiano.* 275 pp. Treves. Milan. 1914. (The leader of the nationalists. Numerous articles in *L'Idea Nazionale, Tribuna, Gerarchia, Politica, Rassegna Italiana.*)

——: *L'unità e la potenza delle Nazioni.* 344 pp. Vallecchi. Florence. 1922. Second edition 1926.

——: *Fascismo Vita d'Italia.* 24 pp. Vallecchi. Florence. 1925.

Costamagna, Carlo: *Manuale di diritto corporativo italiano.* Turin. 1927. (A leading authority on corporationism, member of the Commission of " Solons." See also his articles in *Lo Stato Corporativo.*)

——: *Sistemazione del diritto sindacale nel quadro del diritto moderno.* Vol. I. No. 1. of *Il Diritto del Lavoro.* Rome. 1927.

Croce, Benedetto: *Postille della Guerra.* Laterza. Bari. 1921. (Numerous critical and polemic articles in his *La Critica.* He is supposed to be a " fascist in spite of himself.")

——: *On the Conduct of Life.* (A translation of a collection of *postille.* Not directly related to fascism.)

——: *Elementi di Politica.* 117 pp. Laterza. Bari. 1925. (Has no relation to fascism. Hence the offense it gave!)

Curcio, Carlo: *L'esperienza liberale del Fascismo.* 163 pp. Morano. Naples. 1924. (By a southern idealist; links up fascism with the "historic right wing" of the *risorgimento*.)

De Ambris, Alceste: *I postulati dei Fasci di Combattimento: l'espropriazione parziale.* Bergamasca. Bergamo. 1919. (Prominent syndicalist and follower of d'Annunzio, who deserted fascism and joined the opposition.)

——: *L'evolution du fascisme.* Paris. 1923.

De Falco, Giuseppe: See G. Bergamo.

Delcroix, Carlo: *Un uomo e un popolo.* Vallecchi. Florence. 1928. (A popular veteran and orator.)

Della Torre, Edoardo: *Il concetto sindacalista dello Stato.* 317 pp. Vallecchi. Florence. 1925. (A prominent fascist railroad syndicalist and politician.)

Del Vecchio, Giorgio: *Le ragioni morali della nostra guerra.* 82 pp. Imperia. Milan. 1923. (Rector of the University of Rome. A conservative fascist.)

——: *La Giustizia,* in *Rivista Internazionale di Filosofia del Diritto.* 1926. III.

de Marsanich, A.: See his articles in *Gerarchia, Popolo d'Italia, Roma Fascista, Critica Fascista.* (Prominent among the young polemic writers.)

de Montemayor, Giulio: *La Politica del Vico e quella del Croce.* 31 pp. Alberti. Rome. 1926. (Ex-syndicalist now Professor at the University of Florence. A dilletante on fascist political philosophy.)

Deputato al Parlamento, Un: *Il fascismo.* Milan. 1922. (An excellent brief, critical analysis of early fascism.)

De Stefani, Alberto: *Discorsi.* 275 pp. Imperia. Milan. 1923. (Contains the famous budget speeches of the first fascist Minister of Finance, and also many of his polemics during the early days of fascism in Venetia.)

——: *Documenti sulla condizione finanziaria ed economica dell'Italia.* 545 pp. *Libreria dello Stato.* Rome. 1923.

——: *Decadenza demografica e decadenza economica.* 127 pp. *La Voce.* Florence. 1923.

——: *La ricostruzione economica e finanziaria dell'Italia.* 59 pp. *Libreria dello Stato.* Rome. 1924. (Out of print.)

——: *Vie Maestre: Commenti sulla finanza del 1926.* Treves. Rome. 1927.

——: *Le Riforme Finanziarie.* Chapter in *Mussolini e il suo Fascismo.* Edited by Curt Gutkind. Monnier. Florence. 1927.

Deutsch, Julius: *Antifaschismus.* 118 pp. Vienna. 1926. (Propaganda of Austrian socialists.)

Di Giacomo, Giacomo: *L'Organizzazione sindacale dei lavoratori intellettuali.* 140 pp. Imperia. Milan. 1924.
Disciplina giuridica dei rapporti collettivi del lavoro. 277 pp. *Giurisprudenza del Lavoro.* Milan. 1926. (A good collection of documents and discussions relating to the syndical reform, especially the Law of April 3, 1926.)

Einaudi, Luigi: *Le lotte del lavoro.* 276 pp. Gobetti. Turin. 1924. (By an eminent non-fascist economist.)
Ellenbogen, Wilhelm: *Fascismus — Das Faschistische Italien.* Vienna. 1923.
Ercole, Francesco: *Il carattere morale del nazionalismo.* In *Politica.* Vol. XI. 1922. pp. 193–218. (He is a philosopher who is trying to give nationalism and fascism an idealistic basis.)
——: *La profezia del Fascismo.* In *Politica.* XVIII. 1924. Rome. (reprinted in *Pagine Fasciste.*)
——: *La Politica di Machiavelli.* 1925.
——: *Le Origini dell'Italia Fascista.* Alberti. Rome. 1927.
Evola, J.: *Imperialismo Pagano. (Il Fascismo dinanzi al pericolo euro-cristiano.)* 160 pp. 1928. Rome. (A Nietzschean version of fascism.)

Fabbri, Luigi: *La contrarivoluzione preventiva.* 100 pp. Cappelli. Bologna. 1922. (From a futurist and anarchist point of view.)
Farinacci, Roberto: *Un Periodo Aureo del Partito Nazionale Fascista.* 417 pp. Campitelli. Foligno. 1927. (Collection of his speeches while he was Secretary of the Party, ending with his defense of Dumini at the trial for the murder of Matteotti. The best expression of so-called intransigent fascism.)
Fasci Italiani di Combattimento: Orientamenti teorici, Postulati practici. Milan. 1919.
Fascism: A special number of the *Survey Graphic,* March 1927, containing articles on various aspects of fascism by W. Y. Elliott, A. Fratelli, Silvio d'Amico, Mario Labroca, C. E. Oppo, Arnaldo Mussolini, G. Prezzolini, Edmondo Rossoni, O. Zuccarini.
Fascismo. Avanti. Milan. 1922. (Inquiry by socialists into fascist deeds.)
The Fascist State, by a Special Correspondent of London *Times,* Aug. 16, 17, 18, 1927. (A good statement of recent developments in the syndicates and corporations.)
Federzoni, Luigi: *L'Italia di domani.* L'Italiana. Rome. 1917. (Minister of Colonies, ex-Minister of the Interior, ex-Vice President of the Chamber of Deputies, chief of the nationalist politicians.)
——: *Presagi alla Nazione.* 342 pp. Imperia. Milan. 1924. (A collection of his addresses.)
——: *Paradossi di ieri.* Mondadori. Milan. 1925.

——: *Venti mesi di azione coloniale.* 225 pp. Mondadori. Milan. 1926.

Ferrero, Guglielmo: *Da Fiume a Roma.* (*Storia di Quattro Anni, 1919–1923.*) 141 pp. Athena. Milan. 1923. Translated into English as *Four Years of Fascism,* by E. Dickes. London. 1924. (Analysis, by a distinguished historian, of the political factors in the rise of fascism. He is a liberal and an outstanding figure in the opposition.)

——: *La democrazia in Italia.* 137 pp. *Rassegna Internazionale.*

Ferri, C. E.: *La Società delle Nazioni e l'Italia.* 126 pp. Alpes. Milan. 1924.

I Festeggiamenti e i problemi del rinnovamento Fascista. Civiltà Cattolica. Rome. 1923.

Filareti, Generale: *In Margine del Fascismo.* 421 pp. Unitas. Milan. 1925. (*Nom de plume* of a militant anti-democrat who had hopes in fascism but later was disillusioned. Interesting comments on politics in the south.)

Forges-Davanzati, Roberto: *Fascismo e Cultura.* 41 pp. Bemporad. Florence. 1926. (Typical harangues by a leading nationalist. See also his editorials in the *Tribuna.*)

Formiggini, Angelo Fortunato: *La Ficozza Filosofica del Fascismo.* Rome. 1923. (A humorous treatment of fascist ideology.)

Fortunato, Giustino: *Questione meridionale e riforma tributaria.* 93 pp. *La Voce.* Rome. 1920. (This senator, now too old to be a fascist, has been famous for years for this subject. He regards the north as more or less of an imposition on the south.)

Foscanelli, Umberto: *D'Annunzio e il Fascismo con lo Statuto della Reggenza del Carnaro.* 159 pp. Audace. Milan. 1923.

Freddi, Luigi: *Fascismo: La sua storia — La sua dottrina — La sua organizzazione.* 67 pp. Bemporad. Florence. 1923. (A brief statement by one of the pioneer politicians. Not a critical or historical account, but has some useful facts about the organization of fascism in 1923.)

Gangemi, Lello: *La Politica Economica del Fascismo. Libreria dello Stato, Ministero di Finanza.* Rome. 1926. (An official publication on fascist economic policy.)

Gayda, V.: *La Germania contro la Francia.* Bemporad. Florence. (A statement of changed relations between Germany, France, and Italy since the War. Regular contributor to *Gerarchia.*)

Gentile, Giovanni: *Educazione e scuola laica.* Vallecchi. Florence. 1921. (Leader of the fascist philosophical idealists, chief sponsor of the educational reform, head of Fascist Institute of Culture, and one of fascism's more critical minds. He is fascism's official preacher.)

——: *Il Fascismo al Governo della scuola.* 328 pp. Sandron. Palermo. 1924.

——: *La nuova scuola media.* Vallecchi. Florence. 1925.

——: *Che cosa è il fascismo.* 262 pp. Vallecchi. Florence. 1925. (A collection of his chief addresses.)

——: *I Fondamenti della Filosofia del Diritto, ed altri scritti.* Alberti. Rome. 1926.

——: *Guerra e Fede.* 350 pp. Alberti. Rome. Second edition 1926.

Gianturco, Mario: *La Legislazione Sindacale Fascista e la Riforma Costituzionale.* 190 pp. Imperia. Genoa. 1926. (One of the most extreme of the fascist syndicalists.)

Gigante, M.: *Commento alla legge 3 aprile 1926.* 162 pp. Mantegazza. Rome. 1926.

Gini, Corrado: *The Scientific Basis of Fascism.* In *The Political Science Quarterly,* March 1927, pp. 99–115. (Member of the Commission of " Solons," now head of the Statistical Bureau. A fascist, but has his own theories.)

Giuliano, Balbino: *L'esperienza politica dell'Italia.* 327 pp. Vallecchi. Florence. 1924.

——: *La politica scolastica del Governo Nazionale.* 171 pp. Alpes. Milan. 1924. (A good defense of the Gentile school reform, containing typical bits of fascist philosophy.)

——: *La Formazione Storica del Fascismo.* Chapter in *Mussolini e il suo Fascismo.* Edited by Curt Gutkind. Monnier. Florence. 1927.

Gobetti, Piero: *La rivoluzione liberale.* 162 pp. Cappelli. Bologna. 1924.

Gorgolini, Pietro: *Il fascismo nella vita italiana.* 258 pp. Silvestrelli e Cappelletto. Turin. 1922. (A long rhapsody; but comparatively it is a sober account of the development of fascism. At least it is one of the first. The author is a prominent fascist so-called intellectual, journalist, and organizer of fascist intellectuals.)

——: *La Rivoluzione Fascista.* 144 pp. Silvestrelli e Cappelletto. Turin. 1923. (Contains a number of documents and addresses connected with the March on Rome. Also rhapsodical.)

——: *Michele Bianchi. Profilo.* 30 pp. Imperia. Milan. 1923.

Grandi, Dino: *Le Origini e la missione del Fascismo.* In *Il Fascismo,* with Adolfo Zerboglio and R. Mondolfo, pp. 47–71. Cappelli. Bologna. 1922. (Grandi is a democratic nationalist who came into prominence by this speech delivered at the Rome Congress of 1921. He is now, under Mussolini, Minister of Foreign Affairs.)

Grandi Discorsi Elettorali del 1924. Benito Mussolini, De Stefani, Federzoni, Oviglio, Di Giorgio, Gentile, Corbino, Carnazza, E. Torre, Acerbo, Finzi, Serpieri, Salandra, A. Torre, Delcroix, Paratore, Benelli, Bottai, Benni. 362 pp. Imperia. Milan. 1924. (A good collection of election speeches for the 1924 elections, valuable as samples of the various points of view and conceptions of fascism current in that year.)

Hamburger, Ernest: *Aus Mussolinis Reich.* 47 pp. Breslau. 1924.

v. Hartlieb, Wladimir: *Italien, Alte und neue Werte.*

Hazard, Paul: *L'Italie vivante.* Paris. 1923. (A delightful description.)

L'Italia di Vittorio Emanuele III, 1900–1925. Special number of *Rassegna Italiana,* December 1925. (Contributions by Mussolini and the other Cabinet Members, as well as by a number of directors of important institutions, giving brief summary of developments in various departments during the first quarter of the century.)
Italy's Great War and her National Aspirations. Editors: Nelson Gay, Tomaso Sillani, and Armando Hodnig. With chapters by Mario Alberti, Carlo Corsi, Armando Hodnig, Tomaso Sillani, Attilio Tamaro, Ettore Tolomei. Alfieri e Lacroix. Milan. 1917.

Jannelli, Guglielmo: *La crisi del fascismo in Sicilia.* 50 pp. *Balza Futurista.* Messina. 1924.

Kaminski, Hanza-Erich: *Der Fascismus in Italien.* 140 pp. Berlin. 1925.

Labriola, Arturo: *Le due Politiche — Fascismo e riformismo.* 318 pp. Morano. Naples. 1924. (A veteran syndicalist, former head of C. G. L. and a leading opponent of fascism.)
——: *Il Socialismo contemporaneo. Lineamenti storici. Con un' appendice: La dittatura del proletariato ed i problemi economici del socialismo.* 382 pp. Morano. Naples. 1922.
——: *Polemica antifascista.* 219 pp. Ceccoli. Naples. 1925.
——: *Voltaire, e la filosofia della liberazione.* 332 pp. Morano. Naples. 1926. (A plea for individualism and liberty.)
Lanzillo, Agostino: *Le rivoluzioni del dopo guerra.* 258 pp. Solco. Città di Castello. 1922. (A prominent syndicalist scholar, first Sorelian, then fascist, member of the Commission of " Solons," important also as a Party politician.)
La Legge Sindacale. 94 pp. *Moderna Scuola.* Rome. 1926. (There are now numerous editions of this new labor Law of April 3, 1926.)
Licitra, Carmelo: *La nuova scuola del popolo Italiano.* 173 pp. Alberti. Rome. 1924. (A voluminous young writer of the Gentile school.)
——: *Dal liberalismo al fascismo.* 162 pp. Alberti. Rome. 1925.
——: *La Storigrafia idealistica.* 180 pp. Alberti. Rome. 1926.
Lumbroso, Giacomo: *La crisi del fascismo.* 162 pp. Vallecchi. Florence. 1925. (An excellent, critical account of the dissidence in fascism, 1923–4.)
L. W.: *Fascism: its History and Significance.* London. 1924.

McCormick, Anne O'Hare: *Behind Fascism stands a Philosopher.* In *New York Times* Magazine. September 26, 1926. Several other articles on Fascism in the *New York Times.*

McGuire, C. E.: *Italy's International Economic Position.* Macmillan. 1926.

Magni, Francesco: *I diritti di libertà nel regime fascista.* Cursi. Pisa. 1926. (Develops the irreconcilability between "absolute liberty" and political authority.)

Magri, F.: *La crisi industriale e il controllo operaio.* 327 pp. *Arti Grafiche.* Varese. 1922.

Magrone, Luigi: *La malavita politico-bancaria contro lo Stato Fascista.* 228 pp. *L'Universelle.* Rome. 1923.

Malaparte, Curzio: See Suckert, Curzio.

Manifesti del Nazionalismo italiano. 314 pp. Milan. 1919.

Mannhardt, Johann Wilhelm: *Der Faschismus.* 411 pp. C. H. Beck. Munich. 1925. (The most thoroughgoing history of fascism from 1919 to 1924, which has so far appeared in any language. Though it is wordy and cluttered up with pedantry, it is full of facts and references. A valuable source book.)

Maraviglia, Maurizio: *Il Nuova valore spirituale ed internazionale del l'Italia.* 31 pp. *P. N. F.* Rome. 1924. (A sample of nationalist philosophy.)

Marcuzzi, Antonio: *Letteratura Fascista.* 106 pp. Botta. Turin. 1924.

Marinetti, Filippo Tommaso: *Futurismo e Fascismo.* 249 pp. Campitelli. Foligno. 1924. (A collection of speeches and other forms of futurist violence. Gives an excellent account of the futuristic wing of fascism.)

——: *L'Arte Fascista Futurista.* In *Critica Fascista,* January 1, 1927, p. 3.

——: *Verso un Teatro Anti-psicologico.* In *Il 1919,* August 1926, p. 44.

Marsich, Pietro: *La posizione teorica e pratica del fascismo di fronte allo Stato.* In *Popolo d'Italia,* January 25, 1921. (An important document by an early fascist leader of Venetia, reflecting a point of view which did not prevail after the formation of the party.)

Massuero, F. N.: *Ombre e luci di due continenti.* Alpes. Milan. 1926. (On colonial expansion.)

Matteotti, Giacomo: *Un anno di dominazione fascista — Memorie, fatti, e documenti.* 91 pp. Rome. 1923. (The book that led to his murder.)

——: *The fascist exposed: a year of fascist domination.* Translated by E. W. Bickes. London. 1924. (Also translated into French and German).

Miceli, Giuseppe: His *Rassegna Corporativa,* a department in *Critica Fascista,* gives a good account of current developments in the syndicalist field.

Miceli, Vincenzo: *Il Partito Fascista e la sua funzione in Italia.* 127 pp. Imperia. Milan. 1924.

Michels, Robert: *Der Aufstieg des Faschismus in Italien.* Tübingen.

BIBLIOGRAPHY375

1924. (For many years professor at Turin, now professor at the University of Perugia. An authority on Italian socialism.)

——: *Sozialismus in Italien.* 419 pp. Meyer and Jessen. Munich. 1925.

——: *Sozialismus und Fascismus in Italien.* 338 pp. Meyer and Jessen. Munich. 1925. (Contains an excellent account of the factory occupation at Turin, and many observations on fascism by a sympathetic, but critical scientist.)

——: *Discorso sulla legislazione operaia.* Frankfurt. 1925.

——: *Storia critica del movimento socialista italiano.* 460 pp. *La Voce.* Florence. 1926.

——: *Corso di Sociologia Politica.* Milan. 1926. (Chapter on Fascism.)

Missiroli, Mario: *Il fascismo e la crisi italiana.* 60 pp. Cappelli. Bologna. 1921. (One of the best and most penetrating of early essays.)

——: *Una battaglia perduta.* 381 pp. Corbaccio. Milan. 1924.

Misuri, Alfredo: *Rivolta Morale.* 278 pp. Corbaccio. Milan. 1924. (A detailed account of his revolt from fascism and other incidents in the dissidence movement.)

Mondolfo, R.: *Per la comprensione storica del Fascismo.* Introduction to *Il Fascismo e i partiti politici,* by Grandi and Zerboglio. 35 pp. Cappelli. Bologna. 1922. (A good critical essay.)

Montagnari, Ernesto: *I più grandi siamo noi.* 500 pp. Mondadori. Milan. 1924. (More rhapsody.)

Monti, A. A.: *Pagine reazionarie.* Campitelli. Foligno. 1925. (By a right-wing nationalist fascist.)

Muriello, Raffaele: *Mussolini, his Work and the new Syndical Law.* Macniven and Wallace. Edinburgh. 1926.

Murphy, James: *Syndicalism in Italy.* In *The Edinburgh Review.* 1923.

——: *Fascismo: Reform or Reaction.* In *The Atlantic Monthly.* 1924. (High class scandal-mongering, but contains much first-hand information. See also his other articles in the *Atlantic Monthly,* the *Nation,* and other periodicals.)

Mussolini, Arnaldo: Series of discussions of the Church and the State, between *Il Popolo d'Italia* and the *Osservatore Romano.* September and October 1926.

Mussolini, Benito: *Le Poesie di Klopstock.* In *Pagine Libere,* of Lugano. Vol. II. No. 21. 1908. (An early essay in which he develops the thesis that great men, in their consciousness that they are the chosen champions of the people, become fanatic prophets and dogmatically expound the future aims and destinies of the people and excommunicate all who disagree. Thus they become really reactionaries and forget that their power is derived from the people.)

——: *Il Trentino.* Milan. 1912.

——: *Discorsi politici.* 203 pp. *Popolo d'Italia.* Milan. 1921. (Has been suppressed.)

——: *Diuturna.* 475 pp. Imperia. Milan. 1924. (A collection of his editorials in *Popolo d'Italia* 1914–1922. Many of the most interesting are omitted, but on the whole it gives a fair idea of Mussolini's varying attitudes during these years.)

——: *Fascismo e terra.* In *Popolo d'Italia,* March 19, 1921. (Omitted from *Diuturna.*)

——: *Forza e Consenso.* In *Gerarchia,* April 1922. (Especially important as a theoretical attempt.)

——: *I Discorsi della Rivoluzione.* 106 pp. Alpes. Milan. 1923.

——: *Il mio diario di guerra.* 236 pp. Imperia. Milan. 1923.

——: *La Nuova Politica dell'Italia.. Discorsi e Dichiarazione a cura di Amedeo Giannini.* 3 vols. 241 pp. 230 pp. 510 pp. Alpes. Milan. 1923. 1924. 1926.

——: *As revealed in his political speeches* translated by Baron B. di S. Severino. 450 pp. Dent and Sons. London. 1924.

——: *Fascismo e sindacalismo.* In *Gerarchia,* 5. Milan. 1925.

——: *Discorsi del 1925.* 281 pp. Alpes. Milan. 1926.

——: *Discorsi del 1926.* 398 pp. Alpes. Milan. 1927.

——: *Il Pensiero Fascista.* Alberti. Rome. 1927. (A collection of quotations.)

Mussolini e il suo Fascismo. Edited by Curt Gutkind. Articles by Gino Arias, Balbino Giuliano, Ernest Codignola, Alberto De Stefani, and introduction by Benito Mussolini. 350 pp. Monnier. Florence. 1927.

Mussolini e le Corporazioni. In series of pamphlets *Mussolinia.* Paladino. Mantua. 1927. (Contains notes by Suardo and Panunzio.)

" *Mussolinia.*" Series of pamphlets. Edizioni Paladina. Mantua.

Nanni, Torquato: *Bolscevismo e Fascismo, al lume della critica marxista; Benito Mussolini.* 302 pp. Cappelli. Bologna. 1924.

Naudeau, Ludovic: *L'Italie fasciste ou l'autre danger.* 283 pp. Flammarion. Paris. 1927. (Up-to-date opposition.)

Il Nazionalismo Italiano e i problemi del lavoro e della scuola. Proceedings of the Second Nationalist Convention at Rome, with the political program of the Nationalist Association, framed after the convention by the executive committee, M. Maraviglia and A. Rocco. 204 pp. *L'Italiana.* Rome. 1919.

Nitti, Francesco Saverio: *Nord e Sud.* (An early work of considerable influence.)

——: *Bolchevisme, Fascisme et Démocratie.* 204 pp. *Progrès Civique.* Paris. 1926. Translated into English and enlarged by Margaret M. Green, as *Bolshevism, Fascism and Democracy.* George Allen and Unwin. London. 1927. (By the ex-Prime Minister and the recognized head of the opposition.)

Olberg, Oda: *Der Faschismus in Italien.* 32 pp. Jena. 1923.

Olivetti, A. O.: *Bolscevismo, Comunismo, Sindacalismo.* Caddeo. Milan. 1921. (A veteran exponent of Italian syndicalism now fascist.)

——: *Il sindacalismo come filosofia e come politica. Lineamenti di sintesi universale.* 112 pp. Alpes. Milan. 1924. (Grandiose speculation.)

——: *Sindacalismo integrale.* In *La Stirpe,* 277–279. Rome. 1924.

Le Opposizioni parlamentari nel presente momento politico. 87 pp. Corbaccio. Milan. 1924. (Defense of the Aventine opposition.)

Orano, P.: *Dal Sindacalismo rivoluzionario allo Stato sindacalista.* 29 pp. Camera. Rome. 1925. (A nationalistic syndicalist.)

Oriani, Alfredo: *La Rivolta Ideale.* (First edition 1907.) New edition with preface by Benito Mussolini. 379 pp. Cappelli. Bologna. 1926. (Supposed to be a forerunner of fascism.)

Orlando, Vittorio E.: *Lo " Stato Sindacale " e le condizioni attuali della scienza del Diritto Pubblico.* In *Rivista di Diritto Pubblico.* Rome. January 1924. (The ex-Prime Minister gives his reasons for opposing the syndicalist state.)

Pagano, Antonio: *Idealismo e Nazionalismo.* In *Politica,* August 1926, pp. 201–221, and December 1926, pp. 201–221. (An attempt at reconciling idealism and nationalism).

Pagine Fasciste: I Fondamenti Ideali. Alberti. Rome. 1926. (Collection of important essays on fascist doctrine by Giovanni Gentile, Giocchino Volpe, Francesco Ercole, Giorgio Masi, and Arnaldo Volpicelli.

Pantaleoni, Maffeo: *Bolscevismo italiano.* Laterza. Bari. 1922. (By a distinguished socialist scholar.)

——: *Il Ministero Mussolini.* In *Vita Italiana,* Vol. X, No. 119, p. 360.

Panunzio, Sergio: *Il Diritto e l'Autorità.* U. T. E. T. Turin. 1912. (Left-wing fascist syndicalist, Professor at the University of Rome.)

——: *Il socialismo, la filosofia del diritto e lo Stato.* Solco. Città di Castella. 1921.

——: *L'Auctoritas, lo stato di Diritto.* Solco. Città di Castello. 1921.

——: *Diritto forza violenza.* Cappelli. Bologna. 1922.

——: *Italo Balbo. Profilo.* 50 pp. Imperia. Milan. 1923.

——: *Che cos'è il fascismo.* 85 pp. Alpes. Milan. 1924.

——: *Filosofia e Politica del diritto.* In *Rivista di Diritto Pubblico,* I, No. 4. 1923.

——: *Stato e Sindacati.* In *Rivista Internazionale di Filosofia del diritto,* III, I. 1923.

——: *Stato Nazionale e Sindacati.* 199 pp. Imperia. Milan. 1924.

——: *Lo Stato Fascista.* 177 pp. Cappelli. Bologna. 1925.

Pareto, Vilfredo: *Testamento Politico.* In *Giornale Economico.* 1923. (Pareto's writings have had a direct influence on fascism, as they have on all current Italian politics and social science.)

Pasini, Achille: *Impero Unico. Teoria dello Stato Sinarchico.* 266 pp. Berlutti. Rome. 1924. (Fancy philosophy.)

Pellizzi, Camillo: *Problemi e realtà del Fascismo.* 216 pp. Vallecchi. Florence. 1924. (One of the cleverest and extremest of the fascist youths.)

——: *Fascismo-Aristocrazia.* 197 pp. Alpes. Milan. 1925.

Pennachio, Alberto: *The Corporative State.* Italian Historical Society Publications, Vol. IV. New York. 1927. (Contains documents and charts, as well as a useful discussion.)

Pighetti, Guido: *Sindacalismo fascista.* 254 pp. Imperia. Genoa. 1924. (By a leading fascist syndicalist organizer. Contains some valuable historical references and comments.)

Por, Odon: *Fascism.* The Labour Publishing Co. London. 1924. (One of the best early accounts.)

Preziosi, G.: *Cooperativismo rosso piovra dello Stato.* 322 pp. Laterza. Bari. 1922.

Prezzolini, Giuseppe: *La Cultura Italiana.* 374 pp. *La Voce.* Florence. 1923.

——: *Le Fascisme.* Translated from the Italian by Georges Bourgin. 279 pp. Bossard. Paris. 1925. Enlarged and translated into English as *Fascism.* 1926. (The best and most objective brief account of the general aspects of fascism; contains much first-hand information.)

Puchetti, A. C.: *Il fascismo scientifico.* 136 pp. Bocca. Turin. 1926.

La Reforme Syndicale en Italie. 207 pp. Colombo. Rome. 1926. (Collection and translation of documents relative to the syndical Law of April 3, 1926.)

Relazioni e Proposte della Commissione Presidenziale per lo Studio delle Riforme Costituzionali. 206 pp. *Libreria dello Stato,* No. 324. Rome. 1925. (The report of the Commission of "Solons." A very important document in the history of recent reforms.)

Revisionismo Fascista. 76 pp. *Polemica Fascista.* Rome. 1924. (A collection from the revisionist polemics.)

Ricci, Umberto: *Dal protezionismo al sindacalismo.* Laterza. Bari. 1926.

La Ricostruzione fascista. Novembre 1924–Gennaio 1925. Edited by *Associazione Italiana per il controllo Democratico.* 220 pp. Corbaccio. Milan. 1925. (Contains several important opposition speeches and documents.)

Riforma parlamentare. Editorial in *Critica Fascista,* January 15, 1927, pp. 21–22. (This and a number of other articles in *Critica Fascista* are important among the pleas for the corporate parliament.)

Rignano, Eugenio: *Democrazia e Fascismo.* 129 pp. Alpes. Milan. 1924. (A weak attempt to recall fascism to the democratic fold.)

Rivoluzione liberale, Vol. I, No. 15. Turin. May 28, 1922. (An inquiry by liberals into fascist activities.)

Rocca, Massimo: *Gruppi di Competenza.* 16 pp. *Rinascimento.* Milan. 1923. (One of the fascist pioneers who turned dissident in 1923 and was later expelled from the Party and the country. He organized these groups.)

——: *Idee sul Fascismo.* 357 pp. *La Voce.* Florence. 1924. (Important contribution to fascist ideology.)

——: *Storia di una polemica.* 350 pp. Corbaccio. Milan. 1924.

——: *Finanze e Fascismo.* 225 pp. Ceccoli. Naples. 1925. (Attack on De Stefani.)

——: *Il mio Fascismo.* Ceccoli. Naples. 1925.

Rocco, Alfredo: *Che cos'è il Nazionalismo e cosa vogliono i nazionalisti.* 45 pp. *L'Italiana.* Rome. 1914. (Minister of Justice; nationalist leader; one of the most important leaders of the recent constitutional reforms.)

——: *Ritorno del Medio Evo,* and *Crisi dello Stato e sindacati.* In *Politica,* 1920. (These two articles are among the earliest expressions of fascist syndicalist theory.)

——: *La Dottrina politica del fascismo.* Aurora. Rome. 1925. Translated by Dino Bigongiari under the title *The Political Doctrine of Fascism.* Bulletin of Carnegie Endowment for International Peace, No. 223. Oct. 1926.

——: *La Trasformazione dello Stato. La Voce.* Rome. 1927. (Important exposition of the recent reforms.)

Rossato, Arturo: "*Mussolini.*" Modernissima. Milan. 1919.

Rossi, Cesare: *Il " Memoriale Rossi,"* published in *Il Mondo,* December 27, 1924. Also in *La Ricostruzione Fascista,* pp. 167–179. Corbaccio. Milan. 1925. (One of Mussolini's closest friends and lieutenants attacks Mussolini after the latter had caused his arrest for complicity in the Matteotti murder.)

Rossoni, Edmondo: *Le idee della ricostruzione.* 106 pp. Bemporad. Florence. 1923. (The leader of fascist syndicalism. He has more practical than theoretical ability, as this volume shows. He has written a large number of articles in *Il Lavoro d'Italia* and *La Stirpe.*)

——: *Appunti per la Carta del Lavoro,* in *La Stirpe,* January 1, 1927, pp. 1–7. (His draft for the Labor Charter.)

Russo, Domenico: *Mussolini et Le Fascisme.* 140 pp. Plon. Paris. 1923. (Fair account of the early days.)

Saltelli, Carlo: *Potere esecutivo e norme giuridiche.* Rome. 1926.

Salvatorelli, Luigi: *Nazionalfascismo.* 181 pp. Gobetti. Turin. 1923.

Salvemini, Gaetano: *Il Ministro della mala vita.* 136 pp. *La Voce.*

Rome. 1919. (A distinguished historian, at first favorable to fascism, now an opposition leader.

——: *Tendenze vecchie e necessità nuove del movimento operaio Italiano.* 212 pp. Cappelli. Bologna. 1922.

——: *Dal Patto di Londra alla Pace di Roma.* 450 pp. Gobetti. Turin. 1925.

——: *The Fascist Dictatorship in Italy.* New York. 1927. (Contains a mass of otherwise unavailable material.)

Sarfatti, Margherita G.: *The Life of Benito Mussolini.* 352 pp. Frederick A. Stokes. New York. 1925. (A translation and abridgement of her Italian "*Dux.*" Good for anecdotes, but otherwise has slight historical value. She is an intimate friend of Mussolini, formerly with him in *Il Popolo d'Italia,* now editor of *Gerarchia.*)

Scarfoglio, Edoardo: *Il Popolo dai cinque pasti. Brindisi a Mr. Asquith.* 203 pp. Mondadori. Milan. 1923. (A lively piece of southern energy directed against England. Formerly editor of *Popolo di Roma.*)

Schotthöfer, Fritz: *Il Fascio. Sinn und Wirklichkeit des Italienischen Faschismus.* 224 pp. Frankfurt am Main. 1924. (Little essays, fairly critical, on the fascism of 1923.)

Serpieri, Arrigo: *La Politica Agraria in Italia e i recenti provvedimenti Legislativi.* 284 pp. Federazione Italiana dei Consorzi Agrari. Piacenza. 1925. (In the Ministry of Agriculture. An excellent treatment of fascist agricultural policy, prefaced by a brief, but unusually enlightening account of the rise of fascism.)

——: *Problemi di Politica Agraria.* 80 pp. Alberti. Rome. 1926.

Settimelli, Emilio: *Colpo di Stato fascista?* 95 pp. Facchi. Milan. 1923. (Squadrist and futurist point of view. See also his editorials in *l'Impero.*)

Signoretti, A.: See his many articles on syndicalism in *Lavoro d'Italia* and *La Stirpe.*

Soffici, Ardengo: *Battaglie fra due vittorie.* 211 pp. La Voce. Florence. 1923. (Lively essays by a first rate fascist writer. Also an interesting preface by Curzio Suckert.)

——: *Arte Fascista,* in *Critica Fascista,* October 15, 1926, pp. 383–4.

Spampanato, Bruno: *Divenire Fascista.* 128 pp. Gente Nostra. Naples. 1924. (By a young Neapolitan fascist and journalist. Better than the average.)

Spirito, Ugo: *Il Nuovo idealismo italiano.* 120 pp. Alberti. Rome. 1926. (Prominent among Gentile's disciples.)

——: *La Riforma del Diritto Penale.* 80 pp. Alberti. Rome. 1926.

Sturzo, (Don) Luigi: *Indirizzi politici e riforme costituzionali.* 332 pp. Vallecchi. Florence. 1923. (Popularist leader.)

——: *Popularismo e Fascismo.* 305 pp. Gobetti. Turin. 1924.

——: *Pensiero antifascista.* 280 pp. Gobetti. Turin. 1925.

——: *Italy and Fascism.* London. 1926.

——: *The Italian Popular Party*, in *The Contemporary Review*, June 1926, pp. 730–737. (Outlines causes of the break between fascism and the Popular Party after their brief coalition.)

Suckert, Curzoi (Malaparte): *La Rivolta dei Santi maledetti*. Second edition. 278 pp. *Rassegna Internazionale*. Rome. 1923. (A leader among the "Vocist" group. Sensationally orthodox fascist and radical Catholic. See also his journal *La Conquista dello Stato*.)

——: *L'Europa vivente. Teoria storica del Sindacalismo nazionale.* 127 pp. *La Voce*. Florence. 1923.

——: *Italia barbara*. 126 pp. Gobetti. Turin. 1926. (Among the best of strictly fascist literature.)

——: *Arte Fascista*, and other articles in *La Conquista dello Stato*, December 15, 1926, p. 3.

——: *l'Arcitaliano*. 1928. (A volume of lyrics.)

Syndicalism. In *Costruire*, 1926. (A series of articles on fascist syndicalism.)

Syndicalism. In *Echi e Commenti*. 1925–6. (A series of discussions on fascist syndicalism.)

Syndicalist theory. Series of articles in *Rivista Internazionale di Filosofia del Diritto*. 1924–1926. (Especially the discussion between Panunzio and Costamagna.)

Syndicates and Corporations. A number of valuable articles on this subject appeared in the following numbers of *Critica Fascista*: July 15, 1926, p. 275; August 15, 1926, p. 317; October 15, 1926, p. 395; November 1, 1926, p. 407; and December 1, 1926, p. 445. Also in *Gerarchia*, July 1926, p. 472.

Tancredi, Libero: See Massimo Rocca.

Trevelyan, G. M.: *The historical causes of the present state of affairs in Italy*. Oxford University Press. 1923.

Triaca, Ubaldo: *Le fascisme en Italie*. 57 pp. Paris. 1927.

Turati, Augusto: *Ragioni ideali di vita fascista*. 178 pp. Berlutti. Rome. 1926. (Speeches by the Secretary of the Party.)

——: *Una Rivoluzione e un Capo*. Berlutti. Rome. 1927. (More speeches.)

Turati, Filippo: *Le vie maestre del socialismo*. Bologna. 1921. (The reformist socialist leader, now exiled.)

Uccelli, Oscar: *Il Fascismo nella Capitale della Rivoluzione*. 78 pp. Campitelli. Foligno. 1924.

Valente, Concetto: *La ribellione antisocialista di Bologna*. 222 pp. Cappelli. Bologna. 1921. (By a nationalist participant.)

Valli, Luigi: *Scritti e discorsi della grande vigilia*. Zanichelli. Bologna. 1926. (A pioneer nationalist.)

——: *Il diritto dei popoli alla terra.* Alpes. Milan. 1926. (Nationalist doctrine for international relations.)

Vantaggio, Luigi: *Fascismo e Italia.* Colletta. Messina. 1926. (An anthology.)

Varisco, Bernardino: *Discorsi Politici.* 314 pp. Alberti. Rome. 1926. (A prominent fascist idealist.)

——: *La nuova Italia.* Venice. 1927.

Vecchi, Ferruccio: *Arditismo Civile.* Milan. 1920. (The leader of the *Arditi.*)

Viana, Mario: *Sindacalismo.* 250 pp. Laterza. Bari. 1923.

Villari, Luigi: *The Awakening of Italy, the Fascist Regeneration.* Methuen. London. 1924.

Vitali-Rosati, Uriele: *Il sindacalismo agrario.* 47 pp. Properzi. Fermo. 1923.

Vita Italiana. (This periodical has many useful articles during 1919–1922.)

Volpe, Gioacchino: *Fra Storia e Politica.* 444 pp. Alberti. Rome. 1924. (The leading fascist historian.)

——: *L'Italia che si fa.* Alberti. Rome. 1927.

——: *Per la nuova Italia.* In *Popolo d'Italia,* November 21, 1920. (An early formulation of doctrine.)

Volt: *Programma della Destra Fascista.* 155 pp. *La Voce.* Florence. 1924. (*Nom de plume* for Count Vincenzo Fani; died July 1927. A leader of the right wing. See also his numerous articles in *Gerarchia,* and *Critica Fascista.*)

Zama, Piero: *Fascismo e Religione.* 39 pp. Imperia. Milan. 1923.

Zeitschrift für Politik. 1923. (Contains a number of good articles on fascism.)

Zerboglio, Adolfo: with Dino Grandi. *Il Fascismo,* pp. 1–45. Cappelli. Bologna. 1922. (Contains interesting references.)

Zibordi, G.: See G. Bergamo.

Zuccarini, Oliviero: *Esperienze e Soluzioni. Libreria Politica Moderna.* Rome. 1926. (Editor of a suppressed republican periodical.)

——: *Problemi interni del fascismo.* In *Critica Politica,* October 25, 1926. (See also reply to it in *Critica Fascista,* December 1, 1926, pp. 431–2.)

II. Periodicals

I. Chief Fascist Political Journals.

Critica Fascista: (1923–　). Bi-weekly. Rome. Giusseppe Bottai. Important especially on internal issues within the Party. Recently has published important series of articles on: Syndicalist Reforms, Reform of the Party Organization, Fascist Art (October 1926 to March 1927), Fascist Philosophy.

Il Diritto del Lavoro: (1927–   ). Monthly. Rome. Minister of Corporations. (Giuseppe Bottai.) This official journal of the corporations contains many of the most important articles on the corporate state and in addition has a bulletin of the official Acts and other documents related to the reform.

Educazione Fascista: (1925–   ). Monthly. Rome. Giovanni Gentile. Really a successor to Gentile's *Nuova Politica Liberale,* which, when he became head of the *Istituto Fascista di Cultura* (1925), was transformed into *Educazione Politica* and then (1927) on the wish of Mussolini into *Educazione Fascista.* It is the official organ of the *Istituto Fascista di Cultura* and is devoted chiefly to philosophical and historical studies.

Gerarchia: (1922–   ). Monthly. Milan. Margherita Sarfatti. Founded by Mussolini, still the chief political review of the Party. It carries departments on Religious Thought, Philosophic Thought, and Science, but these are inferior to its more strictly political material.

Politica: (1919–   ). Quarterly. Rome. Alfredo Rocco and Francesco Coppola. Founded by the nationalists. Is far superior to any other fascist political journal. Specializes in foreign policy. Carries a useful record of events.

Rassegna Italiana: Monthly. Rome. Tomaso Sillani. Not strictly speaking a fascist journal. It is a leading political and literary review. Is dominated by the nationalist point of view, imperialistic, and has a special colonial section. Contains many of the most important nationalist articles since the war.

Rivista Internazionale di Filosofia del Diritto. Monthly. Rome. Giorgio del Vecchio. Not strictly speaking fascist. A standard journal of the philosophy of law, edited by the fascist rector of the University of Rome. Contains many important technical discussions on fascist theory of the state.

II. LESSER POLITICAL JOURNALS.

La Conquista dello Stato: (1923–   ). Bi-weekly. Rome. Curzio Malaparte (Suckert). At one time a leading " integralist " paper; but now more or less personal propaganda against the type of fascist represented by *L'Impero.* A lively sheet of high class polemics.

La Corporazione: Weekly. Genoa. Guido Pighetti.

Costruire: (1924–   ). Monthly. Pisa. Darioski (Dario Lischi).

Il Giornale di Politica e di Letteratura: (1925–   ). Monthly. Pisa. Raffaello Giusti and Umberto Biscottini.

L'Italiano: (1923–   ). Weekly. Bologna. Leo Longanesi. This is really Soffici's paper and, like Suckert's *La Conquista dello Stato,* is chiefly bent on ridiculing certain squadrist types.

La Montagna: (1925–1926). Bi-weekly. Naples. Bruno Spampanato. Fascist review, now discontinued.

La Rivolta Ideale: Weekly. Rome. Antonio Beltramelli. Organ of groups of Fascist students in the universities.

Il Selvaggio: Florence. Mino Maccari. Another one of the " Vocist " group of journals.

Lo Stato Corporativo: (1926–   ). Monthly. Rome. P. Marica, Lissia, Santangelo. A new journal devoted to the legal aspects of the corporate reforms. Costamagna is one of its leading spirits.

Vita Nova: (1925–   ). Monthly. Bologna. G. Saitta. The journal of the Fascist University of Bologna. Has an appendix of printed " lessons " in fascist studies for university students.

III. Popular Reviews.

Il 1919: Monthly. Milan. Mario Giampaoli. By the Old Guard of Milan. Has compiled a superficial history of Milan fascism.

La Rivista del Popolo d'Italia: Monthly. Milan. The illustrated magazine of the *Popolo d'Italia.*

La Stirpe: Monthly. Rome. Edmondo Rossoni. Illustrated magazine of the Confederation of Syndicates. Contains many important articles on syndicalism by Rossoni, Signoretti, and others.

Avanguardia: Bi-weekly. Rome. Renato Ricci. Juvenile journal.

Il Balilla: Weekly. Ferrara. Mario Barbieri. Juvenile journal.

IV. Propaganda Weeklies.

(Every town, almost, has its propaganda sheet, run by the local *fascio.* Many of these have been suppressed, being over-abundant and often irresponsible. We list here only a few of the principal ones. There are such periodicals also in many of the Italian centers in foreign countries.)

L'Assalto: Bologna. Giorgio Pini.

Battaglie Fasciste: Florence. Gherardo Casini.

Corriere Latino: Rome. Nicolo Maraini.

Il Nazionale: Turin. Pietro Gorgolini.

La Patria: Rome. Renato Manzini.

Roma Fascista: Rome. Guglielmotti and Foschi.

V. Chief Fascist Daily Newspapers.

(In a sense all papers are fascist, in that none are anti-fascist. Those given here are explicitly fascist and have national significance. The more local papers we cannot enumerate.)

Popolo d'Italia: Milan and Rome. Arnaldo Mussolini. Still the most important, though less authoritative than when Benito Mussolini directed it personally.

La Tribuna. Rome. Forges-Davanzati and others. Fused with the

Idea Nazionale of Corradini, and now one of the best papers of Rome.

Il Lavoro d'Italia: Rome. Rossoni. The organ of fascist syndicalism. A good paper and enjoys a large circulation.

L'Impero: Rome. Carli and Settimelli. The imperialist, squadrist, futurist journal. Headquarters of jingoism.

Cremona Nuova: Cremona. Farinacci. Farinacci's famous sheet. One of the pioneers of fascism. Rivals *L'Impero* for violence.

These are nationally important. They still fall behind such famous papers as *Il Corriere della Sera* (Milan) and *Il Giornale d'Italia* (Rome), which, though they have lost their political independence, still keep up a distinguished journalism.

Chief among the Catholic papers are *L'Osservatore Romano* (Rome), and *Corriere Italiano* (Rome).

VI. NON-FASCIST PERIODICALS.

(Among the few non-fascist periodicals that have not been suppressed, the following contain important discussions of fascism.)

La Critica: Monthly. Naples. Benedetto Croce. This is the foremost philosophical periodical of Italy. It also contains a number of polemic and critical articles on fascism. In general friendly until 1924, since then hostile.

La Critica Sociale: Bi-weekly. Milan. Zibordi. (Now suppressed) Especially a series of articles by Zibordi, Treves, Matteotti, and others on fascism in Numbers 4–9, 1921–1922.

La Riforma Sociale: Ed. Senator Luigi Einandi. Turin.

L'Observateur. Bulletin du Comité Italien de Bruxelles. (No. 1, March 1928.) Opposition propaganda directed by F. Ferrari, Arturo Labriola and A. Zanetti.

INDEX